Queer Externalities

SUNY series in Queer Politics and Cultures

Cynthia Burack and Jyl J. Josephson, editors

Queer Externalities

Hazardous Encounters in American Culture

W. C. Harris

SUNY PRESS

Cover photography and design by Marie Hathaway.

Published by State University of New York Press, Albany

Printed in the United States of America

For information, contact State University of New York Press, Albany, NY
www.sunypress.edu

Production by Diane Ganeles
Marketing by Fran Keneston

Library of Congress Cataloging-in-Publication Data

Harris, W. C. (William Conley)
Queer externalities : hazardous encounters in American culture / W. C. Harris.
p. cm. — (SUNY series in queer politics and cultures)
Includes bibliographical references and index.
ISBN 978-1-4384-2751-5 (hardcover : alk. paper)
ISBN 978-1-4384-2752-2 (pbk. : alk. paper)
1. Gays—United States—Social conditions. 2. Gay and lesbian studies—United States. 3. United States—Social conditions. I. Title.

HQ76.3.U5H3695 2009
306.76'60973—dc22

2008048484

10 9 8 7 6 5 4 3 2 1

for Karl, with love and gratitude

"you married me for it"

It's a very strange feeling. I'm not used to being hated.

—David Levithan, *Boy Meets Boy*

A people as chosen as gays are must erect a ghetto not so much for segregation as for concentration: to learn what gay is. . . . It is not rebellious sex habits that define us as much as the rebel coterie itself, the act of not bothering to adjust to gringo [straight] procedures.

—Ethan Mordden, *Buddies*

Contents

Acknowledgments

A conversation with Donald E. Hall, whose intelligence is matched only by his kindness, made completing this project seem newly possible. Jim Keller and Jim Stacy spurred substantial improvements with perceptive and challenging responses to different parts of this project, while Dawn Vernooy-Epp read more than her fair share, keeping me always conscious of audience and voice. Our decision to convene an impromptu writer's colony in a Philadelphia sublet granted time and space to finish the book. Librarians Berkley Laite, Diane Kalathas, and Signe Kelker of Shippensburg University were obliging in an hour of need, while Burt Kimmelman at NJIT and one of his students, Patricia Egan, brought to my attention some useful work on Internet communication studies.

Thanks for more ambient but still quite material support go to Cynthia Botteron, Laurie Cella, Jennifer Clements, Erica Galioto, David Godshalk, Stephanie Jirard, Sara Grove, Mary Stewart, Kim van Alkemade, and Dawn and Doug Vernooy-Epp—colleagues and friends who have provided conversation, meals, pet-sitting, occasionally forbearance, and generally served as models of professional poise and survival. Arnold Markley and Fred Kogan enriched my time spent in Philadelphia over the past three years; in addition to their wit and friendship, better ciceroni are not to be found. Kate von Goeler has been the truest of friends and conspirators for nearly twenty years. My mother, Judy Harris, remains my most faithful, if naturally most biased, reader. I regret that my father, who died shortly after the publication of my first book, did not live to see the second; his support, love, and example will not be forgotten.

The most salient debt is to my partner, Karl Woelz, who has listened more carefully and contributed more crucially than anyone. First reader of many of these pages, he lent to them his astute eye and sometimes his voice; his candor and insistence on clarity have shaped more than just my argument. A decade after his adventitious arrival on the scene, Karl's love, generosity, and authenticity—not to mention, encyclopedic knowledge of 1980s music—remain my irrefragable constants. (It would be false to my somewhat faded reputation as a show-tune queen not to add, "I must have done something good.") Such loyalty, wit, and understanding are notoriously hard to come by; I cannot imagine my life or my work without him.

It is an honor to be part of the SUNY series in Queer Politics and Cultures. I've been lucky enough to work with a phenomenal group, including Larin McLaughlin, Diane Ganeles, Fran Keneston, Andrew Kenyon, and the team at A & B Typesetters and Editorial Services. Series editors Cynthia Burack and Jyl J. Josephson furnished attentive feedback that, along with generous and frank commentary from the outside readers, was indispensable in bringing the book to its current state; any blame for remaining infelicities or misjudgments rests entirely with me. Finally, I am colossally indebted to Marie Hathaway, whose shrewd eye and clean design actualized Karl Woelz's concept for the cover.

Portions of this book have been previously published. The section of chapter 1 dealing with *Rubyfruit Jungle* appeared in *EAPSU Online: A Journal of Critical and Creative Work* 1 (Summer 2004). Earlier versions of chapters 2 and 3 were published, respectively, in the *Journal of American Culture* 29.3 (Sept. 2006) and in *The New Queer Aesthetic on Television: Essays on Recent Programming*, edited by James R. Keller and Leslie Stratyner (2006). A slightly altered form of chapter 4 was included in *Reading Brokeback Mountain: Essays on the Story and Film*, edited by Jim Stacy (2007). I am grateful for permission to reprint this material. The editors and reviewers for these journals and collections also deserve thanks for their critiques and encouragement.

Introduction

A Hazard of Queer Fortunes

FREE AT LAST? Virtually equal? In June and November 2003, two court cases seemed to promise a true sea change in the legal, and implicitly cultural, status of gays and lesbians: under *Lawrence et al. v. Texas* the U.S. Supreme Court declared antisodomy laws unconstitutional and gestured toward an imaginable rationale for legalizing same-sex marriage; in *Goodridge v. Department of Public Health*, the Massachusetts Supreme Court ruled that denying marriage licenses to same-sex couples violated the principles of equal protection and due process. As of 2007, four states—Vermont, Connecticut, New Jersey, and New Hampshire—had legalized civil unions for gays and lesbians (in the first two cases only, civil union entails the same rights as marriage). Maryland and Colorado later enacted more limited domestic partnership laws. By 2007, California, the District of Columbia, Maine, Oregon, and Washington recognized domestic partner benefits, as did over half of the corporations in the Fortune 500 (such as General Electric, Time Warner, and Viacom).[1] Then in May 2008 California's Supreme Court effectively legalized gay marriage when it annulled its Defense of Marriage Act (DOMA—a state version of the 1996 federal DOMA permitting states, contrary to the Constitution's full faith and credit clause, not to honor marriage licenses from other states—implicitly, those held by same-sex couples). The Iowa Supreme Court took similar steps, declaring the state's DOMA unconstitutional in 2007 and legalizing same-sex marriage in 2009. In 2008, the Connecticut Supreme Court approved gay marriage; by June 2009, state legislatures in Vermont, Maine, and New Hampshire had followed suit. The California decision soon encountered roadblocks. Voters approved Proposition 8, defining marriage heterosexually, in November 2008, and then in May 2009 the same state Supreme Court that had ruled in favor of gay marriage upheld the Prop 8's constitutionality. Meanwhile, New York governor David Paterson declared that New York would honor gay marriage licenses from other states, thereby spurning DOMA and New York's own statute banning gay marriage. In April 2009 Paterson put forward legislation to legalize gay marriage. This embarrassment of victories, however, was met with a backlash that showed the battle for tolerance and equality was far from won. In the 2004 election alone, eleven states banned same-sex marriages, civil unions, and/or the granting of domestic partner benefits. By 2009, twelve states had banned the recognition of any such unions or marriage, twenty states had passed statutory DOMAs, and same-sex-marriage bans had been added to twenty-eight state constitutions.

Queer theorists and activists including Cindy Patton, Lisa Duggan, Michael Warner, Amy Brandzel, and Teemu Ruskola argue that these so-called landmarks constitute, at best, a meager facsimile of progress and, at the worst, a distraction from neoliberal political, rhetorical, and economic strategies that discourage potentially transformative social alliances between disenfranchised groups while promoting "the upward redistribution of resources and the reproduction of stark patterns of inequality" (Duggan, *The Twilight of Equality?* xiv). Ruskola worries that the antihomophobic intentions of the *Lawrence* court are hobbled by speaking "not of 'sodomy' but of 'intimacy'"—that is, by defending, or at least valorizing, gay love and intimacy only *within* committed, implicitly monogamous pairings (236). Much as Michael Warner does in his argument about the ideological and practical costs of fighting for gay marriage, Ruskola holds that cordoning off queer "sex that is not part of an on-going relationship" privatizes homosexuality in a way that not only defines the political potential of mobilizing around sex as "an ultimately political and public issue" but also presents a (to some) soothingly heteronormative version of homosexuality (239, 242). To say that sex and citizenship have nothing to do with one another may prima facie seem tolerant, but it's also a lie. *Lawrence et al. v. Texas* defines "responsibility" and, symbolically, citizenship precisely along sexual lines, "permit[ting] the exclusion of nonnormative sexualities from the 'world of public intimacy,' which may remain reserved for manifestations of normative heterosexuality" (242). More glaring, perhaps, are the actions and words of social conservatives and politicians, such as James Dobson, former Massachusetts governor Mitt Romney, and former President George W. Bush, who, with either open loathing or practiced righteousness, state as a matter of fact that homosexuals are inferior, ungodly, and beyond the pale of civil dispensation. While it is to be expected that homophobic forces will be goaded into more strident and muscular efforts by antihomophobic advances in social attitudes and civil policy, many recent discussions and depictions of homosexuality seem to ignore the invigorated engines of homophobia in favor of rosier yet delusory vistas on both the (queer) present and what constitutes a desirable (queer) future. And, as Lisa Duggan argues in *The Twilight of Equality?* (2003), centrists and even progressives do as much damage, whether by failing to balk at overt homophobia or by remaining oblivious to homophobia's less flagrant, though equally poisonous, manifestations.

In the face of this admittedly, though not inherently discouraging, contradictory present, certain strains of gay thought—utopian, subversive, and assimilationist—persist in forms that may be alluring, yet are unproductive and potentially damaging. Whether encouraged by demonstrable improvements in social and, in some states, legal attitudes toward homosexuality or simply weary of conservative jeremiads, gay and lesbian Americans should stop to consider how queer space continues to be threatened or impinged on—and not just the queer spaces of the ghetto or gayborhood, but the rhetorical and ideological spaces that potentiate critical insight. Even an apparently harmless cultural episode such as the media apotheosis of Ang Lee's *Brokeback Mountain* has a worrisome undertow. Allowing both straights and gays to rejoice in a more tolerant present than that suffered by the film's protagonists, this sympathetic yet dour and tragic depiction of homosexuality is hailed as a sign that tolerance has arrived. Such encounters verge on the hazardous when they are unprotected, that is, when their anodyne character blurs one's awareness—or when one participates in them lacking, or seeking to escape, an awareness—of the boundaries that still bar queers in significant ways from political parity, from cultural presence, and from social personhood. These unmindful encounters also include the erosion, if not active erasure, of other, valuable kinds of boundaries, the differences that mark queers, their pleasures and ethoi, as diacritically yet not pejoratively other. (A promising project in this direction is *What Do Gay Men Want?* [2007], in which David Halperin calls gay men to reevaluate the subjective and political potential of abjection rather than seeking to escape abjection in obedience to psychoanalysis' lingering influence.) More worrisome yet is the extent to which moderate and liberal American queers, under the spell of unrealistic assessments of the communal and national present, and restrictively normative visions of those futures, might find themselves amenable to the sort of quiescence that they might otherwise resist—a submissiveness, advocated by gay conservatives, to a cultural script that fundamentally fails to countenance queers except as symbolic other, docile before roles and institutions for whom their existence doesn't seem to matter so much. The liberal trompe l'oeil of a future in which gayness no longer makes a difference not only forsakes much that's valuable about queerness, it also discomfitingly resembles the right-wing telos of a space where gayness doesn't matter, where it not only ceases to make a difference but where it also ceases to exist.[3]

Taking a popular/cultural studies approach, *Queer Externalities* examines American cultural representations from the current decade that illustrate either an inept appraisal or an insufficient awareness of the ideological, cultural, and sometimes very material muscle wielded—unevenly and incommensurately, from the political Right, Left, or center, from official versus popular discourse—by individuals, subcultures, and ideologies within the larger culture. In particular, I'm interested in looking at moments from the past several years in which the feeling among many queer and even some straight Americans—whether expressed as a "postgay" mentality or a sense that acceptance and visibility have finally, or are very shortly about to, overcome the forces of homophobia—is revealed to be premature, if not chimerical. The cultural artifacts I've chosen to focus on highlight exemplary intersections of queer desire and activism, homophobia, and heteronormativity in American political life, mass media, and literature: *Queer Eye for the Straight Guy*; gay young adult novels by Alex Sanchez, David Levithan, and Bret Hartinger; *Brokeback Mountain*; the 2004 Bush versus Kerry presidential campaign; and the plethora of scandals surrounding outed gay Republicans including Mark Foley, Matt Sanchez, and Ted Haggard. In terms of theory, the book's analyses are underpinned by the work (most recently) of queer theorists including Eve Sedgwick, Lee Edelman, Michael Warner, David Halperin, Anna Marie Smith, Cindy Patton, and Donald Hall, along with an investigation into how certain theoretical perspectives (such as cultural materialism) can heighten our understanding of both the hazardous and animating potential of queer representation. By parsing the multivalent ideological forces humming through these texts and cultural as well as political debates, I hope to show the extent to which the recent decade of scattered legal victories and largely positive gay media visibility has, for many, obscured the menacing antigay rhetoric that continues to structure not just public discourse in general but specific texts and statements in explicitly enunciated, glaring ways.

The book's title, *Queer Externalities*, references a concept borrowed from economics—"externality." In economic terms, an externality is a cost or benefit (respectively, a positive or a negative externality) that is borne not by the participants in an economic transaction but by some other party. Environmentally conscious policies are an example of a positive externality, profiting not any one company but benefiting society as a whole. Conversely, pollution is a negative externality, injuring the larger social welfare without incurring appreciable costs for the company creating the pollution.[4]

Before explaining how the concept of externalities can be applied to contemporary American cultural encounters and the hazards such encounters pose to queer Americans, a comment on my choice of terminology is in order. Borrowing a term from economics for queer analysis seems particularly apt at this historical moment, with the rise of (perceived) queer market niches over the past decade vis-à-vis corporate advertising as well as network and cable television programming. The ways in which corporate entities have been talking to gays has produced as axiomatic the belief that economic interpellation is synonymous with, or as good as, political and legal equality—or even with economic parity. Yet being addressed by a manufacturer hardly translates into the property or inheritance benefits accorded to heterosexual married couples. The equation may be fallacious, but it's had a startling effect on the ways in which queers perceive their power: they have come to see themselves as powerful not because the government legitimizes or acknowledges them but because corporations do. With this in mind, it seems appropriate to adopt an economic term to designate the phenomenon I'm attempting to address. Queers may think that they've arrived because they're being directly addressed and represented in ways measurably less phobic than in the past, but their assessment ignores the extent to which that interpellation is predicated on the whims of ratings, programming executives, marketing wonks, focus groups, and unrelated financial and market trends of corporate entities.

We'll have to wait and see what happens when queers who have felt legitimized by corporate sponsors and the entertainment industry, through shows like *Will & Grace* and *Queer as Folk*, come to terms with the prospect of those shows no longer existing. When this happens, will these queers have (or feel they have) any power? Any recent progress, since the end of the two shows just mentioned, may have already diminished. Once no longer courted in prime time, will these queers and their supposed economic and political power remain? A 2007 survey of GLBT media representation on cable and network television by GLAAD (the Gay and Lesbian Alliance Against Defamation) suggests not. GLAAD's "Network Responsibility Index" bears out the dwindling prospects faced by GLBT audiences with the recent end of long-running gay shows. "Out of a total 679 series regular lead or supporting characters" in the 2006–2007 network season, there were "only nine (9) gay or lesbian [lead or supporting] characters—1.3%—appearing on eight (8) different scripted network programs" (GLAAD, "Where We Are" par. 1). While this is only a slight decrease in the ratio of queer to straight characters from the previous season (a nearly as bleak 1.4 percent), if one also includes recurring characters, the number of gay and lesbian characters is down from the previous season by nearly 30 percent on network shows and down 12 percent on cable programs. Network and cable programmers don't appear to be rushing in to fill that void. Regardless of future increases or decreases in these figures, it bears asking how queers can be said to substantively exist if they exist only as a market segment. Even if some companies continue to address gay audiences as they always have (Absolut Vodka, for instance, has long advertised in gay magazines such as the *Advocate*), that doesn't translate into political or social progress. Yet gay versions of ads (the 2007 Levi campaign that featured a young man eyeing someone in a phone booth: a man in one version, a woman in the other) run only on gay channels or in gay print venues, not on mainstream (i.e., straight) channels, even during a show such as *Project Runway*, which is popular with both queers and straights. When a gay ad runs next to a straight ad on a major network during prime time, for example, one can perhaps talk about more significant progress, that is, progress in which the economic is coterminous with the political, not its inadequate proxy.

To return to the concept of externalities, then, as they occur in queer cultural encounters. The following chapters look at queer externalities, both positive and negative: that is, cultural and ideological side effects generated both by queers and by those seeking to cloak, gloss over, or exterminate queerness. In political terms, for example, homophobia yields a tremendous amount of cultural capital for the Republican Party, right-wing pundits, and some gay members of the mainstream media without cost to themselves (see Richard Goldstein, *The Attack Queers*, for an account of the latter). While this may not exactly seem to be a positive externality in the traditional sense (besides failing to accrue a greater social good, homophobia often seems to benefit its "producers"), most pontifications on the dangers posed by homosexuality are couched in terms of protecting the greater (implicitly, heterosexual) populace. From a less solipsistic viewpoint, of course, homophobia is a negative externality, incurring material as well as symbolic costs not only to queers (in the form of economic inequality, political marginalization, or physical violence) but also to those straights unwilling to inhabit a culture embittered with such rage and invective, to see their relatives, friends, and colleagues disenfranchised, sidelined, or attacked. Objectively assessed, homophobia is a negative externality, exacting ethical as well as tangible costs. Homophobia, of course, emanates from sources other than the most discernibly or flagrantly vitriolic, and part of my project is to elucidate the phobic undertow—the negative externality for queers—of seemingly gay-positive contexts and representations. From a variety of analytic edges (political, cultural, personal, institutional), the term "negative externality" begins to describe the kind of contradiction I've identified between perceived self-interest, or a fantasy of well-being, and collective hazard.

While attention will be given to exceptions (such as the activist camp of *Queer Eye for the Straight Guy*, in which an invigorating queer difference is preserved, and queerness becomes a positive externality), for the most part this book highlights negative queer externalities, the largely unperceived costs for queers (and arguably, for society at large), produced by both homophobic and queer-positive representations of homosexuality. "Queer externality," then, serves as a metaphor for social, political, and cultural behaviors and developments that, though arguably damaging to the larger culture, are potentially even more dangerous for queers. From increased queer visibility in successful mainstream entertainment (such as *Will & Grace* or *Brokeback Mountain*) to outings of conservative religious or political leaders who actively denounce and legally marginalize nonheterosexuals, queerness remains qualified, denied authenticity—as often by those who would redeem it as those seeking to repress or demonize it. Both affirmative and phobic representations meet increasingly jaded reactions, as if to suggest that enunciating queerness is neither as taboo nor as arduous as it once was. *Queer Externalities* analyzes cultural encounters that, despite the warmth with which many in straight and queer communities have welcomed or passively accepted them, are hazardous to the viability of queerness as a locus of personal, social, and political mobilization. Aside from their more obvious personal, immediate costs, these hazards constitute queer externalities by their diminution of sympathy for what gay conservatives and liberal allies alike disdain as outmoded rebellious marginalism.

As tempting as it might be for queers, given certain cultural and political advances, to dismiss separatism as gauche, counterproductive, or no longer necessary, doing so robs us of valuable queer strategies—via essentialism and identification—for resistance, sustenance, and, perhaps occasionally, transformation. Basking in the apparent mainstreaming of gayness means not only to misread the queer past, to mistake interpellation for acceptance, but to write off difference itself, to jettison a queer potentiality for *making* a difference. Rather than solely advocating either ghettoized isolationism or political apathy (many have read Lee Edelman's *No Future* as exhorting the latter), this book advocates the maintenance of an invigorating difference, a consciousness of the hazards of considering that queers have "arrived," and that visibility, whether inspiring or shaming, brings its own hazards.

In *Gay TV and Straight America* (2006), Ron Becker searches for a correlation between the surge in gay- and lesbian-themed storylines on network television shows in the 1990s and the relatively high liberal support, during the same period, for gays and lesbians' effort to fight homophobia and obtain legal parity. Increased media visibility, obviously, does not entail positive representation only. With some exceptions, Becker finds the majority of gay network depictions of gays and lesbians during this period, while far from the wrecked, tortured souls of previous decades, to be reductive, marginal, and exoticizing. At the same time, many of the shows on which these characters appeared were tremendously popular, and networks consistently presented homosexual characters with a frequency (and often, an openness) absent from previous decades. Becker theorizes that "straight panic"—or heterosexual anxiety among liberals and moderates as well as conservatives—about an increasingly visible homosexual population offers the best explanation for the 1990s mixed political and entertainment messages about homosexuality:

> In a climate where identity, history, and values based on the previously unchallenged assumptions of privileged groups were questioned, America was particularly sensitive to the tensions between the rights of a gay minority and the normative power of a straight majority. In fact, that struggle became one of the defining political and cultural issues of the decade. For a culture uneasy about the loss of moral consensus and struggling to deal with the proliferation of social identities, gays and lesbians' demands for social recognition and equal treatment pushed a lot of buttons. Like whites in a post–civil rights era, heterosexuals in the 1990s experienced something of an identity crisis. (31–32)

Becker names "two divergent symptoms of the era's straight panic":

> A conservative backlash worked hard to reestablish heterosexual privilege by justifying and reinscribing traditional moral hierarchies that

> defined gays and lesbians as deviant. Meanwhile, gay-friendly liberals worked hard to accept and to adapt to the new sexual politics by trying to figure out how to be straight (especially a straight man) without the despised homosexual Other as one's point of reference. (32)

Together, these forces—venomous rejection on the one hand and squeamish tolerance on the other—generate a cultural ambivalence that tends to mute, if not countermand, the progress gays and lesbians seem to have made in wooing liberals and some moderates. Faced with homosexuality at nearly every turn, in public debates about marriage, domestic partnership benefits, adoption, and military service, straights in the 1990s got to feel good about being tolerant but also had their anxieties soothed by nonthreatening portrayals of the increasingly visible homosexual on television and in the public forum. In a similar vein, *Queer Externalities* traces, in the current decade, the degree to which both "symptoms" of this cultural ambivalence have become more pronounced. That intolerance, particularly from the New Right, has grown more vehement may not be surprising. Then again, it may be—given the general equanimity and optimism prevailing among many queers and their sympathizers. Weary of Republican and social conservative hate-mongering, and assuming that few rational people are still fooled by their sophistry and brimstone, queer Americans risk being too easily wooed by apparent harbingers of tolerance and equality. To find undue solace in an artifact of queer "arrival" (*Brokeback Mountain*) or an episode of conservative chagrin (the exposure of Mark Foley and the attendant Republican cover-up) may numb the anxieties generated by stepped-up conservative efforts to erase advances toward gay and lesbian parity—but they hardly counteract them. What the present book explores is (1) the homophobia and heteronormativity that fund, subtend, and structure American cultural discourse even when a particular queer representation seems progressive and conscientiously antihomophobic, and (2) the resultant care one must take to differentiate hazardous moments that imperil queer presence from sustaining moments that defilade queers' potential for participation, critical perspective, and, if only in exiguous or local ways, cultural transformation.

Speaking of queers or queer Americans is certain to raise political and intellectual concerns, inasmuch as such terms seem to regard nonheterosexuals—or, more finitely, gays and lesbians—as homogeneous populations, to reify homosexuality and thereby further shore up the already rigid edges of the homo/hetero paradigm. It may be of little comfort that the term's use is antihomophobic (as in queer activism) rather than homophobic (as in the myth of homosexual recruitment). Other readers may demur from my often interchangeable use of "queer" and "gay and lesbian," or from what may seem a reflexive reference to gays and lesbians when the discussions here focus almost exclusively on representations and encounters of male homosexuality. Rather than a semantic imprecision, speaking in the same breath of "gay" and "queer" is meant to gesture toward those ways in which gay experience is representative, though not exclusively so, of queerness in the cultural imagination. Social and religious conservatives are not exactly fond of lesbians, but it's the male homosexual that most haunts and fuels their ethos. Conversely, abjection of the queer in America feeds back into and shapes individual and communal gay self-understanding. Likewise, my terminology is not meant to insist that all gays and lesbians must identify as queer. The ranks of the queer—those who find themselves at odds with one or more norms—include more than those commonly grouped together as the GLBT community. However, contrary to many queer theorists (including Michael Warner, Donald Hall, and David Halperin—with whom I agree on much else), I would argue that sexual norms must be prominent, if not primary, among the norms queers find themselves at odds with. While "queer" is an ideologically flexible category, and while regarding it as such is strategic in terms of coalition building and cultural dialogue, expanding "queer"—queering "queer"—too far weakens the rationale of the category itself (no matter how loose), erodes the ideological cohesiveness of a positionality whose validity lies in its resistance to "regimes of the normal" (Warner, Introduction xxvi). David Halperin puts it in more accommodating terms still: "queer acquires its meaning from its relation to the norm. Queer is by definition whatever is at odds with the normal, the legitimate, the dominant. *There is nothing in particular to which it necessarily refers*" (*Saint Foucault* 62). (For a yet more expansive account, see Carla Freccero 17–20, 29–30.) If queer includes anyone who falls athwart some norm, then doesn't queer risk becoming a regime in itself? Gays, lesbians, and even queers are disparate groups, each of which comprises a broad swath of possibilities and cross-identifications, and the present discussion does not mean to equate the full spectrum of possibilities within any of these parameters of experience with another. *Queer Externalities* does not deal extensively with the intersections of queer studies with, for example, gender or ethnic studies. Hiram Perez and Judith Halberstam, among others, have articulated queer studies' historical disconnect from concerns of race and gender and the need, from multiple angles, to think through more carefully such connections, variances, and possibilities for insight and coalition (Perez "You Can Have My Brown Body and Eat It, Too"; Halberstam "Shame and White Gay Masculinity"). While some might object that the following chapters are "dominated by . . . discussing issues of interest to other white gay men," my project does not pretend to address every issue facing the heterogeneous group loosely referred to as "the gay and lesbian community" (Halberstam, "Shame" 220). My interest lies, rather, in addressing the *homo*geneous, regulatory terms by which queers are interpellated by American culture—terms that are necessarily insufficient, yes, but whose potency to shape homophobic political policy and cultural rhetoric is undeniable. Although rejected by some queer individuals as essentialist and therefore hopelessly inimical to projects of social change—a charge I will return to shortly—these are the same terms that, for their pragmatically motive as well as their curative properties, queers must retain, must engage with without necessarily being globally confined to, if they hope to interact significantly, transformatively, with present-day American political and cultural life.

Up to a point, the cultural conditions represented in and through these texts may stand in for common risks or struggles of queers of various stripes. My concern is predominantly with gay texts and contexts, that is, with representations and interpellations of male homosexuality. Although the ambit of almost any inquiry is restricted in some way, and although an apologia for exclusions has become pro forma, the statement is worth reiterating. The particular inflections and exigencies of lesbian experience are bound to differ in significant ways from those of gay men's lives, and may produce sharply divergent insights and strategies for survival and critique. Yet insofar as (heteronormative) American culture conceives of gays and lesbians, rhetorically, as a single entity—whether corrosive, noble, or merely eccentric—gay men and women share certain political goals vis-à-vis homophobia, heterosexism, and normative conceptions of gender and sexuality. *Queer Externalities* does not aim for truths to be gained from analyzing the antilesbian texture of recent political and literary discourse but rather those truths common to gays and lesbians as targeted populations, caught together in the crosshairs of the larger culture's organizing mythos.

Given that it's become almost de rigueur to eschew essentialisms and identities as restricting and debilitating, my position is bound to seem heteroclite, if not perversely unfashionable. And it is—but not simply for the sake of aberrance or perversity. (It should be noted that essentialism can be understood in more than one sense; the sense in which I'm using it does not extend to arguments such as John Boswell's regarding the existence of homosexuality throughout human history.) Essentialism has taken quite a few hits over the past three decades as feminist, queer, and race studies have problematized—and rightly so—the reductive limits of understanding identity to be elemental or inherent. Gays and lesbians have had reason to be ambivalent about essentialist explanations of sexuality—particularly scientific ones. Simon LeVay's 1991 study of hypothalamic size in gay and straight men promised to reveal what the media dubbed the "gay brain," thereby establishing a biological basis for explaining homosexuality. LeVay's study was widely discredited for its small sample size and LeVay's questionable interpretation of the evidence, yet the idea that such evidence might someday be discovered, in the brain or elsewhere, was both exciting and unsettling. Proof of sexuality's essentialism would refute the phobic myth that homosexuality is a choice and therefore constitutes an irrefutable claim for gay and lesbian rights; indeed, the notional inherence of a person's sexuality has been the cornerstone of the modern gay and lesbian arguments against homophobic violence and legal discrimination. The very same evidence, however, conjures the murderous specter of eugenic detection and elimination. All that being said, however, there are a number of reasons not to write off essentialism so hastily. For one, as Diana Fuss asserts at the outset of *Essentially*

Speaking (1989), "The bar between essentialism and constructionism is by no means as solid and unassailable as advocates of both sides assume it to be" (xii). While Fuss's insistence that "an essentialist theory of identity (which sutures over the dislocating operations of the psyche) is ultimately *not* a secure foundation for politics" sets her argument apart from mine in distinctive ways, it's my position that the "steady and localizable" character of "political work" can be, as Fuss believes, compatible with identity's inherent "internal disorder" and instability (105). In fact, identity's—and indeed, representation's—capacity for fragmentation permits both critiques of homophobic rhetoric and strategic deformations of heteronormativity, sustaining queers' capacity for survival as well as intervention. Fuss herself admits as much:

> There is an important distinction to be made between "deploying" or "activating" essentialism and "falling into" or "lapsing into" essentialism. "Falling into" or "lapsing into" implies that essentialism is inherently reactionary—inevitably or inescapably a problem or a mistake. "Deploying" or "activating," on the other hand, implies that essentialism may have some strategic or interventionary value. . . . [T]he political investments of the sign "essence" are predicated on the subject's complex positioning in a particular social field and . . . the shifting and determinative discursive relations which produced it. (20)

Though ultimately my investment in the political is material in a way that Fuss might reject as "reifying," the following discussions pay sufficient attention, I hope, to "shifting and determinative discursive" status of queerness in American culture to honor the "differences and inconsistencies in the production of stable political subjects" (106, 104). (For previous attempts to strike a balance between deconstructed and strategically essentialist senses of "queer," see Butler, *Bodies That Matter*, 229; and Spivak and Rooney.)

If my position appears retrograde to some, it will perhaps prove refreshing to others. Given the dead end to which mainstream, assimilationist, single-issue gay and lesbian politics has led us, there's value to be gained from returning to past insights—like the importance of remaining critically aware of American culture's ultimately heteronormative agenda—insights mainstream gay and straight culture have rejected as backward, polemical, impolite. *Queer Externalities* issues from a controversial yet frank conviction that visible and distinct gay and lesbian communities and identities are not impediments to our progress, relics of our political past. Choosing to identify as gay or to participate in a gay community is a matter of individual taste. Many gay men vehemently insist that they are "not into the gay scene," meaning, usually, that they do not frequent or do not feel comfortable in gay neighborhoods or bars—that is, publicly gay places. This is not to say that such a position is inherently heteronormative, unexamined, or co-opted. "Gay" is ultimately a space, a sheath, and I can put it on or not. Regardless of my willed affiliation, however, the larger culture still considers me gay. I may choose not to go to gay bars, circuit parties, or pride marches, but I still have sex with men. In these terms at least, being gay can never be apolitical. Without identifying as gay, I am still tarred with the same homophobic brush—even if being closeted or refusing to call myself gay exempts me from homophobia's more direct blows.[5] And media visibility, mixed legal gains, and a relative increase in tolerance (toward the idea of gay and lesbian equality) in no way guarantee the permanence of a gay and lesbian presence in the public sphere, nor do these ensure against the attrition of our presence or the reversal of those developments. Anna Marie Smith says as much in *New Right Discourse on Race and Sexuality* (1994), an analysis of homophobic and racist public policy and discourse in Britain from 1968 to 1990:

> What the left often fails to recognize is that homosexual, gay and lesbian identities cannot be taken for granted, for, as historical constructs, they developed only in certain contexts, and will disappear in other contexts. It is true that many lesbian and gay activists remain suspicious about any attempts to enforce the normalization of gay and lesbian; they, like Foucault are proponents of endlessly creative sexual movements which would celebrate the multiplication of non-authoritarian differences. However, there is a quite a difference between, on the one hand, the weakening of lesbian and gay identities and their displacement with new identities through our own creative practices, and, on the other hand, the marginalization of our political movements and the destruction of our entire culture by homophobic forces. Although we need to be on our guard against the rigidity of identity games, this does not mean that we ought to abandon our efforts to consolidate our fragile gains in the face of tremendous authoritarian bigotry. Again, we can only engage in the exploration of creative identity games once we have fortified enclosures against homophobic forces through defensive identity games. (237)

I am somewhat more cautious than Smith about the power of isolated acts in altering paradigms of sexuality, at least telically or in the short run: such transformations, as David Halperin argues in *How to Do the History of Homosexuality*, seem to require an accrual of time and subversive play beyond the reaches of the individual and the horizon of the present. What's more, exerting pressure on identity and roles in an attempt to reconstruct them or shift an entire paradigm (although this may not be what Smith means) seems like so much energy wasted, energy that might be channeled more productively toward grappling for agency in the polity that recognizes gays and lesbians by those identities. I concur with Smith on the dire need and the protective as well as productive ("creative") utility of "fortified enclosures" and "defensive identity games."

Shying away from the notions of identity and essentialism as entirely outmoded or inhibitive vehicles for queer life and mobilization is an injudicious move away from a paradigm that permits play and offers real protections that, as this book substantiates, are still sorely needed in a culture where homophobia is not only pervasive but escalating in putatively liberal or neutral contexts, and to lessening public objection. (In "Why Did Armey Apologize?: Hegemony, Homophobia, and the Religious Right?" Smith contends that the New Right has made homophobia more palatable, that is, less obviously offensive by disguising it as an objection to "special rights," a crusade against the inequality embodied, supposedly, by gay antidiscrimination laws. Smith's adept analysis of homophobia's greater infiltration of the public sphere through right-wing rhetoric will be returned to in chapter 2.) In *New Right Discourse*, Smith trenchantly observes that conservative objections to the promotion of homosexuality—by its sheer visibility, usually—are so vehement precisely because queer identity, whether we conceive it as concretizing, unstable, or somewhere in between, *is* politically effective. It might seem counterintuitive, but antigay conservatives are right on one count: "[H]omosexuality survives only to the extent that it is promoted. . . . [L]esbian and gay identities . . . profoundly depend upon political intervention, and . . . if homosexuality were politicized, it could indeed have a tremendous subversive effect on the 'normal'" (Anna Marie Smith, *New Right Discourse* 238). Visibility, identification, and the sort of adulterated essentialism recommended by *Queer Externalities* are crucial to queer survival and—just perhaps—instrumental to queering, or transforming, the social.

One need not be so apologetic about recommending essentialism, however, for the argument has been made before—though perhaps forgotten—that essentialism is immanently adulterated. To regard identity, by contrast, as unilaterally essentialist, hierarchical, or oppressive, is, according to Cindy Patton, to willfully misunderstand the nature of identity—that is, to forget that identity is not purely an intellectual concept but one that operates also in the real world and therefore, whatever else it is, must on some level be understood materially. Whatever identity seems capable of being, it must also be doable. And it is, as gays and lesbians know from their own lived experience. In "Tremble, Hetero Swine!" (1993), Patton cautions queers against the then-fashionable flight from essentialism by insisting that holding onto differences can be essentializing in one sense but thoroughly pragmatic in another. Queer theory, inspired by poststructuralism and social constructionism, sought the promise of escape from the oppressive history and limitations of Western (white, male) subjectivity by alleging that the true nature of identity—constructed, unstable, contingent—undermined all modes of identification as unsound, backward, essentialist. Essentialism became what institutions do to individuals, an imposed, policing mechanism. And it's not that identities can't be that. It's just that their other characteristics—motility, agency—are being shortchanged. Patton compellingly asserts:

> A . . . fundamental principle of identity discourse seems to have been lost from view in the debate about postmodernism and postidentity politics. Implicit in the differing modes of identity construction are claims about political formation, about forms of governmentality, about the difference between modernity and postmodernity. To the extent that groups like ACT UP or Queer Nation have, largely due to their sophisticated use of cynical media practices, been associated with postmodernism, other forms of gay political labor have implicitly been identified as "bad old modernist." But more than standing for a discovery of the self, identities suture those who take them up to specific moral duties. Identities carry with them a requirement to act, which is felt as "what a person like me does." There is a pragmatic, temporal aspect to identities, whether we believe in them or not. The requirement to *act* implicit even in transient identities means that those who inhabit them feel they must do something and do it now. This produces a kind of closure, but that does not mean that identities are or become effectively essential: the stabilization of identities appears to be ineluctably essentialist only when we treat them in the realm of the imaginary, with its apparent promise of infinite possibilities for performance and reperformance. Instead, I propose . . . that we treat identities as a series of rhetorical closures linked with practical strategies, implicit or consciously defined, alliances and realliances that in turn affect the whole systems for staging political claims. (147)

Not all identity constructions are essentialist all of the time. Not all essentialisms are bad. More exactly, essentialism is not what we have made it out to be: it is not, as a matter of course, exclusive of the pragmatic, the incidental. What makes the situation more dire—and the reappraisal of essentialism more vital—is that homophobic institutions and individuals engage with essentialist identity constructs. And so it is there, through such modalities, that antihomophobic work—personal, cultural, political work—must, on some level, be undertaken. In Patton's words, "Quotidian uses of identities must be understood in the context of a struggle to control the general rules of identity construction. The plainly essentializing logics within this field must be viewed as options deployed in a deadly game of queer survival, not as 'foundations' for 'identity'" (167). Similarly helpful is Patton's use of the term "deontic closures" to specify those "performative and pragmatic dimensions" of identity (as opposed to its "imaginary dimensions" as conjured by the specter of "essentialism"), to underscore the way in which gay and lesbian identities "carry with them a requirement to act." But the implication of Patton's argument is broader, it seems. Identities not only "suture those who take them up to specific moral duties" (calling out phobic exclusions in social discourse, for example); they also present a moral obligation, which can be taken on or rebuffed, to those outside the "rhetorical closures" of one's identity position. These obligations, or opportunities, exist then on both sides, potentiating "alliances and realliances," permitting both the polemical and the affiliative moves integral to "staging political claims." Contrary to Eve Sedgwick's concern, in *The Epistemology of the Closet* (Axiom 4), over the punitive repercussions of essentialist (as well as constructionist) theories of homosexuality, Patton suggests that that tension—the resonance of identity both as debated and as lived—is in fact the energizing contradiction of queerness. And it's a contradiction as capable of spurring social change as of sheltering embattled lives, as given to crossing boundaries as to fortifying them. Furthermore, when Patton says that identity discourse "produces a kind of closure," we might reasonably extend this to mean literal as well as rhetorical enclosures. The "gay community"—as a bloc and as a geographical space, as a gayborhood—has permeable but remnant boundaries. Being true to the complexities of human experience (rather than merely being sloppy), one can regard "gay" as both internal and external to "queer," "queer" as simultaneously a labile anticategory, slur, and insignia.

Refusals to queer identification can be mild, made in the name of privacy or as a statement against "labels." British pop musician Mika "actively markets himself to a gay audience" yet is leery of "acknowledg[ing] his own sexuality" (Juergens, "Mika: Why Don't the Gays Love Him?" par. 1). Known for his "Freddie Mercury falsetto . . . and defiantly flamboyant posturing," Mika appeared on the July 2007 cover (ironically) of *Out* magazine, but not to out himself (par. 1). Like the caption for the cover photo ("Mika: Gay/Post-Gay/Not Gay?"), Mika's responses to questions about his sexuality were evasive: "Anybody can label me, but I'm not willing to label myself. . . . Anybody who says that I don't talk about sexuality or that I don't politically sexualize my music because of taboos, because of being afraid of [not] selling records, is completely wrong. . . . Why pigeonhole myself like that? Will it change? Possibly" (qtd. in Hilton pars. 3, 5, 7). Like characters Molly Bolt and Jason Carillo (from *Rubyfruit Jungle* and the *Rainbow Boys* novels), Mika squirms at the apparent imprisonment of labels. But the complaint about being "pigeonhole[d]" is rarely the principled stand it facetiously pretends to be. What principle that might be, in any case, is unclear; one seldom hears threnodies about the personality-immuring effect of other identifiers (for example, "pro-choice," "emo," or "evangelical"), or at least not as loudly. It's not so much the case that Mika doesn't like labels. The label he doesn't like is "gay." Mika himself acknowledges that, in the wake of Elton John and George Michael, being an openly gay musician is hardly the automatic career killer it was once feared to be.[6] Simply put, in the words of gay blogger Brian Juergens,

> [t]he story here is that we have a gay-vague celebrity *aggressively* marketing himself to us while telling us that we are part of a society with whom he would not want to identify. He constantly refers to not wanting to be "labeled," which is beyond offensive to those of us who don't

> see sexuality as a label, but rather a fundamental part of who we are. Does it define us? No—not any more than "tall," "Hispanic," "enthusiastic," or "big-boned" would. ("Mika: In Which We Decline" par. 2)

In response to Mika's pejorative association of "being labeled" with homosexuality, Juergens adds, "I wasn't aware that your sexuality was something that you could (or would want to) 'move past'" ("Mika: 'Post-Gay'" par. 7). While it's true that "gay" is not inherently limiting, unlike the other nonlimiting descriptors Juergens uses above, it constitutes a more integral part of gay experience, if only as a result of the homo/hetero paradigm that defines all of us, especially gays and lesbians, by our sexuality. One doesn't have to be "into the gay scene," but one needs to be allied to it. It's ethically incumbent on queers to acknowledge that affiliation. Not to do so—by reticence or by default—is collaborationist.

Rejections of gay identity also come in more clamorous, less evasive forms. Jack Malebranche's *Androphilia: A Manifesto: Rejecting the Gay Identity, Reclaiming Masculinity* (2006) presents itself as a "book for men who love men but are sick to death of the gay community" (x). Malebranche claims to speak on behalf of "men who rarely have their feelings about homosexuality and gay culture in print," a silent majority of everyday Joes who, stereotypically masculine in almost every way, just happen to be sexually attracted to men:

> Gays would like to believe that those same-sex-inclined men who want little or nothing to do with the gay community or who disagree with gay ideology are a few isolated self-hating Roy Cohns. I believe they are legion. And I don't think most of them hate themselves or hate being attracted to men. But because these men are busy living their lives without wrapping themselves in their sexual identity, because they are busy simply *being men*, they go unnoticed. (x, xi)

Claiming to be marginalized by those who themselves are marginalized, Malebranche ignores the existence in gay communities of men who belie his false, blunt dichotomy between "living one's [implicitly normal] life" and being gay—men who do not confine themselves to a gay ghetto, or for whom being gay doesn't necessarily (or only) mean riding on a pride float in nothing but short shorts and leather boots. Furthermore, Malebranche's own screed against gay identity disregards the import of his own trajectory into and then out of the gay community:

> While I've always been critical of the gay hive mind, I haven't always been the outsider I am now. I spent a significant portion of my life traveling in gay circles, hanging out in bars and gossiping with queens. In the early 1990s, I was a go-go dancer in New York City's club kid scene. I ran around in elaborate costumes and makeup. I've shaved my

> body, colored my hair, and pierced my eyebrow. I've been a fashion fag and an enthusiastic pop-culture addict. I've challenged gender constructs. I've done drag. I've talked the talk and fagged out with the best of them. I've been to backrooms, leather clubs, bear bars, hipster hangouts and circuit parties. I even marched in a gay pride parade once. I know the gay community from inside out. . . . I know what the gay lifestyle has to offer.
>
> . . . Eventually, I realized that while I was experiencing many things in the gay world, I was shutting out so much more, I was living in a gay bubble, dissociated from nongay men, cut off from a part of myself that was distinctly, unmistakably male.
>
> . . . Men who love men have a place in the world beyond the gay world; they have a place in the world of men. (xi–xii)[7]

Is there something about certain sex-related professions that turns its gay practitioners into conservatives, if not career homophobes? Malebranche was a go-go boy. Jeff Gannon, who ran a partisan Republican Web site and regularly attended White House press conferences (and perhaps performed other services while there), was an escort. Matt Sanchez, darling of the Right's campaign against liberal bias in higher education, was formerly a gay porn star. (Gannon and Sanchez are discussed in chapters 2 and 5, respectively.) If not explicitly Republican, Malebranche has made the same arc, from gay to "androphile" (read: "postgay"?), from sex worker to a conservative (in matters of gender at least). Equally striking, and more immediately relevant, is his failure to countenance other ways of being gay, almost a refusal to conceive of club queens and "normal" same-sex–oriented men as possibly ever cohabiting the same culture or subculture, of being capable of moving between subcultures, or of inhabiting both in turn. For Malebranche, to walk into a gay bar is to be trapped in a "bubble," wholly "dissociated" from straight men, from masculinity, unless one is strong enough to go hyperbutch as he did and cross back over to Jordan's manly side. Despite the existence of gayborhoods, gay and lesbian bookstores, bars, and community centers, such spaces are open to and often frequented by straights as well as queers. Gay bathhouses and adult bookstore backrooms are more restricted, but on the basis of gender; their clientele include gay as well as bisexual (and some straight) men. All of these establishments still exist within larger heterosexual spaces; gay men must move through and inhabit straight spaces every day; we live there. As a character from Terrence McNally's *Love! Valour! Compassion!* says, "[S]traight people. . . . There's too goddamn many of them. I was in the bank yesterday. They were everywhere. Writing checks, making deposits. Two of them were applying for a mortgage. It was disgusting. They're taking over. No one wants to talk about it but it's true" (58). It's facile to conceive of gay experience as hermetically sealed off from the larger culture. Yet this is the scenario—and the dichotomous set of extremes—conceived of both by the larger culture and, as Malebranche's diatribe attests, by some gay men themselves. Malebranche is right on one point: association with gays or a gay subculture is entirely a matter of individual choice. It's also a matter of opportunity and access. One can be gay and associate with few to no straight men, or with almost exclusively straight men. But the insistence of *Queer Externalities* is that the option of a largely gay space is worth preserving, whether or not one lives in a gayborhood, frequents gay bars, or has many gay friends. Association is a choice, but affiliation should not be. Malebranche may express himself more bluntly than Mika, but the sentiment is at base no different. Distaste for homogeneity stems from, or translates into, an antipathy for homosexuality. It amounts to the same in the end.

As much as it might rile those like Malebranche, the perceived (and, on some level, actual) militancy of a project such as mine is inevitable in the current climate. Neither is it contrived. And while ghettoized isolationism without an ameliorating political, social interestedness seems misled, ghettos themselves are not the shallow, alienating oubliettes that apostles of the "post-gay" movement would have us believe (as if American culture in general were not as capable as gay subculture of being shallow or alienating). This is hardly to say that gays or lesbians who don't live in or near urban areas with a visible and significant queer population are somehow inauthentically queer. But gayborhoods—indeed, any safe, reserved real or rhetorical space for queers—are valid and necessary, as some minimal space cleared, even if not entirely or permanently, of the overwhelming ubiquity and righteousness of straightness. A historically semipermeable neighborhood, the gay ghetto stands as and stands in for the conscious attempt to regulate intercultural transactions, to monitor, perhaps deflect or queer, the flow and impact of heteronormatively vectored energies. It's in this way that my argument is likely to seem perverse, for recommending the maintenance and intermittent embrace of what many queers view as a liability, a relic of a radical past. Whether taken literally (visiting a gay ghetto) or figuratively (holding open some space for abstention or resistance), the gay ghetto is valuable for what it keeps in and out on both sides. Likewise, some queer externalities may yield simultaneously negative and positive dimensions. The gayborhood needn't (and probably shouldn't or can't) circumscribe one's sociocultural environs, account for one's only positioning. But it should be acknowledged for its utilities, relied on periodically for its saving capabilities and ludic allowance.

It's not my intent to advocate what David Van Leer calls a strict margin/center dichotomy in reference to queers and straights, or heteronormative culture and queer subcultures. Here I concur with Van Leer's comment in *The Queening of America*: "Whatever the perks of empowerment, I doubt that anyone aspires to occupy 'the center' as such or that 'the margins' are where minorities feel themselves to live—either as exiles or as cultural insurrectionists. And no critique of the inside/outside dichotomy admits the extent to which persons, indifferent to referentiality, often experience their position simply as 'here'" (9). As nonrepresentative of most queer (and nonqueer) persons' lives as dichotomous models (margin/center, homo/hetero) may be, they do hold powerful attractions: the lure of making it from one side to the other and the lure of thinking that one might abolish the paradigm altogether. While they may not (perceptibly) structure one's everyday experience, the representational plinth is there, an ideological force that exists regardless of one's attempts to disavow it.

Weighing in on the constructionism/essentialism debate in order to declare one's fealty to one side or the other (if not both) has become de rigueur for discussions in queer studies—and for good reason. Queer theory has illuminated the historical embeddedness of sexual identity: rather than a universal, transhistorical category, what we usually mean when we refer to homosexuality refers not so much to certain behaviors and desires but to an *alignment* of behaviors and desires particular to Western culture from the mid-nineteenth-century onward.[8] On the other hand, the modern gay and lesbian movement's arguments against discrimination, the activist "recovery" of a gay past (Plato, Michelangelo, etc.), and most gays and lesbians' senses of their own sexuality all rest on a conviction that sexual identity is not a choice but an inborn part of one's person, like eye or skin color—a rationale that constructionism would seem to undermine. Eve Sedgwick famously tried to bracket this impasse in *The Epistemology of the Closet* (suggesting "minoritizing" and "universalizing" as terms with less baggage as homophobic cudgels than constructionism and essentialism). However, David Halperin has argued the inescapability and continued relevance of the constructionist/essentialist model—with a slight yet convincing alteration. In *How to Do the History of Homosexuality*—a seminal work in queer theory on the order of Sedgwick's *The Epistemology of the Closet*—Halperin proffers a "rehabilitated constructionist approach": "readily acknowledging the existence of transhistorical continuities, reintegrating them into the frame of the analysis, and reinterpreting their significance within a genealogical [that is, historicized] understanding of the emergence of (homo)sexuality itself. A constructionist history of homosexuality . . . can easily accommodate such continuities. . . ." (106). Halperin's innovation in the long tug-of-war between constructionists and essentialists is to delineate the shifting alignments of same-sex desires, acts, and gender behavior—the "long historical process of accumulation, accretion, and overlay"—that constitute "sexuality" uniquely at different periods in history.[9] My reading of Halperin, a reading that informs much of *Queer Externalities*, is that sexuality may be thought of as historically constructed, but that within that, our range of movement—the options for willed reconfiguration of elements that make up those categories—is limited. Historically embedded and culturally constructed, sexual identity is essential within a paradigmatic moment (such as our present homo/hetero paradigm)—changeable, but not by individual will or in a visible way in any single moment or series of moments. As with the evolutionary theory of punctuated equilibrium, the transformation or *re*construction of sexualities is a slow, accretive, and not (entirely) conscious or intentional process.

That's not to say that revision is impossible.[10] Advocating the preservation of certain boundaries, even permeable ones, is bound to strike some as backwardly essentialist. Shoring up the notion of a gay ghetto, rhetorical or real, may seem counter to current activist impulses. A position like mine may also come under philosophical scrutiny. In *Bodies That Matter*, for example, Judith Butler (most famous for *Gender Trouble* and her theory of gender performance/subversion) voices concern over the essentializing tendency of gay and lesbian identity politics. "[A]ttribut[ing] a false unity to heterosexuality," a relational understanding of homosexuality—as *not* heterosexuality—"paradoxically . . . weaken[s] . . . the very constituency [gay or lesbian identity] is meant to unite" (113). Inasmuch as gay and lesbian identities can be seen, far from problematizing heterosexuality, as confirming the larger framework (homo/hetero) to the exclusion of other positions (not limited to bisexuality), it is certainly worthwhile to think through

> the potential cruelties that follow from an intensification of identification that cannot afford to acknowledge the exclusion on which it is dependent, exclusions that must be refused, identifications that must remain as refuse, as abjected, in order for that intensified identification to exist. This is an order of refusal which not only culminates in the rigid occupation of exclusionary identities, but which tends to enforce that exclusionary principle on whomever is seen to deviate from those positions as well. (116)

Butler cautions against the tendency, under the homo/hetero paradigm, to "disavow a constitutive relationship to heterosexuality" in order to escape heteronormativity's association of homosexuality and abjection," a disavowal "enacted as a political necessity to *specify* gay and lesbian identity over and against its ostensible opposite, heterosexuality" (113). If anything, the following chapters show the obduracy with which queers are both definitionally bound to and abjected by the stipulations of heteronormativity. Blindly embracing or simply misreading negative queer externalities, instead of "disavowing" the double bind between homosexuality and heterosexuality, at once romanticizes that bond and fantasizes that the boundary differentiating gay from straight can be erased or is well on its way to being so. In my reading, contemporary queer culture, far from renouncing a constitutive relationship with heterosexuality, sometimes seems hazardously enthralled by its fundamentally homophobic totems.

It seems feasible (and advisable) to be sensitive to the historical contingency and adverse consequences of certain models of identity formation, even to work queerly toward a more equitable construction, and yet at the same time value the appreciable auspices and pragmatic sense of an essentialist model. There's a more than academic distinction to be made between reification and a commitment, as David Van Leer phrases it, to "risk[ing] essentialism [in order] to forestall explanation" (10). Van Leer, rather than "deconstruct . . . the homosexual/heterosexual binarism" by "exploring the indeterminacy of sexual identity," allies his work with

> recent revisionist accounts in African American and feminist scholarship that, at the "risk of essentialism," discover a social reality behind the constructed categories of "female" and "race." . . . Even on those days when I do not think that the homosexual/heterosexual dichotomy is here to stay, I am not convinced of the practicality of dismantling it unilaterally. Deconstructing difference might problematize homosexual identity yet leave heterosexuality blissfully unaware that its universality was under attack. (9)

"Deconstructing difference" might also encourage queers to think that its punitive powers have also vanished—been overcome—with the toppling of the paradigm, even if difference's dismantling is only rhetorical. My book examines contexts in which either assimilating (crossing from margin to center) or escaping the identitarian game altogether (which sometimes amounts, all the same, to a kind of assimilation) seems deceptively easy—obliquely exacting a compensatory price, an exclusion on some other front—or is revealed to be stubbornly elusive. As William Turner notes in *A Genealogy of Queer Theory* (2000), an individual "must articulate resistance within the terms of the identity, because the identity itself, or the definition of it, provides the supposed justification for oppression" (54). Being queer, like queering work, merits our energetic engagement. Turner puts it in more dire—yet undeniably practical—terms:

> People who live in a political culture that predicates rights and political legitimacy on one's status as an autonomous, responsible individual build oppositional political programs around the deconstruction of the subject only at their peril. As a theoretical critique, it may make sense to argue that the use of the identity categories "woman" or "lesbian" serves only to reinforce the very ideological and political structures that gave rise to sexism and lesbophobia in the first place. As a matter of daily resistance and practical strategies, this theoretical critique serves only to point out more clearly the terms on which everyone must negotiate power differentials: One who surrenders personal identity also surrenders all claims to resistance, even to meaningful existence within the political realm. (91–92)

We should beware, especially, of the intimation that queering is no longer needed or is too excessive, has already been adequately accomplished or is simply indecorous, offensive.

Queer negative externalities may of course stem from less obvious sources. The real and rhetorical militarization produced, by paranoid fiat, through Bush's War on Terror and invasion of Iraq have cemented the risk of contamination and infection as the national idée fixe. The "liquid bomb" plot in the summer of 2006, when rumors of a planned terrorist attack temporarily halted air travel, ratcheted fear of contaminants, particularly fluids, even higher. A few scientifically informed commentators explained the impracticality, if not near impossibility, of making a bomb with the chemicals in question while on board an airplane: triacetone triperoxide is so unstable that it would have to have been kept chilled until the plane was airborne, then titrated drop by drop during the flight; the fumes given off by the titration would attract other passengers' attention immediately, and, if the suspect sought the privacy of the bathroom, the fumes would have asphyxiated him in such a confined space.[11] But fear makes for better copy than reason, so most Americans never learned how unfeasible the ostensible plot was. The Transportation Security Administration issued a new set of safety measures regarding the transport of liquid on commercial air travel. A masterful combination of *Catch-22* and *Mission Impossible*, the rules required that any liquid, from shampoo to contact solution to soft drinks, be in containers no larger than three ounces and that all these containers be sealed in a transparent ziplock bag and offered for inspection at security. One is likely to be struck by the irony that an administration famous for fabricating a motive for war and illegally tapping citizens' phones would require transparency of its citizens. Gay readers are likely to find a yet more direct parallel: in the 1980s the real and continuing crisis of AIDS turned semen and blood from erotic and life-giving fluids into potential instruments of mass destruction. Although the threat in the "liquid bomb" plot seems chimeric, the parallel is there: everyday substances may harbor death-dealing agents.[12]

Lest homosexuality be eclipsed as the ultimate threat to civilization, however, a news story in summer 2007 reestablished gayness as a threat—although, this time, the threat was to our enemies. CBS reported that, in the military's efforts to develop nonlethal weapons, an Ohio Air Force lab proposed in 1994 "that a bomb be developed that contained a chemical that would cause enemy soldiers to become gay, and to have their units break down because all their soldiers became irresistibly attractive to one another" (Plante pars. 6, 4). Under the Freedom of Information Act, this proposal was uncovered through a request by the Berkley Sunshine Project, a nonprofit organization dedicated to fighting the post–cold war proliferation of biological weapons. A spokesperson for the Department of Defense "indicated that the 'gay bomb' idea was quickly dismissed" when first proposed (par. 7). As ludicrous as the idea of scientific research on aphrodisiacs may be, the gay bomb proposal reemphasizes American culture's phobic association of homosexuality with death, blight, and destruction. This incident also resonates with the theme of recruitment and the Right (addressed in chapter 5). Since Anita Bryant's 1977 Save Our Children Campaign, American social and religious conservatives have fought the gay and lesbian movement's push for equality and nondiscrimination with the specter of homosexual recruitment (that is, gays and lesbians adopting and then brainwashing or seducing children in order to make more homosexuals). A gay bomb relocates the origin of that threat. Instead of gays trying to "turn" straights, now it's heterosexuals (since, officially, there are no homosexuals in the military) trying to gay other straights—which, were it not in an attempt to rout the enemy, might almost seem progressive. As in so much American rhetoric, homosexuality remains a destructive force. Even though the gay bomb plot intends making gays as an *annihilating* creative act, it also belies straights' claims of noninvolvement in the propagation of homosexuality, unveiling the myriad ways in which queers are heterosexuals' representational—and literal—progeny. As the Village People sang, echoing the Uncle Sam military recruiting slogan, "They want you! They want you! They want you as a new recruit." Playfully accessing gay fetishes for the military and its uniforms as well as the homosexuality anecdotally endemic to the Navy, the lyrics also parody an implicitly heteronormative patriotism: "Come on, protect the motherland . . . Come on, and make a stand." Reversing the usual accusation of recruiting against gays, "In the navy" discloses the forcefulness with which we are all constantly being recruited, queers and straights alike, by normative categories of nation and sexuality.

Gay bombs and hazardous fluids suggest that the continued debate, within the gay and lesbian movement, between assimilation and separatism is not so easily settled. The choice is not so clear. Each strategy brings its own payoff and its own price. And each—assimilation and separatism—can often be found nested within its apparent antithesis. As Didier Eribon observes in *Insult and the Making of the Gay Self*,

> The idea that some kind of sexual "subversion" would necessarily be linked to politically progressive attitudes is an idea that needs to be abandoned. . . . [O]ne can be (more or less) "subversive" as regards sexuality and (more or less) conservative politically speaking. . . . It is clear, then, that we have to proceed on a case-by-case basis, always inquiring into the true content of what is called "subversion," inquiring as to what is to be subverted, and why, and even if there is anything whatsoever being subverted at all. (124)

The conservative impulses of some gays and lesbians may be unsurprising, but it's worthwhile considering their impact on queers of all stripes in a decade when homosexuality has become legal, more visible, and yet more unspeakable as a position of alterity—a distinct point of view not entirely divorced from norms (which seems impossible) but with some critical perspective on them. The hazard is not just that gays and lesbians are becoming too suburban, adopting kids and moving to Jersey (or becoming more amenable to domestic and reproductive norms) but that they feel generally accepted even as certain cultural chants against homosexuality have hardly abated and, from some influential quarters, have crescendoed. Considering queer encounters on a "case-by-case basis," as Eribon recommends, is, on some level, the aim of this book. Texts and developments that feel subversive may turn out to be quietly, covertly vectored toward assimilation. Those that smack of collaboration may, in fact, be capable of deferring or even splintering the accomplishments of their avowed normative projects. (This volatility is exacerbated by the diametrically conflicting ways gay conservatives and gay liberals conceive of progress—respectively, as assimilation and subversion.) Eribon writes,

> Consider . . . some of the "assimilationist" demands that one finds being made by gay and lesbian movements in many countries around the globe. Leo Bersani has described them quite cruelly (but justly) as revealing a "desire to demonstrate that we too can be good soldiers, good parents, good priests." Are such demands not necessarily shaped from the inside by the "unrealizable" quality of gay identity? That quality of gay identity—however it is conceived—introduces a slippage into any assimilationist project, any project that has as a goal to allow one to inhabit the social order. For no gay person will ever be accepted according to the established set of values into whose sanctum he or she may sometimes entertain the silly illusion of being admitted. This is shown . . . in all of the baroque arguments adduced by all the social and cultural agents of homophobia against the manifest desire of gay men and lesbians to be granted normal rights and normal forms of institutional recognition. These agents and their agencies repetitively reproduce a violent discourse that asserts on every occasion that gay people represent a great danger to society and to civilization. They thereby at least perform the service of reminding anyone worried about the "conformism" of assimilationist programs, that even those very programs contain the capacity to induce a kind of social and cultural instability—*one that homosexuality will always carry with it*—in the institutions that, some day or other, are going to have to make a place for it. (124–25; emphasis added).

If an inherent instability characterizes assimilationist as well as subversive projects, gay efforts at assimilation, or texts that seem to promise it, should not be so worrisome, for, if Eribon is correct, gays can never truly assimilate no matter how hard they try. Yet deluding ourselves into thinking it possible, or not freighted with enervating, unforeseen commitments, is hazardous enough to merit prophylactic, critical resistance. The discussions in *Queer Externalities* might warrant qualifying Eribon's final thought in the passage above, however. "[I]nstitutions" will not "*have* to make a place" for homosexuality or its "capacity to induce instability" because both homosexuality and the corrosive threat it supposedly represents are the constitutive, sacred core of heteronormativity, the sun around which all its satellites revolve and which imbues them with their coruscating glory.

By explicating an array of texts, products, incidents, and narratives, the following chapters attempt to spell out the ways in which certain cultural, political, and textual processes, as negative externalities, undermine the queer community—such as the now commonsense conviction that essentialisms are always bad, or that entertainment visibility and measured social and legal progress have rendered (queer) political identities archaic, if not unnecessary.

Chapter 1 juxtaposes Rita Mae Brown's 1973 coming-of-age novel, *Rubyfruit Jungle*, with gay young adult novels from the current decade in order to make two interrelated observations about the continued appeal of apolitical utopianism for queer audiences. First, while *Rubyfruit Jungle* is usually understood as a piece of lesbian/feminist literature, it can better be read as an antipolitical novel that repudiates its lesbian appropriation through a protagonist who doesn't like labels and rejects identifications with any group or community. Brown's brand of calculated political solipsism finds an odd parallel in gay political writing of the 1970s, where reaction against the prescriptive capacity of any role (straight or gay) leads to an abandoning of identity altogether. Second, a number of authors within the burgeoning field of gay young adult fiction are selling a utopian—or q-topian—vision of American life to both young adult readers and their thirtysomething counterparts. But these headily gay-positive q-topias are riven by a worrisome, unacknowledged contradiction: although in the worlds imagined by Sanchez, Levithan, and Hartinger, gays win acceptance on a par with their heterosexual peers through little or sometimes no effort, those worlds and the desires of their queer characters remain immured in the very totems and rituals by which heteronormativity historically propagates its autochthonic sanction. While soothing to queer readers weary of or indifferent to the fight for political and economic equity, q-topian narratives such as these are delusory and irresponsible negative externalities. Reaching a moment when gayness seems to no longer matter may be a laudable objective in the struggle for tolerance, but the "end of gay," we must remember, is equally amenable to those on the Right and the middle of political and moral spectrums who would like nothing better than our silence, passivity, and disappearance.

Turning to politics, chapter 2 investigates the role of masculinity, Francophobia, and a specifically right-wing notion of tolerance in the gay-baiting of John Kerry during the 2004 presidential campaign. Not limited, as one might expect, to Republican and conservative journalists and pundits, swipes at Kerry's masculinity and sexuality circulated in mainstream news outlets, demonstrating homophobia's basal imbrication in American (heteronormative) culture. Whether relying on coded insinuation or outright name-calling, media coverage of Kerry traded heavily on facile equations between "flip-flopping," effeminacy, and homosexuality—as opposed to Bush's hyperphallic, bellicose persona. More disturbing is the extent to which this stunningly naive yet *au fond* heteronormative model of gender and sexuality structured public discourse well beyond the 2004 campaign. Even as polls show increased tolerance among Americans for gay and lesbian equality (but not marriage's legal and economic privileges), efforts of conservative Christian and even federal officials continue to undermine tolerance for queers or simply edge them back toward public invisibility. Is there perhaps some perverse correlation between tolerance of queers and a willingness to tolerate antigay slurs as ridiculous and therefore harmless? Or have expressions of tolerance, from any direction, been poisoned by the conservative reframing of homophobia as a pseudodemocratic championing of equality against "oppressive" antidiscrimination policies?

In highlighting the queer representational anxieties stimulated by the first openly gay makeover show, *Queer Eye for the Straight Guy*, chapter 3 demurs from most critics in regarding the show as engaged in generating a positive queer externality, a ground for parsing the commonalities and the sharp disjunctures between gays and straights. Negative reactions to the show extend from concerns over the commodification of queerness to unease with gay stereotypes. The admittedly commercial nature of the genre within which the show's hosts complicitly operate does not, I argue, exclude the possibility of all critical engagement. I also contend that much of the negative criticism leveled at *Queer Eye*—opposition to the visibility of gay interior decorators, hairdressers, and sissies—is ultimately an assimilationist drive, a move to censor all but a narrow spectrum of the queer community: those straight-acting, professional fags who don't discomfit heterosexuals, and the stigmaphobic queers who seek to placate them. It's by camping it up with gay stereotypes, admitting what's true as well as erroneous about them, that *Queer Eye* not only claims a place in public discourse for the marginalized (lispers, femmes, and nellies) but also foregrounds gay desire in its typically most repressed (and for queers, most dangerous) venue: desire for the public male body. Whereas the shame and disgust for effeminacy present in most initial reactions to the show betray a cultural discomfort with homosexuality that transcends class, party, and even sexual orientation, *Queer Eye* honors gay desire at the same time that it punctures clichés such as the predatory homosexual.

Chapter 4 implicates *Brokeback Mountain*—the film, its reviewers, and the author of the source material, Annie Proulx—in a tragically truncated gay representational universe. The popularity of a gay cultural product is explicable, here, as a function of a particular kind of repudiation (or impossibility) of unapologetic queerness. Critical effusion over the film fails to question its fundamental inability, if not unwillingness, to envision gay happiness. Although *Brokeback* tells its story poetically and wistfully, the fact remains that Proulx and the filmmakers chose Ennis's tight-lipped isolation over Jack's willingness to imagine a life for the two of them (about Jack's death Proulx has said, "there was nothing I could do about it. It couldn't end any other way"). Hailed as a breakthrough in gay representation, *Brokeback*, frankly examined, is a joyless, hackneyed rehearsal of the doomed gay love story with which queers—and straights, for that matter—are all too conversant.

Chapter 5 traces American political and moral conservatives' reliance on the myth of gay recruitment to one of its watershed moments: Anita Bryant's 1977 Save Our Children crusade. But aside from simply being a bogeyman used to scare voters with the prospect that gays and lesbians want to turn children gay, it turns out that the Republican Party itself practices recruitment—of gay men. Like most of the "homocons" and "pink elephants" outed over the past several years, Mark Foley, Ted Haggard, and Matt Sanchez are notable as closeted gay men (or heterosexually identified men secretly having sex with men) who either worked in vocally homophobic political or religious organizations and/or themselves aggressively pursued gay-bashing rhetoric or legislation. Although most commentary on Foleygate referred to Foley incorrectly as a "pedophile" (as opposed to an "ephebophile"), coverage of the scandal demonstrates how closely, and how phobically, male homosexuality and pedophilia—and thus homosexuality and recruitment—continue to be associated in the American mind, despite repeated studies identifying almost all pedophiles as heterosexual (at least in their primary, publicly acknowledged relationships with another consenting adult). While it may seem mystifying that someone would labor on behalf of an organization that actively seeks their disenfranchisement, if not eradication, the figures of the closet (Sedgwick) and the pariah (Dillard) suggest the particular ideological convolutions requisite for gay conservative identity. Perhaps identifying primarily as conservative and conceiving of identity as exclusively public in nature allows someone like Senator Larry Craig to be sincere when he says, "I'm not gay, I've never been gay," to sincerely think of himself as heterosexual. The frequency with which gay conservatives are being "caught out" points not simply toward the arrogance of power or some deep psychological conflict, but rather toward the incompletely fathomed (and, for better and for worse, unfathomable) dimensions of the closet and its convoluted, shifting relations to both public and private lives. In addition to paralleling the Right's dependence on the gay recruitment myth, the closet's liability to colonization—in this case, by the Republican Party—underscores the totalizing, recruiting ambition of heteronormativity, its inclination to arrogate ideologies, representations, and even bodies for its own purposes, regardless of the negative externalities created for queers and others who stand athwart its norms.

Far from an argument for the embrace of an undiluted essentialism, *Queer Externalities* advocates an identitarian substrate on which the exigencies of history, time, and individual desire might exert both consolidating and splintering forces, capable of both fortifying and decentering identities.

1

At the End of the Rainbow

Q-topian Literature and the Lure of Apolitical Identities

FINE BY ME is a nonprofit organization, familiar to many high school and college students through their "gay? fine by me" T-shirt campaign, dedicated to battling homophobia. The success of this organization, and the popularity of its T-shirts, is oddly juxtaposed, however, with the political apathy of many young queers and their allies. Bracketing other cultural factors that have worked to depoliticize this population (along with many other Americans), this chapter looks at titles from the recent surge in gay young adult novels, such as Alex Sanchez's *Rainbow* series, David Levithan's *Boy Meets Boy* (2003), and Brent Hartinger's *Geography Club* (2003)—novels in which queerness is at once capitalized on and subsumed, normalized in gratifying feel-good narratives that relinquish a historically queer defiance of norms and stabilization as well as a pragmatic awareness of a wide variety of oppressions.

The early 2000s saw another development, parallel to and concomitant with the proliferation of gay titles for the young adult (or YA) market: the publication and prominent in-store marketing of gay adult titles by Kensington Publishing Corporation. In 2006, independent publisher Kensington's romance, fiction, and nonfiction titles—under the imprints Kensington, Pinnacle, Zebra, and Citadel—made up 7 percent of American mass market paperback sales. Deciding to expand their romance audience to include gay readers, the company began issuing novels such as Andy Schell's *My Best Man* (2000) and Timothy James Beck's *It Had to Be You* (2001). Due to its market share, Kensington was able to buy space for these and similar titles on the front display tables at megastores such as Barnes & Noble. During the gay literature boom of the 1980s—AIDS fiction and mainstream gay literary fiction—the book megastore did not yet exist. Even if it had, it's doubtful that merchants would have displayed a cluster of elegiac AIDS novels front and center, particularly in the early to mid-1980s when, courtesy of popular magazines and newspapers, the public face of homosexuality was the spectral "AIDS victim" (to use the anxiogenic parlance of that moment). Thus, Kensington's gay romance line marks the first opportunity for gay readers to see gay books conspicuously displayed in a public, mainstream consumer venue.

In contrast to Kensington's romance line, scaled back in 2007 due to disappointing sales, the future of gay young adult novels—the subgenre on which this chapter focuses—seems more promising. Publishers' loyalty to gay fiction is historically fickle, as evidenced when St. Martin's purged its lagging gay backlist in the late 1990s, yet the fact that major houses such as Simon and Schuster, HarperCollins, and Knopf (who have published Sanchez, Levithan, and Hartinger) are competing for this niche market suggests that the current cycle of gay literary success, though shifted to a younger demographic than in the past, has not yet run its course.[1] Scholastic has issued several titles, including David LaRochelle's *Absolutely, Positively Not* (2005) and Brian Malloy's *Twelve Long Months* (2008). Even Kensington, after its bid for the adult romance market, has turned to gay young adult fiction—such as Robin Reardon's *A Secret Edge* (2007) and *Thinking Straight* (2008) and Frank Anthony Polito's *Band Fags!* (2008).

Garnering prominent display space (both in megastores and infinitely smaller gay and lesbian bookstores) as well as critical praise, these recent gay YA novels are most productively read against the background of another extremely successful title, Rita Mae Brown's lesbian classic, *Rubyfruit Jungle* (1973). Not only is labeling Brown's novel "lesbian" somewhat questionable (the main character refuses to identify with any sexual community—gay, bi, or straight), but the model of sexuality embodied by Brown's protagonist, Molly Bolt, is utopian to the point of being unimaginable. As admirable as *Rubyfruit*'s rejection of labels might be from the perspective of a certain strand of queer theory—emphasizing the need to move beyond rigid systems of identification and develop understandings of sexuality's lability and expansiveness beyond the homo/hetero paradigm and beyond object choice—the lure of an identity without identity politics often amounts to simply apolitical identity. While this is what attracts young queer readers (and here I use "queer" in the sense of anyone who finds themselves at odds with regulatory cultural norms), it's a risky pleasure. The taste for ego-stroking reads like *Rainbow High* and *Rubyfruit Jungle* is also whetted by the rhetoric of the nationalized gay and lesbian political movement that, through vehicles such as the Human Rights Campaign and the Lambda Legal Defense Fund, emphasizes laudable goals of legal equity on issues of health care, property and custodial rights, and protection from discrimination, but does so in a civil-rights–inspired language based in sameness (we're as human as you are) and vectored toward assimilation (we're just like you).

For the purposes of this chapter, I have chosen to focus on gay YA novels, that is, novels written by gay men and featuring gay male protagonists. While some might find the transition from a 1970s lesbian novel to gay YA novels from the early 2000s problematic, the decision is based on methodological as well as commercial factors. Part of my argument is that even though *Rubyfruit Jungle* has long been cherished as a lesbian literary touchstone (it seemed a vast improvement over tortured predecessors such as Radclyffe Hall's *The Well of Loneliness* [1928] and Vin Packer's *Spring Fire* [1952]), calling *Rubyfruit* a lesbian novel feels odd inasmuch as its protagonist, Molly Bolt, eschews identification with any group, lesbians included. The anti-identitarianism and utopianism of Brown's novel are what connects it to novels such as *Rainbow Boys* and *Boy Meets Boy*. It is the heady optimism and apolitical ethos of *Rubyfruit* that these other more recent novels hearken back to, just as certain strains of current gay and lesbian activist thought evoke (if not consciously draw on) gay and lesbian liberationist ideas of the 1970s.

Examining the queer political language and interests contemporary to *Rubyfruit Jungle* and recent gay YA fiction contextualizes what is both so tempting and so illusory about identity without politics—queerness with little or no drama—particularly because identity so conceived encourages political apathy, diminishes consciousness of material injustice and inequities, and transmits the imperiling message that queers value the pith and substance of straight culture more than their own. Practically speaking, the attempt to imagine certain kinds of gay utopias—in which homosexuality is so accepted as no longer to matter, no longer to be homosexuality (as oppositionally defined)—amounts to a form of assimilation that, even in spite of itself, tends to serve the agenda of queer disappearance.[2]

Reading these gay YA novels is part of a larger effort to trace a noticeable shift, on the part of many straight and queer Americans over the past decade, toward a different sort of "fine by me" attitude than that envisioned in the "gay? fine by me" T-shirt campaign. Novels such as *Rainbow High* or *Boy Meets Boy* posit a level of tolerance and acceptance that doesn't match reality—which parallels a popular, though not universal, assumption among some gays and straights that the struggle toward tolerance is nearly, if not yet fully, won. Furthermore, such novels offer gay and gay-friendly readers a calming vision of a futuristic, utopian, and ultimately misleadingly gay-friendly world. And if gay readers are soothed into thinking that homosexuality no longer elicits (or will very soon cease to elicit) retaliatory acts, rhetoric, and resistance, then heterosexuals of various stripes might also welcome such an outlook. Moderate and liberal heterosexuals would feel cheered and psychologically assuaged by the nominal success story of yet another embattled minority. Sadly, the end toward which the liberal fight for tolerance is typically vectored—the day when difference is no longer pejoratively recognized—would also mollify those conservatives riled by the advent of tolerance.[3] In this instance, a liberal victory would also be a conservative one, solving the complaints of both camps and leaving queers the only losers. For the day when difference is no longer pejoratively recognized is hazardously close to the idea (embodied in certain conservative and religious scenarios as well as in the "postgay" movement) of difference—of "gay," if not gay people—disappearing altogether.[4]

Dr. Molly Feelgood; or, How *Not* to Stop Worrying and Love *Rubyfruit Jungle*

While it might seem strange to begin an examination of contemporary gay YA novels by discussing a novel published three decades ago—and, moreover, a novel routinely described as a "lesbian classic"—*Rubyfruit Jungle* was, and remains, one of the most popular gay or lesbian utopian texts of the post-Stonewall era. Rita Mae Brown is a highly successful, openly lesbian writer. Many of her novels, including *Rubyfruit Jungle*, feature lesbian content. Several of them are best sellers, but *Rubyfruit*—first issued in 1973 by Daughters Publishing, a small lesbian press, and picked up by Bantam in 1977—has been continuously in print for over thirty years. An achievement for any novel, this sort of longevity is sadly rare and especially commendable for a gay or lesbian title.

In my own experience teaching *Rubyfruit Jungle*, and the classroom experiences of some of my colleagues, student responses are uniformly glowing, if not downright fervid. Even from students not given to superlatives, infrequent or inactive readers who rarely seem to be moved by literature, the response almost invariably includes the words "the best book we have read in this class," if not "the best book I have ever read." Almost without exception, Molly Bolt, the novel's plucky protagonist, charms the socks off readers, regardless of background, sexuality, or gender. This novel's ability to elicit unmeasured praise is more than anecdotal, however. Take the following excerpt from a gay and lesbian literary encyclopedia published in 1997, almost a quarter century after the novel's first printing. The entry on Rita Mae Brown, by Beth Kattelman, concludes:

> Even though she has had a long and varied career, Brown is still best known for her semiautobiographical, picaresque novel, *Rubyfruit Jungle*, in which she introduces the headstrong young lesbian, Molly Bolt. Molly feels no need to apologize for her lesbianism and storms through society with her openness and honesty, refusing to conform to the expectations of either the dominant heterosexual society or the New York lesbian subculture. The novel espouses a doctrine of radical individualism that runs counter to much post-Stonewall lesbian literature that emphasizes communitarianism. *Rubyfruit* has sold millions of copies, and is one of the best-selling gay-lesbian books of all time. . . . Brown articulates a lesbian voice that resists categorization: nonetheless, a voice that began the tradition of the lesbian picara, the proud lesbian "hero." (119)

This entry reflects not only *Rubyfruit*'s power to speak to many different constituencies but also its largely unquestioned place of honor in the lesbian literary pantheon. As will soon become clear, referring to Brown's novel as a "lesbian classic" (which Kattelman is hardly alone in doing) or Molly Bolt as a "lesbian 'hero'" makes little sense (118, 119). Molly does not exactly "refuse to apologize for her lesbianism." She has sex with women but refuses to "label" herself a lesbian and, as Kattelman observes, rejects the embrace of urban lesbian subculture—a subculture that was the reason many lesbians left their hometowns to move to Manhattan. Part of what charms the readers of *Rubyfruit* with whom I've had the most contact (college students, mostly straight with a slim queer minority) is, very likely, what has attracted gay and straight readers since 1973: an uncompromising individualism that resonates with women's liberation rhetoric of the 1970s as well as with the mind-set of nearly any teenager, in the 1970s or now.

There's certainly nothing wrong with a good read, and Brown's long-term success is remarkable. Still, it's worth thinking about the cost at which queer visibility is gained in *Rubyfruit Jungle*, particularly since it is a cost most readers fail to recognize. That cost is especially visible against the background of both the feminist and the lesbian and gay liberation movements of the early 1970s. Sadly, *Rubyfruit Jungle* takes the liberationist impulse of those movements, the rejection of socially prescribed gender roles and sexualities, and ends up selling out what might seem to be its primary audience in order to garner the attention of wider audiences—adolescents, heterosexual men and women. Whether intentionally or not, this is a novel that everyone can read, and Molly Bolt is a character nearly everyone can identify with—an odd state of affairs for a book that's also considered one of the staples of twentieth-century lesbian literature. How does Brown manage to speak to lesbians at the same time she speaks—and quite fluently, it would seem—to gay men, straight women, bisexuals, and straight men?

Molly Bolt is an attractive character in part because she says what is on her mind; she uses profanity; she is sexually frank. But she's also a fundamentally (almost pathologically) evasive character: Molly is the nonconformist par excellence. *Rubyfruit* is a noncommittal novel, written in the heat of the feminist and gay liberationist early 1970s, when all roles, identities, and labels seemed utterly prescriptive, inherently repressive, tainted with history, indistinguishable from the patriarchy that perpetuated them. *Rubyfruit Jungle* engages readers because it taps into the ultimate solipsistic fantasy: being oneself, answering to no one, being allowed to explore one's world and identity without boundaries, without being forced to define or to make choices. By examining some of the rhetorical strategies Brown uses to give her novel the widest possible appeal—and looking more closely at precisely where Molly Bolt's outlook diverges from feminists such as Adrienne Rich and gay liberationists such as Carl Wittman and the Radicalesbians—this chapter argues that *Rubyfruit Jungle* attracts readers with the lure of a utopian space that in the end cannot be imagined. The discussion will then turn to newer YA novels, also utopian, that imagine an alluring world where homophobia has been erased, but a world that should not be desired because it is also a world where indifference to heteroegeneity slips effortlessly into homogenization, where blindness toward difference too easily dovetails with indifference toward the liminal and disenfranchised.

Brown's novel has received little critical attention aside from the original industry reviews and the perfunctory, rarely analytical inclusion in histories of lesbian literature.[5] From a literary critical perspective, this neglect is unfortunate, for literary criticism discerns—in high and low culture, regardless of so-called literary merit—the inner mechanism of textual desire, the solutions to hard cultural problems sought under narrative auspices. One of the only serious critical assessments of *Rubyfruit Jungle* was made in the mid-1980s by Leslie Fishbein. Fishbein offers a corrective for what she sees as the wrongheaded view of the novel's contemporary critics, for whom the novel is a "celebration of lesbian feminism" (155):

> The novel is completely narcissistic and selfish. It is an utterly individualistic tale that has no social consciousness or sense of commitment to a lesbian community. When lesbians are portrayed in groups, they are viewed as butches or femmes, as sexual predators. . . . The novel never evokes lesbian support networks or genuine gay friendships. The only oppression it seeks to correct is Molly's own. In that sense, *Rubyfruit Jungle* becomes the perfect document of the ME generation: it takes the new selfishness and makes it both gay and good. (158–59)

Fishbein's observations are well grounded: Molly makes a number of friends during her picaresque journey, but she retains few; she sleeps with both women and men, though she says she enjoys sex with women more. Relationships with women provide Molly some of her deepest insights into her own identity, yet she refuses to commit to any community—straight or gay. Beneath a prickly exterior of maverick sexual humor, denial of community is perhaps her core value. This is nonconformity in the strongest possible sense. In Molly's own words, "'You are for sure getting yourself screwed on rules other people make'" (70). More than simply an antidote to somber and parodic representations of lesbianism of the past (Hall's *The Well of Loneliness* is a prominent example), *Rubyfruit Jungle* rejects the concept of roles altogether.

Molly Bolt might appear to be a lesbian, but she identifies herself as such only once, and has heterosexual relationships throughout the novel. When the women she sleeps with describe themselves as lesbians, Molly asks why they have to "give it a name." When a lesbian approaches Molly in a gay bar and asks whether she's a "butch" or a "femme," Molly denounces these terms as she does all other categories. Molly has arrived at the bar with Calvin, a gay African American homeless ex-football player who is the first person she meets on arriving in New York City, with no place to stay herself. "'All I want is a drink or two,'" says Calvin, "then I have to go out and hustle for a place to stay tonight. Too damn cold in that car. Who knows, maybe some lady will be kind and put you up without having you put out. Oh, here comes a bull and she's heading straight for you. Christ, go to bed with her and she'll crush you."

Sure enough this diesel dyke barrels down on me, slams on her brakes and bellows, "Hi there. My name is Mighty Mo. You must be new around here. . . ."

[After brief banter, Mo asks me,] ". . . are you butch or femme?"

I looked at Calvin but there wasn't time to give me a clue for this one. "I beg your pardon."

"Now don't be coy with Mighty Mo, you Southern belle. They have butches and femmes down below the Mason-Dixon line, don't they? You're a looker baby, and I'd like to get to know you, but if you're a butch then it'd be like holding hands with your brother, now wouldn't it?"

"Your tough luck, Mo. Sorry." Sorry, my ass. Lucky she spilled the beans.

"You sure fooled me. I thought you were femme. What's this world coming to when you can't tell the butches from the femmes." . . . She slapped me on the back fraternally and sauntered off.

"What the flying fuck is this?" [I ask Calvin.]

"A lot of these chicks divide up into butch and femme, male-female. Some people don't, but this bar is into heavy roles and it's the only bar I know for women. I thought you knew about that stuff or I wouldn't have sprung it on you."

"That's the craziest, dumbass thing I ever heard tell of. What's the point of being a lesbian if a woman is going to look and act like an imitation man? Hell, if I want a man, I'll get the real thing, not one of these chippies. I mean, Calvin, the whole point of being gay is because you love women. You don't like men that look like women, do you?"

"Oh me, I'm not picky as long as he has a big cock. I'm a bit of a size queen."

"Goddammit. I'm not either one. Now what the fuck do I do?"

"Since you're here, you'd better choose sides for a warm bed. . . . It's not that bad for one night."

"It seems to me that if say I'm femme then the Mighty Moes of the world will descend upon me, but if I say I'm butch then I have to pay for the drinks. Either way I get screwed."

"The human condition." (146–48)

This scene resounds with dissonance and, like the rest of the novel, reveals more about the fragility of its philosophical stance than it means to. Most noticeable to gay readers, perhaps, is the inconsistency of Molly's comprehension of gay and lesbian slang. Molly employs certain terms with ease ("diesel dyke" and "bull") yet is inexplicably ignorant of basic gay jargon such as "butch" and "femme." Similarly, the novel's attempts at camp humor (much of it male) are either solecisms or jarringly incongruous: Molly claims she could "beat out Bette Davis for acting awards," and elsewhere calls a closeted lesbian a "'closet fairy'" (129, 128).[6] Brown is carefully punching tickets, attempting to garner as wide and diverse an audience as possible. As with the overdetermined "underclass" characterization of Calvin (a gay, black, homeless ex-football player), Molly's selective ignorance of lesbian slang in the bar scene suggests a certain opportunism in Brown's approach: speaking to communities in their own language but playing to the outsider. This is the antialliance position Fishbein speaks of, but Brown's endorsement of it creates strong doubts about the wisdom and integrity of honoring *Rubyfruit* as a treasured work of lesbian literature, at least one treasured by lesbians.

The final exchange between Molly and Calvin is revealing in a different way: "'if I say I'm femme then the Mighty Moes of the world will descend upon me, but if I say I'm butch then I have to pay for the drinks. Either way I get screwed,'" to which Calvin responds, "'The human condition.'" Calvin's terse reply smacks of gay-bar humor about the grim reality of Molly's currently homeless condition. Given the fact that *Rubyfruit* is not one of those novels that calls into question its protagonist's point of view, and given Molly's clear possession of center stage in this scene, it seems that Brown expects us to be shocked at Calvin's brutal objectivity and revolted by his acceptance of role-playing. Nonetheless, Calvin's words hit home, despite their throwaway delivery. The notion that having to "choos[e] sides" is the "human condition" touches on a reality that Brown, or at least Molly, seems determined to avoid: the roles and identities and labels that social and intimate lives spend so much time negotiating. In the immediate context, choosing sides may be a matter of expediency ("for a warm bed"), but—wise-old-queen humor aside—choosing sides is, as Molly repeatedly finds, a human compulsion. Her insistence on "the real thing, not one of these chippies" is, as Jonathan Dollimore has pointed out, an extension of the "charge of inauthenticity to one's own kind" (94). Of course, Molly refutes the very terms of Dollimore's reading: the lesbians in the bar on Eighth Avenue are not her "own kind"; rather, she herself, Molly would insist, belongs only to *her* own kind. This claim to membership in a class of one's own is epitomized by what might be the novel's watch cry: "'I can't like anybody if I don't like myself'" (36). Liking oneself in this context appears to depend on being not just authentic but uniquely so, for, to Molly's eye, butch and femme lesbians are playing parts that are no better than those of heterosexual women and men. They are still acting. Molly claims that only she is not acting a role, that only she is being herself—in short, that only she is truly authentic.

What is most fascinating about this scene is that Calvin, though dismissed by Molly's uncompromising individualism, seems to speak the truth, a truth that resonates longer than Molly's own "free to be me" diatribes. Earlier in the novel, when one of Molly's female lovers inquires whether "'you're queer,'"

Molly lashes out: "'So now I wear this label "Queer" emblazoned across my chest. Or I could always carve a scarlet "L" on my forehead. Why does everyone have to put you in a box and nail the lid on it. I don't know what I am. . . . Do I have to be something?'" (107). Calvin says "yes," and I would argue that some part of Brown herself, though outvoted, agrees with him. The violence of Molly's diction ("carving" initials and words into one's flesh, being "nail[ed]" up in a coffin) exaggerates, a bit histrionically, the potency and permanence of discursive representations that, though undeniably formidable, are always attempting to construct and stabilize a fluctuating entity.

Though Molly Bolt seems dismissive of her, Mighty Mo speaks what was for many in the gay liberation movement a damaging heterosexist myth (but was perhaps also simply a politically incorrect truth). Mo knows what she wants: she wants a femme. Pursuing another butch is a waste of her time. While one might say Mo has internalized a restrictive paradigm (which was a compulsory code of social behavior for many, though not all, pre-Stonewall lesbians), the fact that this butch prefers only femmes does not mean that all butches feel the same. As Calvin, the self-proclaimed "size queen" implies, everyone has their predilections; being butch is Mo's. Further, it is interesting that Brown overlooks the possibility that exists at the heart of an apparently stagnant milieu: Mighty Mo has to ask Molly about her role, which is to say that roles are not always legible, determinable—and by extension, not determinate. A role does not define the extent of a person or dictate in perpetuity the full range of her behavior. Although Mo might have assumed Molly was a femme, this is, as Mo says, a "'world [in which] you can't tell the butches from the femmes.'" Once again, minor characters in the novel demonstrate an elasticity about gender and sexual roles, and a variability within those roles, which Molly repudiates and of which the novel itself seems to remain wholly ignorant.

Free at Last?

While Molly's desire to transcend anything that resembles the current social construct may seem naively idealistic, in 1973, when the novel was first published, such idealism seemed to hold serious promise for foundational, wide-reaching social and political change in the eyes of both feminists and the men and women within the gay and lesbian liberation movement. Certainly, an indictment of the existing social order and the gender roles it inculcates could be found in statements by almost any gay liberation group. Take, for instance, Carl Wittman's "Refugees from Amerika: A Gay Manifesto," one of the movement's founding documents:

> We are children of a straight society. We will think straight, and that is part of our oppression. One of the most fucked up of straight concepts is inequality. Straight (also, white, male, capitalist) thinking sees things

> always in terms of order and comparison. A is before B, B is after A. . . . This idea gets extended to male/female, on top/on bottom, spouse/nonspouse, heterosexual/homosexual; boss/worker, rich/poor, white/black. Our social institutions cause and reflect this verbal hierarchy.
>
> We have lived in these institutions all our lives, so naturally we mimic the roles. . . . [W]e are becoming free enough to shed these roles which we've picked up from the institutions which have imprisoned us. (Wittman 161)

Words like these echo throughout the 1970s, from Wittman's 1970 manifesto to Adrienne Rich's landmark 1980 essay, "Compulsory Heterosexuality and Lesbian Existence." The list of institutions rejected by queer and feminist liberationist critiques for perpetuating a set of restrictive roles usually begins with marriage and the nuclear family, both of which dictate heterosexuality as the normative paradigm. Marriage is shunned, to use Wittman's concise Marxist formulation, for its encouragement of "propertied attitudes" (162). Unsurprisingly—though it seems from our present perspective, problematically—this critique ends up questioning not just prescribed gender roles and sexual identities but also the viability of *any* concept of gender or identity. Molly Bolt's insistence on sexual freedom is consistent with Wittman's attack on monogamy: marriage makes "promises about the future, which we have no right to make and which prevent us from . . . growing" (Wittman 162). Worse yet, marriage is founded on "inflexible roles . . . which do not reflect us at the moment but are inherited through mimicry. We have to define for ourselves a new pluralistic, role-free social structure" (162). Despite these similarities, however, Rita Mae Brown goes further than any gay liberation activist in asserting independence from community in any form—further than Phyllis Katz (author of "Smash Phallic Imperialism") or separatist groups such as the Radicalesbians ("Leaving the Gay Men Behind") and the Gutter Dyke Collective ("This Is the Year to Stamp Out the 'Y' Chromosome"). Even in writings of the most radical separatist, one finds some commitment to a common cause, to a polity of the like-minded.[7]

While there is surely fault to be found with institutionalized heterosexuality, the difficulty lies in getting outside the system, being able even to think outside it. The real difficulty for these liberationists was theorizing not just a viable, nonessentialist form of social construction beyond the present one, but a new set of concepts. Wittman's discussion of bisexuality is a case in point:

> The reason so few of us are bisexual is because society made such a big stink about homosexuality that we got forced into seeing ourselves as either straight or nonstraight. Also, many gays got turned off to the ways men are supposed to relate to women and vice-versa, which is pretty fucked up. Gays will begin to get turned onto women when 1) it's something that we do because we want to, and not because

> we should; 2) when women's liberation has changed the nature of heterosexual relationships.
>
> We continue to call ourselves homosexual, rather than bisexual, even if we do make it with the opposite sex also, because saying "Oh, I'm Bi" is a cop out for a gay. We get told it's okay to sleep with women, too, and that's still putting homosexuality down. We'll be gay until everyone has forgotten that it's an issue. Then we'll begin to be complete people. (159)[8]

In language deliciously of its time, Wittman makes an early and laudable insight into the shared animus of gay and lesbian liberation and feminism. But this insight is not without its logical problems: for one, if bisexuality is the inherent human condition, that does little to obviate the distinctions on which the objectionable categories are based. Bisexuality is no less predicated on essentialism than heterosexuality or homosexuality; how is assuming everyone is bisexual an improvement over assuming everyone is straight? Whereas the second paragraph above is on one level a prescient comment on the divergence (or at least complex relation) between sexuality and sexual activity, it also pinpoints, perhaps unconsciously, the counterintuitive catch-22 that Molly Bolt demands. Gay men find themselves, in Wittman's world, in the confusing dilemma of identifying as gay in spite of their present sexual activity in order to further the movement (gay liberation) that somehow is attempting to pave the way for an adequate recognition of bisexuality. The idea of a sect dedicated to its own eradication may seem odd, though not uncommon. What is worrisome, however, is the disingenuousness Wittman would ask of men, whatever their sexual preference, the dishonesty on which the gay liberation movement seems here to be founded: being bisexual but pretending to be gay for the sake of gaining political critical mass. And if one is actively bisexual, in what sense is saying "I'm bisexual" a "cop out"? The referent of "we" in the second paragraph continues to slip in the last two sentences: "We'll continue to be gay until everyone has forgotten that it's an issue. Then we'll begin to be complete people." Is Wittman suggesting that men who currently identify as gay are simply in denial, or only shamming, refraining from sex with women until "real" gay men—who they're (it seems) pretending to be—have won equity? By comparison, Brown's take on bisexuality is less confusing than Wittman's. After having sex with her longtime friend Leroy, Molly makes a hedging declaration ("maybe I'm queer") but immediately commits to sleeping with "twenty or thirty men and twenty or thirty women before I decide" (70).

A world without labels and roles is a very pleasant fantasy, but it's largely that. Reality, at least the reality of women's and lesbian's lives even today, doesn't work that way. The one ground on which Fishbein seems to praise the novel is its moving beyond the "stereotype of lesbianism being a parody of straight life" (156): "Denied knowledge of nurturing friendship and support networks among lesbians by the distortions of existing lesbian literature and the historical denial of lesbianism, lesbian culture in the 'old days' parodied straight culture in its emphasis on butch and femme" (155). Yet the praise is merely perfunctory, for Fishbein is quick to point out that, despite a commitment to "celebrati[ng] . . . the joys of lesbian life," "lesbians are . . . viewed [by Molly and by extension Brown herself] as butches and femmes, as sexual predators" (158–59). Any illusions the novel has in terms of transcending parodic depictions of lesbianism are undone by its remaining mired in both the argot and the concepts of lesbianism as parody. Despite the fact that "butch" and "femme" fail to exhaust the possibilities for lesbian sexual and behavioral roles, these images of the self are still emphatically operative. Lesbians still reference, enact, and embrace as well as trouble these stereotypes. But they play within them, as well as outside them. The key—not visible in 1973 and perhaps not yet in 1984 when Fishbein writes—is not to fall into the trap of assuming that roles such as butch and femme are finally definitive, that once chosen or even flirted with, they stick irrevocably and define the shape of one's inner and outer lives indefinitely. Butch and femme roles might stand for any set of identitarian positions (sexual and binary, or otherwise); and, like being a bossy leather bottom or a dominant foot fetishist, these positions continue to structure, in various permutations, human sexual lives. They do not provide a pattern that those lives would otherwise lack; they provide a pattern, and pleasure is taken in what they contain as well as what they allow.

Certainly, not all individuals commit themselves to a discrete sexual identity, nor should they be compelled to. By the same token, while in a perfect world no one would be judged or categorized according to arbitrary categories, in reality they are. The last thirty years have raised awareness of roles, binarisms, and their arbitrary character, yet there seems to be little chance of roles themselves disappearing altogether. Those are the categories we have to work with; if we throw them out, where do we go from here? How do we talk about ourselves, negotiate our lives and desires in terms that anyone but each individual would, by him or herself, understand? Furthermore, in casting aside labels such as "lesbian" and "feminist," don't we risk losing sight of the tremendous amount of work still to be done in advocating for and guaranteeing nondiscrimination and equal treatment? Ultimately, the weakness of this vision is not Brown's alone but that of a movement. What neither Brown nor Wittman foresees—perhaps what neither would accept—is the notion that consciousness of hierarchy permits subversion and transformation of the system on its own terms.[9]

It's important to distinguish Brown's and Wittman's bristling at the reified nature of sexual identity under the homo/hetero paradigm from queer theory's deconstruction of identity as nonstatic.[10] *Rubyfruit Jungle* is understandable as a flight from what Judith Butler describes as the "tacit cruelties that sustain coherent identity [such as] the abasement through which coherence is fictively produced and sustained" (*Bodies That Matter* 115). Indeed, Molly's disavowal of any of the subcultures she encounters could, perhaps generously, be read as anticipating Butler's critique of the centrifugal, fragmenting direction in which identitarian politics and feminist/queer/race theory analyses often push one. Yet this reading is finally too generous. Where queer theory affords and encourages resistance, play, and revision within a range of behaviors and ideas outside received delimitations, Molly Bolt wishes to play without engaging with other players, without choosing (even temporarily) specific tools. She wants to play, but only a game no one else has ever played, and she seems reluctant to play it with other people. Rather than inhabit roles and positions, Molly—immaturely and unproductively—wants to take her marbles and go home.

Does any of this bring us closer, then, to grasping *Rubyfruit*'s relevance for and popularity with present-day readers—both straight and GLBT youth? "Crossover" enthusiasm for gay-themed texts from straight readers manifests, on one level, the rejection of previous generations' attitudes toward homosexuality; at the same time, it signals two pitfalls—one for gay and lesbian literature, and the other for the readers themselves. The debate on the meanings and conditions of mainstream success for gay and lesbian writers deserves further elaboration (though critics of such success can rest easy, given the lack of sincere support from the major publishing houses).[11] Still, what does it mean when one of the most popular lesbian novels of the last fifty years continually eschews alliances, and acknowledges no sense of community with lesbians or women—even though straight women and gay men constitute a generous segment of its readership? Could the novel's popularity across identitarian lines imply a commitment to assimilation, despite its vociferous individualism? The issues here are complex enough to merit further discussion, but *Rubyfruit Jungle*'s ambivalence toward community in any form is relevant to the current crisis of gay and lesbian publishing, and concomitant issues of where gay and lesbian literature belongs, to whom it's marketed, and what sorts of narratives and genres various publishing houses are willing to support (erotica, crime novels, boy-gets-boy novels, self-help books).[12] Also worth considering in this context is the success of lesbian novelist Sarah Waters, whose most compelling and well-crafted narratives, *Affinity* (1999) and *Fingersmith* (2002), are also those in which lesbianism or sexuality is not the central or constant focus (as opposed to 1998's *Tipping the Velvet*). *Fingersmith*, especially, is a nineteenth-century narrative that brackets modern standards of sexual identification and depicts women who love women as agents enlisted in heterosexual plots of suspense and intrigue. It is difficult to separate the power of Waters's storytelling from the *Rubyfruit*-like attractiveness of a world in which lesbians are not just lesbians (as if that were an impoverished space). Finally, to what extent can *Rubyfruit*'s popularity with straight readers, as well as twentysomething gay and lesbian readers, be attributed to the miring of American social culture and personal identity, for the past thirty years, in a static notion of individuality without connection, alliance, or responsibility to anything beyond the self?[13]

What would a world without roles, without identities, look like? How would it function? Such a space certainly never gets realized in the novel; how could it, when it's cognitively unintuitable? According to Steven Seidman, the unintuitable character of a sexual future unburdened by identitarian attributes was, at least conceptually speaking, the liberationists' Achilles' heel: liberationists

> challenged the dominant sexual/social regime by juxtaposing to it a polymorphous, androgynous ideal of a liberated—constraint-free—humanity. Wouldn't a liberated humanity, however, require stable identities, social roles, and normative constraints? Liberationists conflated the critique of rigid roles and identities with the critique of all identities and roles as signifying domination. In a word, liberationists projected a radically individualistic, utopian concept of emancipation. They lacked, moreover, a credible strategy to transform a stable, socially anchored gay/straight identity regime into a postidentity liberated order. (129)

If Seidman regards a "postidentity model" as "lack[ing] credibility today," it's important to note—in terms of *Queer Externalities'* larger argument about identity and politics—that he is equally critical of certain poststructuralist readings of identity, specifically, attempts, via queer and gender theory, to read identity as inherently unstable and always and everywhere subject to radical subversion. I concur with Seidman absolutely when he asserts,

> Identity constructions are not disciplining and regulatory only in a self-limiting and oppressive way; they are also personally, socially, and politically enabling; it is this moment that is captured by identity political standpoints that seems lost in the poststructural critique.
>
> ... [I]f, indeed, identity categories have enabling, self- and socially enriching qualities, then the issue is less their affirmation or subversion than analyzing the kinds of identities that are socially produced and their manifold social significance. In this regard, I would follow the poststructural move that recommends viewing identity as a site of ongoing social regulation and contestation rather than a quasi-natural substance or an accomplished social fact. Identities are never fixed or stable, not only because they elicit otherness but because they are occasions for continuing social struggle. . . . As disciplining forces, identities are not only self-limiting and productive of hierarchies but are enabling or productive of social collectives, moral bonds, and political agency. . . . [P]oststructuralism's own troubled relation to identity edges toward an empty politics of gesture or disruptive performance that forfeits an integrative, transformative politic. (134–35)

What Seidman pinpoints is the repeated disconnect—frequently worried over in queer academic and activist writings of the early 1990s—between idealism and practice, between the social constructionist revelation that identities are culturally contingent, historically prone to hierarchy, and the activist understanding that essentialism not only makes propriodescriptive sense but is crucial to forging a life on the ground, vying for greater agency, engaging with the world as we find it, and, hopefully, transforming it.

It's understandable then, that, from the vantage point of the early 1970s, the possibilities of working within the roles we're to some extent stuck with might have seemed slim to none. What's worrisome about the enthusiasm of *Rubyfruit Jungle*'s present-day readers is that their sympathies for Molly's fight to "just be herself" are unconnected to the feminist and gay liberation critiques of patriarchy and the politics of gender roles. Without a sense of the complicated history of liberationism in the feminist and lesbian movements of the past thirty years, these new readers of the novel are encouraged to indulge in the most counterproductive sort of escapism: one radically divorced from the world in which identities and labels still exist, the world in which any transformation of identity will have to be tested, if not developed in the first place. The question for contemporary readers of the novel is one that's unpopular to bring up, unlikely to be taken seriously, much less answered: Does Molly Bolt's rebellion against everything—reminiscent of Holden Caulfield's finding phoniness wherever he looks—constitute a substantive insight that can be put to use in transforming or even navigating social reality, or is this another trapdoor opening into the oubliette of feeling good about oneself for being unique in a culture where individuality has become the sine qua non of existence?

"Anything Less than Confetti-and-Sparklers Acceptance"

While no one can predict whether the *Rainbow* novels, *Boy Meets Boy*, or *Geography Club* will enjoy the print longevity of *Rubyfruit Jungle*, the volume, success, popularity, and visibility of a new wave of popular queer novels bear examination. Aside from the decision by some publishers such as Kensington to aggressively market gay titles, as well as the extent to which queer titles are enjoying the wider boom in YA literature, the appeal of titles such as *Rainbow High* and *Boy Meets Boy* results from factors beyond the mastery of a genre's conventions. Though not all to the same degree, authors such as Alex Sanchez, David Levithan, and Brent Hartinger emotionally pitch their writing at the apparent industry standard, portraying characters in their late teens as imagined from an adolescent point of view. This perspective would be less problematic, though only slightly, if the books' intended audience were young adults, that is, twelve- to eighteen-year-olds. But allusions to historical events and pop culture references that are unfamiliar to most teenagers born in the late 1980s clarify the ways these books speak to two audiences at once: queer teens, and those who were queer teens in the 1980s. Surely this latter group of thirtysomethings and fortysomethings is the readership Sanchez and Levithan are addressing by having their characters, present-day teens, reference Truman Capote, Oscar Wilde, Erasure, and 1980s Madonna. However, familiarity with Stonewall, Depeche Mode, and 1980s films (e.g., John Hughes's *The Breakfast Club* and Cameron Crowe's *Say Anything*) are not the only lure for those older than the ostensible YA target audience.

If *Rubyfruit* queered the Bildungsroman, these boy-novels queer the straightest narrative of late twentieth-century American pop culture: high school. High school, which of course reserves some of its cruelest gauntlets for queers, serves then as the therapeutic revisiting of a primal scene—if not the earliest scene of gay-baiting and ostracism, then perhaps the most torturous, as one's straight counterparts embark on the culturally sacralized path of heterosexual courtship. Like *Rubyfruit*, the boy-novels generally promise the untroubled pleasures of apolitical identity. Whereas the former may eschew identity politics out of an impulse (common to Stonewall era liberationism and present-day queer theory) to resist the regimentation of desire and the reductiveness that identity politics tends to effect, these more recent books do not so much renounce identity politics as take their givenness for granted. And that may amount to the same risk. For in assuming the efficacy of identity politics, visibility, and coalition building, these novels fail to question whether other mechanisms for alliance and change may exist, much less what other identitarian modalities the present model obscures, and, of most concern, what resistances, reverses, and failures the civil-rights/coalition model of GLBT politics has perennially failed to avert, dissolve, and overcome. Grown complacent with a reified public identity (interpellated equally by the vitriol of Fred Phelps and the courting of corporate advertisers), queer Americans may find in novels such as *Rainbow High* and *Boys Meets Boy* a heartening, telic reassurance: once a critical mass of visibility, of education, is reached, tolerance is a given. Amid the recent YA boom, Brent Hartinger's *Geography Club*—the focus of this chapter's final section—is one of the few to doubt the imminence of "anything less than confetti-and-sparklers acceptance" (7).

The parallels between the ethos and trajectory of Brown's novel and those by Sanchez and Levithan are convoluted but crucial to comprehending the empty promise and misleading pleasures of certain brands of utopian thinking. Molly Bolt wishes for a place where she can be whoever she wants to be and be roundly accepted for it, without allegiance to any group or community; Sanchez's and Levithan's characters, with token exceptions, find precisely that. What's distinctive about the boy-novels is that they lack *Rubyfruit*'s antisocial impulse. In fact, they are, if anything, compulsively social, longing for acceptance and mainstream inclusion. In a sense, then, the boy-novels are both utopian and normative. Contextually, this chapter suggests the relevance of timing to the success of Brown's and recent gay YA titles. In the early 1970s, during the birth pangs of what would become the contemporary American gay and lesbian movement, gay liberationists such as Wittman rejected roles and institutions wholesale. In the early 2000s, as many gays and lesbians have become both depoliticized and more content with positive attitudinal shifts in the culture, the same wishful escape into a world uncomplicated by affiliation has become, once again, increasingly appealing. But this newer utopian trend is more misleading and conflicted than Brown's: Sanchez's and Levithan's novels look forward to a gay-friendly future but contain a more confusing relation to heteronormativity.[14] Nominally resisting compulsions to adhere to sexual and behavioral norms, these authors' characters nonetheless remain worryingly enamored of some of those very norms, the institutions and conventions in opposition to which queer desires are historically defined.

Sanchez and Levithan conjure an atmosphere of acceptance as eerie in its excess and suddenness as it is falsifying in its ease and totality. In terms of how these novels answer certain political or cultural desires, I argue that, while the conflicted and what I call unpremeditated utopianism of such texts may be motivated by the desire to map out a queer-friendly world for today's queer youth (and in so doing, rewrite the pain of one's own high school years, formative as some might argue that experience is), such rewriting does young queer readers a disservice by eliding the numerous, weighty roadblocks on the path toward GLBT equality as well as delivering a unidirectional, somewhat unqueer sense of what that future is, and a sense that that future is singular. These novels' particular utopian vectors may well constitute a reaction against the continuance of inequality, discrimination, and hate crimes. And that, one might object, is the modus operandi of the utopian text: to depict, as Thomas More first defined the term "utopia," a "good place" that is also no place. By definition, utopian texts vault toward futures that can't always be imagined from the present. But imagining a world elsewhere without positing how one might approach it, at least incrementally, is not a pleasure queers can presently afford. Sanchez and Levithan in particular ignore More's central ironic insight: that liberation is not antithetical to the continuance of some forms of abjection (slavery, in More's text). For just as More's ideal society, which has abolished money, overcome the evils concomitant with class and property, and instituted free health care and education, nonetheless condones slavery, the utopias—or "q-topias," as I prefer to call them—sketched by Sanchez and Levithan remain hazardously beguiled by forces and traditions antagonistic to their interests, if not existence.

Pulling Yourself Up by the Jockstrap

It's not that homophobia doesn't exist in novels such as *Rainbow High* or *Boy Meets Boy*. It's that homophobia exists as minimal, token resistance and crumbles, for the most part immediately, in the face of logical and emotional appeals—the same appeals that, in the hands of gay activists, have historically done little to win over neutral audiences, let alone committed homophobes. The pace of acceptance may be exaggerated (perhaps for dramatic effect), yet concerns about its price and conditionality rarely cloud the blithe ether in which these characters by and large exist. Levithan's *Boy Meets Boy* takes place in a future when queers are, with one exception, so widely accepted that the only possible drama becomes a gay version of the historically heterosexual romance. Sanchez's trilogy—*Rainbow Boys* (2001), *Rainbow High* (2003), and *Rainbow Road* (2005), in which three high school seniors narrate their final year together—grafts its own vision of tolerance onto characters whose status as athletes (and often, whose ideals and desires) could not be more normative.

Although Sanchez's *Rainbow* novels are not futuristic, acceptance is still largely there for the taking. When protagonists Jason Carillo and Kyle Meeks come out, support manifests itself almost instantly, marginalizing if not transforming homophobia by a sort of attitudinal alchemy. Muddling the ideality, however, is the fact that two of the three protagonists—in fact, the two who come out—are jocks. Jason Carillo is the school's star basketball player, and Kyle Meeks, a member of the swim team; both Jason and Kyle come out during the first novel, *Rainbow Boys*, Kyle preceding Jason. The third protagonist of the trilogy, Nelson Glassman (or "Nelly," as the school's jocks have nicknamed him), is out before the first novel begins. A somewhat stereotypical finger-snapping queen complete with a camp idiom and neon-colored hair, Nelson thus wins peer acceptance only when a member of the group who formerly teased him (the jocks) comes out—and to cheers of support and accolades for bravery, no less. The somewhat incestuous coupling of the two gay jocks seems indicative of the compromised progressivism of Sanchez's novels, the intensity with which they fetishize stasis as much as change.

Denial and intolerance are not wholly absent. Jason's father once beat Jason for kissing a boy at ten years old and regularly calls his son "fairy boy," "pansy," and "queer" (RB 27).[15] But this abusive alcoholic, one of the *Rainbow* novels' few irredeemably bad guys, is easily vanquished, deserting his family when an openly gay Jason finally strikes his father back. Kyle's parents are comparatively much more supportive: his mother is almost instantly accepting; his father comes around when he learns that his son's boyfriend is Jason, a star athlete. When Kyle tells his father that Jason defended him and Nelson from gay-bashing peers, Mr. Meeks

> gave an impressed nod and handed Kyle the ice pack. "I think he's someone you should spend more time with."
>
> Kyle tried not to grin.
>
> His dad called the insurance people, beaming as he told them his son had been in a fight. (RB 203)

A gay son who gets in fights is a source of pride, whereas until this point Kyle's father had been stereotypically resistant to (though not homophobic about) his son's sexuality. Grateful for his father's approval, Kyle nonetheless can't help feeling slighted at the terms on which that approval has been brokered: "Although [he] never doubted his father loved him, he could tell Jason was the type of son he'd always wanted Kyle to be—self-confident, popular, winning" (RH 55). Speaking about his father, Kyle tells Jason directly, "'I think he likes you better than he likes me'" (59). Sanchez hardly suggests that Mr. Meeks loves his son solely for who he's dating. To his credit, Kyle's father confronts the swimming coach about tackling homophobia among Kyle's teammates. Yet none of this makes it less troubling—or makes the novel seem less enamored of the norm—that the implicit sting of a gay son is here ameliorated by that son's having a butch, athletic boyfriend. Mr. Meeks hardly seems a practicable or admirable model of acceptance when what renders his son's coming out palatable is its failure to negatively impact Kyle's social status or gender value (i.e., when, essentially, nothing he himself values changes) and the acquisition of a surrogate son who's true to all the norms his own son falls short of. Jason may be gay, but he's implicitly a better athlete who plays a butcher sport.

It's additionally telling that moments of tension—and later, acceptance—between Kyle and his father hinge not just on Kyle's sexuality but on attending sports events. In one argument, after a Redskins game, Kyle realizes the specific outlines of his own closet:

> "I never wanted to come to this stupid game to begin with."
>
> His dad shot him a hurt, angry look. "Then why didn't you say so?"
>
> Kyle crossed his arms, unable to explain it: how he felt guilty when his dad had his hopes up; how he didn't want to disappoint him. That was a big part of why it had taken him so long to come out.
>
> "You never asked, Dad. You think just because you like something, I will too. I never liked football, or hockey, or any of those things you think I should like."
>
> "Then why'd you come to all those games with me?"
>
> Kyle stared out the window. He'd gone to all those games because he wanted to be with his dad. He wished he could say that.
>
> "From now on," his dad said softly, "I won't ask you to come with me anymore."
>
> Kyle should've felt relieved and happy, but he didn't. (RB 105)

The cultural assumption Kyle bucks against is not merely that fathers expect sons to share their interests, but that fathers expect sons to be athletic, masculine, and straight. Tracing the umbilical double bind that oppositionally defines homosexuality and heterosexuality, masculinity and effeminacy, Kyle refuses to masquerade any longer as a sports fan in order to model what he assumes is (and correctly so, it appears) his father's ideal of heteronormative masculinity. Surprisingly, however, Kyle's resolution to stop attending sports events with his father is momentary: by the end of the first novel, he caves. Rather than negotiate new terms for their relationship, Kyle accepts the old ones, with one modification. When Jason asks Kyle to watch one of his games, Kyle has the "brilliant idea" of asking his father to attend also: after "giving Kyle a cautious, inquisitive look . . . he broke into a huge smile. You would've thought the prodigal son had come home" (RB 207). While Mr. Meeks may well have become less uncomfortable with his son's gayness in time, this quicker reconciliation is staged as a homecoming. And this homecoming is doubly fraught with traditionary, normative force: coming home to the father (as in the biblical homily about patriarchal benevolence) and returning to one's alma mater for, among other festivities, a football game. The sport may be different (basketball rather than football), and the game Kyle attends with his father does not occur during homecoming weekend, but the ideological alignment—of athleticism, forgiveness, and the twentieth-century school pageant of nostalgia for a primary site of heterosexual subject formation—is significant. Sanchez admittedly radicalizes the paradigm, with father-and-son bonding over an athletic event featuring the latter's gay lover. Yet the question remains whether this advance is capable of countermanding the aegis of athletics and the (heterosexual) family. Is the "quick, secret, glorious smile" Jason flashes Kyle from the court "quick" and "secret" because Jason hasn't yet come out, because Kyle's father is there—or the weighty combination of both (RB 208)?

Sanchez's *Rainbow* world is not utopian to begin with. Kyle finds the word "QUEER" spray painted on his school locker (RB 129). School bullies regularly harass Nelson and, as already mentioned, physically attack him and Kyle. At least one door in the school has the word "FAG" crudely etched into it (RH 94). In the name of not upsetting Jason's teammates, Principal Mueller urges Jason to delay coming out until after the state championship game. For the most part, however, the atmosphere sparkles with support. As the girlfriend of one of Jason's teammates exclaims after learning Jason has come out to his coach, "'It seems like everyone's coming out all of a sudden'" (RH 64). A jock coming out has exponential force, apparently. In *Rainbow Boys* the school board votes unanimously to allow the creation of a Gay-Straight Alliance at Walt Whitman High. (Given that Sanchez names the school after the author of gay utopian poems such as "I Dreamed in a Dream," utopianism is perhaps to be expected.) In *Rainbow High* the principal permits same-sex couples to attend the prom, where Nelson and his date, Jeremy, dance together. Acknowledging the pleasure some queer teens might derive from this inclusion of their desires in official/social discourse, one may yet feel it needlessly limiting to conceive of gay happiness within such conventional parameters, or rather to imagine that the queering of rituals and spaces will not be met with personal or institutional resistance and muzzling[16] or, alternatively, that their queering might not (or should not) have some transformative impact. In other words, it's at once unrealistic (though rosy) to imagine that deeply ingrained rituals can be effortlessly and instantaneously co-opted (when, in fact, many schools routinely ban the prom attendance of same-sex couples), and also disheartening that Sanchez's characters fail to look beyond the identificatory positions cultural institutions such as high schools are designed to inculcate (as if those positions are, in the moment, being discovered rather than (re)created and (re)inscribed). That gay teens might seek to queer those forms most immediate to them should neither be surprising nor a matter of reproach. The next section of this chapter returns to the more worrisome matter: their unquestioning and unreflective affection for such forms (and on prescribed terms). For now, one question worth holding on to is whether or not, by multiplication, malleability, or cross-identification, one can visualize queerness in forms that dispute, interrogate, or disturb larger cultural forces, or at the very least remain aware of one's tendencies toward complicity and reification in even the queerest venture.[17] Utopian texts, whether satisfying or not, raise a second question: can alternatives be located beyond ghettoization on the one hand and enervating realism on the other?

The oblique, exclusionary logic by which q-topia is produced in the *Rainbow* novels—jock apotheosis and queeny marginalization—suggests that for Sanchez the answer to the second question is no. High school athletics in Sanchez's q-topia do not uniformly celebrate homosexuality. Kyle's swimming coach grossly mishandles Kyle's coming out. When "'one of [his] teammates objects to having to shower in the same room as someone who proclaims he's gay,'" Kyle volunteers to shower at home instead, and Coach Sweeney accepts his solution (RH 87). Unable or perhaps unwilling to navigate what she refers to as "'uncharted territory,'" she unfairly burdens Kyle with solving the problem that she implies he has caused. The homosexual is obliged to solve the difficulties, to mitigate the nuisance, his or her presence occasions. As prejudicial as Coach Sweeney's course of action may be, one suspects it would be adopted by many high school, if not college and professional, athletic directors.

It's at this point that the conflicted nature of Sanchez's q-topia appears most glaringly. When Kyle comes out in *Rainbow High*, he is asked to be unobtrusive. When Jason comes out, however, the tide suddenly turns. Coach Cameron is as supportive and empathetic as a social worker. Suggesting only for a moment that Jason may be suffering the stock adolescent sexual confusion, Cameron quickly becomes Jason's staunchest advocate—conferring with the Gay-Straight Alliance's faculty sponsor (lesbian art teacher Ms. MacTraugh) and supporting Jason's decision to come out to his team before the state finals (not afterward, as the principal asked). When Jason asks Cameron why he's being so supportive—a nod perhaps to straight male coaches' reputation as less than gay-positive—Cameron replies, "'For the same reason I sent you on the court all those games. . . . Because I believe in you'" (RH 124). Though heartwarming, it's unclear what "believ[ing]" in Jason means in this context—belief in his sexuality? Belief in Jason's confidence that he's gay? The scenario becomes yet more enchanted when Jason finally comes out to his team. Less realistic, perhaps, than Cameron banning the use of homophobic slurs by his players is the threatened punishment for disobedience: "'First time, you get a warning. Second time, suspension,'" even "'right before [the] championship [game]'" (130). The difference sexuality makes in our culture, especially in homosocial environments, evaporates under Cameron's interdict. Players who have previously used gay slurs apologize to Jason. No one expresses discomfort over showering with him. Some even kid him about having preemptively suggested, during his coming out speech, that "'none of us handsome studs is your type . . . [so] who is?'" (131). A gay utopia in which queerness is subsumed without a ripple into an institution for which the always shifting dividing line between homosocial and homosexual is constitutive seems collaborationist, if unconsciously so. Gay-positive policies and attitudes in sports, or in many other institutional environments, would be welcome. What's oddest about Sanchez's brand of utopianism is that he presents a social environment both before and after its transformation without any evidence of a catalyst. There is no methodology, it would appear, except visibility—which seems to abolish homophobia ipso facto. Evidently a brief chat "about name-calling and respecting others" works wonders as well: after Kyle's coach borrows this revolutionary strategy from Coach Cameron, the swim team homophobe, Charlie, stops taunting Kyle, who no longer has to shower at home after practice.

Part of Jason's mojo, of course, is that, aside from his sexuality, he conforms to almost every other social norm. He's a leader, he's masculine, and he's popular enough to survive the coming-out gauntlet with his high school persona unscathed. Watching Jason chat with girls and known homophobes—all popular, one assumes—Kyle hits on a dispiriting truth. A gay jock is not the same thing as a jock who happens to be gay. After Jason comes out to his team—and, implicitly, to the entire school—Kyle observes him from afar in the lunch room, surrounded by a "crowd of girls":

> . . . [Kyle] watched as two of the school's biggest, loudest homophobes approached Jason's table. *Uh-oh.* Kyle dropped his spoon. Was there going to be a fight?
>
> He stared in disbelief as the guys actually shook Jason's hand, wedging themselves into the packed harem of a table.
>
> "Am I seeing things?" Kyle asked. . . . "[T]hose guys hate gays!"
>
> "Jason's still a jock." Nelson shrugged. "Being a jock trumps being gay."
>
> "What about me?" Kyle protested. "I'm a jock."
>
> "Nah, swimming's different. Besides—nothing personal, but you just don't have that whole spit-and-scratch-your-nuts charisma."
>
> Kyle watched as Jason laughed with the homophobes. (RH 144–45)

There's no implication that Jason is laughing at homophobic jokes. What goads Kyle is the fact that jocks and homophobes alike accept a gay Jason in a way they do not accept a gay Kyle. Kyle doesn't play a sport where stereotypical demonstrations of masculinity like spitting and nuts scratching are expected. Swimming is effete; basketball is manly. But as Nelson pointedly observes, it's not just the type of sport Kyle plays. Kyle is not as butch as Jason. Acceptance, it turns out, is awarded unevenly in this q-topia, evincing an untroubled complicity with normative (hetero)masculinity. Though perhaps true for Jason, the notion that "'being a jock trumps being gay'" rings false in Kyle's experience. Shortly after Jason has identified Kyle on camera as his boyfriend and kisses him during a postgame television interview, Kyle asks him,

> "Your day suck as much as mine?"
> "Not really." Jason smiled. "Mostly a lot of handshakes and celebrations."
> Kyle stared at him, incredulous. "No one's hassled you about . . . ?" He glanced over his shoulder and whispered, "About saying we're boyfriends? About our kiss?"
> Jason gave a shrug. "Coach said it hadn't been the brightest thing to do. The guys on the team kind of hooted and whistled. . . . But they do that with everyone. It's no big deal."
> Kyle listened, flabbergasted, shaking his head.
> "Why? What did they say to you?"
> Kyle hesitated, feeling a little weird about repeating some of the stuff guys had said, feeling weirder about the fact that they'd said it to him and not to Jason, and feeling most weird that he hadn't been able to do anything to stop them.
> "Just stupid stuff. . . ."
> "Like what?" Jason insisted.
> "Like calling me—" Kyle forced himself to say it, "—your bitch."
> Jason . . . squared his shoulders. "If anyone said that to me, I'd beat the crap out of them."
> Though Kyle knew that was true, it made him feel like a wimp in comparison. He'd hoped for a little more sympathy.
> "Well," Kyle hissed "that's probably *why* they didn't say it to you. Besides the fact that you're the school hero." (RH 207-08)

Other than losing an athletic scholarship (he later obtains one to a less prestigious university), Jason encounters few consequences upon coming out. In place of name-calling, ostracism, or gay-bashing, Jason is greeted, in his words, "'[m]ostly [by] handshakes and celebrations.'" (It's true that Jason's alcoholic father walks out on him and his mother, but it seems clear that this event—like the argument in which Jason finally stands up to his abusive, homophobic father and strikes him back—was a long time coming and contingent on other factors than Jason's homosexuality.)

Jason's coming out—in contradiction to Nelson's or Kyle's—is further lauded in the final novel in Sanchez's trilogy. The premise of *Rainbow Road* is that a Los Angeles gay and lesbian high school has invited Jason (not Kyle) to address its student body. Given that Walt Whitman High is somewhere in northern Virginia, Jason's fame has spread quickly and far. In *Rainbow High* no sooner does Jason announce he's gay than he finds "'notes shoved through the slats of my locker . . . telling me I've given *them* courage'" (RH 150). As Kyle tells him, "'Everyone thinks you're a role model'" (RH 83). But as star player on a high school basketball team, wasn't he already a role model? An anonymous letter from the captain of a wrestling team from another high school, a boy who's seen Jason come out on local television, thanks him for "inspir[ing] me" (RH 236). Oddly, visibility has not been universally efficacious: the writer hopes he will be "brave enough" to come out someday, but for the time being, still fearful of losing his friends, he will continue to lie (236). Not knowing Jason personally, he can't know that, in fact, Jason's friends haven't shunned him. Or perhaps, the closeted wrestler already knows, as Kyle is just discovering, that not all athletes wield equal clout.

Coming out and gay visibility themselves can be successful in confronting homophobia and effecting change, but such change is not always for the better, and it is rarely instantaneous. Without advocating silence and hiding, one can be more realistic—and wise—about one's vision of queer futures, much less a q-topia. What does one gain—and more possibly, what richer, less normative alternatives does one foreclose—when the abatement of homophobia depends largely on the efforts of jocks? Not only is this unlikely (only a handful of professional athletes have come out, and then only after retirement), but it feels more than slightly reactionary. As the more flamboyant Nelson complains, "'I'm queer too! Where's my TV debut? . . . Jason, Jason, Jason.' Why did everyone keep making such a big whoop about him? As if he was the first high school student to ever come out? So what if he was a sports champ? Did that make him superior?" (RH 163, 194). The answer to the last question is apparently yes, for even though Sanchez can conceive of why it might gall a "Nelly" Glassman (or anyone for that matter) that tolerance hinges on the coming out of a straight-acting jock, Sanchez imagines precisely this scenario. Furthermore, while Sanchez may register Nelson's complaint, he devotes much less time to it than the present discussion might suggest—as if to suggest that Nelson's point of view may be sympathetic but that this is simply the way things are.[18]

If Sanchez's portrayal of queer teenage love relies most heavily on the apotheosis of the jock, giving yet more face time to a group that has already enjoyed more than its share, the motive is strategic. Aside from allowing gay adult readers to dust off long-ago fantasies of scoring with the quarterback, the gay jock scenario serves as a gentler, less polemic alternative to the strategy of outing pioneered by Michael Signorile in the 1980s. In a practice criticized by many straights and gays, Signorile outed public figures (especially politicians) whose homosexuality was either largely unknown or known to associates and insiders but not the general public in an attempt to combat a structured public discourse about homosexuality that trades at once in invisibility and gross stereotypes. Yet the objective of outing, at least as practiced by Signorile, is not merely to embarrass closeted persons by airing their dirty laundry or, in the case of officials making political hay of family values rhetoric or pursuing antigay policies, by broadcasting their hypocrisy. The hope, rather, is that outing prominent celebrities, politicians, and other public figures will trigger, by critical mass, the realization that the crusade against homosexuality is senseless (that is, unethical) or impractically Pyrrhic (victory would mean decimating one's own ranks). In *Rainbow High*, Jason comes out voluntarily, actuating the erosion of homophobia that political outings have, puzzlingly, failed to set in motion. An understandable narrative impulse thus amounts to a facile bit of magical thinking: if the jocks come out, gay-baiting will cease altogether because no one would dare taunt these deities of the teenage demimonde. If the most respected or influential individuals in a culture or organization (in high school, jocks) come out, they can, as GSA sponsor Ms. MacTraugh proclaims, "'help . . . change the world'" (RH 235). Without producing a nationwide conversion to gay positivity, within the microcosmic setting of the novel the entire social structure—a structure that is an American student's world for twelve years—changes. But, practically, this kind of seismic change seems far from likely, at least with so little action or opposition. Nelson may claim that "'being a jock trumps being gay,'" but one suspects that in reality the opposite would be true, that being a member of an abject class would compromise, if not nullify, the advantages arrogated by members of an elite.

Discovering a queer among the ranks of high school jocks also serves an individually therapeutic purpose. For gay adult readers who were taunted as teens by their peers, jocks were likely to have been among the name callers. Thus, the possibility of these jocks having been secretly gay provides adult readers a form of catharsis—and, depending on one's tastes, a little erotic frisson to boot. The fantasy indulged by *Rainbow High*, however, may not simply be the efficacy of openly gay athletes, but their coming out in the first place. Homophobic pressure surely bears down more forcefully within an all-male homosocial environment, much less an athletic one, peppered as such settings are by what sociologist C. J. Pascoe, in *Dude, You're a Fag: Masculinity and Sexuality in High School* (2007), dubs "fag discourse." (The conclusions of Pascoe's analysis, though not its content, are naturally indebted to a long feminist discourse on the subject, dating back to Suzanne Pharr's *Homophobia: A Weapon of Sexism* [1988]. The insights provided by Pharr's destabilizing model of gender identity with respect to queer-baiting [see especially 16–26] have come to permeate the humanities and social sciences to the point of no longer seeming to require acknowledgment.) Pascoe's study, by scrutinizing gender, race, and sexuality discourses at a northern California high school, evidences the likelihood that "fag discourse" might well weather the demise or at least decline of antigay homophobia—since this discourse functions also to mark, regulate, and narrate the masculinity of nongay boys and men:

> Fag is not only an identity linked to homosexual boys but an identity that can temporarily adhere to heterosexual boys as well. . . .
>
> *Homophobia* is too facile a term with which to describe the deployment of *fag* as an epithet. By calling the use of the word *fag* homophobia—and letting the argument stop there—previous research has obscured the gendered nature of sexualized insults. Invoking homophobia to describe the ways boys aggressively tease each other overlooks the powerful [naturalized] relationship between masculinity and this sort of insult. . . .
>
> Fag is not necessarily a static identity attached to particular (homosexual) boys. Fag talk and fag imitations serve as a discourse with which boys discipline each other through joking relationships. Any boy can temporarily become a fag in a given social space or interaction. This does not mean that boys who identify or are perceived to be homosexual aren't subject to intense harassment. Many are. But becoming a fag has as much to do with failing at the masculine tasks of competence, heterosexual prowess, and strength in any way revealing weakness or femininity as it does with a sexual identity. This fluidity of sexual identity is what makes the specter of the fag such a powerful disciplinary mechanism. It is fluid enough that boys police their behaviors out of fear of having the fag identity permanently adhere and definitive enough so that boys recognize a fag behavior and strive to avoid it. (53–54)

Even if Sanchez was not speaking to adult as well as YA readers, the sheer optimism of his fictional world seems too counterfactual to be gratifying.

Visibility's impact is, historically and at present, far too haphazard, dependent as it is on circumstance, context, and a host of other factors. The intent is hard to fault: for Jason, coming out "was about all those players who would come after him, no longer having to endure homophobic slurs" (RH 189). This is not to diminish the circumstantial value of being out: visibility is a commendable, often efficacious move. But Sanchez fails to question what that move does and does not effect, what complications and reversals it may generate even as it occasions a positive reorganization of one's person and environment.[19] Coming out produces virtually no consequences here. It fails to produce the political, inevitably activist effects outlined by Didier Eribon in *Insult and the Making of the Gay Self* (2004). My reading of the boy-novels, then, concurs largely with Eribon's opinion that an assimilationist reliance on queer utopianism is both chimeric and disabling:

> One should not believe that a glorious future is looming on the horizon, one in which homosexuality will be considered as "normal" as heterosexuality, one in which homophobia will have disappeared along with the stigma attached to the category of homosexuality, one in which there will be merely a continuum of practice and behaviors, each as normal as all the others. Such a utopia—one no one really believes in—is a chimera whose only function is as part of an effort to cause the gay movement to lay down its arms, to turn to a kind of self-effacement—the only form of "assimilation" allowable today, and one endlessly called for.
>
> Homosexuality is perpetually disturbing. It causes worry and perturbation. It produces rejection and hatred. Still, that idea developed by gay movements in the 1970s, according to which there would be a strong link between homosexuality and revolution . . . seems merely a pipe dream or a silly article of faith. Such ways of thinking and speaking had a considerable importance in creating the gay and lesbian movement, but they have more to do with wishful thinking than with analysis, or with a firm grasp on reality. . . . [H]omosexuality can happily dwell hand-in-hand with a whole range of conservative, reactionary, elitist, and nationalist ideologies. . . .
>
> Still . . . whatever [a gay person's] political positions may be, however socially or politically conformist he or she may be, however willing to submit to dominant values, established norms, and the institutions that reproduce them . . . it nonetheless remains the case that the world to which that gay man or that lesbian would assimilate is the world of insult. It is a world in which that person has been called or might potentially be called a "stinking faggot" or a "dyke" and in which he or she will consequently always be, in one way or another, marginalized or ostracized. (. . . [S]uch assimilation is an impossible project, a trap gay people set for themselves, and . . . one's time is better spent turning one's back on the kinds of claims whose aim would be to integrate gay people to the social order and, instead, learning to enjoy the benefits of marginality.) (118–20)[20]

Eribon makes a convincing case for not jettisoning gay identity as a necessary but merely expedient stage in cultural evolution, as the "postgay" movement—initiated by former *Out* magazine editor James Collard—espouses.[21] Eribon's sharp reading serves as a sobering reminder of the hidden enervating polemic force of a certain strain of gay utopian thinking—even in the hands of gays. I would argue that, far from opposing the queering of sexuality urged by those such as Donald Hall,[22] Eribon advocates a gay (or one might better say, queer) positioning that is neither fully assimilationist nor wholly separatist: "The point is to choose identification with the group insofar as that produces freedom and individual autonomy and to refuse that identification once it begins to produce alienation and conformism" (140).

It may seem counterintuitive to deny the activist urge of Sanchez's trilogy, for his novels take real strides toward a more enunciated, officially condoned presence (gay prom dates, approval of a GSA). But if the praxis of visibility pursued by the *Rainbow* series fails to produce sufficiently activist effects, this is partly due to a failure to be cognizant of the effect it *is* producing (assimilation), the telos toward which it is heading (disappearance). To aim for a horizon where gayness is no longer problematic (even productively) is to head toward a space where a discourse of sexuality exists without critique, without conscious play or resistance—toward a space without homosexuality. The first factor accompanying and fueling this drive toward an identitarian event horizon is an aggressively antirealist utopianism, one that so far fails to match reality as to be both incredible and impractical. This has been the subject of the present section. The other significant factor, the focus of the following section, is an unresolved (and inevitably unrequited) crush on the very norms Sanchez's characters are at once fleeing from and seeking refuge in.[23]

The irreducible question regarding utopianism, finally, would be its appropriateness. Without prescribing that art must be always useful, practicable, one might well interrogate the helpfulness of art that proceeds so against the grain of reality—especially when that art addresses (if not solely) queer and questioning teens and their allies. Is it not incumbent on such art to offer more than an emotional purge, to offer, instead, some manner of praxis?

Virtually Normalized

In 1995, gay conservative Andrew Sullivan predicted the mainstreaming of gay and lesbian Americans away from, in his view, a flawed and unproductive identity politics. Granting gays and lesbians the right to marriage, for instance, "is not a radical," he argued, but "a profoundly humanizing, traditionalizing step. It is the first step in any resolution of the homosexual question" (*Virtually Normal* 185). Sullivan may profess that he holds to both liberal and conservative ideals, but his position is at its core traditionalist: "a politics that tackles the heart of prejudice . . . while leaving the bigots their freedom," that "banishes the paradigm of victimology and replaces it with one of integrity" (185). Beneath the radical patina of much gay-positive YA fiction—if not the radical feeling that gay YA literature exists in the first place—lurks an addiction to heteronormativity, to the rituals, norms, and rites tenaciously scripted as heterosexual. A novel such as *Boy Meets Boy*, by David Levithan, would initially appear to have bypassed the need to steer clear of the siren song of norms. While the unequalled hyperbole of the q-topia imagined by Levithan earns it a place in the present discussion, Sanchez's *Rainbow* trilogy is a still richer source for understanding the intentions and hidden costs of certain kinds of gay utopian thought.

Set in the future, at a not quite credible, ultratolerant high school (think *The O. C.* meets *The Jetsons*), *Boy Meets Boy* centers around the romantic tribulations of sixteen-year-old Paul; his new boyfriend, Noah; and Kyle, who previously broke up with Paul to go straight but who, having declared himself a bisexual, renews his attentions to his ex. Cliques may forever characterize high school life, but this novel is so overloaded with love and acceptance for the historically lame and outcast of adolescence that it's a bit nauseating. Paul's school features a drag queen cohort, led by Infinite Darlene, aka Daryl Heisenberg, who also happens to be the star quarterback. "There are few sights grander at eight in the morning," Paul comments—and, one might add, less credible—"than a six-foot-four football player scuttling through the halls in high heels, a red shock wig and more than passable make-up. If I wasn't so used to it, I might be taken aback" (25). No one else is taken aback, either—certainly not the openly lesbian principal, and not Daryl's coach or teammates. Perhaps his becoming an even better athlete since "he started wearing false eyelashes" explains their placid acceptance (26). As both star quarterback and homecoming queen, Darlene participates in the Homecoming Pride Rally in both female and football drag: a "pink bail gown, covered in part by her [football] jersey" (34).

Bracketing the token homophobia embodied by the zealously religious parents of Paul's friend Tony, attitudes about both gender and sexuality have generally undergone sweeping adjustments—and in a nonurban small town, no less. "If anybody notices" when two men or two women hold hands in public, "no one cares" (84). The local Boy Scout troop, objecting to the organization's antigay stance, renounces its charter and forms the alternative "Joy Scouts" (84). PFLAG, or Parents, Families, and Friends of Lesbians and Gays, "is as big a draw as the PTA" (142). In a series of events still more outlandish, Paul's kindergarten teacher writes on his report card that he "is definitely gay and has a very good sense of self" (17). Apparently free of the heterocentricity of subject formation, by second grade Paul comes out, in third grade he becomes the first openly gay class president when his opponent's fag-baiting backfires, and in sixth grade he founds his elementary school's first Gay-Straight Alliance (21). (The principal even broadcasts Gloria Gaynor's "I Will Survive" and New Order's "Bizarre Love Triangle" over the PA system following the Pledge of Allegiance.) The number of firsts in which Paul plays a central role confusingly suggests a world in which receptivity and tolerance exist in advance of and without solicitation. My objection to this starry-eyed q-topia is not a curmudgeonly objection to tolerance per se. My point is not that Levithan's teenaged queers should be required to suffer like their predecessors but rather that constructing a queer field of dreams does little to change the fact that, in the present, everyday world, queer teens still suffer daily and that, regardless of (and, indeed, because of) mixed attitudinal shifts and legal decisions regarding homosexuality, the heterosexual texture of discourse leaves them always ready to be reviled and marginalized.[24]

Boy Meets Boy's treacly sentiment may be as off-putting as it is unrealistic. Its dependence on norms, however, is more disconcerting. Levithan's gay characters seem uncritically fixated on monogamy. Granted, this is a YA novel, so it well might be unreasonable to expect a discussion of queer commentary (from Carl Wittman to Michael Warner) on the "tyranny of coupledom" as yet another artificial paradigm that draws a morally inflected line between good and bad sex, between meaningful and empty (if not downright destructive) encounters. Still, modeling unquestioning obeisance to normative monogamy does queer teen readers no favors. Such a text implies that if queers have sex monogamously, as straights ostensibly do, we too can enjoy all the trappings of the grand (heterosexual) romance narrative writ large on every facet of Western culture. Paul, who admits that he's "not used to being hated," speaks of Noah as "the one my heart was made for" (28, 166). Given our habitation within a heterocentric discursive system, to ape normative forms such as the romance narrative without attempting to revise, resist, or queer them is to cheerfully accede to an impotent, othered abjection. Although Levithan seems to have defanged heteronormativity through inversion, what happens when punitive norms are no more?—that is, when certain behaviors and ideas are no longer norms. Can the absence of norms itself become normative? Are norms not, on some level, inescapable? In *Boy Meets Boy* what makes "our country such a strange and unbelievable place" is not a quarterback drag queen but Paul's father's job as a director of philanthropy for a corporation that funds school programs (80). What does it mean, from the vantage point of queer social history, for queer to become the norm, or at least to become unhesitatingly accepted?[25] More immediately, given these q-topian conditions, why are characters such as Tony's parents still homophobic? How have they alone escaped being transfigured by the otherwise ubiquitous gay rapture?

Corseting these texts' ability to be truly utopian is a normative fixation, a fixation that typifies the assimilationist impulse of a gay and lesbian movement committed both to subversion and separatism. Like Levithan, Sanchez gives adult gay readers the straight romance they were not allowed in high school: the visible courtship, the unabashed declaration of one's love. "It suddenly struck" Kyle, for instance, that "[h]e had actually kissed the boy he loved. And that boy had kissed him back" (RB 138). Nelson, characteristically less sentimental than Kyle, is surprised, yet not displeased, to find himself behaving in a recognizably heterosexual way: "The weird part is that even though [Jeremy and I] didn't have sex, I really like him. Now I understand why girls hold out when they're going with guys. It makes you want the other person even more" (RB 226).

Even in the midst of coming out, of asserting one's difference, characters such as Jason and Kyle yearn toward the very norms and rituals against which their desires are culturally defined. Still wrestling with his sexuality, Jason assures himself that "if he ever did make it with another guy . . . it would be with someone normal like Kyle" (RB 33). Implicitly, that "someone" would not be like Nelson, whose father inquires, "'Why can't you just be normal?'" (RB 221).

Kyle's plans for his and Jason's future—gay marriage, adoption, and "liv[ing] happily ever after"—are as worrisome for their normativity as for their dissonance with the reported apathy of younger gay demographics toward marriage and adoption rights (RH 26). If Kyle's "life's dream" is "to someday marry the guy he loved, have a house, raise kids," it's perhaps more surprising that the less traditional Nelson thinks of a boyfriend as "'someone to hold hands with. I want to take him to the prom. This is our freaking senior year, Kyle. I want the whole rite of passage thing'" (RH 230, 48). This is young queer life visualized in the most traditional, unimaginative terms.

The more conservative (and very likely, related) moments of Sanchez's trilogy turn on the pathologization of casual sex and the mimicry of traditional family roles. The Radical Faerie sanctuary visited in *Rainbow Road* grants the boys their first exposure to the notions of open relationships and casual sex. A humpy, partnered faerie named Horn-Boy invites Nelson for "'a walk in the woods'" and, one assumes, some al fresco sex (75). Although he formerly understood "why girls hold out," this time Nelson is intrigued. But the more norm-loving Kyle intercedes:

> "You can't sleep with someone you just met."
>
> "Why not? It's just sex."
>
> "It's *not* just sex," Kyle said in a low voice, embarrassed that [people] walking by might hear them. "It's *never* just sex. You're trusting a guy with one of the most special parts of you—and you need to know him first."
>
> "Oh, Kyle!" Nelson swung his arms around him. "You're so old-fashioned."
>
> "Plus," Kyle added, "you were stoned. . . . First it's rum, then it's pot, what's it going to be next? Crack?"
>
> "Yeah, boy crack." Nelson gave a sly grin. "You're overreacting, Kyle." (RR 82–83)

High school libraries might well ban a YA title that advocates casual sex, but the other reactionary trappings of Sanchez's novels suggest that the casual sex sermonette is not merely politic or calculated. In *Rainbow Road* Sanchez takes Kyle's "overreacting" to its Freudian extreme, oedipalizing his three protagonists in stale near-Victorian terms. As they drive cross-country together, they morph into a nuclear family. Jason, the father figure, "knew he was a better person because of Kyle. . . . He only wished that he could be more the guy Kyle wanted him to be and not do so many stupid, impulsive things" (180). Nelson, the mischievous son, brings a bottle of rum along for the road trip; Kyle soon pours it out. In Nevada, the irrepressible Nelson almost incites a gay-bashing when he proudly tells a "creepy" local whose truck sports a "TERRORIST HUNTER'S PERMIT" sticker that "'we're queer, butch'" (172, 173). What would the nuclear family be, though, without Mother (or "'Mother!'" as Nelson repeatedly labels Kyle) (151, 234). Nelson complains about his "controlling" nature, and "Mother" herself frets over "the two of them [Jason and Nelson] acting completely out of control" (136, 169). When "Mother" reproves Nelson for smoking pot with the Radical Faeries, Nelson objects, "'You're not my mom!'" (75). The *Rainbow* trilogy ends with its gay main characters safely coupled off, leaving the text's more interesting, liminal characters (the transgendered B. J. and a sissy boy named Esau) to fade like a heat-addled vacation memory.

In their discussions of bisexuality, Sanchez and Levithan seem, by contrast, to eschew discursive constrictions on sexuality, specifically, the homo/hetero binary. Though it's by now clear this aversion is hardly the only mark of affiliation between *Rubyfruit Jungle* and *Boy Meets Boy* or the *Rainbow* novels, it is perhaps the most visceral and patent one. When Jason attends a Rainbow Youth meeting in the first chapter of *Rainbow Boys*, he is still dating and sleeping with Debra, and his lingering attraction to women returns as an occasional plot point. Kyle, who identifies firmly as gay, eyes Jason's possible bisexuality as a Damoclesian threat to their relationship. Jason, on the other hand, clings less to heteroeroticism than what he calls the "simpl[icity]" derived from the company of women *and* men—of a nonhomosocial crowd that might include bisexuals and straights as well as queers (RR 129). Here Jason's craving for the normative exceeds Kyle's. Jason doesn't mind going to a gay dance club but is happier at one with a "mixed crowd. You couldn't easily tell what was what. Jason felt more comfortable that way. . . . This was simpler" (129). Jason enjoys spending time with a female same-sex couple he meets at a club because they refer to themselves not as lesbian but as "heteroflexible" (RR 130), and "he could identify with that" (129). Far from striving to abrade norms, this scene reveals the extent to which bisexuality risks remaining squarely within the given discursive grid of options, opting for both halves of a binary without troubling their contours or the limitations of the binary as a whole.

A corresponding discussion of bisexuality from *Boy Meets Boy* arrives, though discontentedly, at a similar conclusion about the difficulty of resisting categories that are themselves resistant. Paul, trying to help his ex-boyfriend Kyle come to terms with being sexually attracted to both men and women, offers the simplest diagnosis:

> "So you're bisexual."
>
> Kyle's face flushes. "I hate that word. . . . It makes me sound like I'm divided."
>
> "When you're really doubled."
>
> . . . I know some people think liking both guys and girls is a cop-out. Some of Infinite Darlene's biggest rivals save their deepest scorn for the people they call "dabblers." But . . . I don't see why, if I'm wired to like guys, someone else can't be wired to like both guys and girls.

"We could call you an ambisexual. A duosexual. A—"
"Do I really have to find a word for it?" Kyle interrupts. "Can't it just be what it is?"
"Of course," I say, even though in the bigger world I'm not so sure. The world loves stupid labels. I wish we got to choose our own. (180)

Kyle decidedly resists prescribed labels more than a character such as Jason does—though both characters chafe at them with the passion of Brown's heroine, Molly Bolt. But the pessimism of *Boy Meets Boy*'s narrator, Paul, about the outcome of such resistance is telling: one may balk at labels and the limited repertoire of types they imply; one may even desire, behave, and affiliate in ways sharply dissonant with one's label or with the palate of available categories; but it's unclear to what extent one's private sexual activity is capable of trumping one's discursive public (self-)representation, to what extent an individualizing act of identification (such as polysexual) can avoid being subsumed by a communalizing one (such as lesbian). The implicitly voluntary act of identification must always contend with interpellation's countering force.

According to clinical developmental psychologist Ritch Savin-Williams, however, labels such as "heteroflexible" constitute an attempt by present-day teens to problematize simple notions of identification. In *The New Gay Teenager* (2005), Savin-Williams surveys data from studies (including his own) of teen sexuality over the past decade.[26] One of his conclusions is that many teens, "loathing . . . labels [gay, lesbian, bisexual, straight] and the implied sexual scripts they seem to dictate," have coined terms that aspire toward less rigidity (168). Included among these terms, used mainly by women to express "physical or romantic attractions to other women" include *ambisexual*, *bi-queer*, *heterosexual-identified lesbian*, *heterosexual with questions*, *not straight*, *pansensual*, *polyfide*, *polysexual*, *questioning*, and *unlabeled* (168). Savin-Williams greets the adoption of these terms, alongside older terms such as *dyke* and *lesbian*, as "indicat[ive of] a greater flexibility (and, I might add, creativity) in sexual labeling" (169). Reminiscent of Molly Bolt's refusal to identify with any extant group, these teens' efforts are perhaps not so pioneering as they or he might wish to think. Savin-Williams's optimism prevents him from observing that a nonaffiliative category such as *not straight* is still a category. By describing oneself as unlabeled, as indescribable, one is nonetheless labeling oneself. A nonlabel is a label. Even to refuse a label acknowledges the fact that bodies and selves exist within—are created by and themselves involved in creating—multiple discursive networks. Subjects exist by description; a negative description (not X or Y or Z) is a description even so. More practically, labels, despite routine condemnation by adolescents, teens, and others lacking a secure sense of self, are not authoritarian dicta that quash every facet of one's personality.

Savin-Williams reads this pluralization of (or abstention from) affiliation—along with "disconnects" for teens "between behavior, identity, and sexual orientation"—as part of a larger, positive social and cultural trend (21). Following gay historian John D'Emilio, Savin-Williams asserts:

> Today, no particular "gay agenda" exists, and sameness with the mainstream trumps differentness. Perhaps this has always been true. In some circles, "gay" has become merely another marketing niche to exploit. The gay image is less edgy, less different, more integrated. . . . To be treated like everyone else is the new revolution. Dare I propose that the ultimate goal is to recognize the ordinariness of same-sex attractions?
>
> . . . Whether this melding of previously separate gay and straight cultures is inevitable, unavoidable, and even desirable is a controversial topic. It is not just cultural conservatives who fear the inevitable. Some gay activists also long for the days when they could live their lives apart from mainstream culture. . . . Those most politically involved in the battle for gay rights frequently regret the homogenization that aping straight culture is doing to gay people. . . .
>
> . . . D'Emilio . . . attacks the identity politics of the gay community, in part because it results in an us-versus-them mentality. Focusing on uniqueness blinds gay people to the possibility of building coalitions with subsets of heterosexuals, such as women, people of color, and immigrants. . . . [G]ay activists. . . seem intent on imposing their radical politics on all nonheterosexuals. As a result, gay adults have stopped listening to their gay children, to the new generation. Unsparing in his criticism of those who glorify gayness as a means of identification, D'Emilio favors not gay marginality but the incorporation of the social changes won by gay people into existing institutions and mainstream politics.
>
> Thus, what we should be heralding is the integration and normalization of homoeroticism, resulting in the near disappearance of the gay adolescent and the emergence of sexually diverse young people. We must move . . . [toward] a recognition . . . of the *ordinariness* of same-sex attracted individuals. The "new gay teenager" reinterprets gayness to signal the end of being gay. (17, 21)

Regardless of whether one is inveigled or aggravated by this sort of thinking, it's incumbent to consider certain questions: Is the "integration and normalization of homoeroticism," the "end of being gay," truly imminent, much less "inevitable"? And if so, isn't it worth asking whether such a development is desirable, much less possible (and on what terms)? The persuasiveness of the "postgay" ethos is its invocation of an alluring but false dichotomy between subversion and assimilation, one that has energized and split gay movements since their inception in late nineteenth-century Germany. But as Michael Warner points out in *The Trouble with Normal,* such a point of view fails to consider results of gay marginality other than exile, to consider marginality as possibly sustaining and invigorating.[27] At the same time, the "incorporation" advocated by D'Emilio and Savin-Williams seems little different than assimilation. And assimilation that fails to preserve the wisdom of the previously marginalized amounts simply to co-optation. For how can one be confident that the transformations wrought by the "new gay teenager" on sexual discourse or behavior will not, following Foucault, be overwhelmed?

Clearly, Savin-Williams, D'Emilio, and others would concur that the "end of being gay" will soon be upon us, and, indeed, that "normalization" is the optimal and logical end (in both senses) of the modern gay and lesbian movement.[28] If neither queers nor straights any longer recognize differences based in sexuality, so the logic goes, there will be no need for ghettos, gayborhoods, even gay and lesbian activism, because discrimination will have ceased to exist. This line of thinking also exaggerates the degree both of gay culture's marginalization and its assimilation; the truth lies somewhere in the excluded middle. American cultural attitudes and laws toward queers have patently shifted and, overall, improved in the past fifty years, yet gay and lesbian meeting places, rituals, and experiences remain uniquely marked—out of the way, set apart, and protected, out of choice and/or concession to the workings of identity politics. Such delineations are, however, only partial, applying differentially over the duration and topography of one's life. Further, notwithstanding the ways queers are marginalized, ignored, or abused by the larger culture, how "separate" or unrelated can "gay and straight cultures" be, inhabiting as they do the same discursive and, most of the time, social space?

Yet even if sexual habits have changed significantly, the predominant social (i.e., public) identification for Americans is heterosexual. Increasing numbers of Americans may be desiring and acting under these more labile notions of sexuality, straining toward a less rigorous consonance between identification, orientation, and activity. They might well have been doing so long before now. But "having fun" in a public restroom with other "bi/married" men is not guaranteed to translate into open political or social discourse/advocacy. On the one hand, the proliferation of Internet hookup sites has permitted individuals of all tastes and identities to more easily find like-minded others. On the other hand, while the Internet may have decreased the sense of isolation felt by young questioning teens, and while cyberinteraction allows the creative, identity-flexible experimentation extolled by both Savin-Williams and Carl Wittman, this communal solidarity is conditioned at least partly on queer social fragmentation, on the further erosion of a public (and queer communal) forum. Identifying online as "discreet" (or, in an unintentionally ironic misspelling, "discrete") may mean not only "my girlfriend (or wife or husband or parent) doesn't know" but also "no one knows." The malleability of identity illustrated by the proliferation of cyberselves is not innately liberatory.

Savin-Williams expects that when "heteroflexible" teens grow up, they will not fall into old patterns but transform them. And while historians of sexuality such as David Halperin (*How to Do the History of Homosexuality* 104–37) have documented that social discourses of sexuality shift over time, these shifts typically involve the realignment or reconfiguration of a limited set of available terms. It remains to be seen whether, when the teens mentioned by Savin-Williams grow up, they will seek out the given heteronormative patterns (married or unmarried coupling, monogamy, procreation). Perhaps these teens will not run to these normative channels, if they can create new models of adult sexual behavior, orientation, and identity besides those now in place. What if, in their twenties or thirties, these same teens find themselves drawn, for various reasons, to the very identities they eschewed a decade or so earlier? Despite the sophistication of Savin-Williams's approach, one might ask whether what one ends up doing isn't merely sophisticating the now discredited model of an adolescent sexually experimental "phase."

Kyle and Jason certainly conceive of adult happiness in none other than heteronormative terms. So if the current generation of teenagers is, as Savin-Williams observes, apolitical and also doesn't recognize what it sees as restrictive categories, there remains no answer to the question of how self-identified gays and lesbians are to obtain the rights they currently lack. The civil-rights, identitarian model surely has its limits, but it's unclear what would replace it. How effective would an alternative model be, say, in rallying against homophobic violence and discrimination? If, in another decade or two, very few thirty- to forty-year-olds see themselves as gay or lesbian, or even as queer—but simply pretty much like anyone else—will there be shock or even response to a murder such as Matthew Shepard's? Or will such murders somehow cease? What we currently think of as gay and lesbian identity has been extant in the West for roughly 150 years;[29] queer identity, for just under twenty. Realignments in the components of sexuality (including desire, morphology, and identity) have periodically occurred in the past and will surely occur again. But until they do (or even as they're occurring, since lucid assessment requires retrospect), it seems hasty to jettison the paradigm within which so many gays, lesbians, and bisexuals have articulated their sexual, political, and social selves (and by which they have been articulated). Queer theorists such as Donald Hall urge resistance to the homo/hetero paradigm's reductive impulse, but resistance is not escape. To judge from the marketability and success of utopian gay YA literature, the *Rubyfruit*-like dream of jettisoning that paradigm by arrant force of will, of escaping it altogether, continues to enchant some queers. Those who find such a vision more hollow than enchanting, however, are those still grounded in and seeking to remedy the continuing (if not widening) rift between pro-gay and antigay opinions and policies.

"'What it's like to have to hide'"

At first glance Bret Hartinger's *Geography Club* might seem very close to *Boy Meets Boy* or the *Rainbow* trilogy. Although Russel Middlebrook, the novel's gay protagonist, and Min, Russel's bisexual best friend, are self-professed "Nerdy Intellectuals," their love interests (Kevin and Terese, respectively) are both athletes

(8). Given the iconic status of jocks in high school social life and in gay adult fantasy, perhaps it's to be expected that Hartinger succumbs to the fantasy not just of jocks turning out to be gay but of their falling in love with the brainy and socially marginal. And what's not to love about Kevin, one of the novel's two closeted jocks? He flashes his "flexing" "dimpled ass" on his way to the shower after baseball practice, and he gushes like a moony adolescent: "'I wanted to kiss you. Ever since that first night when we met here? I wanted to kiss you then'" (127). Occasionally Kevin sounds, jarringly, more like a moony adult: "'And your hair. . . . I've never seen hair this color before either. It's the color of autumn leaves'" (128). But the teen jock ideal holds—totemically irresistible, it would seem.

Refreshingly, though, Hartinger's vision of queer life is neither so utopian nor blithe as that of the previous novels. The gazebo in the park where Kevin and Russel furtively meet stands next to a methanous swamp, insinuating, as early as the first chapter, the crude whiff of reality. With a less clouded vision than Levithan or Sanchez, Hartinger frankly maps out the extent to which heteronormativity, miasmically, isolates as well as co-opts queers. He's also more honest about the ambivalence and complicity many queers may experience toward norms, and their power as both deterrent and lure.

Geography Club soberly depicts the range of peer attitudes about homosexuality and the unpredictable, reasonably dreaded consequences of coming out. In the same conversation in which Russel comes out to his best friend, Min, he learns that she herself is bisexual and that her lover is Terese, a female jock. But Terese, undoubtedly like most real jocks, knows or fears the repercussions of coming out, so she and Min have been secret lovers, rendezvousing for the past three years at a downtown warehouse and covering their trail with the necessary lies. As Kevin, Russel's love interest, says, "'being popular'" comes with enormous "'pressure,'" "'especially when you're jock'"—pressure to be, among other things, straight (41). For queer or questioning jocks, that means "'keeping a secret'" (41). What distinguishes *Geography Club* from Sanchez's and Levithan's novels, however, is that in this case jocks are not the only ones fearful of coming out or being outed. Russel, Min, Kevin, Therese, and Ike (another founding member) call the after-school group they form a Geography Club rather than a gay support group because none of them are out—and only Kevin and Therese are jocks, or are considered "the most popular" (3). That members of high school's lower and upper echelons share a paranoid need to conceal the true nature of their club suggests that their motive is less shame than fear of repercussions. And why would their fear be so great had they not heard, perhaps daily, the "fag discourse" wielded by male teens, had they not been schooled in a curriculum that celebrates the naturalness and universality of heterosexuality and (if only implicitly) the poverty and pathos of being gay? As Russel so succinctly declares in the sequel to *Geography Club*, titled *The Order of the Poison Oak* (2005), "Let's face it: being openly gay at age sixteen really, really sucks" (3). "[E]ver since I'd come out, my high school had suddenly felt like a very dangerous place," he adds, "and I had the defaced locker and anonymous E-mails to prove it" (3).

Geography Club, then, is no novel of shame. Queer characters' secrecy stems not so much (or at least, not explicitly) from a sense of worthlessness as from a near certainty that, because the larger culture devalues nonheterosexual desire and sex, publicly identified queers will face social exile. Of course, being closeted constitutes its own exile, as club members commiserate at their inaugural meeting:

> "We're all alone," I said.
>
> . . . Then Therese said, "Man, that's true."
>
> "Sure can't tell your family," Kevin said. "My dad would go feral."
>
> "Mine too," Min said. "I'm not even sure my mom knows what 'gay' is. And even if I could get her to understand that, how do I ever get her to understand 'bisexual'?"
>
> "Can't tell your friends either," Ike said. . . . Even if they say they're radical. They're not radical about this. Not when they're still in high school."
>
> . . . [Therese said,] "It's like you can never really relax, not when you're with other people. I mean, if they knew the truth, would they still be your friends?"
>
> . . . "It's like you're always wearing a mask or whatever," Ike said. "Your family, even your friends, you can't let them see the real you." (39–40)

Like society in general, high school students are not as uniformly tolerant as one might hope—despite the growth of gay-themed network and cable programming and the establishment of gay-straight alliances. Rather than a predictable coming-out story, this novel sympathetically roughs out the defensive functions of the closet. Though the club's members may currently feel alone, the club's formation tempers that solitude somewhat. Coming out publicly would likely underscore and make more palpable their exile; worse yet, it would risk destroying their fragile, nascent community.

Hartinger ably traces the queer sense of inhabiting a terrain whose boundaries and markings have been drawn by others, along with the sense that, by and large, those boundaries are queers' to redraw for themselves. Topographic and espionage-related imagery characterizes much of the novel. While appreciative of having the other geography clubbers to talk to and "learn about the places I wanted to go," Russel feels he hasn't "actually set foot outside my door. The terrain of my own heart, the landscape of love was still entirely unexplored" (124). Outside of their meetings—in the highly segregated world of the school cafeteria, for instance—Russel and the other members are once again "citizens of different countries" (54). Min describes her closeted relationship with Terese as a "'perfect, special place that only we could get to,'" but also dark and unlit

(70). Espionage is an equally compelling and apt figure for the closet. As Ike says above, "'It's like you're always wearing a mask'" (40). Allowing his friend Gunnar to believe he's made out with a girl, Russel remarks to the reader, "As a master liar, I knew people believed what they wanted to believe" (121). The novel's opening provides the most sustained analogy between spying and being gay in a less than friendly straight world:

> I was deep behind enemy lines, in the very heart of the opposing camp. My adversaries were all around me. For the time being, my disguise was holding, but still I felt exposed, naked, as if my secret was obvious to anyone who took the time to look. I knew that any wrong action, however slight, could expose my deception and reveal my true identity. . . . The enemy would not take kindly to infiltration of their ranks, especially not here, in their inner sanctum.
>
> . . . I was in the high school boys' locker room at the end of third period P. E. class. I'd just come from the showers, and part of the reason I felt naked was because I *was* naked. I'd slung my wet towel over the door of the locker and was . . . eager to get dressed and get the hell out of there. Why exactly did I feel the . . . locker room . . . was enemy territory—that the other guys were rival soldiers in some warlike struggle for domination?
>
> . . . [T]he fact that I even thought about getting naked with a guy in a sexual way was something that Kevin [and other P. E. classmates] Brad and Jarred and Ramone would never understand. I wasn't the most popular guy [at school] . . . but I wasn't the least popular either. . . . But one sure way to *become* the least popular guy was to have people think you might be gay. (1–2, 3–4)

Not only is homosexuality coded throughout the culture, even now, as secret and furtive, but as both C. J. Pascoe and Eve Sedgwick point out (in *Dude, You're a Fag* and *Between Men*, respectively), the rumor of queerness, especially in homosocial environments, is as damning as the reality.

The embattled social and rhetorical condition of homosexuality is made clearest by heterosexual colonization of the private queer space these five teens have made for themselves. The five original members purposely name their club after the most boring subject they can imagine, deceiving administrators and discouraging other students from joining. The plan to maintain a secret, safe queer space soon goes awry when a straight student named Belinda shows up to one of the meetings, wishing to join. Unable to turn Belinda away without outing itself to the entire school, the club accepts her. During the first meeting Belinda attends, open exchange about being gay ceases: "We were speechless. . . . [Her] addition basically meant the end of the Geography Club" (109). At the very next meeting, the others worry whether Belinda can be trusted to keep their secret, and, ominously, Belinda appears just as Russel is bemoaning the oppressive ubiquity of heterosexuality: "'Why can't there be just one place for gay kids, where we don't have to hide who we are? Hell, straight people have the whole rest of the world. They go around holding hands and kissing and talking about "my-boyfriend-this" and "my-girlfriend-that." And they say *we* shove our lifestyle in *their* faces?'" (136–37).

Although it soon becomes clear that Hartinger doesn't seem to view this as a moment of colonization, and while the expansiveness of "queer" beyond definitions of sexual orientation is a valid, often savvy tool for coalition building, it bears asking: is a private gay space—a support group, a closet, a bar—colonized by the entry of straights who may or may not be allies? What costs or strings come with an appeal to strength in numbers, to affiliation? And how crucially does a GSA differ from a GLBT support group (like the Rainbow Boys meeting in Sanchez's trilogy)? The question facing Hartinger's characters—a question with which gays and lesbians have historically wrestled—is the interrelation and potential mutual exclusivity of and conflicts between external affiliation and internal solidarity. The outing of the Geography Club, its forced transformation into an openly labeled GSA, implies some doubt that gays and lesbians can find sufficient support (emotional or political)—or that they can find the same kind of support—in a community set apart as opposed to some more integrated entity.

Straight though she may be, Belinda proves a benign addition to the group. Walking into the room just as Russel is complaining about the invasion of the club's queer space by an outsider (quoted above), Belinda immediately realizes what she's joined is not a club devoted to studying geography. To gain the trust of the other members, she establishes her queer credibility—taking "queer" in the loosest sense possible—by "outing" herself as the child of an alcoholic. Like queers, so the strained analogy goes, she is used to hiding:

> "People are always talking about their families. . . . How they all went out to Chuck E. Cheese for pizza, or how they just got back from Disneyland. The whole world has to tell me over and over how normal they are, and how different they are from me. And I have to just sit there and listen, because no one wants to hear the truth, that my family never has been to Disneyland and never will go. . . . So I know what you mean when you talk about people always shoving something in your face. And I know what it's like to have to hide."
>
> . . . Belinda had something in common with the rest of us. She was a good liar. (138–39)

In Hartinger's eyes, Belinda's confession dispels the specter of the end of free queer dialogue. As soon as she finishes her story, she agrees to leave the group and keep its true purpose secret. Convinced that her experience with lying somehow qualifies her as queer, the club's original members invite her to stay: "The

Geography Club wasn't really about being gay, we all seemed to agree. It was ultimately about something else, some sense of being an outsider, a vagabond, with no place to call home. Whatever it was about, Belinda obviously qualified as a member" (139). So queer space belongs to any outcast, anyone with a secret? Michael Warner, Donald Hall, and others have convincingly argued that "queer" applies to individuals who find themselves at odds with cultural norms, though the norm or their nonnormative behavior is usually related in some way to sex, gender, or desire. Hartinger's expansion of "queer" attempts to appeal to straight readers and promises the political weight of alliance across difference, yet he goes too far. The "something" Belinda feels she shares with her gay peers, even if analogous to what queer teens face, is importantly not the same. Not all secrets are commensurable. Children of alcoholics may carry a substantial emotional burden, but as a category of person neither they nor alcoholics are culturally reviled, made political fodder out of, or economically disenfranchised. Alcoholics' offspring do not hide in the same way and for the same reasons as gays and lesbians. (In *The Order of the Poison Oak* the analogy that dominates the novel, to its detriment, is an equation between homosexuality and difference of almost any kind—in this case, being a burn victim.) Contrary to Hartinger's logic of infinite lability, queering the group in this case de-queers it. If almost anyone deviates from some norm, then why do we still rail against norms, still feel their pressure? If nearly everyone is "queer" in some way, what distinguishes the group from society at large? One feels Hartinger is slightly torn over the prospects of assimilation versus subversion—a conflict which, as mentioned above, Didier Eribon dismisses as an ideological cul-de-sac, an identitarian excluded middle.

If norms have deterrent and invasive power, they also tempt queers with promises of inclusion—as Hartinger deftly explores by outlining a moment of queer complicity in heteronormativity. In the subplot to Russel and Kevin's sub rosa romance, Russel's straight best friend, Gunnar, asks Russel to do him a favor. The girl Gunnar is interested in, Kimberly, will go out with him only if Russel agrees to take out Kimberly's friend Trish. At the novel's outset, Gunnar attests to the unmatched cachet of heterosexuality when he sets out to get a girlfriend, largely for strategic reasons:

> Gunnar sighed. "Every popular guy I've ever known has had a girlfriend or a dog. . . ."
>
> "You don't want a dog," I said. . . .
>
> "Fine, forget the dog, but I *do* want a girlfriend!" . . .
>
> "Because it means you're not a loser."
>
> "Exactly! And don't deny it, because you know it's true." (26)

When Russel agrees to "whatever [he] can do" to help Gunnar, the helpful homo routine kicks into gear. It's not enough that every facet of the culture reflects back, facilitates, and rewards heterosexual coupling; it also requires gay men's help. Russel admittedly has his own romantic plot line, but in the scenes with Gunnar the queer protagonist is reduced to a selfless sidekick.[30] Worse yet, after two double dates with Gunnar, Kimberly, and Trish (during which Trish has pressed Russel to have sex), Russel initially refuses to go on a third date, but caves when Gunnar blackmails him with the threat of being thought gay:

> "What's the problem? Don't you think she's nice? . . . Don't you think she's good-looking? . . . What's the real reason?" The boldness still hadn't left [Gunnar's] eyes.
>
> . . . "It's just not there," I said at last. "I don't feel anything for her."
>
> "For her? That's funny. 'Cause I don't remember you feeling anything for anyone else either. . . . I can't remember you ever being interested in *any* girl."
>
> Suddenly, I was sweating . . . the cold, clammy sweat of fear.
>
> . . . "It just seems funny" [Gunnar said]. ". . . I think people might think that's funny." (151–52)

Rather than be outed, Russel submits to a third date. But efforts to remain closeted by embracing heterosexuality end up backfiring: when Russel refuses to have sex with Trish, she and Kimberly spread the rumor—which in his case, of course, happens to be true—that he's gay. Despite his best efforts, Russel is "[s]uddenly . . . The Gay Kid" (194). What makes the whole episode a more dispiriting exercise in queer co-optation is that Gunnar, Russel later learns, has known (read: assumed) Russel was gay for the past five years. Despite this presumed knowledge and without the slightest regard for Russel's discomfort or dignity, Gunnar asked him to participate in, and later gay-baited him into, heterosexual pretense.[31] Russel, after all, at this point wants to remain closeted, so dating Trish provides the perfect cover. But he quickly regrets his decision, dreads each date, and finds himself threatened, by one of his best friends no less, with being labeled queer. Neither Russel nor Hartinger seem sufficiently perturbed by Gunnar's conscious, homophobic manipulation.

Next to this episode, the novel's strongest illustration of the lure and force of norms—and, for queers, their usually hollow promise—is Russel's "defection" from the "Nerdy Intellectuals" to the jocks. This unexpected arc is perhaps the narrative's most commendable element, one that sets it apart from *Boy Meets Boy* and the *Rainbow* trilogy. After Belinda joins the Geography Club but before she gains the group's trust by spilling her own secret, Kevin asks Russel to join the baseball team; if they can't talk freely in the club any longer, he reasons, at least they can spend time together on the team. Even though there are obviously other ways they could spend time together, Russel readily agrees: "Kevin Land was happy I'd joined the baseball team, and that was all that mattered! Was I pathetic or what?" (112). This moment of introspection aside, Russel feels surprisingly at home in what had previously seemed like "the opposing camp" (1). The "spy in hostile territory" now "laugh[s] and jok[es] with the best of them" (146). Experiencing a "strange sense of camaraderie" with boys around whom he'd always felt an outsider, he is no longer intimidated by the homosocial atmosphere or its antigay underpinning. The benefits of assimilation are what one might expect: "Now people I had never spoken to before, people who I didn't think even knew who I was, called out my name in the hallways. Even some teachers . . . had a little glint in their eyes when they talked to me" (153). As delightful as this all is, a reader might wonder if, with this "one tiny compromise"—"part of what relationships were supposed to be about," Russel assures himself (134)—Russel has not been doubly colonized, first by heterosexual dating and now by sports. Of course, heterosexuality and sports are practically consubstantial, as Gunnar illustrates (in the scene already quoted) when he intimidates Russel into a third date with Trish: "It just seems funny. . . . [A] big baseball star like you, but you don't have a girlfriend?" (152).

Russel soon finds that assimilation and normativity exact a price beyond the marginalization of one's erotic and romantic life. Entering "paradise," the "Land of the Popular" and the straight, means not only remaining closeted but bullying others in order to police the lines between the popular and unpopular (159). As a jock, Russel's expected to join in ridiculing Brian Bund, a generic school outcast (but not a gay one), and he does. The taunting in this case does not turn homophobic, and Russel assures himself he wouldn't have participated if it had. But given the ease with which this queer outsider joins the "opposing camp," his confidence in the voluntarism of complicity—in selective collaboration—may be unwarrantably optimistic. Collaborators such as Russel who are also double agents jeopardize their license to choose which acts they will and will not carry out as part of their cover. Like saying no to a date with a girl, refusing to call someone a queer would invite scrutiny of one's own hetero bona fides. Hartinger is clearly sympathetic to motives for remaining closeted in a hostile environment, yet he also stresses the costs of not being out. Less a categorical indictment of the closet, the novel instead limns the unavoidably complex boundary relations queers must negotiate in a heteronormative culture. Rather than advocating the utopian dissolution of all distinctions between gay and straight, *Geography Club* stands apart from the other novels discussed in this chapter by highlighting the extent to which some of those distinctions are sustaining and/or indelible, and thus the extent to which the q-topianism of Brown, Sanchez, and Levithan is a detrimental endeavor, a negative externality that yields illusory pleasures by shearing homosexuality of its critical relations to normativity.

For Hartinger, being out fails to dissolve homophobia almost instantly (as it does for Sanchez and Levithan). Yet more shrewd is the observation that the impetus of regulative cultural forces can alternatively expose and protect those trying to elude as well as hide behind them. When Russel's bisexual friend, Min, witnesses Russel harassing outcast Brian Bund, she suggests inviting Brian to join the Geography Club, anticipating correctly that such a move will upset those members with more to lose from being outed (jocks Kevin and Terese). Threatened by this proposed addition to the club—more members only increases the threat of discovery—Kevin, Terese, and Russel vote against Brian's admission. (Min, Belinda, and Ike vote for his admission, but without a majority, the motion fails.) The vote is also a mandate against admitting yet another heterosexual. Despite Russel's attempt to cement his pact with normativity by voting not to admit Brian to the club, the rumor (started by Trish and Kimberly) that Russel is gay makes short work of both Russel's popularity and his relationship with Kevin. To shield himself from guilt by association, Kevin turns on Russel, accusing him of "want[ing] a big ol' sausage" in front of fellow jocks while flashing the kind of "cruel sneer" typically reserved for outcasts.

Having been disqualified as one of the chosen at the end of the novel, Russel's status nevertheless remains ambiguous—and, in terms of my argument about queer externalities, authentically so. Although not gay himself, Brian asks school permission to form a Gay-Straight Alliance (an uncloseted one, that is) after Russel, remorseful over making fun of Brian, befriends him. Russel further redeems himself when Kevin agrees, once Brian (not Russel) is rumored to be gay, to continue their closeted relationship. Russel finally decides that the ethical and practical costs of assimilation outweigh its benefits and dumps Kevin. This is qualified redemption, however. One might argue that Russel refuses to stay in the closet, but that's not exactly true. Kevin's comfort with being both gay and homophobic (even if only deflectively) "had changed the way I looked at him" (222), and makes Russel unwilling to love "in [a] darkened warehouse" as Min and Terese have done for five years. But, conversely, it doesn't perturb Russel that, after Brian's application to start a GSA,

> people still didn't think of me as gay. Brian was The Gay Kid (even if he wasn't really gay). I was just being nice to him. I guess people couldn't quite grasp the fact that at a school of eight hundred students, there might actually be more than one gay kid. I couldn't complain; just a couple of months before, I'd thought there could only be one gay kid (me!). Besides, now for the first time in my life, homophobic ignorance was working to my advantage. (224)

There's nothing wrong with deriving strength from an impending (if somewhat premature) sense of solidarity. But Russel clings rather wistfully to the smokescreen of a GSA (in which members could be gay or straight), and he's in no haste to correct the misidentification of Brian as "The Gay Kid." Russel is clearly on his way out of the closet,[32] but this moment of nostalgia stands as a reminder of the medial condition that is perhaps endemic to homosexuality in its present cultural form: closet-adjacent, poised between queerness and normativity; not yet acclimated to the critical distance marginality can afford, and not yet comfortable with the complicity that even liminality entails.

Q-topian thought is not intrinsically otiose. Without some objective, however pragmatic or visionary, the queer community is likely to founder. Indeed, questions regarding the present shape, mutual awareness, and activist investments of the queer (or gay and lesbian) community or communities are vexed ones. They are questions without clear answers, and decreasing numbers of queer Americans seem interested in the admittedly contentious work of sorting through them. A more highlighted (and, compared to decades past, less caricatured) gay presence in entertainment media and more blatant niche marketing seems to be enough—seems to be "fine by me"—to many queers at present, especially younger queers. The decriminalization of sodomy in 2003 failed to generate much excitement, despite the legal and symbolic momentousness of the decision. The beleaguered, vicissitudinous battle over same-sex marriage seems to interest younger queers even less, whereas their older counterparts, after local and state battles, may be weary of the fracas (or wary of its repercussion and/or the objective itself). It's to such a diverse audience of queers, weary of setbacks and postponements—or of rallies and agitation—that a vision such as that offered by Sanchez, Levithan, and (in some moments) Hartinger is likely to appeal. For these novels promise a world *at the end of* (or after) *the rainbow*, beyond the struggles against homophobia and marginalization, beyond what some might feel to be the prescribed stations of identitarian rhetoric. More than simply a positive message aimed at teen readers, the cultural encounters investigated in the following chapters reveal other moments of queer as well as straight Americans looking to a time or place after a frustrating present—a present, when it comes to homosexuality, seemingly deadlocked between liberality and obloquy. Certainly, the political rhetoric discussed in the next chapter stands to remind queers, as Belinda says in *Geography Club*, "'what it's like to have to hide,'" or at least, what it's like to need a place of refuge from the homophobic animus that, sirocco-like, still gusts through the culture. Insights such as those offered by Hartinger—about the seductive charm of complicity, and the bitter resistance of norms to our best intentions to queer them—might be kept usefully in mind as we move from the social microcosm of high school to, in the next chapter, a wider arena of politics and cultural debate, where the stakes are higher, the rhetoric more vindictive, the impact more widespread and consequential.

2

"In my day it used to be called a limp wrist"

Flip-Floppers, Nelly Boys, and Homophobic Political Rhetoric

By the summer of 2004 Republicans had succeeded in branding Democratic challenger John Kerry a "flip-flopper." Less than a month before the election, that transformation seemed a fait accompli: as Rob Christensen noted in the Raleigh *News & Observer*, despite Kerry's Theodore Roosevelt-like "San Juan Hill moment . . . in Vietnam," "the Republicans have saddled [him] with less rugged images of him wind-surfing, being vaguely French, and being the master of the flip-flop" (pars. 11, 12).[1] Queerly enough, among the issues Kerry was accused of flip-flopping on was gay marriage. Despite the applicability of "flip-flopper" to Bush himself in terms of policy (the creation of a 9/11 Commission and the creation of a Homeland Security Department, to name but two instances), this single sound byte typecast the presidential hopeful as indecisive, spineless, and unmanly. Setting aside Kerry's astute deconstruction of Bush's so-called certainty as bullheaded solipsism and of "flip-flopping" as altering one's course when reason and reality demand it, I would like to examine the gender stereotypes and homophobic rhetoric on which Republican strategists relied to denigrate Kerry in the public eye and to crystallize, by contrast, Bush's image as machismo nonpareil—the farthest thing from a limp-wristed flip-flopper one could ask for. The importance of understanding what the Republican National Committee (RNC) and their supporters accomplished in emasculating and queer-baiting Kerry lies in its effect on the election's outcome, which itself can be measured not merely by preelection polls and media coverage but also by the jarring resonance of campaign homophobia in postelection Republican policy. Queer-baiting Kerry dovetails into baiting queers.

Homophobic rhetoric is hardly a new phenomenon in American campaign politics; challenging the manliness of one's opponent has long been part of that mudslinging game, as has discrimination and intolerance against gays and lesbians. As Canadian journalist Stacy Lorenz observed on Election Day 2004, "a longer view of the gender rhetoric surrounding presidential elections reveals a preoccupation with manhood in much earlier periods" (par. 2). Of Lorenz's examples, the 1840 election contest between the incumbent president Martin van Buren and Whig challenger General William Henry Harrison is the closest parallel to the 2004 race. Despite Whigs' emphasis on their candidate's "manly virtues" (as a military hero from the 1811 Battle of Tippecanoe), Democrats dubbed him "Granny" Harrison, caricaturing him as "a senile, feeble old woman" (pars. 4, 7). In retaliation, Whigs attacked Van Buren as a "champagne-drinking aristocrat who wore ruffled shirts . . . and ate fancy meals prepared by 'French cooks'" (par. 6). Aside, however, from the fact that being manly and being French have been opposed in the American imagination for more than a century, the 2004 campaign marks a definite advance in the use of gender rhetoric as mudslinging. Candidates in past presidential campaigns may have been mocked as insufficiently masculine—Adlai Stevenson was nicknamed "Adelaide"; James Buchanan, called a "granny of an executive" (pars. 13, 10)—but there are few if any previous instances in which a candidate's sexuality has been questioned, at least so openly and unabashedly.

The stark and minatory innovation over campaign rhetoric of the past is the convergence of politics as usual with a serious agenda for regulating public debate and codifying as law the erasure of queers from the civil and cultural landscape. A largely unbroken silence in public forums toward recent acts of censorship and intimidation makes the advance, whether downplayed as pandering or simply ignored as hollow rhetoric, additionally chilling. And, following Lisa Duggan in *The Twilight of Equality?: Neoliberalism, Cultural Politics, and the Attack on Democracy* (2003), that's precisely the aim of mainstream American political rhetoric since 1980—the dawn of neoliberalism.[2] Duggan argues that among the direst failures of progressives in the past three decades has been their failure to understand the sleight of hand by which, since Ronald Reagan, reactionary policies on the economy, class, and minority rights have been enacted, fairly evenly, over the course of both Republican and Democratic administrations. It was an ostensible liberal, after all—Bill Clinton—who approved North American Free Trade Agreement, passed welfare reform, and signed DOMA and "Don't Ask, Don't Tell" into law. It does little good—in fact, it does much harm, Duggan suggests—to get mired in Republican versus Democratic positions, since to a certain extent they're indistinguishable. For example, Democratic support for civil unions is not incompatible—quite to the contrary—with Republican support either for a federal marriage ban or for leaving the issue to state prerogative. As this chapter (and *Queer Externalities* in general) demonstrates, the effacing and disciplinary forces vectored at queer Americans course throughout the cultural, political, and social spectrum, originating from putatively well-meaning sources as well as plainly homophobic ones, moderate as well as conservative, Democratic as well as Republican.

Looking back on the 2004 election, Riki Wilchins writes in the *Advocate* that "[g]ay rights, women's rights, and gender rights are now at the fulcrum of the culture wars just as black civil rights were in the '60s and '70s. We are in for a long and difficult public debate . . . [one that] will require addressing familiar issues in new ways, particularly around gender. The ongoing crisis in masculinity—and hatred of femininity—was nowhere more evident than in this year's elections" (par. 2). It's this symbiosis between "anxious masculinity" and hatred of all things feminine that psychologist Stephen Ducat investigates in *The Wimp Factor: Gender Gaps, Holy Wars, and Anxious Masculinity* (2004). Ducat traces the palpable influence of homophobia and what he terms "femiphobia" on American political discourse during the presidential administrations of Clinton and the two Bushes. Charlotte Hooper's *Manly States* (2001) surveys the intersection of identity studies (masculinities and feminism) and international relations studies in an attempt to chart the connections between international relations, gender roles, and popular culture. Focusing on the "significant" but largely neglected role that world affairs play in the production of identities," Hooper reminds us that "masculinities are not just domestic cultural variables: both political events and masculine identities are the products of men's participation in international relations" (80). Besides illuminating the interplay between the national, the subnational, and the international, as well as between various competing models of masculinity ("the elevation of some types of masculinity over another"), *Manly States*' most apposite insight for the present discussion is the reciprocal (rather than one-way) causality that pertains between international relations and masculinities (220). Considering how consequential posturing over the Iraq War and the War on Terror was both to Bush's first term and to the 2004 presidential campaign, Hooper's examination of "changes and challenges" to "hegemonic masculinity" through the lens of international affairs helpfully reminds us that masculinity's role and mechanism in American politics are shaped by forces external as well as domestic (224). Most importantly, Hooper's progressive take on masculinity studies emphasizes the fluidity and multiplicity of masculinity—the masculinities (bellicose/irresolute; manly/faggy) we see in especially combative play and slippage in the Kerry-Bush presidential race.

Republican rhetoric from the 2004 campaign shows the trend plotted by Ducat only growing stronger, more toxic, and (I would argue) more specifically homophobic. If, as Lakshmi Chaudry wrote in May 2004, "the penis rules when it comes to presidential elections," then making informed decisions or ever changing one's mind is as good as being gay. While anyone modestly versed in gay studies or women's studies, if not any critically thinking adult, knows effeminacy to be an unreliable index of homosexuality, many ideologues, media strategists, reporters, and Internet pundits routinely collapse gender into sexuality without blinking.[3] In a culture rife with metrosexuals and, compared to twenty years ago, flush with gay media presence (*Queer Eye for the Straight Guy*, *Will & Grace*, *Queer as Folk*, *Six Feet Under*, *Boy Meets Boy*), somehow being unmanly, being vulnerable to being pegged as gay, is still as good as being gay.[4] As in high school gym class, "unmanly" equals "sissy" equals "queer." This chapter delineates the homophobic rhetoric that underlies the flip-flopper label as well as the supplementary imagery that was disseminated in regard to both Bush and Kerry to solidify the latter's image as a cultured, verbose, wishy-washy, timid nelly boy—in short, a homosexual.[5]

The title of this chapter, "In my day it used to be called a limp wrist," is borrowed from Mart Crowley's 1968 play *The Boys in the Band*, which, after the Stonewall Riots a year later, seemed to capture the most unattractive features of a pre-Stonewall gay consciousness dominated by self-loathing and insecurity. That the play equally represents a diversity, resilience, and deep camaraderie rarely seen in gay literature before or since is an important but tangential argument. The character who utters the "limp wrist" line is Emory, the self-professed "nelly queen": an effeminate, mincing gay man who might seem stereotypical outside the spectrum of homosexuality with which Crowley is careful to surround this truth teller. Like most truth tellers, he makes others uncomfortable; in the homophobic vernacular, he "flaunts" his sexuality—as if heterosexuality is not flaunted, indeed, flogged, from every commercial, every film, nearly every public deed and moment in the American landscape.[6] The line referenced by my title occurs while Emory is "reading" a dim-witted male prostitute (whom Emory has bought for the night as a friend's birthday present) for trying to renegotiate the terms of his hire:

> COWBOY. I hurt my back doing my exercises and I wanted to get to bed early tonight. . . . I lost my grip doing my chin-ups and I fell on my heels and twisted my back.
>
> EMORY. You shouldn't *wear* heels when you do chin-ups.
>
> COWBOY (*oblivious.*) I shouldn't do chin-ups—I got a weak grip to begin with.
>
> EMORY. A weak grip. In my day it used to be called a limp wrist. (43)

Although considered by some a dated relic of the gay canon, *The Boys in the Band* remains timely because the ideological battles it delineates—over what and who count as masculine, what does not, and the tremendous political and representational stakes riding on where those lines are drawn—still rage furiously, inside the GLBT community and within straight culture.

Examples of homophobic rhetoric as well as homoerotic resonance in the 2004 campaign are almost too numerous to catalog, much less analyze, but the first two sections of this chapter focus on three salient examples—dealing with the French, the sissy, and locker room penis envy—of the shrill relentlessness with which homophobia was leveraged by shills for the Right bent on savaging a presidential challenger. Turning to two postelection outbreaks of this emboldened homophobia (one from a federal mental health agency, the other from family-values demagogue James Dobson), the third section limns a pernicious new alliance that may have been forged, or at minimum cemented, between queer-baiting humor and actual policy targeting queer voices and rights.

Freedom Fags and Limp-Wristed Leaders

As Ben Fritz and Brendan Nyhan observe, writing online for *SpinSanity*, Kerry's political "adversaries [sought] to capitalize on anti-French sentiment created by the war [in Iraq] and portray him as aloof and opposed to America's interests" (par. 2). Journalists and faux journalists were not alone: Commerce Secretary Donald L. Evans joined the fray with the observation that Kerry "looks French" (Millbank par. 2; J. C. par. 2)—a sound byte originated by an anonymous Bush adviser speaking in April 2004 with the *New York Times*, and then obligingly parroted by, among others, FOX News anchors and guests, Rush Limbaugh, *Washington Times* editor in chief Wesley Pruden, the *Wall Street Journal*'s James Taranto, and ABC's Cokie Roberts.[7] Pronouncing that Kerry, if elected, would be America's "first French president" is transparently calibrated to galvanize rabid patriotism and xenophobia, but representative stories by online amateur commentators state categorically what FOX News anchors merely insinuate with their sneering pronunciation of the word "French" (see *Outfoxed*), elucidating the rhetorical link in the popular mind between being French, being un-American, and being gay. Surely every producer and consumer of news intuited the subtext of the "French connection," but Frank Rich alone seemed brave enough to spell out the infantile logic behind these attacks: "Mr. Kerry was said to appear 'French.' (That's code for 'faggy.')" (par. 7).

Such an equation is explicit in "Men Are from Mars, John Kerry Is from Paris," an article by Jim Manion posted at *Mensnewsdaily.com*, an online oubliette of chauvinism one might think had been left behind in the 1950s or at least in the Robert Bly workshops of the 1990s. As the title of Manion's piece suggests, in the chauvinist universe of *Men's News Daily*, being unmanly makes John Kerry not only French but female. Kerry's genealogical connection to France, along with his wife's wealth, renders him "the ultimate male whore" (par. 41). With a lack of subtlety that seems characteristic of those in the grips of gender panic,

Manion lambastes Kerry for "throw[ing] a baseball like a little girl," "throw[ing] a football like a little girl," for being not just unathletic but "limp wristed" (pars. 3, 4). Many of Manion's barbs are obviously tongue-in-cheek:

> John Kerry has never told Theresa to "pull my finger";
> John Kerry has few, if any, broken bones . . . ;
> John Kerry has no idea what it means to be the breadwinner;
> John Kerry does not have a favorite beer;
> John Kerry has never ridden a bull;
> John Kerry has never tipped a cow . . .
> John Kerry has never tested the theory that the human generation of methane can be flammable;
> John Kerry has never worn the pants in his family, relying instead on the right bank account . . .
> John Kerry has a French flag tattooed on his buttocks (per John Edwards). (pars. 19–24, 29–31)

Despite the feeble attempt at humor, one feels that Manion is still serious in equating the crudest banalities with masculinity. And as the last item in this absurd litany illustrates (crassly suggesting that Kerry and his running mate are lovers), the transition from gender to sexuality is seamless. To be less than hypermasculine, or rather, less than an inebriated frat boy, is to be emasculated, feminine, homosexual.[8] And lest one think Manion's sophomoric brand of homophobia anomalous or unrepresentative of mainstream media coverage, the *New York Times* ran an editorial by *Texas Monthly Magazine*'s creative director, Scott Dadich, who found room in his pop-psychological yet otherwise thoughtful typographical analysis of Bush and Kerry campaign ads for some good ol' Texas-style queer-baiting:

> On a typical drive to work, I encounter no fewer than five typefaces used in as many different Kerry-Edwards logos. One is stretched out; another is condensed. One looks masculine; one looks feminine. In contrast to Mr. Bush's aggressive sans-serif font, Senator John Kerry's multitudinous font choices center on the use of thin, *delicate-looking*, "girlie-man" type. No wonder some voters think he's a vacillating wimp. (par. 5; emphasis added)

Apparently even typography can be faggy. (In that case, Dadich might want to reconsider the butch credentials of Bush's "sans serif"—a font whose name, regardless of its appearance and in spite of the effort to butch it up with the adjective "aggressive," sounds precariously effete and definitely French.) And once again, variation ("multitudinous") is for indecisive, spineless sissies.

For Manion, masculinity is proudly, dourly monolithic:

> Men are from Mars. We are simple creatures. We are wired in a simple way. What we lack in sensitivity, we make up for in courage and resolve. What we lack in shopping skills, we make up for in providing for our family. . . . We will protect our families and our country with our very lives. And we will do so without a second thought, and despite protests from home.
>
> Some of us have survived the feminist movement intact. We resist emasculation, yet we give in to small displays of love for our mates on occasion, like holding their purse in a crowded mall. . . .
>
> John Kerry is not from Mars . . . [but] from a different place. A place where a man can be a man without being a man. . . . A place where the male persona no longer exists, being replaced by an asexual multicultural template. A place where what a man says is more important than what he does. A place where appearance trumps substance.
>
> . . . Kerry is not from Mars. He is from Paris. . . .
>
> Yes, gay Paris. (pars. 32, 34, 36, 39, 40)

Manion is so blinded by a hackneyed castration anxiety that holding his wife's purse requires rhetorically hefting his testicles to confirm their presence; presumably, his terror prevents him from clarifying how making a man hold a purse is a blow for feminism.[9] And it would probably not occur to Manion that not all men "are wired" in the same "simple" way, that some men are gay, that some are effeminate and straight. The defining characteristic of the passage in terms of a homophobic assault on Kerry is unimaginatively simplistic: Kerry is sensitive (expressive rather than active), emasculated (married to a wealthy woman), and—once again—French. If he finds Kerry superficial, the effort Manion puts into safeguarding his genitalia blurs his perception of the Bush machine's deft image control. Kerry's public image is surely not rugged enough for a man's man like Manion, whose vicarious enjoyment of presidential machismo distracts him from the shame that being a cooperative spouse patently causes him (or men like him). The author defines men as soldiers and cowboys ("provid[ers]" and "protect[ors]" stolid with "courage and resolve"), the two figures on whom Bush's "war presidency" mythos was squarely based. The Western cliché of the man of few words underlies the childishly anti-intellectual complaints about the grammatical complexity of Kerry's speech and praise for Bush's plainspokenness.[10] Manion is testimony that angry white men who feel they have no clear enemies left (or rather, no more permissible targets) make excellent heavies, if for no other reason than that they eschew reason and appear to spend little time reflecting on the consequences of their own or others' actions (because that would be weak, feminine).

Being less than masculine in the most limited, stereotypical way also disqualifies a man from being a good leader for Bernard Chapin, another contributor to *Men's News Daily*. Chapin's article "Maureen Himmler" sets out to skewer Maureen Dowd for bemoaning the war-blown hypermasculinity of both Bush's and Kerry's campaign imagery. To his credit, Chapin comprehends Dowd's thesis: "the real reason that she wrote this piece ["Gotta Lotta Stigmata," *New York Times* 24 Aug. 2003] is to call to the reader's attention how silly it is for politicians to have to prove that they possess manly characteristics" (par. 7). The problem is that he fundamentally disagrees with her: "are masculine virtues intrinsic to good leadership? Absolutely" (par. 8):

> A government exists to defend its people. That's it.
>
> [U.S.] armed forces are not ruled by newspaper columnists. They are ruled by a commander in chief. When the commander in chief is an indecisive free-rider, national security is compromised, just as it was during the Clinton Administration.
>
> . . .What good can a crying, blubbering male do for the people he is paid to protect? No good whatsoever.
>
> Politicians try to depict themselves as being masculine figures for good reason. A masculine man acts purposefully and forcefully—which is integral to providing a meaningful defense of one's land and people.
>
> . . . [I]n times of terror . . . [the] capacity to stoically deal with adversity and to unemotionally deal with crisis are invaluable traits.
>
> . . . I could care less about how [George Bush] appears on an aircraft carrier. What I care about is that he possesses the manly virtues of strong decision making and that he understands that those who bow before tyrants will be tyrannized by them forever. (pars. 9–14)

In a refreshing moment of insight, Chapin admits that masculinity can be simulated ("depict[ed]"), and not always successfully. He fails to comprehend, however, how this vitiates one's ability to distinguish real "manly virtues" ("what [he] care[s] about") from simulated ones. "[H]ow [Bush] appears on an aircraft carrier," literalizing his status as commander in chief, inevitably informs any assessment of his "virtues." Indeed, because abstractions cannot be perceived unless palpably rendered, how can one be sure the phallic pageant that symbolizes "manly virtues" did not in fact create them? The fact that by the time of Chapin's article Saddam Hussein's capability of launching a surprise nuclear attack on the United States at a moment's notice had been thoroughly disproved seems to have little impact on Chapin's logic. Quick, unconsidered action is good, period, no matter the reality or level of threat. Because Chapin equates logic and reason with emotion, all of which are bad, and action with a lack of emotion, his rhetoric is unwisely, if tellingly, ham-fisted: he fails to see how his warning not to "bow before tyrants" lest one be "tyrannized by them" might apply as equally to Bush as to Hussein. Even one blind to Bush's litany of civil rights violations at home and abroad should be capable of imagining that an unhesitating, aggressive leader who never seeks advice or fails to strike against the faintest rumor of a threat might also lash out at the loyal. Tyrants are historically not above tyrannizing their own subjects. Indeed, home is where tyranny tends to start.

Though less anxious than Manion, Chapin finds room for homophobia in his portrait of manly leadership: "crying, blubbering male[s]" make bad leaders because, the implicit schoolyard logic goes, crybabies are not men. Crybabies are sissies. While not automatically labeled as homosexual, they are never entirely free from suspicion.[11] Since, legally speaking, homosexuals do not exist in American armed forces, it would seem that (by Chapin's logic) soldiers never cry or feel fear. Some tangled chain of logic such as this lay behind campaign ads questioning Kerry's heroism in Vietnam, if not the mere fact of his service. The demonstrably fallacious ads sponsored by the paradoxically named Swift Boat Veterans for Truth questioned not merely the fact of Kerry's service record but its spirit, impugning his heroism, honor, and manliness. Confronted with evidence that it was this group's credibility, not Kerry's war record, that was dubious (this, after two weeks of aggressively uninvestigative journalism from mainstream media outlets), the Bush reelection apparatus began conjuring doubts about Kerry's manhood in future conflicts, whether facing another 9/11 or the next Saddam Hussein.[12] Sissyphobia so permeated the Swift Boat donnybrook that the satirical Web site *Broken Newz* ran a story regarding Kerry's antiwar activism after returning from Vietnam under the headline "John Kerry Has No Recollection of Throwing Medals Like a Girl" (Tanner). In this mock interview, Kerry cries when asked about his "feminine throw." He recalls routinely being "picked last place as a child for sports" and "flinch[ing] and scream[ing]" when a Nerf football was thrown at him (pars. 16, 19). Whether Tanner's piece formally qualifies as satire or not, *Broken Newz* touts itself as the "Internet's Premiere Satire News," implying that the fault or vice being exposed here is Kerry's effeminacy, his unmanliness. Humor that trades on the playground dictum that only the class faggot gets "picked last" is as irresponsible as it is puerile.

While Chapin and Manion are clearly conservative hacks, it is noteworthy that they are low-level ones. Whether their spoutings receive financial assistance from those with more political, journalistic, or economic pull (as was the case, at least in the latter sense, with Jeff Gannon's Talon News) seems irrelevant; it is enough that Chapin and Manion are *rhetorically* funded by others, that they speak to an audience for whom their overstatements, vitriol, and bald counterfactuals require no argument. Their confidence, along with a shared language of social and political conservatism, attests to their having found a ready audience. Speaking for the "common man" is at least in part a marketing affectation, yet comments such as theirs seem as valid a barometer as one is likely to find, if not of the "popular imagination," then of the form in which certain political perspectives are being popularized. Dismissing Manion's and Chapin's tirades as nugatory would be to ignore a phenomenon that seems powerful and potentially damaging regardless of whether it is cause, effect, or both. (And, given the echo-chamber character of current television news, the Möbius-strip connectivity of Internet journalists, commentators, and bloggers, and the tireless message discipline of what David Brock calls the "Republican noise machine," ferreting out sources and causes has become increasingly onerous.) Trickle-down gender panic and homophobia, at least in these examples, show little sign that distance from an ostensible origin diminishes their force.

Eyeing the Presidential Package

Perhaps the most fascinating, if slightly sickening moment in the phallic contest for the presidency came on May 8, 2003, during a broadcast of NBC's *Hardball with Chris Matthews*. Matthews and guest G. Gordon Liddy were discussing Bush's landing on the *USS Abraham Lincoln* for the infamous "Mission Accomplished" press conference. As Mark Crispin Miller aptly describes it in *Cruel and Unusual*, Liddy giggled "like a schoolgirl" over George Bush's genital package in his flight suit—suggesting that it was Bush's enormous endowment, not the ill-fitting parachute harness, causing the noticeable bulge in the president's crotch (Miller 155). Liddy brayed that those who criticized the press conference as a costly, *Triumph of the Will*–inspired spectacle were driven by

> envy. I mean, after all, Al Gore had to go get some woman [Naomi Wolf] to tell him how to be a man.
>
> And here comes George Bush. You know, he's in his flight suit, he's striding across the deck, and he's wearing his parachute harness, you know—and I've worn those because I parachute—and it makes the best of his manly characteristic.
>
> You go run those—run that stuff again of him walking across there with the parachute. He has just won every woman's vote in the United States of America! You know, all those women who say size doesn't count—they're all liars. Check that out!
>
> . . . [H]e's coming across as a—well, women would call in on my [radio] show saying, what a stud, you know and the guy—they're seeing him out there with his flight suit, and he's—and they know he's an F-105 fighter jock. I mean it's just great. (Liddy; also qtd. in Miller 153, 154)

Although less genitally fixated than Liddy, Matthews also waxed exuberant over the camaraderie between troops and commander in chief: "It's pretty impressive bonding. . . . I mean, they did win the war together." In both men's charged, compulsive excitement we are witnessing the return of the repressed, which should be no surprise in a photo op (and early election campaign stop) built on the very sort of homosexual "double bind" famously postulated by queer theorist Eve Sedgwick in *Between Men: English Literature and Male Homosocial Desire* (1985).[13]

Sedgwick argues that the homosexual double bind—and thus the homoerotic subtext of same-sex situations commonly regarded as wholly free of sexual energy—becomes visible when one traces the frequent and

> important correspondences and similarities between the most sanctioned forms of male-homosocial bonding and the most reprobated expressions of male homosexual society. . . . [T]he fact that what goes on at American football games, in fraternities, . . . and at climactic moments in war novels can look, with only a slight shift of optic, quite startlingly "homosexual," is not most importantly an expression of the psychic origin of these institutions in a repressed or sublimated homosexual genitality. Instead, it is the coming to visibility of the normally implicit terms of a coercive double bind. . . . For a man to be a man's man is separated only by an invisible, carefully blurred, always-already-crossed line from being "interested in men." (*Between Men* 89)

Of course the stakes are so high (in what seemed destined to be the central image of the 2004 Bush campaign triptych) and the register so shrill that the Liddy-Matthews repartee reads as anxiously and simultaneously homosexual and homosocial without even a "slight shift of optic." Liddy attempts to cordon off homoerotic desire (women see "a stud," while men see an "F-105 fighter jock"), yet the double-entendre of his own word choice ("jock" means both athlete and jock-strap) draws the gaze back to what male viewers are supposedly not looking at.

Liddy's nervous yet ebullient homoeroticism is voiced, as Sedgwick argues is usually the case, through a triangulated (in this case, hypothetical) female whose spectral presence should be—but, of course, seems incapable of being—enough to sanitize the heterosexuality of the man so jubilantly giving voice to homosexual desire. The triangulation of gay desire by Liddy reveals the intensity with which homoeroticism circulates in ostensibly homosocial or heterosexual environments. By comparison, Kerry's cosmopolitanism leaves him vulnerable to what Sedgwick calls the "structural residue of terrorist potential, of *blackmailability*, of Western maleness through the leverage of homophobia" (*Between Men* 89). Sedgwick extends this line of argument in *The Epistemology of the Closet* (1990):

> [A]t least since the eighteenth century in England and America, the continuum of male homosocial bonds has been brutally structured by a secularized and psychologized homophobia. . . . [T]he arbitrary and self-contradictory . . . nature of the way *homosexuality* . . . has been defined in relation to the rest of the male homosocial spectrum has been an exceedingly potent and embattled locus of power over the entire range of male bonds, and perhaps especially over those that define themselves, not *as* homosexual, but *as against* the homosexual. (185)

By this line of reasoning, straight men devote unrelenting energy to contests of machismo—in sports, boardrooms, wars, elections, and endless other competitions—because the threat of male-male relationships being construed (much less unmasked) as anything more than friendship or rivalry is constant. Fag jokes or references to "dropping the soap" are most common in contexts (locker rooms, communal showers) where men might be in danger of exhibiting desire for one another. Invoking the specter of homoeroticism in order to denounce and disavow it, then, would seem to be the ineradicable counterpoint of homosocial and thus heterosexual culture.

Politics has long involved a citizen's or subject's emotional and psychological identification with a leader. When both the citizen and leader in question are male, identification is inherently narcissistic and, perhaps abstractly, homoerotic. When the leader in question bases his credibility on bellicose phallic supremacy and, more concretely, on the fetish of military uniform, and when the eye is forced to crotch level by two black straps outlining and bunching together a codpiece's worth of fabric, the male spectator's view is unavoidably homoerotic. Men watching Bush land on the *Abraham Lincoln* cannot help but look at his crotch, and some of them, like Liddy, respond by frankly admiring the presidential package. This sort of behavior is atavistically tribal: he with the largest penis is the biggest and implicitly greatest man. As Diana Fuss observes in *Inside/Out: Lesbian Theories, Gay Theories*, "Sexual identities are rarely secure. Heterosexuality can never fully ignore the close psychical proximity of its terrifying (homo)sexual other, any more than homosexuality can entirely escape the equally insistent social pressures of (hetero)sexual conformity. Each is haunted by the other" (4).

What makes the double bind of homosociality yet more bizarre is that blindness to homoerotic undertones of one's own words or actions is often accompanied by a perspicacity, or rather penchant, for spotting homosexuality in the actions and words of others. Matt Drudge, a Republican operative who passes off libel and rumor as news, presents with this symptom in his Internet report from July 8, 2004, "Can't Keep Hands Off Each Other."[14] In what even for Drudge constitutes a new nadir in yellow journalism, he targets images of causal contact between Kerry and Edwards on the campaign trail (all of which Drudge must know to be staged photo ops) as evidence the two are lovers. Drudge writes that "'candidate handling' has become the top buzz on the trail. . . . 'I've been covering Washington politics for 30 years. I can say I've never seen this much touching between two men, publicly,' e-mailed one wire photographer" (pars. 3, 5). Drudge is neither credible nor a journalist (nor is Dennis Miller, anecdotally credited with starting this rumor on its way), so there is no reason to believe the anonymous quote authentic. If indeed a fake, the quote is all the stranger for the (one assumes unintentional) nod it gives to a rampant private homosexuality: saying one's never seen "this much touching between two men, [pause], publicly" implies that one has witnessed a lot of same-sex intimacy behind closed doors. And considering that Drudge himself was outed as gay back in 2000, it seems safe to infer that he has. What Sedgwick calls the "endemic and ineradicable state of . . . male homosexual panic"—panic at being called or thought queer, especially given the incessant potential for slippage between the homoerotic and the homosocial in male-male bonds—seems to require the queer-baiting of others (*The Epistemology of the Closet* 185). The practice of preemptive homophobia by those who have themselves already been outed, such as Matt Drudge, calls for further, possibly unintuitable explanation.

Drudge was not alone in relying on homophobia to denigrate the Democratic ticket.[15] A plethora of Internet postings painted the Democratic running mates as bedmates: "The Kerry Gay Conspiracy Revealed," "Are John Kerry and John Edwards Gay?" (musically accompanied by "It's Raining Men"), "Kerry & Edwards in Love" (accompanied by Marvin Gaye's "Let's Get It On" and featuring animated photos of Kerry cupping Edwards's ass and of the two French kissing), and "They Aren't Gay—They're FABULOUS!" Regardless of their appearance on humor Web sites (some of which are clearly partisan, others not), these postings validate the homophobia on which right-wing muckrakers such as Drudge trade. Worse yet—and a sign of homophobic rhetoric's ascendancy through the journalistic ranks—is Jodi Wilgoren's *New York Times* piece "Part Butler and Part Buddy, Aide Keeps Kerry Running," which profiles Kerry's "factotum, or 'body man,'" Marvin Nicholson, Jr. (par. 11). In Wilgoren's words, Kerry is "comfortable being catered to. A social loner, he is happy with an aide half his age" (par. 6). Compiling a titillating collage of suggestive details, this article does not simply paint Kerry as pampered but explicitly marks the candidate and his aide as homosexuals: "at night, [Nicholson] often stays by [Kerry's] side until he is ready to go to sleep. . . . When Mr. Kerry stays overnight at supporters' homes, it is Mr. Nicholson who accompanies him; in Iowa once, they shared a bathroom. 'I've seen him in his underwear,' Nicholson said, declining to discuss the topic further" (pars. 8, 19, 20). Lest the latent homoeroticism in the notion of a "body man," or body servant, escape some readers, Wilgoren harps on the suspicious proximity of two male bodies during various states of undress and possible nudity. The implication that indubitably straight men are not intimate in such ways, whereas only gay men are, fails to gel with the fact that straight male roommates routinely share bathrooms and often see one another in their underwear. Ignoring this universally known reality, Wilgoren tips the balance with the image of Nicholson hovering at Kerry's bedside, part Florence Nightingale, part gay lover—waiting, in either role, to minister to a man's body in a way that, to the homophobe, unmans both participants.

Lee Edelman's forceful new contribution to queer theory, *No Future: Queer Theory and the Death Drive* (2004), allows us an even sharper insight into the force with which homosexuality impinges on the collective heterosexual imagination. As diatribes of the Family Research Council or Reverend Fred Phelps evince and insist, any "refusal to embrace the genealogical fantasy that braces the social order cannot . . . be a matter of social indifference" (Edelman 44). "Queer sexualities," Edelman contends, following Sedgwick, "are linked to the conceptual coherence of heterosexual desire" (43). This constitutive dependency might explain the antipodal articulations of homosexual desire in mainstream culture: either vilification and repudiation, or eroticism expressed with self-conscious humor or incognizant earnestness. Drawing on postmodern and psychoanalytic theory, Edelman's watershed argument is that

> homosexuality, understood as a cultural figure, as the hypostatization of various fantasies that trench on the antisocial force queerness might better name, is . . . thought as a threat to the logic of thought itself insofar as it figures the availability of an unthinkable jouissance that would put an end to fantasy—and, with it, to futurity—by reducing the assurance of meaning in fantasy's promise of continuity to the meaningless circulation and repetitions of the drive. Lacan . . . himself makes clear the risk at which such jouissance puts reproductive futurism when he observes that "the end of jouissance . . . does not coincide with what it leads to, namely the fact that we reproduce."
>
> That risk informs the cultural fantasy that conjures homosexuality, and with it the definitional importance of sex in our imagining of homosexuality, in intimate relation to a fatal, and even murderous, jouissance. . . .
>
> . . . [Little can alter] the all pervasive-fantasy [of what Edelman terms "reproductive futurism"] within which [queers'] meaning is always a function not only of what we do with our genitals but also of what we *don't* do: a function, that is, of the envy-, contempt-, and anxiety-producing fixation on our freedom from the necessity of translating the corrupt, unregenerate vulgate of fucking into the infinitely tonier, indeed sacramental, Latin of procreation. (39, 40)[16]

In brief: heteronormativity, to retain its normativity, requires a formulation of homosexuality as extrasocial, as culture negating and life negating. Anti-gay-marriage activists—who are, Russell Shorto remarks, simply the newest face of antigay activism—spout the same, unfounded revival-tent stereotypes: homosexuality is a "hedonistic way of living, one devoted to partying, drugs and wanton sex that ends, often in illness and early death" (41). In 1997 Gary Bauer, of the Family Research Council (FRC), pronounced that "those who practice homosexuality embrace a culture of death." Seven years later, FRC publications were still "lin[ing] up studies and statistics to link homosexuality with cancer, alcoholism, mental illness, suicide and reduced life span, in addition to H.I.V./AIDS and other sexually transmitted diseases" (Shorto 41). Cindy Moles, Southern California area director for Concerned Women for America, speaks consciously from the position that marriage is the sacred vessel of culture and that homosexuality is its sure destruction—that is, certain death: "'Look at the Netherlands, where same-sex marriage is legal. Those marriages last an average of 1.5 years, and during that time there are an average of eight outside partners. That's not a solid foundation for our country'" (qtd. in Shorto 64). Perhaps it is not surprising that Moles, Bauer, and others have been too enthralled with their own self-righteousness to see that without queers they, in some fundamental sense, could not exist, much less have anything to denounce. As Edelman elucidates, this abjection of the queer is—paradoxically, and troubling in terms of heteronormativity's supposed stability—internal, if not elemental to, the social order to which it is so threateningly antagonistic. Yet whether or not abjection of the queer is a native social impulse, this impulse has recently been recognized, by some, as a legitimate basis for law.

Michael Warner's *The Trouble with Normal* (1999), a socially vectored petition to reclaim a "queer ethic of dignity in shame"—not to barter away queer authenticity by desexualizing homosexuality in an attempt to gain cultural acceptance and political equality—bears strong affinities to Edelman's work (Warner 37). Both advocate not rejecting but embracing the stigma traditionally associated with gay sex and identity (Warner 35–40, 46–50, 65–75). But Edelman, unlike Warner, holds out little hope that such a "frank embrace of queer sex in all its apparent indignity" might subvert the "damaging hierarchies of respectability" on which heteronormativity is predicated, might "change the self-understanding of . . . [a] culture" that is stigmaphobic to its core, not just against queers but against them most of all (Warner 74, 50). "Rather than rejecting, with liberal discourse, this ascription of negativity to the queer," writes Edelman,

> we might . . . do better to consider accepting and even embracing it. Not in the hope of forging thereby some more perfect social order—such a hope, after all, would only reproduce the constraining mandate of futurism, just as any such order would equally occasion the negativity of the queer—but rather to refuse the insistence of hope itself as affirmation, which is always affirmation of an order whose refusal will register as unthinkable, irresponsible, inhumane. . . . When I argue, then, that we might do well to attempt what is surely impossible—to withdraw our allegiance, however compulsory, from a reality based on the Ponzi scheme of reproductive futurism, I do not intend to propose some "good" that will thereby be assured. . . . My polemic thus stakes its fortunes on a truly hopeless wager: . . . that attending to the persistence of something internal to reason that reason refuses, that turning the force of queerness against all subjects . . . can afford access to the *jouissance* that at once defines and negates us. Or better: can expose the constancy, the inescapability, of such access to jouissance in the social order itself, even if that order can access its constant access to jouissance only in the process of abjecting that constancy of access onto the queer. (4–5)

Like Warner, Edelman adjures an awareness that abjection of the queer is the mother's milk of normative culture and, ironically, of reproductive futurism—the fantasy that the future of civilization rests in the cradle, in sex that is always about something, always productive of a future (which, according to cliché, children are). This is the invidious distinction on which antigay crusaders rest their lances, the comforting, corrosive lie on which homophobia in any venue organically depends: that even for the infertile and the elderly, heterosexual intercourse is freighted with the potential to create life, stave off death, endow meaning where, for queers, there allegedly is none. To return to Edelman's linguistic analogy ("the corrupt, unregenerate vulgate of fucking" versus the "tonier . . . sacramental Latin of procreation" [40]): If heterosexual intercourse were ever no more than that, if straight fucking failed to transcend the vulgar, simply pleasurable confines of the act itself, if it were not always buttressed with the narrative through line of children, family, and futurity, then straights would be no better than queers. Shorn of its apotheosizing constellation of myths, straight sex would be reduced to—or rather, revealed to be no more than—fucking. Anyone can do *that*. Shoring up the distinction between straight sex and every other kind of sex—as a putatively natural distinction freighted with the most profound difference (receptacle of romance, creator of life, sustainer of nations)—is, as Edelman and Warner point out, the Sisyphean labor of American heteronormative culture.

Brave New Homophobia

Another calculated assault on Kerry's ability to "command," that is, to be a man, involved outright homophobic caricature—and an especially sophomoric brand, at that. Immediately following the first Bush-Kerry debate, FOX News correspondent Carl Cameron quoted from Kerry's remarks at a postdebate rally: "Women should like me! I do manicures," "Didn't my nails and cuticles look great? What a good debate," and "I'm a metrosexual—[Bush is] a cowboy" (qtd. in "FOX Chief Political Correspondent"). The only problem is that Kerry never said any of this. Cameron fabricated the quotes and posted them as part of his official FOX coverage of the Kerry campaign.[17] Portraying Kerry as homosexual in style—or even metrosexual, since the FOX story pretty much equates the two—is second only in homophobic virulence to Wilgoren's "gay butler" piece. And as the examples provided here suggest, this particular contest of masculinities has also been framed as a battle of real men against sissies and nellies, straight against gay.

I would not go so far as to suggest that all evocations of masculinity are homophobic (perhaps just nearly all) or that every instance of homophobic rhetoric in the 2004 presidential campaign was directed at American gay men. The flip-flopper moniker was used to taunt Kerry and no one else. But in a culture as drenched in masculinity as ours, the suggestions that "flip-flopper" carries—vacillation, hesitation, timidity—cannot but resonate with the homophobic infrastructure of heteronormativity. Real men do not fear. Real men are not queer. Real men hit a baseball and fire a gun with confidence. Within this ethos, a leader rules either with an iron fist or a flexible—that is, a limp—wrist. Again, I would never suggest that slurs against candidates' masculinity are new to politics. The months following Bush's reelection, however, manifested a brave new homophobia; this, perhaps, should be no surprise after the reelection of a candidate whose platform contained elements (namely, the Federal Marriage Amendment) as homophobic as his rhetoric. In the same election, a majority of citizens in eleven states approved amending their state constitutions to ban same-sex marriage, civil unions, and, in many cases, domestic partner benefits. The postelection confidence of a brave new homophobia seemed to bode ill for queer civil rights, conjuring instead the wistful prospect of a return to queer silence and absence.

To be fair, opinion is divided about the influence of homophobia on the election's outcome (see Carolyn Lochhead), but an accurate judgment depends on what one means by outcome—that is, whether one means who won (which presidential candidate) or whether one means *what* won, what ideology was affirmed, looming larger than a single candidate. While the eleven state ballot initiatives defining marriage heterosexually and preemptively banning gay marriage and/or civil unions constitute a Melvillean "'No' in thunder" to pro-gay-marriage developments in Massachusetts, California, and New York, the argument that "gay marriage [was] Kerry's undoing" or that so-called moral issues were the deciding factor is a hasty bit of punditry refuted by most commentators—including Karl Rove himself, on *Meet the Press* five days after the election (qtd. in Collingsworth par. 1).[18] The notion that "the most important issue to voters was not terrorism, but moral values," to quote Ann Coulter, does not sustain scrutiny (par. 13). In reaction perhaps to exaggerations such as these, other commentators tried to put the homophobic state initiatives in perspective: marriage amendments may have "won by lopsided majorities in all 11 states where they were on the ballot," but Coulter, like others who echoed this right-wing talking point, fails to mention that most of the amendments passed in red states the Democrats never (or, at best, faintly) expected to carry. Writing off any states, much less one-fifth of the nation, as too backward to ever entertain the idea of queer equality may afford a smug self-satisfaction with one's own liberal credentials, but the victory is Pyrrhic, and not merely rhetorically speaking. Apathetic acceptance of inequality does little psychologically to stem the tide of homophobic retrenchment and, concretely, it renders turning back that tide that much more difficult, both legally and culturally. Thus, while the tangible effects of the election and its homophobic rhetoric on the progress of GLBT issues may seem mixed and not irreversible, I would contend that the gestalt effect of the election, at least for the four years following, was in fact to embolden homophobia, to whet the confidence of those whose hatred—legally and socially unacceptable when voiced against any other minority—masquerades in the cowardly guise of moral tenet, religious belief, or free speech. Russell Shorto says as much (though he attributes the view to gay activists, as if the view is partisan rather than just factual): the groundswell of anti–gay-marriage activism can be chalked up to the fact that "gay marriage serves as a vessel for containing opinions that many social conservatives have but which in the past they might have felt were socially unacceptable to voice" (41).

Two incidents hard on the heels of the election bear representative witness to the impress of such rhetoric in other contexts. In February 2005 the Suicide Prevention Resource Center was asked by Bush appointees at the Substance Abuse and Mental Health Services Administration (SAMHSA) to "remove the words 'gay,' 'lesbian,' 'bisexual,' and transgender' from . . . material" used in the center's upcoming conference, which was funded by SAMHSA. What made the request more outrageous was the fact that the conference in question was called "Suicide Prevention Among Gay/Lesbian/Bisexual/Transgender Individuals" (Brandt par. 1; see also "HHS Backs Down" and Susan Forrest). Technically, federal officials never said the content of the workshop was objectionable (suicide prevention among GLBTs), yet censoring the title of the conference suggests that, in some minds, it should be. At the very least, a homophobic administration is willing to help GLBT persons as long as no one finds out about it. Bureaucratic muscle-flexing here betrays a desire not just to return queers to the closet (or keep them there) but to deep-six the very words that refer to them, that hint at their existence—and not flamboyant terms such as "nelly" or "queen," but the most clinical descriptors. SAMHSA officials agreed to allow the conference to go forward if its title were amended to "Suicide Prevention in Vulnerable Populations" and if all GLBT terms were eliminated from the workshop description ("HHS Backs Down" par. 9). Fortunately, after quick and vocal protest from openly gay Congressman Barney Frank (D-MA) and a "flood [of] complaints," SAMHSA decided to permit the use of the offending words (Brandt par. 14). The outcome of this incident, however, fails to diminish not merely the attempt to restrict access to professionals who counsel suicidal GLBTs but the *1984*-like effort to police language, to purge public discourse of the words for certain persons and, by extension, to purge public spaces and the public mind of their existence.

A more confident wave of homophobia also made itself felt in child psychologist and family values demagogue James Dobson's assault on popular children's cartoon character Spongebob Squarepants. Founder of the Christian Right think tank Family Research Council (the Washington, DC, lobbying arm of Dobson's organization Focus on the Family), Dobson commands substantial influence nationally: he reaches an audience of over 200 million with his daily radio show and was regularly consulted by President Bush and White House strategist Karl Rove on matters of policy and election strategy. Speaking at a 2005 inaugural week event in Washington, DC, Dobson did not, as media sound bytes suggested, claim that the cartoon character himself was gay but rather that Spongebob is "promoting homosexuality." The wide-eyed undersea-dwelling sponge appears, along with other children's television characters, in a "video put out by the 'We Are Family Foundation,' which is intended," according to the foundation's press release, "'to promote tolerance and diversity to America's children'" by emphasizing "'our common humanity and the vision of a global family'" (The Plaid Adder par. 3). Dobson's crusade rests on what passes for logic with right-wing organizations such as the Family Research Council. As the *National Business Review* reported after speaking with FRC officials, "A 'homosexuality detection expert' at the . . . Family Research Council told the NY Times [*sic*] that words like 'tolerance' and 'diversity' are part of a 'coded language that is regularly used by the homosexual community'" (The Plaid Adder par. 6). Online commentator The Plaid Adder states that

> the very concept of tolerance—the idea that we should all try to live together in peace and harmony instead of being constantly at war with each other—is now obnoxious to the religious right. Tolerance is a *bad thing*. Tolerance, in fact, will make your children gay. And since being gay is absolutely the worst thing that could possibly happen to them, we must fight all tolerance anywhere it lurks. . . . (par. 7)

Dobson has been wily enough to claim that he never meant to discourage tolerance, but not enough so to keep him from contradicting himself, or at least appearing to do so (I'll return to this apparent tergiversation in a moment). The Plaid Adder continues:

> The problem is not with acceptance or kindness, certainly. But kids should not be taught that homosexuality is just another "lifestyle," or that it is morally equivalent to heterosexuality. Scripture teaches that all overt sexual activity outside the bonds of marriage is sinful and harmful. Children should not be taught otherwise by their teachers, and certainly not if their parents are unaware of the instruction. (par. 10)

Separation of church and state is for Dobson little more than a shibboleth of the Left, an atheist myth. Still, it boggles the mind that the religious Right thinks "diversity" and "tolerance" are code words for the "gay agenda"—an insistence on tolerance for homosexuality only, not tolerance of racial, religious, and ethnic diversity as the rest of us might naively have thought. As Dobson's radio audience of 200 million Americans knows full well, their leader is right about one thing: queers are the last whipping boy of the culture, or at least the one it is still acceptable to flog in public.[19] Among all the differentials of otherness (race, gender, religion), we are the single locus that has not been legally brought within the fold; and, as Lee Edelman suggests, because the multitudes who differ along those other axes still hold in common a (hetero)sexuality, perhaps we never *can* be—that is, not psychologically and therefore possibly not legally as well. Dobson's invective would be ludicrous were its intent not deadly serious:

to eliminate any positive discussion of homosexuality from educational contexts and thus to ensure that children receive one uniform message—a negative one—with no pesky talk of Christian doctrines such as love and acceptance blocking the hate-mongering signal. The equally absurd concept that there exists anything like a "homosexuality detection expert" conjures the McCarthyesque image of eyes from which no one can hide, eyes policing all public and private space to ferret out the infidel homos in hetero clothing whose sole mission it is to destroy America.[20] Apparently no one at the Family Research Council, except maybe the homosexuality detection expert, is familiar with the concept of gaydar (or in straight parlance, "it takes one to know one"). It is debatable as to which of the impulses demonstrated here is worse: to erase homosexuality, even the mention of it, from public discourse (like SAMHSA); or to silence selectively, like Dobson, allowing solely toxic images of homosexuality to circulate in the bloodstream of the body politic.

Although it's easy to write off what Dobson is peddling as simple homophobia, doing so would be to miss the nuance of his position. It's a position he's not alone in adopting. Anna Marie Smith's "Why Did Armey Apologize?: Hegemony, Homophobia, and the Religious Right" (2001) brilliantly dissects the Right's largely successful bait-and-switch strategy of distracting Americans from concrete economic and political problems with illusory moral crises. Smith (156–63) accredits the Right's success in part to the new approach they learned to take with traditional hot-button issues related to race (affirmative action) and sexuality (antidiscrimination, education, and same-sex marriage). While hardly granting "holy dispensation" to queers, homophobes in the religious Right have learned that "unmodified homophobic bigotry is acceptable" as long as they construct their "bigotry in some nominal fashion with reference to liberal democratic values" ("Armey" 163). Members of the religious and political Right have made a quantum leap in their war on homosexuals by pitching it as a crusade against "special rights." The reality of heterosexism is obscured by a diversionary cover story: the "special rights" demanded or already enjoyed by homosexuals in fact oppress heterosexuals and thereby violate the notion of general democratic equality. This is a common conservative means of short-circuiting antidiscriminatory policies: by claiming they're actually discriminatory—against heterosexuals, men, or whites, depending on the policy under discussion.

As Anna Marie Smith spells out, such claims are part of a larger trend within right-wing discourse. The "parasitic tendencies" of the religious Right, along with neoconservatism and the "new racism," have been

> quite successful in constructing frameworks for right-wing indentifications with such key signifiers as "freedom," "equality," "democracy," and "tolerance of difference." The religious Right, neoconservatives, and new racists do not mount a singular attack against liberal democracy as the Far Right has done; for the most part, these groups claim instead that

> they are the real defenders of liberal democracy. They construct their exclusions of women, people of color, the unemployed, the poor, and lesbians and gays as demands for a "return" to an "egalitarian" social order and a "renewal" of "democratic rights" against the imaginary foes of leftist cultural forces dedicated to the promotion of social engineering, a redistributive state, and a reverse-racist affirmative action apparatus.
>
> The American Right redefines "freedom," "equality," and "democracy" in a possessive individualist and exclusionary manner that rules out as incoherent the radical moments of the civil rights, black power, welfare rights, feminist, and sexual liberation struggles. Ultimately, the Right's corruption of democratic values would allow it to reconcile its peculiar "democratic" discourse with the perpetuation of virtually every form of inequality. Together, the religious Right, the neoconservatives, and the new racists have subversively borrowed the language of the civil rights struggle, eviscerated its radical meanings, and stuffed it with profoundly antiegalitarian connotations. ("Armey" 150–51)

Via this bifurcated semantics, the demand not to be discriminated against constitutes a demand to be treated differently than others; a law that awards equality to gays and lesbians, such as a law against firing someone because of their sexuality, produces inequality because it provides a special protection. Never mind the fact that straights don't need such protection; wielding the term "equality" as a blunt instrument doesn't allow for such subtleties. It's not the case, then, that religious and political conservatives are less homophobic but, rather—as Cynthia Burack skillfully details in *Sin, Sex, and Democracy: Antigay Rhetoric and the Christian Right* (2008)—that they've learned to moderate their rhetoric, to frame their traditional antigay message in more politically centrist language, a democratic double-talk that still reaches the base while appealing to alienated Democrats and others who would be turned off by blatant homophobia.

So how does this clarify Dobson's gay-bashing of Spongebob? Is there actually any nuance there? On one level, Dobson's speech, as quoted earlier, is transparently intolerant. But it's equally important that Dobson, when accused of intolerance, claims that he intended nothing of the kind. Is he contradicting himself, or just lying? As boggling as it might seem, he is in fact doing neither. Dobson is both discouraging tolerance and embracing it. The solution to this puzzle lies in the Right's recent overhaul of its message. Translating homophobia into an appeal to democratic values has been a successful strategy, but it creates a rather disorienting dissonance. A word such as "tolerance" is burdened with two divergent meanings, which the Right is trying to market as consonant: the mainstream, democratic connotations of nondiscrimination and liberal individualism, and the New Right, homophobic connotation of proselytism or recruitment—the peddling of homosexuality by predatory queers. When the FRC spokesperson refers to "tolerance" as "part of a 'coded language . . . used by the homosexual community," he's being a bit disingenuous (The Plaid Adder par. 6). If "tolerance" has a "coded" meaning for anyone, it's Dobson, not gays and lesbians. "Tolerance" panics Dobson because, like other members of the Right, he assumes it means two things. One is the acceptance of difference, legally enforced or not (in the form of antidiscrimination laws); the other is the promotion of homosexuality—that bogeyman of the Right. The first definition is one queer activists would likely agree with. If one defines "promotion," as Smith does in *New Right Discourse*, as "political intervention" [238], queers would, oddly, find themselves agreeing with the Right on both counts (seeking intervention toward radically different ends, of course). This is not its meaning for the Right, though—at least, not its most terrifying one. For Dobson, to accept difference as legitimate is to promote what is different, to sell difference as attractive: in short, to recruit for the "other team." Dobson detests tolerance because presenting queerness as not abnormal—as no less "normal" than heterosexuality—brings into question the latter's cultural centrality, its right to be called the "norm." And there Dobson is correct; that's precisely the intent. What uniquely terrifies the Right about questioning heteronormativity, however, is the "possibility that homosexuality may be accepted as legitimate, as a 'norm.' [Homophobic] discourse instead names homosexuality as a false 'norm,' its family relations as simulacra and attempts to make a distinction [in referenda on same-sex marriage] between the pretender and the real thing" (Anna Marie Smith, *New Right Discourse* 204). Even though "the very necessity of [drawing] such a distinction is indicative of its impossibility," when the Family Research Council or the Concerned Women for America speaks out against tolerance of homosexuality, what they're really upset by is, to their mind, the promotion of homosexuality (204). To call "tolerance" a gay code word is to suggest that queers seeking "tolerance" are, in truth, seeking something else—recruits. Suggesting that queers are using the word duplicitously is a projection, since it's the accuser in this case who's engaging in double-talk. Calling "tolerance" a gay code word diverts focus from its function as a right-wing code word, a signal to the conservative base that "special rights" and "promotion of homosexuality" are on the verge of destroying their families and communities. But it also attempts to deform the meaning of "tolerance" for those outside the base, to recruit other Americans to their authoritarian cause. This is how Dobson can object to tolerance and at the same time claim not to discourage it: he's talking (somewhat schizophrenically, it might seem) to two different audiences, engaging in two antithetical discourses simultaneously.

There's yet another, equally enlightening way to look at Dobson's broadside. And that's to see his claim—not to be intolerant even while objecting to tolerance—as not duplicitous but forthright. Perhaps without understanding that he's doing so, Dobson's apparently Janus-faced position exemplifies the tainted character of tolerance itself. Although it is often considered to be an ideal tool for deterring physical persecution by mitigating tensions over differences in race, culture, religion, nationality, or sexuality, political scientist Wendy Brown proposes that tolerance, at least in Western liberal democracies, tends to function quite differently (5). Brown's thesis in *Regulating Aversion: Tolerance in the Age of Identity and Empire* (2006) is apt to strike one as counterintuitive, but such a reaction only proves the West's "uncritical embrace of tolerance across a wide ideological field" (5). Far from a panacea to deter violence against historically persecuted populations, Brown argues that tolerance tends to mask *in*tolerance, to perpetuate and often implement inequality. More crucially, despite the good intentions of some individuals, tolerance serves as a tool of subjection: "even an individual bearing of tolerance in nonpolitical arenas carries authority and potential subjection through unavowed norms. Almost all objects of tolerance are marked as deviant . . . by virtue of being tolerated, and the action of tolerance inevitably affords some access to superiority" (14). Tolerance operates as a "disciplinary strategy of liberal individualism," such that its

> [d]esignated objects . . . are invariably marked as undesirable and marginal, as liminal civil subjects or even liminal humans; and those called upon to exercise tolerance are asked to repress or override their hostility or repugnance in the name of civility, peace or progress.
>
> . . . This regulatory individuation of the deviant, the abject, the other, suggests a further implication of the normalizing work of contemporary tolerance discourse. Tolerated individuals will always be those who deviate from the norm, never those who uphold it, but they will also be further articulated as (deviant) individuals through the very discourse of tolerance. (28, 44)

This seems absolutely on target: tolerance induces the very abjection it purports to overcome. If one pauses to think about it, tolerance is not something gays and lesbians, people of color, Muslims, or members of other traditionally (or more recently) persecuted groups are typically called on to exercise. Who's always being asked to be or coached into being tolerant? Whose fears of the Other, implicitly or transparently, is tolerance education meant to soothe? Straight, white, bourgeois Christians.

Brown's analysis seems eminently, if ironically, applicable to Dobson's Spongebob fatwa. In this light, Dobson doesn't give up anything when he says he's not discouraging tolerance. It turns out he's not even being duplicitous. By intolerantly railing at gays and lesbians, he's merely tapping into the bitter core of tolerance discourse. The same split occurs in America's conflicted attitudes about gay rights versus same-sex marriage: "the state sees and enjoins homosexuals from marrying, [while] the (heterosexual) citizenry averts its glance and tolerates homosexuality in its midst"—thus confining tolerance to "a civil and individual . . . practice" but stopping short of making it a "state practice" (99). Socially, we're told, in poll after poll, Americans favor equality for gays and lesbians, yet politically the still quite strong opposition to same-sex marriage among heterosexuals blocks and disables the ability to implement that equality in any other than a nominal fashion.

That's not to say that all forms of tolerance are to be abjured: "The recognition that discourses of tolerance inevitably articulate . . . belonging and marginality, . . . and that they invariably do so on behalf of hegemonic social or political powers, does not automatically negate the worth of tolerance in attenuating certain kinds of violence or abuse" (10). The latter brand of tolerance is a moral practice; Brown's subject and target is tolerance as a "political practice" (11). For gays and lesbians, tolerance functions not merely as another kind of discrimination. It also marks queers' exclusion from the nation: advocating "tolerance of homosexuals . . . as an alternative to full legal equality . . . opposes tolerance to equality and bids to maintain the abject civic status of the homosexual" (10–11). The tolerance extended to gay and lesbian Americans marks the painfully "limited reach of liberal equality claims," the extent to which "the Other remains outside a norm of citizenship" (75).

This disclosure of tolerance's hidden phobic lining fits in well with queer theory's embrace of the abject as exhorted by Michael Warner, David Halperin, and Lee Edelman. Embracing difference or culturally ascribed abjection with the aim of overcoming or dissipating it would be both naive and ineffective. As Brown points out, it's by voicing respect for cultural difference that tolerance discourse masks the "workings of power," the processes by which sexuality, gender, and race have been "produc[ed]" and enshrined as supposed facts—constructed to conceal the legal and social inequalities they codify. At first glance, recommending that queers accept their degraded status might seem to run counter to what Brown is saying: isn't embracing one's own abjection just encouraging a regime of tolerance, playing into its "regulatory" and "normalizing" work (44)? But it's not quite the same thing, as a recurrence to Lee Edelman's argument in *No Future* will clarify. Instead of combating homophobia with tolerance education—an endeavor Edelman and Brown regard as futile—queers would do well to accept our culturally contemptible status (our identification, for Edelman, with hedonism, death, and the destruction of civilization). We should do so, the argument runs, not because such characterizations are true but because through them we are able to point to the cheat of hegemonic social and political discourse, the hollow center of heteronormativity. Accepting the ascription of abjection isn't the same as asking to be tolerated. If anything, it's to show up tolerance for the sham, the tool of subjection and normalization, it really is. The cultivation of abjection advocated by queer theory, then, stands distinct from assimilation on the one hand and the tolerance discourses Brown is critiquing on the other. Instead of playing into tolerance's game, embracing queers' abject status can actually assist in uncovering the hegemonic deployment of tolerance, by drawing attention to the unpredictable effects of even the most repressive rhetoric. It's part of my larger argument that significant queer work can be accomplished, not by jettisoning identity categories as purely repressive but by mobilizing essentialisms in a pragmatic, strategic manner, whereby their "naturalness" is never naively taken for granted but problematized as a discursive effect—an effect that can still lodge substantial claims for personhood as well as critique current models of social and political belonging. That being said, another key point of *Queer Externalities* is that, regardless of difference's constructed nature, its discursive effects are still quite real. Those effects can be painful, punitive, even murderous (as well as, on other occasions, shielding, preservative, efficaciously subversive).

If there have been more than a few missteps in the Right's homophobic cotillion, these have come mainly in the form of an epiphenomenonal queering that confuses but does not (or at least not yet) seem in danger of derailing the Right's gay-baiting efforts. In a refreshing counterpoint to the gay-baiting examined here are the outings—by their own actions or by the Signorile-like activism of Mike Rogers and John Byrne—of a number of conservative Republican politicians and officials over the past few years: Congressman David Drier (R-CA), chair of the House Rules Committee, who employed his lover at a salary higher than former Bush White House Chief of Staff Andy Card; Congressman Ed Schrock (R-VA), coauthor of Virginia's 2004 law forbidding private companies from granting domestic partner benefits, who dropped his bid for reelection after his phone sex conversations with other men were posted online; Arthur Finkelstein, the veteran GOP operative who assisted the rise to power of those such as Jesse Helms and who married his longtime male partner in Massachusetts not long after that state legalized same-sex marriage; Jim West, mayor of Spokane, Washington, author of antigay city legislation, who was busted for seeking underage male sex partners on *gay.com*; Ken Mehlman, head of the 2004 Bush/Cheney campaign and later RNC chairman; Jay Banning, chief financial officer and director of administration of the RNC since 1983; and, as mentioned earlier, infamous blogger and conservative gadfly Matt Drudge. Whether or not outspokenly homophobic in attitude or in legislation, those listed here are fascinating examples of what one might call a collaborating-minority syndrome: working for an organization (in this case, the GOP or the Bush administration) publicly committed on state and federal levels to retrenching or preemptively negating queer civil rights.

Another notable inductee to the gay Vichy Hall of Fame is Robert L. Traynham, director of communications for vehemently homophobic former Senator Rick Santorum (R-PA), prominent champion of the failed Federal Marriage Amendment. "According to PageOneQ, an online gay and lesbian publication . . . Traynham," who has worked for the senator since 1997, "said that he was an 'out gay man who completely supports the senator'"—the same senator who routinely rails against homosexuality as a cancer eating away at the nation and who, in a 2003 jeremiad, warned that decriminalizing sodomy would lead to "man on child [and] man on dog" sex (Steve Goldstein par. 2; Santorum par. 19). Traynham, who also happens to be African American, seems untroubled by his party's overt program of opposition and neglect toward the two communities to which he belongs. For his part, Santorum was characteristically schizoid, asserting that his employment of Traynham "'squares very clearly with my public positions on every other issue, which is that I treat people fairly, I treat people equally, I treat people with dignity and respect, and irrespective of what they may or may not do outside of work'" (Krawczeniuk par. 3). Santorum also lamented that "'my staffs' [*sic*] personal lives are considered fair game by partisans looking for arguments to bolster my opponent's campaign. Mr. Traynham continues to have my full support and confidence as well as my prayers as he navigates this rude and mean spirited invasion of his personal life'" (Steve Goldstein par. 6). It seems that privacy cloaks only what *Republicans* do "outside of work." Politicians of every other stripe are subject to smearing—and even impeachment—on the basis of their private lives; ordinary citizens, to the infringement of rights and privileges guaranteed to every other citizen.

Such gaffes notwithstanding, the homophobia boiling up through the campaign rhetoric of the 2004 presidential race, on the force of Bush's reinstatement, soon crested and turned back toward the shore, stronger and more brazen. What it is able to wash away, and how many respond in the effort to stem its progress, remains to be seen. Especially disheartening is the fact that outings of antigay Republican politicians and the revelations of hypocrisy in their stances on "moral issues" so central to their rhetoric—in the rare instances when these stories make it onto major networks, much less make headlines—do not seem to shake the faith of their benighted constituencies. Tenacity on that order suggests that the quiet passage in September 2005 of a long-overdue expansion of federal hate crimes laws covering sexual orientation, though indisputably an important foundation, may not of itself be an ample bulwark.[21] What political or critical difference might be made by more high-profile outings, in 2005 and 2006, of yet more Republicans and social conservatives will be considered in the final chapter.

On the other hand, some hope may stand to be derived from postelection legal challenges to anti–gay-marriage and anti–civil-union measures in six states, including Nebraska, and, in June 2006, from the resounding defeat of the Federal Marriage Amendment, resurrected by the GOP to reenergize a disaffected fundamentalist base for midterm elections. June 2007 also gave hope, to some, that at least one political gain by gays and lesbians would not be overturned. Conservative efforts by groups such as the Concerned Women for America and the Massachusetts Family Institute to secure a legislative ban on gay marriage—legalized by the Massachusetts Supreme Court in 2003—seemed to have finally met defeat. After four years of conservative demands and legislative deadlock, the State House finally produced a bill that would outlaw gay marriage and annul the nine thousand or so marriage licenses issued since the state began issuing licenses in 2004. The decision by nine legislators formerly in support of the ban to change their votes finally gave supporters of same-sex marriage a clear victory, at least for the time being.

On the basis of such legal (as well as broad cultural) shifts, Richard Mohr predicts the "collapse of the taboo" against homosexuality in the United States. In *The Long Arc of Justice: Lesbian and Gay Marriage, Equality, and Rights* (2005), Mohr contends that "gays and lesbians are making rapid progress. . . . America has passed a crucial turning point on gay issues and is undergoing important structural changes that bode well for the long haul" (3). Without naysaying the good news that equality seems more possible than in the past—seems, to many, inevitable—I am a bit more cautious. Mohr's assertion, for example, that "however successful as politics, the conservatives' antigay strategies necessarily trip over themselves as a cultural project" may overestimate the ways in which antigay activists' having to discuss gay issues subverts their own efforts, as well as underestimate the umbilical cord by which homophobic rhetoric nourishes, and is capable of accomplishing, political as well as cultural projects (7).

The kind of mudslinging routine in political campaigns can, as we've seen in the 2004 presidential race, serve a dual purpose. Republican queer-bashing does more than tar one's opponent with the same brush as the party's bête noire, the homosexual. It deepens the GOP's hold on American popular consciousness by combining the effete, the foreign, and the faggy in a tincture sure to offend the senses of voters across the spectrum, from the party faithful to swing voters and conservative and centrist Democrats. And while the impact of queer-baiting Kerry on the election's outcome may be difficult to parse out from a complex tangle of other factors, chipping away at alliances among Independent and Democratic voters by aiming at America's Achilles heel (particularly in wartime) has had concrete, diagnostic repercussions. Name-calling by playground bullies is nothing new to queers. But implying that a presidential hopeful might be less than "all man" insinuates homophobia in a way that avoids issues where the Republican stance might offend: locker-room digs impugning one's heterosexuality are juvenile and crass yet not as repugnant as direct attacks on queers. However, it's been my contention in this chapter that oblique, atmospheric homophobia is conspecific with, and equally as corrosive as, frontal polemics against gay and lesbian civil rights—not that many on the Right are above such direct attacks. But disseminating antigay hatred, even in contexts where it seems ludicrous, hard to take seriously, squares the force of more palpable concomitants, such as barring legal parity by outlawing domestic partner benefits. Republican queer-baiting's overdramatic, conspicuous character also distracts one from an extralegal, perhaps more ominous state of affairs: that, for the leadership in both parties, gays and lesbians are not really on the map.

A seemingly counterfactual statement such as this requires some explaining. First, note that I say "leadership" not "leaders," since a few candidates, such as former president Bill Clinton and current president Barack Obama when he was running for the presidency in 2008, went beyond party silence or neutrality and took positive stands on gay and lesbian issues. Granted, with Clinton gay positivity quickly faded. Although the homophilia of his 1992 campaign was, very likely, window dressing, Clinton faced both broad institutional prejudices (in Congress, at the Pentagon, and from the party machinery) and a centralized nonrepresentative gay leadership (the Human Rights Campaign (HRC), most prominently) determined to reduce gay and lesbian rights to two single-issue causes: gays in the military and same-sex marriage. On the local level and in limited instances, politicians have addressed concerns of gay and lesbian constituents, but in national politics queers are simply not on the map. To put it more baldly, queers don't exist in national politics.

Second, it's true that gay and lesbian issues—lack of access to basic property and personal protections and the form in which such protections might be secured, either marriage, domestic partnerships, or civil unions—have been a fulminating point in national, state, and local races for the past decade. While this kind of limelight may feel progressive ("they're talking about us, finally!"), the legislative pileup of states rushing to pass statutes and constitutional amendments banning same-sex marriage, civil unions, and/or recognition of domestic partnerships suggests otherwise. Furthermore, the blinkered manner in which gay and lesbian rights have been discussed in this period puts all its weight, questionably, behind single-issue politics and legislative/juridical channels, to the effect that other issues and channels have received little attention—at least from organizations well-funded and centrist enough to stake out a significant media presence, national organizations such as the HRC and the Lambda Legal Foundation. (See Lisa Duggan's analysis of neoliberal—essentially, conservative—trends in national gay politics in *The Twilight of Equality?*, chap. 3.) Discussions taking place below the national level have been inaudible to the general public. Thus, it seems fair to say that gay and lesbian issues in any substantive complexity (which would include issues specific to gays and lesbians of color, transgender issues, and poverty in the gay and lesbian community) are not on the political map of either party. It's also fair to assert that "gay and lesbian," the voting bloc by which the GLBT community is improperly and incompletely addressed, also excludes queers: those gays and lesbians who for one reason or another don't affiliate with "the community" or whose relationships, ways of having sex, gender status, advocacy of sexual diversity, or critical relation to normativity puts them at odds with a label as reductive as "gay or lesbian." This isn't to say that forums that propose to speak to or from "the gay and lesbian community" are not problematically exclusive. Rather, the only queers on the radar, the only ones taken seriously by either political party and by the courts, are those who are monogamous, coupled, middle class, usually white—in short, those "normal" enough to be nonthreatening to the politicians and voters being asked to defend them or grant them certain civil rights.

Finally, given the phantasmatic register in which most public political discussion occurs, one might say that queers, or even gays and lesbians, exist mainly as a rhetorical effect, a hot-button issue on which candidates, depending on the year and the direction of the political tide, must weigh in. While the personal motive for individual candidates to do so may be deeply sincere, there's a strategic motive as well: to put oneself in a position to bait one's opponent with either benighted prejudice or doom-laden liberality. In national politics, queers are invisible.

Queer-baiting Kerry and baiting queers proved an advantageous marriage for Republicans in the 2004 presidential race, working the bellows to fan homophobia not just in an attempt to sway the election (by pandering to certain voters without intending to act on their interests) but as part of a larger, incremental trend toward gay erasure. In future races gay marriage need not even be a presidential campaign issue, since, as with abortion, the right-wing has mobilized its forces more effectively on the state level through amendment referendums. At least for now, despite *Lawrence et al. v. Texas*, queer Americans are at risk of existing more vividly in the homophobic lexicon, in fag jokes, between the lines of heterosexual definitions of marriage, and less and less visibly as real people.

More than a few are likely to balk at a statement such as the last one as willfully contrarian. Their reluctance is understandable. In the most literal sense, of course gay men and women exist. We know them, some of us. We have lesbian friends, gay coworkers. We even see a few real-live ones on television, as on *Queer Eye for the Straight Guy*, the subject of the following chapter. My immediate interest, however, is not in debating in what ways reality shows mediate their subjects, and with what degree of deliberateness. My point is more that the flesh-and-blood quality of real gay men and women is clouded by its inability to dispel the fog of phobic counterrhetoric. Such images are not limited to the preposterous caricatures circulated by right-wing bullies such as Dobson but include those generated by liberal capitalism: the equally exaggerated, sanitized image of a mainstreamed, unified gay and lesbian populace, less a citizenry than a commercial and multicultural demographic.

At first glance *Queer Eye* might seem to provide gays a visibility that's worse than erasure. Yet if we look closer, beneath the product placement and the exfoliant, we find mediation not merely between gay men and straight men, between the hosts and their weekly fashion victim. Rather, we find a more complex sort of mediation, a brokering between flesh-and-blood gay men and a spectrum of representations and stereotypes, an imaginary articulated, in concert or in reply, by straights and queers. The insight of *Queer Eye*, despite the consumerist drive inherent to the makeover-show genre, is that queers themselves can populate the cultural imaginary with their own stereotypes and, by inhabiting gay caricatures both parodic and abject, can offend, amuse, or provoke both straights and themselves. For, as Wendy Brown's work suggests, a productive relation to contemporary political culture requires more than a callow belief that tolerance leads inevitably to equality, that address means inclusion. Uncoupling gay life from the regnant homophobia of American culture may not be entirely possible, but it may not be unreasonable to attempt moments, if not more sustained episodes, of negotiated disengagement, to deviate not merely in spite of complicity but by way of it.

3

Queer Eye on the Prize

Homo Hands and the Activism of Camping

SINCE THE SUMMER 2003 premiere of the Bravo network's runaway hit *Queer Eye for the Straight Guy*, in which five gay men dubbed the "Fab Five" make over the world "one straight guy at a time," there has been an inordinate amount of handwringing over what this new makeover represents or fails to represent about gay men and the potential boon or harm it poses to the struggle for GLBT rights in America.[1] For example, according to sociology professor Melinda Kanner, the show "presents us with a preparation in which gayness has become domesticated, unthreatening, and constructive to the interests of heterosexual fulfillment" (37); similarly, Terry Sawyer, music and TV critic for *popMatters*, complains that "Bravo seeks to show gay men as materialistic vamps, style clowns with cock-centered worldviews who see conversation as opportunity for *Three's Company*–level double entendres" (par. 2). Negative reactions of industry critics and everyday viewers,[2] or at least the volume of such reactions, may have been fueled by unfortunate (or, to others, perhaps felicitous) timing. For the summer of 2003 also witnessed a landmark Supreme Court decision: *Lawrence et al. v. Texas* struck down sodomy laws as discriminatory and unconstitutional, thus correcting *Bowers v. Hardwick*, the Court's 1986 decision that upheld sodomy laws and gave the Court's imprimatur to the treatment of gays and lesbians as second-class citizens. Then, in November 2003, the Massachusetts Supreme Court handed down an equally groundbreaking decision asserting the legality of same-sex marriage. Most often, naysayers to *Queer Eye for the Straight Guy* faulted the show for relying on gay stereotypes. Although the connection was not voiced,[3] perhaps the fear was that the dissemination of what some felt to be stereotypical images of gayness—and on a tremendously popular show with straight as well as gay viewers—would precipitate a backlash and deal a fatal blow to revived debates about GLBT equality and same-sex marriage at the very instant when progress on those issues seemed within reach.

Casting the debate in such starkly polarized terms might seem to obscure the fact that not all gays and lesbians deem marriage part of a "progressive" agenda. Michael Warner, among others, has vocally criticized the narrowness of the marriage debate, which eclipsed alternative forms of establishing household and rights of property and person, as well as larger social justice issues (the discriminatory basis on which certain rights are accorded only to the married). My focus, however, is not so much the myopic mishandling of gay rights issues by well-heeled, socially conservative organizations such as the HRC (who proclaimed that all gay and lesbian Americans really wanted was military service and marriage) or Lambda Legal (whose exclusive focus on the courtroom Lisa Duggan criticizes as slow, if not ultimately counterproductive). As Duggan writes, a focus on "courtroom litigation, legislative battles or electoral campaigns" ignores assertions by earlier gay activists regarding the "limits and false promises of the 'equality' on offer through liberal reform—equality disarticulated from material life and class politics, to be won by definable 'minority' groups, one at a time" (*The Twilight of Equality?* xviii). Such criticism is relevant inasmuch as it's possible to see *Queer Eye* as complicit with (or simply not resisting) a larger national retreat from addressing equally pressing issues: for example, issues of privacy in the face of the "shrink[age of] the spaces of public life," or legal parity framed not just as a gay and lesbian issue but as having the potential for a much broader and stronger progressive alliance along multiple axes of identification and political philosophy. Far from being "disarticulated from material life," *Queer Eye* would seem to be naively, apolitically—and in some minds, injuriously—complicit with consumption. Yet it's my contention that whether engagement with the market necessitates forfeiture of the political, whether capitalism and heteronormativity fully negate camp's potential for mockery and interrogation, is a question with more than one answer.

This chapter examines a range of responses to *Queer Eye*—sharp critiques along with sometimes heady accolades—and parses, in particular, claims that the show is a shallow market-penetration device devoted to hawking merchandise and that it promotes reductive stereotypes, analogous to those of minstrelsy, of gays as servile, predatory, or jejune. My overall claim is that the show's most vehement critics, whether they balk at stereotypes, sexual innuendo, or merchandising, are advocating assimilationism—advocating the maintenance of what Michael Warner in *The Trouble with Normal* (1999) calls "hierarch[ies] of respectability" and "shame" (49, 24). This policing action is not always conscious, is often far from malicious, and may perhaps be felt necessary to guard the snail-like progress of gay rights from the whiplash of ignorant homophobes.

And the motives behind negative responses to sissies such as Carson Kressley and Jai Rodriguez may be as diverse and complex as "'internalized homophobia,' in-group hostility, or simply . . . the [heteronormative] perspective unconsciously embedded in so much of our thought and perception" (Warner, *The Trouble with Normal* 89). But motive and awareness make little difference. The effect is the same.[4] Rather than take individuals to task merely for their opposition to the show, I think it's important to note not just the analytical or historical errors that undermine their accusations but the unexamined attitudes, lurking beneath the surface of this outcry, which pose a more insidious and significant threat to the attainment of equity and the integrity of queer identity.

"Pagan Adoration"

Allegations of commercialism against *Queer Eye*, while not entirely baseless, are overly alarmist. Richard Goldstein, a writer for the *Village Voice*, insists "[t]here are more product placements in this show than on the Home Shopping Network" ("What Queer Eye?" par. 2). Terry Sawyer is equally hyperbolic: "Every scene involves a close-up on a store front, a label, or a smartly designed tube of styling gel. I hope that most gay people are rich as well as peerless aesthetic fascists, because *Queer Eye* consistently equates good taste with ridiculous expense" (par. 10). Aside from the overexaggeration that weakens their point, Goldstein, Sawyer, and others seem, inconceivably, to have forgotten the corporate marketing forces that structure almost every single televised moment, not just commercials themselves but the invasive product placement now integral to most reality shows (see Dixon). It's true that in a moment of high-end excess, food and wine expert Ted supplies pricey foie gras for a wife's belated birthday party. Overall, Thom Filicia, an interior designer, takes the straight men to midmarket chains such as IKEA, Hold Everything, and Pier 1. And if some of the spas and furniture and clothing stores the Fab Five patronize are high-end, one cannot forget that *Queer Eye* is filmed in New York City, not Des Moines. The charge that the show hawks predominantly high-end businesses makes little sense if we consider that most of its audience lives outside Manhattan or other areas where many of the regional chains if not specialty stores exist.

It might seem that part of the worry over *Queer Eye*'s commercialism stems from the gay and lesbian community's fairly recent love affair with mainstream corporate culture. This heady courtship over the past decade or so has purchased mainstream visibility and economic clout with the coin of diminished (or at least less confrontational) calls for political equity. As Alexandra Chasin points out in *Selling Out: The Gay and Lesbian Movement Goes to Market* (2000), the queer community has been a marketing target since the early 1990s spawned the myth of the DINK (Dual Income, No Kids): because lesbians and gay men have no children (supposedly), any queer, partnered or not, has a significantly larger chunk of discretionary income than a heterosexual with children. While it might seem that some gay or lesbian couples without children, depending on other factors such as education, income bracket, and race, might well have more cash on hand than either straights, gays, or lesbians supporting one or more children, the DINK myth is rendered problematic by the skewed sample on which the original marketing reports were based: "disproportionately, the politically active and the affluent" (Baker 13).[5] Economist M. V. Lee Badgett's corrective study, "The Wage Effects of Sexual Orientation Discrimination," found that, "after taking differences in education, age, and other factors into account," "gay/bisexual men . . . earned 11% to 27% less than similar heterosexual men" whereas "lesbian/bisexual women . . . earned 12% to 30% less than similar heterosexual women" (Badgett, "Beyond Biased Samples" 69). Advertisers paid little attention to this correction, however, as they continued to target gay and lesbian consumers. In response to this continuing trend, Chasin reminds us that economic clout does not necessarily translate into political authority: the notion that "private consumption can ever do the work of progressive political action" is a "myth" (244). Swimming in the mainstream market, queers become as anesthetized as heterosexuals, focused more on the best cell phone plan than the cost of health care, an illusory middle-class tax cut, or "compassionate" moves to segregate gays and lesbians in the separate but equal paddock of civil unions.

Yet some critics of *Queer Eye* hold the show responsible for single-handedly prostituting gay men to corporate America. Kanner writes that

> the underlying premise of the show [is] that all it takes to lead a happier romantic life and have greater personal fulfillment is an improved ability to consume goods. . . . The growing link between gayness and consumerism is disconcerting. The gay movement of the 1970's and 80's found gay people acting as a potentially disruptive force, challenging the straightjacket of compulsory heterosexuality and fixed gender roles. If, in contrast, our energies are focused on finding the perfect sofa or optimizing our highlights, can we still be acting as a progressive force for necessary social change? (37)

"*Growing* link"? Kanner seems not merely to have avoided opening a mainstream magazine for quite some time, but also to have mistaken the show as being aimed solely at gay viewers. Terry Sawyer, apparently attempting to rescue gay men from being portrayed as materialistic, errs on the side of excess: "It would be better to broaden the representations and deny that being gay has any consistent content at all than to write a show that portrays gays as moral savages who live their entire lives in pagan adoration of high-end hair products" (par. 13). Aside from evoking an offensive image of primitive societies as backward worshippers of inert objects ("moral savages" in "pagan adoration"), Sawyer ignores the fact that, thanks to marketing machinery, a significant number of straight men currently use gel or other hair products. Alonso Duralde, reviewing the *Queer Eye* soundtrack, which includes the *Queer Eye* theme song along with other pop music tracks, snidely dismisses the show's "whole you-should-buy-this ethos"—a profoundly ironic observation to make in the slick, ad-glutted pages of the *Advocate*. What distinguishes *Queer Eye* from any other network show, straight or gay, or from queer media organs such as the *Advocate* and *OUT*, both of which devote as much time as *Queer Eye* to the hawking of pricey merchandise and the creation of consumer "needs"?

Consumerism has certainly levied a deadening weight on the American republic (if a word that implies a sense of public debate is still applicable), but it makes no sense—indeed, it seems perceptually impossible—to single out *Queer Eye* as the lone culprit. Unfortunately, the illusion that a television show, whatever its content, is not always also a market-penetration device is no longer sustainable. Nonetheless, I would argue that the presence of product placements on *Queer Eye*, which constitute an urban, semiaffluent style that not all gays or all men desire, does not invalidate the transformation, each week, of one heterosexual man's self-image. What matters in this transformation is not so much a trendier haircut as it is the modeling of alliances between two groups (straight and gay men) whose acknowledged mistrust, ignorance, or fear of one another has helped keep homophobia faceless, monolithic, and powerful.

Lispin' and Swishin' for the Heterosexual Massa

The second recurrent criticism is that *Queer Eye* trades on stereotypes, disseminating reductive images of gay men and providing visibility only in stale formulae regularly used to sustain homophobic cultural attitudes. Like other minorities, queers harbor a long-standing, warranted paranoia regarding stereotypical representation. Equally strong, though perhaps unwarranted, are the pressures that weigh on mainstream representations of a minority, particularly the imperative of diversity—with the result that any single image is by default reductive, exclusive, and (so the logic goes) stereotypical.[6] Yet to compare *Queer Eye* to the minstrelsy of Step and Fetchit, as more than one observer has done, seems unmerited. Kanner cautions, "Perhaps gay people are next to be relegated to the status of an entertainment class, much as black performers have been throughout the 20th century" (37). When Christopher Kelly, writing for the *Miami Herald*, "[w]elcome[s us] to the rise of the gay minstrel show," it's true that he has *Will & Grace* and *Queer as Folk* in his sights along with *Queer Eye* (par. 3), but the latter draws the heaviest fire:

> It may seem a bit unfair to compare shows like *Queer Eye* . . . to the minstrel show tradition, which, in its best-known form, featured white actors in blackface, grossly exaggerating African-American stereotypes and dialects for the amusement of mostly white audiences.
>
> But much like, say, the 1950s television version of *Amos 'n' Andy*—which featured black actors—shows like *Queer Eye* peddle entirely

> in stereotypes, and then write off their offensiveness as good fun. (pars. 10–11)

The accusation of minstrelsy is historically inaccurate and analytically unsound. Camp, unlike minstrelsy, has usually been enacted by gay men for other gay men (or for a gay-friendly audience). As Cathy Griggers remarks in "Lesbian Bodies in the Age of (Post)mechanical Reproduction," straights have typically (mis)read camp as superficial, tasteless, or demeaning: "gay and lesbian subcultures have always understood [it] as a style of everyday cultural politics and survival and not as prepolitical (a reading commonly produced by straight 'politicized' subjects)" (188). Minstrelsy was rarely performed by African Americans for an African American audience. Furthermore, the object of camp is arguably not the denigration of an entire group (as when performed by whites in blackface), and its result is not self-denigration (as with the black stars of the television version of *Amos 'n' Andy*). Minstrelsy's only purpose was the maintenance, by ridicule, of an image of black Americans as childlike fools who deserve the second-class citizenship a biased polity assigned them. The aim of camp, by contrast, is to trouble—always at the hands of queers—the naturalized categories of gender and sexuality, and the presumed hegemony and integrity of those categories in a heteronormative culture.[7]

At times, camp humor may seem little better than sophomoric. For instance, when Carson squeezes a tube of skin ointment too hard and accidentally squirts it all over Ted and that week's guest, John Zimmerman IV, Carson's tag line is "Oh, I had no idea . . . I was that close" ("Queer Eye for the Skate Guy"). But this is gross-out humor with a difference: two of the participants are gay, and their graphic projection of queer sexuality—literally—onto other male bodies, gay and straight, provides the edge, the inflection, that is part of what defines camp. More often than not, however, camp turns on gender inversion (which raises the specter of stigma so disconcerting for many straights and some queers). When Carson originally discovers a large collection of creams and ointments among a professional male skater's toiletries, designer Thom Filicia quips, "He's got a dry vagina" ("Queer Eye for Skate Guy"). Some jokes, outwardly sophomoric, are camp because they accentuate gay desire, if only humorously—as when Ted, referring to an unwashed jockstrap the boys have found and soaked in a pot of water, says, "We're gonna fry that. Would you like some soy sauce with that?" and Carson replies, "There was already some soy sauce on it. Was it soy sauce or *boy* sauce?" ("Hair Today, Art Tomorrow"). The frank sexuality of the Fab Five, which deserves its own analysis, is the subject of the final section of this chapter.

And while in *Queer Eye* camp humor might seem to have been drafted in service of the norm (commercialism and/or heterosexuality), isn't it possible for camp irreverence to maintain its integrity within the matrix of consumer/popular culture that Richard Goldstein and Sawyer portray as absolutely oppressive? Since the time of Oscar Wilde, if not before, camp humor has been one of gay men's strongest weapons against hypocrisy and the concept of "normal." The Fab Five's camp humor is not only important in terms of gay history but also crucial to the success of the show's project. I would argue that irony and innuendo are in fact responsible for the success of *Queer Eye*, and for its central achievement: keeping open (within a heteronormative consumer/pop culture) a space in which authentic connections between straight and gay men and culture can be forged and sustained—and not just between the show's participants but between the homosexual and heterosexual men and women who bond while watching it together or talking about it at work the next day.

Another version of the complaint about stereotypes is that the show confines its gay stars to the role of "body servants" to heterosexual men (Richard Goldstein par. 7). I find this interpretation, which quickly becomes a refrain in commentary about *Queer Eye*, uniquely puzzling, not just in its origin but in the tenacious grip this trope seems to have on some version of gay communal memory. Goldstein, Kanner, and others hold that, because gay men have been enslaved for too long (to straight women, supposedly), *Queer Eye* constitutes a step backward in queer history. Goldstein sarcastically supposes "it's a sign of progress that this interchange [between gay and straight men] looks plausible, but it's a measure of how far we *haven't* come that the meeting must be staged on stereotypical ground" (par. 6). He continues,

> The makeover show is a perfect setting for this hedged entente. It offers the illusion of a power exchange within very stylized confines. The queers fuss while the straight guy gets fussed over. Aside from a requisite hug when the work is done (and a playful slap when homo hands stray below the belt), the attended one never touches his attendants. Doesn't this resonate with the most primitive view of gay men? Haven't fags always been consigned to the role of body servant? Aren't they supposed to have a doting eye for the straight guy?
>
> And as faux women, aren't they expected to be obsessed with style? (par. 7)

It is unclear what period or context Goldstein has in mind, in which gay men served as straight "body servants" (although the choice of words recalls the stereotypically predatory gay man, precisely the "primitive view of gay men" to which Goldstein objects). Goldstein's reaction to what he views as distasteful sexual baiting is significant, and I will return to this topic in the concluding section.

Writing in the *Gay and Lesbian Review Worldwide*, Kanner attempts a more informed analysis:

> For many decades, some otherwise marginalized gay men have found their way into the mainstream, into the seats and rooms of money and influence, as mascots, mostly for the amusement of straight women. Straight society seems to be able to tolerate a certain amount of

> gayness, but only in confined quarters. We need theatre, we need dance, we need hairdressers and florists, after all, to enhance the lives of heterosexual married women and their men. Traditionally, gay men serve, entertain, and please. But the accomplishments of gay men outside these domains have rarely been celebrated in the public forum of the mainstream media. (36)

One of the flaws in Kanner's position is a striking blindness to those gays who were not stylists, interior designers, or confidants, and so who were always marginalized. Even if the "mascot" (or lapdog) scenario were accurate, wouldn't interacting with straight men—the traditional bogeymen for gays—be an advance? What is most offensive about this analysis is the failure to consider that these "mascots" did not live their entire lives "performing" for straight society but had lives and, more emphatically, a subculture of their own, and that these highly visible gay men were well paid for their services and wielded a certain amount of expertise and power within their domains. This male underclass that exists only to "serve, entertain, and please" does not resemble the interior designers and stylists I knew as a child and a gay youth. And if one's definition of a "mascot" is someone who exists merely to enhance the lives of a more privileged set, then those in the swelling ranks of the American service sector equally qualify as lapdogs.[8]

Inspiration for applying the "lapdog" myth to *Queer Eye* may be partly due to the fact that these gay men appear to play second fiddle to their straight counterparts, allowing their skills to be co-opted in service of the broken-record heterosexual narrative: getting the girl. Kanner describes it as a sort of homosexual serfdom:

> After sprucing up the straight man's body, house, and cuisine, the Fab Five return to their loft—a sort of queer superhero Bat Cave—to eavesdrop on the unfolding of a gaily enhanced straight romance. Now, as in earlier times, the powers and talents of gay men are being pressed into the service of heterosexual privilege. Remedial therapy in personal care, fashion savvy, and dating service are all directed at a straight guy's romantic life. (36)

Christopher Kelly, in part quoting Bob Thompson, director of the Syracuse University Center for the Study of Popular Television, concurs with Kanner:

> The straight couple whose home they have invaded looks upon them with both superiority and delight. They are the ersatz king and queen, welcoming their jesters to court. . . .
>
> Talk about reaffirming heterosexual primacy: the Fab 5 are the literal fairy godmothers who help straight dudes hook up, and who then return to their own beds alone.

> . . . "In the end, who's the hero . . . ?" Thompson asks. "It's the straight guy. He's the guy who needs to be rescued, so he can either get the girl or the gallery showing. And then they leave before the climax, and they have to watch it on the periphery. Talk about being marginalized—they literally have to watch the climax of the show from the margins.
>
> . . . They can't even stay to take their bows." (pars. 2, 7, 22)

Among the oddities in this passage are the monarchical imagery (few of the houses and apartments look anything like a "court" when the Fab Five first arrive) and the insinuating tone (is Kelly indignant, or is he suggesting that the Fab Five should be indignant, about being banished from the straight man's presence without "hook[ing] up"?). Although Kelly takes exception with *Queer Eye*'s use of stereotypes, he himself evokes one of the oldest and most homophobic: the oversexed gay man, incapable of interacting with a straight man without making sexual advances.

Questions of tone aside, if one accepts the premise of the show, and further recalls that impressing a girlfriend is not the goal every week, Kanner's statement requires qualification. And a gallery showing, which Kelly mentions, is hardly the standard telos of the heterosexual male narrative. Anna McCarthy, writing in a 2005 *GLQ* forum on "Queer TV Style," faults the show for "marriage merchandising," selling "marriage and domestic consumption" as the "necessary elements of civility," and furthering the neoliberal project of "outsourc[ing] state functions to private institutions, like marriage and the family" (99, 98). Like Kanner, McCarthy exaggerates the centrality of marriage proposals to the show, given that in the first season only one episode ends with the straight guy popping the question. Girlfriends and wives may be the prevailing motivating force behind these straight men's decision to clean up their act, but they are not the universal impetus. Sometimes the straight men are out to please family members other than their spouses; professionalization for career advancement is often a concomitant motive. What Kelly, Kramer, and McCarthy fail to acknowledge is the fact that monogamous romantic pairing is the heterosexual narrative, not the Fab Five's mission. If many of the straight guys are married, in a serious relationship, or seeking to be, that speaks to heteronormativity's motive principle (as well as stricture), not homosexuality's. Carson, Thom, Kyan, Jai, and Ted are helping heterosexuals fulfill their own quest, their unexamined reenactment of the heteronormative ur-text. The easy retort is that a makeover show hardly seems a proper forum for serious debate about civil rights and equity, much less an instrument suited to progressive organization or political action.[9]

But one needn't hedge so defensively. On the contrary, *Queer Eye* delivers a more serious critique than most have been willing to credit. Jaap Kooijman assures us there's more going on than genuflection to heterosexual norms. Far from limiting gay men to the "traditional role of the fashion designer," Kooijman points out, "[w]hat makes *Queer Eye* stand out . . . is that the 'straight guy' is the object of the 'queer' makeover, rather than the conventional heterosexual woman" (106). Furthermore, although negative responses to the show typically regard camp as an inept means of polemic, camp—conceived of more generously—might serve as a catalyst, not an impediment. The queens on *Queer Eye* are camping, but some viewers, even gay ones, may not consider the show camp. The Fab Five are far from ironic about consumption, yet what they're camping is inept straight consumption. They might be corporate shills, yet they're also campy about bad style, about being less than fabulous. And although they're giving away the gay trade secrets to looking or feeling fabulous—and the overarching ideology of emotional rehabilitation through superficial alteration—the show's premise nonetheless carries a keen bite. That premise is that the distress call that opens each episode (where the hosts get briefed on the current hapless straight man) lingers long after the final transformation, a queer judgment on a pallid, imaginatively impoverished heterosexuality. Sasha Torres concurs, also in the *GLQ* forum, that *Queer Eye*'s critique is devastating. Instead of "put[ting] its queer protagonists in the service of heterosexual coupling," the show underscores the "perpetual incompetence of the heterosexual family":

> Surely the profound inability of the straight guys to perform the simplest domestic tasks, their abject impotence in the care of the self, indicates, week after week, a crisis in the reproduction of heterosexuality so enormous that the Fab Five's interventions constitute at best a drop in the bucket. In other words, even as the show positions queers as just the thing to ease the straight guys' transition from unkempt bachelorhood to happy coupledness, it suggests, sotto voce, the inadequacy of such coupling, and of the heterosexual families such coupling initiates, to teach heterosexual men how to live.
>
> After all, the most basic premise of *Queer Eye for the Straight Guy* is that heterosexuality constitutes its own undoing. It is "straightness"—as incompetence in housekeeping, grooming, and relating to others—that constitutes the obstacle to the putatively desired heterosexual outcome: getting the girlfriend to understand that she is appreciated, to move in, to agree to marry. A similarly fundamental premise of the show is that women cannot teach straight guys the things they need to know in order to be with a woman. When the guys' mothers are interviewed about their sons' bad domestic habits, they roll their eyes, indicating that they gave up on this project years ago. We are given the sense, in episode after episode, that the long-suffering wife or girlfriend has already tried, without success, to get the straight guy to clean the bathtub. It follows, then, that only men can impart these lessons; that it is as crucial that the Fab Five are gay *men* as that they are *gay* men. (96)

Queer Eye ironizes heterosexuality's naturalness by camping its failure to shine effortlessly as the culturally foundational artifact it supposedly is.

Still, who's to say that one can entirely separate the pleasures of capitalist consumption from the queer pleasure of looking good by simultaneous effort and apparent effortlessness? In *Working Like a Homosexual: Camp, Capital, and Cinema* (2002), Matthew Tinkcom's queer reading of Marx explores the notion that pleasure (guiltless as well as complicit) might exist coextensively with critical (dis)engagment. Analyzing the films of Vincente Minnelli, Andy Warhol, Kenneth Anger, and John Waters, Tinkcom argues for camp's potentially critical relation to labor and capital. Camp, Tinkcom asserts, is a "force of production" for consciousness of one's "capacity as an actor in history and politics" (19, 24). He continues:

> Marx's recognition of human self-consciousness as "other" to itself is fundamental to his account, and it is not, as he suggests, an otherness steeped only in negation; otherness from the world as a thinking creature and from the social subjects who surround us has its own rewards of knowledge, and camp is one such reward.
>
> . . . [Camp involves the] discovery by subjects that the irregular dispersal of value under capital not only entails knowing where capital's cultural logics are fraught with incoherence but provides the opportunity for such subjects (in this specific case, queer men in the American metropolis) to offer their own visions of how even the most homogenized of expressions, such as the Hollywood film, might be tampered with.
>
> . . . [Q]ueer male camp is the consciousness, expressed through the terms of value in its multiple registers and fluxes (i.e., in the terms of the political economy that Marx identifies), of not only how queer men labor within the world but how they labor effectively to ward off the homophobic stances that they encounter on all too common a basis, and, through their labor on the commodity, stage in deflected fashion such forms of affect in the world. (25–26)

To speak then, as Anna McCarthy does, of the "theft of queer cultural capital in the name of marketing" (100) passes too hastily over the point that critical consciousness of one's cultural status—and attempts to alter it—must first (if not perhaps invariably) be expressed in situ, "through the terms of . . . political economy." Consumption, like labor on behalf of capital—(and for Tinkcom, camp is "work-as-play" (13)—does not forestall camp's disarticulation of heteronormativity's "incoherence[s]": a queer vivisection that lays bare its constructed organicism, that exposes the consistent failure of heterosexual coupling (if not coupling in general) to live up to its surety as a primordial, perdurable dictum. Camp is capable of shielding against homophobic attack, of rooting out places where "even the most homogenized of expressions," such as heteronormative romance or the makeover show, are "fraught with incoherence," interstices where they "might be tampered with." In other words, one can allow for partial (if not complete) divergence of the show's agenda from that of Carson and company.

It is only natural to worry these days, as even Tinkcom does, about queers' capacity for cultural critique:

> Increasingly it becomes evident that gay male subcultures are not the place to seek such insights, or more generously we might say that they are not the *only* place to discover camp at work now. One measure of the depletion of gay male political culture has emerged in the tendency of same-sex political movements in the past few decades toward an increasingly banal discourse of human property rights, as the relatively affluent gay male (and lesbian) urban sector goes about their business of making or acquiring children, becoming fascinated with the gyrations of property value, and consuming the most sentimental proclamations of celebrity culture seldom without giving a sense of the contradictions at hand. In this light, such political alliances seem unhelpfully to reveal themselves as class formations first and citizens of an impoverished critical capacity second. (190)

Here Tinkcom is very much in line with Lisa Duggan's analysis of the American gay and lesbian community's unexamined cathexis with neoliberalism, and the implicitly bourgeois, white, male nature of the liberal subject, such that the more vexed, if not blocked, approach of the nonbourgeois, nonwhite, and nonmale to "America" goes dangerously unexamined and thereby compromises gays and lesbians' argument against discrimination. But, like Tinkcom, I also feel that, while there is still much work to be done in parsing the complicated intersections of queerness with race, class, and gender, the existence of such blind spots does not invalidate all queer critique. Tinkcom continues:

> Hardly satisfying, though, is a shortsighted decision that such middle-class, mostly gay white gay men are responsible for an enfeebled critical imagination in the face of capital's reorganized forces, now branded in so much corporatized culture as "globalization" and "interconnectivity." Nor does it help much to remark that the expanded public sphere of "sexual politics" means that the conditions for camp intellectual production have changed so profoundly as not to mean that sexual subject might forge a critical capacity for understanding value's wild career, at least, not in the secretiveness and jeopardy that characterized prior historical moments. Be that as it may, even the social formations that have given rise to the expression of sex/gender difference as so much glossy consumption find themselves reaching a point of exhaustion. . . . Too facile is the insight that the new-consumer possibilities of Rainbow Visa cards and the active

> recruitment of brand-name vodka drinking as an expression of gay "pride" come at the cost of camp's ferocious delights. . . . (190–91)

In other words, the fact that *Queer Eye* appears to enshrine marriage, heterosexuality, or even a privatized neoliberal conception of citizenship does not blunt or repudiate the censure made possible when camp inhabits and labors in—and for queers, simultaneously, to the side of—those very structures and ideas. Nor does compliance with cultural or ideological forms preclude repetition with a difference. Deference may encompass dissidence, perhaps even potentiate it. Dissent, redecorate, repeat. Camp can be arch, of course, but it may also be mordant. And, as the final section of this chapter argues, sexual play may also labor for an earnest end: conquering not bodies but ideology.

Where many have spurned the *Queer Eye* queens as cheerleaders for assimilation, it's my contention that those who disparage the show so vehemently are—unconsciously or not, perhaps unintentionally, and often counter to their declared intentions—advocates for assimilation. While it seems unwise to conclude that allegations of stereotyping necessarily have assimilationist underpinnings, in this instance it seems true. Assimilation into the mainstream is a common strategy of minorities attempting to gain legal equality by winning social acceptance. For the GLBT community at least, acceptance has all too often been translated into acceptability; the latter is easier to obtain, but becoming acceptable is surreptitiously more costly than being accepted. Presenting a nonthreatening, desexualized, unflamboyant face to the public may be politically expedient, but it is also incompatible with the gay and lesbian community's commitment to diversity, tolerance, openness, and critical engagement with norms—unless that commitment is to be jettisoned. And yet for decades before Stonewall, being versed in style and culture was gay men's province, artistically and socially.

Hemal Jhaveri, writing for *PopPolitics.com*, exemplifies the way in which concern over stereotyping may mask nervousness about traits, behaviors, and personalities that jeopardize assimilation because they are socially (read: publicly) unacceptable: "By clinging to existing stereotypes, and mainly seeing all gay people as savants of style, we marginalize them and dilute the complicated lives of many. In ignoring gay men's sexuality, we project a condescending tolerance of a lifestyle, implying that homosexuality is well and good, unless it actually involves sex" (par. 8). If I may bracket for a moment the question of the Fab Five's asexuality, it's illuminating to note that Jhaveri, in speaking out against marginalization, is doing some marginalizing of his own. (The use of "we" is vague and worrisome, regardless of Jhaveri's sexuality, which is unindicated.) Is there no longer a place for interior decorators and hairdressers in representations of GLBT persons?[10] Are men who happen to have "stereotypically gay" occupations not rounded in other, individualized ways? Is effeminacy not acceptable, even within a queer setting? Leanne Potts, reporting on negative reactions to the show, suggests negative answers to all these questions: "Critics say the show panders to the widely held belief that all gay men are flaming style mavens. Tom Shales of the Washington Post [*sic*] said the show encouraged a 'patronizing mentality' while Latisha Frederick, an attorney active with the Albuquerque Lesbian and Gay Chamber of Commerce, says the show 'perpetrates stereotypes, both gay and straight'" (par. 23). Accusations about stereotyping are yet more disconcerting, more perniciously dismissive, when one considers, as surprisingly few seem to have done, that in spite of their moniker the Fab Five are not fictional characters. They are real people. The fact, then, that Jhaveri speaks in the same breath of real people (the Fab Five, Chip and Reichen from *The Amazing Race*) and fictional characters (Jack from *Will & Grace*, Keith and David from *Six Feet Under*) suggests either a facile confusion between reality and representation or a discomfort with realities that he does not want represented.

Ultimately, negative gay reactions to *Queer Eye*—especially criticism of its stereotyping, camp, or sexual inneundo—seem driven by shame. The subtext is that mincing fairies like Carson only detract from the image of the "good homosexual" that gays have sought to cultivate in the public eye in order to earn respect and, it is hoped, political equality. This reaction may be understandable in light of the ways gays have been depicted in the past through film and television. The problem is that censorship of negative stereotypes is a blunt and inadequate instrument of political progress. The problem is not the campy queen himself but how he's represented and to what end: as a shallow stock character, or as a more fully realized character who also happens to be queeny. Furthermore, as a reality show, *Queer Eye* problematizes the urge toward shame-based censorship. Do we really wish not to see camping queens because it perpetuates stereotypes among homophobic straight viewers, or simply because camp makes us, as individual gay men, uncomfortable? And are we uncomfortable because these queens are camping it up, or because they're doing so in front of "company," in front of the straights we're trying so hard to impress. If the latter is true, then our reaction is less indignation at homophobic clichés than shame about homosexuality in general. And gay shame originates in—and reflects back—the disgust expressed by straights about homosexuality.

A number of philosophers, including Aurel Kolnai and Winifried Menninghaus, have investigated the origins and mechanics of disgust. Among the more recent and useful of these accounts is Martha Nussbaum's *Hiding from Humanity: Disgust, Shame, and the Law* (2004). Nussbaum admits that although the emotion of disgust may have had value "in our evolutionary past" as a "policing" mechanism for "bounding off a group against its neighbors and promoting clannish solidarity" (102), it also has a long history of being used "as a powerful weapon in social efforts to exclude certain groups and persons" (107). As a form of "social engineering," disgust at homosexuality has less to do with personal "vulnerability and shame" and more to do with distancing oneself from a particular group by associating it with some threat or repulsive object (110, 109). Like xenophobia, homophobia posits one group as the sole obstacle to "an unrealizable romantic fantasy of social purity and turns our thoughts away from the real measures we can take" to address concrete social problems (107). Disgust is "problematic" as a basis for law because "[n]ext door to the fantasy of a pure state is a highly dangerous and aggressive xenophobia" (107)—and what could be more foreign to the nation, in such a fantasy, than homosexuality? What could seem more foreign to the mythical normal American family than gays and lesbians, who must make their own families without legal protection or cultural sanction? What could destabilize heteronormativity more than gay and lesbian couples, whose sexual lives don't depend on the production of children for their cultural legitimacy? By extension, Nussbaum suggests that disgust over gay marriage stems not from distaste over queers tying the knot, or even jealous regard for marriage's cultural cachet, but from the conviction that "something is wrong with heterosexual marriage, and gays and lesbians are somehow to blame" (259). Opponents of same-sex marriage irrationally cite falling birthrates in European countries that permit gay marriage—as if gay sex, rather than women choosing to have fewer children, was the culprit.

More useful still is a passage by Nussbaum that could apply as easily to gays objecting to effeminacy on *Queer Eye* as it could to heterosexuals in "moral panic" over the queer threat to civilization:

> What exactly are we saying [by expressing disgust over a certain group]? That the presence of such people and their acts in our community will cause its downfall? Why should we think this? Because we don't like them? That is hardly a sufficient reason for legal regulation. And if we were to uncover and state what really seems to be in the background, namely, "We have chosen these people as surrogate animals in order to distance ourselves from aspects of animality and mortality that appall us," then that reason, once brought out into light, would provide absolutely no ground for legal regulation. Instead, it would prompt the further question, "Why don't we criticize ourselves for treating a group of people in such a blatantly discriminatory way?" *The real content, in short, would prompt criticism of the disgusted rather than of the constructed cause of their disgust.* (123; emphasis added)

Discriminatory disgust—disgust whose motive force is "social engineering"—inevitably tells us more about those experiencing it than the objects of their disgust. Objectively viewed, this kind of disgust also exposes the "constructed" or fabricated nature of its cause. Thus, gay viewers of *Queer Eye* repulsed by its display of effeminacy and camp must at least consider the possibility that they're simply parroting the larger culture's distaste for the homosexual. But they may be deflecting the repungnance that heteronormativity seeks to induce in them by projecting it onto "bad queers," queers who "give the rest of us a bad name." In so doing, they mark themselves as "good homosexuals," and they further heteronormative culture's ambition: subsume those who can pass (the good homosexuals who aren't too faggy in their affect or profession), and expunge those whose difference sets them too much apart and challenges the norm's putative universality.

Assimilation into the mainstream appears to require both a near total erasure of difference and a kind of identitarian eugenics to weed out traits, occupations, or behaviors that have been deemed too embarrassing for public view. As gay software engineer Fred Jarina says, "Of course there are some gay stereotypes represented on the show. But there are gay people like that out there. Why should we as gay people be embarrassed by it?" (qtd. in Potts par. 24). If anyone is advocating stereotypes, it seems to be the very individuals who criticize the Fab Five for embodying them; these critics would have us reject a whole host of negative stereotypes for the sake of a single, blanched image: what David Leavitt, in his short story "The Marble Quilt," calls the "'good faggot'"—someone who is not an embarrassment to those at the head of the table or to those who have just recently gained a place at it (495). The commotion about *Queer Eye* proves that assimilationism is alive and kicking: it requires that diversity, the watch cry of the GLBT movement, be absorbed into uniformity—heterosexual or straight-acting uniformity. No nellies, femmes, or lispers need apply. I would argue that what's occurring in *Queer Eye* by contrast, is not assimilation but integration, an interleaving of gay and straight lives and sensibilities: the creation of a new landscape whose only threat is its novelty, its bravura navigation of what many gays and lesbians assumed for so long—and it seems, sadly, still assume—to be forbidden territory. Richard Goldstein evinces both this uneasiness, and just perhaps the hope of moving past the stigmaphobia from which it issues, when he observes that *Queer Eye* "allows straight and gay men to relate to each other with an ease that seems at once moving and strange, like a sci-fi film from the 50's. But this is not a forbidden planet; it's a world in the making" (par. 10). Despite what Goldstein says, it still in some way feels forbidden.

"Homo Hands" and the Activism of Camping

If the mood evoked by *Queer Eye* is "moving and strange," however, it is so because of the show's flirtation with the forbidden. The show's genius is the way its stars establish a richly ambivalent and complex—to many critics, downright frustrating—relation to stereotypes of gay effeminacy and sexual predation. The American Film Institute ranked the show as one of 2003s nine "moments of significance" because it "brought gay culture to the national fore by spoofing *and* celebrating stereotypes, and unlike other reality shows, [doing] so in a winning and genuine manner that developed a bond between the gay and straight men" ("AFI's Top Film, TV, Moments of 2003" par. 26; emphasis added). As Michael Giltz reports for the *Advocate*, "Thom [Filicia] . . . resisted being an interior designer because he thought it would embarrass his parents, while Carson [Kressley] avoided fashion because it seemed too gay. [Both are] excited that a new generation of kids, both gay and straight, can grow up seeing their careers celebrated" (44). By highlighting men whose occupations' stereotypical gayness brands them pariahs in a nominally diverse gay and lesbian movement, *Queer Eye* is activist in the best tradition of queers reappropriating images and words (including "queer") that have been used to marginalize gays as well as occupations (such as hairstylist or interior designer) which gays themselves have marginalized. Bruce Steele, also writing in the *Advocate*, suggests that

> by playing into gay stereotypes, the Fab 5, paradoxically, lay them to rest. They're so personable and sharp and real that the clichés they embody are magically reconstructed as richly human, without the tiniest swatch of shame. . . .
>
> Winning gay and lesbian marriage rights . . . will be an uphill effort for years to come, but in a few short weeks *Queer Eye* has high-glossed over centuries of prejudice and fear. It's "We're here, we're queer" with a sensible dose of altruism. . . .
>
> And one of the ultimate joys of *Queer Eye* is this: The Fab 5 are reshaping how America sees gay people not because they chose to be activists but because they chose to be designers and gourmets and groomers—to straight eyes, the gayest jobs on the planet. They don't even seem to know or care that they're fighting the good fight, which makes them elusive targets for our enemies.
>
> Who would have thought throw pillows and chocolate mousse could be among the most powerful weapons of social change? (43)

Although Steele gets right the covert activism of focusing the public's attention on five men with "the gayest jobs on the planet," it seems hasty to say the show has "high-glossed over centuries of prejudice and fear," or much less, could attempt to do so. In their rush to crown the Fab Five the new Great Gay Hope, Steele, along with other critics such as Jhaveri, Johnson, and Potts, is quick to characterize these goodwill ambassadors as wholly, and unrealistically, nonthreatening. While I am certainly not questioning the sincerity (or success) of the show's attempt to reach straight viewers, to view the project as anodynic is to miss what makes it a unique and especially promising meeting ground for straights and gays: the overt sexuality that, along with camping, makes a significant portion of both audiences so deeply, if unadmittedly, nervous.

The fear is that sexualized homosexuality will only exacerbate the historic estrangement between heterosexual and homosexual men. The straight men are "subjected to no small amount of ribbing and flirtation," "alternately poked at and shoved aside by the team's flood of energy" (Johnson par. 4); the Fab Five constitute a "slashy bitchpit," whose "hissy onslaught" their "makeover candidates . . . weather . . . with steel-plated patience and courtesy" (Sawyer par. 6). Among the most vocal is Christopher Kelly, who denounces *Queer Eye* as "execrable—a catalog of homosexual stereotypes, played to a throbbing, techno-disco beat, that also systematically denies its gay stars their complexity and their sexuality. From first scene to last, they trill and fuss, displaying their talents at traditionally effeminate tasks. The straight guy . . . stands back, endures some innocuous flirting and emerges as the ultimate hero stud" (par. 6). Kelly's nervousness about the show's humor leads to the odd conclusion that the Fab Five are at once oversexed ("trill and fuss") and neutered ("denie[d] . . . their sexuality")—an ambivalence best summed up in the phrase "innocuous flirting." Dismissing gay flirtation with straight men as "innocuous" misses the reality that it is still taboo, seen by some as inappropriate, and, around the wrong crowd, dangerous. The implication is that the straight man is embarrassed, while the Fab Five have embarrassed an entire community by reinforcing the stereotype of the sex-obsessed nelly queen. Kelly insinuates as well that gay men who "trill" like queens should be ashamed, too, or at least ashamed enough not to trill in mixed company. And I think this chagrin is at work in almost every discussion of *Queer Eye*. As Michael Warner asks, "Can it be very surprising if those who are most concerned with winning respect"—whether queers themselves or heterosexuals concerned on their behalf—"might find themselves wishing that their peers in shame would be a little less queer, a little more decent?" (*The Trouble with Normal* 50).

Perhaps it is this feeling of shame that deters critics from citing specific examples of the show's sexual humor. Checking on Tom Kaden in a dressing cubicle, Carson exclaims, "Oh dear God, it's huge . . . the belt" ("Make Room for Lisa"). In many but not all of the episodes, Carson is likely to address the straight man with some version of the following: "If at any time today, you want to make out with me, just let me know" ("Make Room for Lisa"). Carson may not be flirting in earnest, but his jokes hardly shy away from the specifics of gay male desire. When Kyan and Carson accompany Adam Zalta to a day spa, Carson goes over the man's back with an exfoliating brush, observing, "It's just like currying my pony. My Pretty Pony"; when Kyan asks, "Does that feel good?" Carson adds, "Wait till I brush your *ass*" ("A Great Mess in Great Neck"). Standing back to see how an outfit looks on another man, James M., Carson remarks, "God, you're so hot. If I didn't know you, I'd try to lure you to a roadside rest area" ("Training Day"). Whether referencing anal sex or queer public sex culture, Carson ambiguates the nonthreatening atmosphere that he also sincerely fosters.

While Carson may be the most sexually verbal (for which he has received the brunt of criticism), none of the Fab Five refrains from physical contact with the straight men. Even though the touching is never predatory, whether it occurs in conjunction with a compliment or not, this physical contact seems to produce the most unease in critics and viewers.[11] Goldstein, in a passage quoted earlier, remarks on the "playful slap [from the straight man] when homo hands stray below the belt" (par. 7). The incident to which he's referring occurred in the first show aired, when Brian Schepel jokes about keeping a tally of how many times Carson tries to help him tuck in his shirt; but even then it is a playful slap. To understand the degree of Goldstein's discomfort, one needs to review the entire sentence from which this comes: "Aside from a requisite hug when the work is done (and a playful slap when homo hands stray below the belt), the attended one never touches his attendants." Goldstein's assertion is simply not true: the straight men routinely "allow" themselves to be touched and flirted with, and some of them even respond in kind. While shopping for tableware with Thom at Pier 1, Tom Kaden says, "Next thing you know, I'll have a boyfriend" ("Make Room for Lisa"). Kaden, later referencing Carson's flirting while helping previous guests get dressed, offers to help Carson with *his* fly. We're left, then, to speculate: is the mere fact of physical contact so embarrassing that it must be denied? Or is it the mixed signals of the Fab Five—sexual innuendo and flirtation side by side with matter-of-fact conversation and neutral physical contract—that have to be misstated rather than discussed openly? I cannot know which is the case with Goldstein, but if it were the latter, he would at least have fathomed the show's method even if he regarded it as madness. Carson, for example, is both embodying a stereotype (as if to say, "you expect this of me, the loud nelly queen") and also camping his own performance ("you don't know that I am like this")—in short, fulfilling and lampooning our expectations, holding both the cartoon and its possible reality in ambivalent tension. What few seem to consider (or perhaps what most refuse to consider) is that Carson is genuinely like that, even if (and this is the mindblower for many heterosexuals and some queers) he is not always like that. By telling a man he has dressed, "you're hot," Carson is, on the one hand, simply admiring his own aesthetic creation. On the other hand, "you're hot" stands as an index of the constantly lurking prospect of gay desire for the male (in this case, heterosexual) body. Never fully acknowledged or dismissed, this erotic potentiality is constitutive of gay male experience, a constant hazard of pleasure and/or fear that the far-from-neutered *Queer Eye* reminds us is inescapable whenever gay and straight worlds meet (see Kooijamn 106).

Queer Eye succeeds because it is more than a public relations campaign, periodically re-marking the differences between gay and straight culture as it paves over others. Admirers have at times hastened to gloss over the show's subversive embrace of the queen and the sexualized gay man. Kanner writes, "In each episode there's a flirtation and a sexually provocative scene, usually launched by Carson and understood to be playful and harmless when taken in context" (37). The flirtation on *Queer Eye* is playful, and perhaps harmless in the sense of not being a real sexual advance (though notice how many critics single out Carson, the most unapologetic about his mannerisms or desires). As Ben Patrick Johnson perceptively notes, the show's producers

> approach their audience on multiple levels. They put on a noisy big-top show while engaging the pathos of both sides of what has long been a broad cultural divide. In the process, *Queer Eye* runs a certain risk of perpetuating stereotypes—the lisping gay man, the predator, the mincing, bitter, cultural aesthete. But the show's title includes a former gay

> slur, queer, which has been appropriated by the gay political movement as a term of prideful self-identification. Not surprisingly, the show, like its title, speaks from a position of empowerment. (par. 12)

Johnson skirts the show's real daring, underplaying sexualized queeniness in an attempt, once again, not to alienate readers for whom "queer" or "queen" is unthinkable as a "term of prideful self-identification."

As Bruce Steele points out, the purpose is in fact to resurrect stereotypes, to flaunt gay sexuality and celebrate the erotic charge of the male body: "They even effortlessly refute the canard of the predatory gay man . . . : They slap and tickle, and everyone gets the joke. Flirting is just good fun, not a sexual assault. In a way that must drive [Supreme Court Justice] Scalia crazy, the Fab 5 are both aggressively sexual *and* nonthreatening" (43). I would suggest, however, that *Queer Eye* succeeds precisely because it punctures mutual, unspoken tensions between gays and straights as well as the merchandising shtick that is the show's financially obligatory window dressing.[12] It is partly gay men's fear of being sexual, being whole people, around straight men, that maintains the distance between the two. The same fear—as stigmaphobia—keeps gay men constantly monitoring the language and mannerisms of themselves and others, and creates the impulse to distance themselves from anyone (read: queens) who behaves inappropriately (read: who femmes out) in front of the heterosexuals. Yet the straying "homo hands" to which Goldstein refers are reaching for a prize more complex than "empowerment," a state of actualization and exchange that is less static. The show's sensibility refuses to sugarcoat the still appreciable gap between two cultures (or rather, between two different concepts of dignity and normality).

The Fab Five's camp humor and active sexualization (of themselves and straight men), coupled with their sincerity and objective advice, is their bravest, most subversive, and thus politically effective, act.[13] This is unapologetic camping: their flirting is not innocuous; flirting with straight men is sexualizing them, at once dismissing and embracing the stereotype of the predatory queen. For admitting that straight men have bodies and that gay men are attracted to men is both to reject the notion that gay men lust after every straight man they meet and also to admit that, given the fact that straight men have the bodies to which queers are physically attracted, this is not always necessarily untrue. Still, despite the Fab Five's sexualized and sexualizing patter, some critics continue to judge them as "sexless." Anna McCarthy writes in *GLQ*: "They may tease their subjects, but there is no chance that they will get to sleep with them" (99). Well, of course, they won't, at least not on camera; yet I'd argue that actual gay sex need not be imminent for the suggestion of it—as with Carson's ejaculatory joke about the squirted ointment, both playful and graphic—to rankle the ease of American masculinity, disconcert its presumption that desire is safely heterosexual and within its control.

The bravura of this dangerous move—acknowledging gay sexual desire for men's bodies—lies in its innovation: camping not in the safety of a gay bar or the privacy of a circle of friends but in front of straight men and straight viewers; and (again in contrast to minstrelsy) camping not for the amusement of others at one's own expense or the expense of one's community but for the edification of others. Aggressive camping, including flirtation, means bringing to the fore what potentially may embarrass both the camping queen and his audience, saying not just "this is who we are" (which smacks of entreaty) but also "this is who we *can* be." It is this ambiguity that very possibly liberates because it threatens, extending a friendly hand on the basis of the common ground shared by gays and straights while, with the other hand, retaining a firm grasp on what will always, for better and for worse, set us apart. As Carson Kressley is quoted as saying in an *Advocate* interview, "'We're not cartoonish, and we're not pretending to be supergay or superstraight or whatever. We're just being ourselves. I'm not going to make any excuses for who I am, and I don't think any of these guys are either'" (qtd. in Steele 44). Being afraid of nelling out or letting slip a "she" in reference to a man defeats the purpose of being out in the first place. The Fab Five are welcome if rare counterevidence to Michael Warner's statement that "homosexuals were and still are afraid to be seen as queer" (*The Trouble with Normal* 65).

The risk is that some viewers, particularly some straight men, will not be disarmed by "good-natured bitchiness," much less willing to believe that the show's premise is "sincere rather than ironic" (Kanner 35).[14] It would be naive to forget that, despite pronounced shifts in cultural attitudes, some people will always be offended by queers—and this is not limited to those who will always hate them as well. Heteronormativity is profoundly deep-seated, inscribed too indelibly to be overcome, whether in a single moment, a television show, or a movement. Even among the liberal and gay-friendly, some will inevitably be put off—by this gesture or that joke. Moments such as these jar us out of thinking we are fundamentally the same, reminding us that not every jagged anomaly can be subsumed in a sea of bland uniformity, for that seems deadly to a polity framed in checks and balances, sustained by friction and conflict. Genuine tolerance brings passions and aversions into sharp relief and requires us to navigate them, not blithely countenance them. Self-editing by queers does heterosexuals the disservice of believing that in our heart of hearts we want just to be normal; and queers themselves, the disservice not so much of believing that we can as believing, contrary to a long communal tradition of critiquing the "natural," that anyone can.

Vociferous reactions to *Queer Eye*, negative or positive, confirm the clarity with which the show delivers truths that many viewers, acclimated to a normalizing gay and lesbian movement, find unacceptable and regressive. Those truths are that gay men are not straight; that norms are invidious; that gay men, according to the best realizations of a collective past predicated on "resist[ing] normalization," are not normal; and that alliances that are possible between straight and gay culture do not eradicate those alliances that are not (Warner, *The Trouble with Normal* 143). *Queer Eye* is an antidote to a notion targeted by Michael Warner in *The*

Trouble with Normal and all too evident in the responses to *Queer Eye*: namely, that "the way to overcome stigma is to win acceptance by the dominant culture, rather than to change the self-understanding of that culture," to question the "desire for a conformity that . . . can never be fully achieved," to resist a "betrayal of the abject and the queer in favor of banalized respectability" (50, 43, 66).[15] I am not lauding a sort of victim pathology, espousing opposition for its own sake, and I am not saying *Queer Eye* does so, either. On the contrary, I believe *Queer Eye* teaches us the value of retaining a sense of what is absurd, fabulous, unifying, alienating, nonnormative, disruptive, and even banal about our lives and desires, gay or straight.

I want to close, and also look forward, by referring to a question raised earlier: what is the relation of consumption and critique, of capitalism and camp? Even if settled here, the question persists in discussions of other gay cultural artifacts, such as *Brokeback Mountain*, the subject of the next chapter. The connection of queerness and capitalism is one that can be vexed and yet also made quite easily. *Queer Eye*, undeniably, is about gay men teaching straight (and gay) men how to consume more. Yet to reject outright what the show has to contribute to queering the norm is to insist on anticapitalism as the benchmark of resistance or alternative politics/identity formation. Though they're hawking consumer goods (and, I repeat, what network or cable personality isn't peddling a sponsor's product, at least by proxy if not more directly?), the Fab Five are undeniably less servile, and more troubling—in a positive sense—than the "sexless" or "handmaiden" labels would suggest. One can do work, while inhabiting an ideological position, that is not entirely necessarily beholden to that ideology. One can do queer work—and, I'd argue, effectively so—while working within a capitalist framework. Even progressive political action has to begin by addressing consumers, if only to rouse them, reshape their conceptions about the status quo. This isn't to say that queer work is going to be effective in every way or to everyone's satisfaction. *Queer Eye* fails to trouble what continues to be the disconcerting nonrepresentative public/mainstream face of gay and lesbian Americans: that is, affluent gay white males. And of course, since the overarching metaphor of this book—externality—derives from economics, it's not unfair to question why the main example I've provided of a positive externality continues (or fails to worry) a disturbing trend of the gay and lesbian community's acceptance of economic address in lieu of concrete political rights/inclusion. My response to this objection would be that, if *Queer Eye* fails on some levels (for instance, failing to contemplate alternative logics of relation), it succeeds on others. Camp as activism works both to defuse straight male anxieties about queer desire and to stimulate those anxieties, by refusing to desexualize gay men. As a positive queer externality, the camp activism of *Queer Eye* may not embody or produce political power, but its rhetorical push opens a space in which others might realize such power. And as chapter 4 demonstrates that's precisely the kind of space that *Brokeback Mountain* seeks to incarcerate, the galvanizing aporia it attempts to corral.

4

Broke(n)*back* Faggots

Hollywood Gives Queers a Hobson's Choice

BROKEBACK MOUNTAIN (2005) has allowed legions of well-meaning Americans to wax rhapsodic over how moving this story of "universal" love is, or even to empathize with the tragedy of gay love banned from speaking its name in a benighted time and place. Daniel Mendelsohn's careful analysis of the film's marketing and reviews lays bare the extent to which assessments of *Brokeback* as a universal story in fact marginalize or closet the narrative's experiential gay core—presumably out of a "desire that [it] not be seen as something for a 'niche' market but as a story with broad appeal" (par. 2). Critics have routinely hailed the film as "a human story" where the "two lovers just happen to be men": generic, euphemistic diction that obscures or seeks to excuse a possibly discomfiting divergence from the master narrative of heterosexuality (qtd. in Mendelsohn par. 2).

Similar critical acts of erasure are ubiquitous. "This slow and stoic movie, hailed as a gay Western," writes Anthony Lane in the *New Yorker*, "feels neither gay nor especially Western: it is a study of love under siege" (par. 5). Richard Alleva holds that *Brokeback* is "not a gay movie. This superb work of art is about the tragedy of emotional apartheid, and none of us, no matter our sexual orientation, is ever safe from the way life conspires to make us put our hearts on ice" (par. 10). Ignoring the fact that the crux of *Brokeback* is that sexual orientation does matter, even reader letters, such as the following one from *Commonweal*, take up the mantra of universality: "the themes of love, loss, and regret are universal and transcend mere sexual orientation. This is why the film has such broad appeal. As a gay man, I can watch a film of *Romeo and Juliet* and cry just as much as I did watching *Brokeback Mountain*. Love is love, heartbreak is heartbreak. . . . That . . . the star-crossed lovers are both men is secondary" (Anziulewicz). Yet Jack and Ennis are not Romeo and Juliet. They are two men, not a man and a woman. Ranking Ennis and Jack with canonical figures such as Shakespeare's young lovers obscures the disparate origin, weight, and breadth of the interdict each couple faces: opprobrium from potentially every member of one's culture versus simply from one's family.[1] As Mendelsohn puts it,

> The real achievement of [the film] is not that it tells a universal love story that happens to have gay characters in it, but that it tells a distinctively gay story that happens to be so well told that any feeling person can be moved by it. If you insist, as so many have, that the story of Jack and Ennis is OK to watch and sympathize with because they're not really homosexual—that they're more like the heart of America than like "gay people"—you're pushing them back into the closet whose narrow and suffocating confines Ang Lee and his collaborators have so beautifully and harrowingly exposed. (par. 15)

Jack and Ennis may bear little resemblance to gay characters American mainstream film has given us to date—witty sidekicks, AIDS victims, serial killers. But bracketing them with the Capulets and the Montagues brackets off homosexuality as incidental, when what precipitates *Brokeback*'s primary conflict is Jack and Ennis's homosexuality.[2]

Of the multitude who have weighed in on *Brokeback*, Roger Ebert travels furthest toward a gay vanishing point. Jack and Ennis's "tragedy is universal," Ebert wrote in the *Chicago Sun-Times*. "It could be about two women, or lovers from different religious or ethnic groups—any 'forbidden love'" (par. 3). As Mendelsohn points out, Ebert's analogy is "seriously misguided" (par. 8). Lovers from different religious or ethnic groups may be hated or persecuted, but, unlike queers, they have not been taught "beginning in childhood" to "despise *themselves*" as "unhealthy, hateful, and deadly" (Mendelsohn par. 8). Interracial or interfaith couples may still find themselves subject to violence, intimidation, and prejudice (though, in many parts of the country, arguably less so than in the past), but that violence comes from without not within: "[B]ecause they learn to hate homosexuality so early on, young people with homosexual impulses more often than not grow up hating themselves: they believe there's something wrong with themselves long before they can understand that there's something wrong with society" (Mendelsohn par. 9). Asserting that Jack and Ennis could be "two *women*" or any other culturally sundered lovers might seem to scotch the erasure accomplished by the phrase "any 'forbidden love.'" Yet inclusion is, in this case, not really inclusion; the universal category ("'any . . . love'") trumps and subsumes the specific (gay love).

Refusing to see difference, politically correct as the intent may be, can be a more benign form of closeting. As Vito Russo trenchantly wrote two decades ago in *The Celluloid Closet*, queer art that attempts to be or is described as "universal" might be better characterized as pandering and/or inauthentic:

> The Hollywood trap is that the success of a film is judged by whether or not it reaches a mass audience. The gay activist trap is that a film is judged by whether or not it succeeds in persuading that audience to accept homosexuals. Neither of these barometers is valid or important. Both encourage the making of films in which acceptance of homosexuals is based on the notion that they are just like everyone else. . . . Yet this is a false premise that never works. You can't plead tolerance for gays by saying that they're just like everyone else. Tolerance is something we should extend to people who are not like everyone else. If gays weren't different, there wouldn't be a problem, and there certainly is a problem. (271–72)

It is crucial that the lovers in this case are homosexual. Effacing difference does away with the need for tolerance, begging the question of why Ennis and Jack feel out of step with almost everyone except one another. Andrew Holleran, author of the iconic gay novel *Dancer from the Dance* (1978), who admits *Brokeback*'s kinship with straight classics of American literature likewise concerned with "the dream we fail to realize," nonetheless ends his review of the film on a note of specificity: "I'm not sure why *Brokeback* is so moving. . . . I think it has something to do with its being what [screenwriter Larry] McMurtry called it: a 'tragedy of emotional deprivation.' This is surely a universal experience, but at a certain point in life most gay men seem to conclude that it's the particular fate of being gay" (12, 15). McMurtry's words resonate with queer experience because the "particular fate of being gay" involves much more than emotional deprivation. Being queer in America, especially in recent years, involves being simultaneously included and excluded—made more visible and treated more humanely by enough organizations and individuals to make the stark, invidious political and economic inequities still endured by queers and the continuing debate about the threat queers constitute to marriage, children, and American (religious) values that much more demoralizing. If *Brokeback* is to have substantive value for American viewers, it seems vital—though oddly forgotten by most reviewers—not to forget that it is a story about gay Americans.[3]

An Ambivalent Polemic

Of greater concern, however, is an equally rankling aspect of the film's apotheosis, one that seems to have gone unremarked. *Brokeback* is an irreducibly ambivalent work. From one angle, it reads as an antihomophobic polemic against the deforming and stunting impact of homophobia, which the film subtly implies may be endemic to heterosexuality rather than sadly anomalous. Yet it takes minimal effort to see *Brokeback*'s potential to serve also as an antigay polemic, a cautionary tale about homosexuality not homophobia. (This is not to accuse author Annie Proulx, screenwriters Larry McMurtry and Diana Ossana, or director Ang Lee of conscious or intentional homophobia. Part of my argument touches on the extent to which homophobia courses throughout the most carefully antihomophobic discourse.) *Brokeback* stands as an antigay polemic inasmuch as it depicts, albeit in the tragic register, the deleterious effects of violent homophobia as well as heteronormative imperatives to marry, to perform one's gender and sexuality in prescribed ways. While *Brokeback*'s tragic register is meant to elicit our sympathy, and while its content may deserve sympathy, none of this should distract one from the brutal nonfictionality of the story: victimized, marginalized, and disenfranchised queers populate America's present as well as its past. Likewise, we should be careful to distinguish the brutality of Jack's death (imagined by Ennis as a gay-bashing), a brutality necessary to Ennis's terrified vision of the world, from the unnecessary brutality of Proulx's decision, as the writer, to kill off Jack, when Ennis's emotional and erotic isolation is long complete, and complete without such a price being paid. Determining the film's status as polemic requires elaboration in order to clarify both how necessary and how otiose and unnecessary its doubly tragic ending is. Whatever the antihomophobic intent of Lee's film or Proulx's original story, or to whatever extent viewers have generously read in them an antihomophobic intent to the exclusion of other, rebarbative messages, we should not blind ourselves to the homophobic energies circulating in these texts and the culture that produced them.

Ang Lee has delivered a sad film, but one that is finally all the sadder for its eliciting pity rather than empathy, tears rather than anger. On some level, empathy is what a film about gay life can never elicit from a straight audience. But one can fault *Brokeback* insofar as its tone remains elegiac, unconscious that its tragic conclusion is not inevitable. Indeed, the film's setting—the West, the 1960s and 1970s—is unfamiliar to contemporary urban and suburban audiences, thus reifying the distancing potential of tragedies about minority populations, further hollowing out the catharsis the film has provided for so many. As media contretemps over dubbing *Brokeback* "the gay cowboy movie" have shown, the resonances produced by a slippery text risk undermining, if not overwhelming, its potential as a gay-positive polemic.

Fit to Be Tied

Brokeback is, in fact, eerily descriptive of the present state of gay Americans. What seems troublingly apropos is Ennis Del Mar's sense that, outside of the open spaces "up on Brokeback," there is no place in the world he knows for him and Jack Twist to love one another—no place that is not inimical, hostile, murderous. Proulx's choice of temporal setting seems hardly accidental: the love story spans two decades, from pre-Stonewall 1963 to 1982—the dawn of AIDS and an era of governmental indifference to treatment and research. As Proulx comments, "Although there are many places in Wyoming where gay men did and do live together in harmony with the community, it should not be forgotten that a year after this story was published Matthew Shepard was tied to a buck fence outside the most enlightened town in the state, Laramie, home of the University of Wyoming" ("Getting Movied" 130). Although less extreme but in the same vein, gay men are still vilified by the culture—if not outright, then by the bare fact that, regardless of not everyone's taking it seriously, pundits and policymakers are still debating whether gays and lesbians deserve the human rights accorded to the republic's other citizens. If queer Americans are included in significant ways that they patently were not twenty years ago—ranging from media visibility to tolerance and spotty legal victories—they are fundamentally still excluded as Americans, denied basic equity of treatment and rights of property.

Ennis himself constitutes the closet, that deforming nexus of homophobia and heteronormativity as learned, felt, and enforced by queers and the alien culture into which they are born (and alien home as well, unless they are raised by same-sex parents). Coming out, then, involves not so much overcoming that nexus—homophobia and heteronormativity seem too deeply imbricated to escape by one act or by one person's repeated acts of coming out—as much as reorienting oneself toward it, disengaging from the psychologically and emotionally oppressive effects of its force through counterdiscourse or through counterinvestment in and revision of stereotypical images and behavior. According to Andrew Holleran, *Brokeback* "indicts both kinds of homophobia: the external and internal. As awful as the homophobes are who litter the film . . . it's equally about gay men's self-censorship, their internalization of what is expected of a man" (14). What a number of critics read in Ennis as not just internalized homophobia but the fatalism of classical tragedy seems more problematic than simply either (Draz 12; Holleran 14). It's true that Ennis fears homophobic retaliation, but the words conveying his fear ("I doubt there's much we *can* do. I'm stuck with what I got here") also relay the cognitive poverty that comes from not being able to conceive of an alternative to the heteronormative rubric, much less to articulate his thoughts or desires in recognized cultural discourse (McMurtry and Ossana 49). Unable to conceive of "two guys livin' together," merely of stealing infrequent, furtive moments "in the back of nowhere," Ennis rejects Jack's proposal of "a little ranch together somewhere" (54, 52). It is not merely a dearth of (nonvirulent) models for same-sex love that has obliterated for him the possibility of "some sweet life" (52). When he was a boy, his father took him to see the battered, genitally mutilated corpse of Earl, a gay rancher who lived openly with his lover and business partner. Recounting the sight to Jack ("they'd took a tire iron to him . . . drug him around by his dick till it pulled off"), Ennis recites the lesson clearly intended by the rancher's assailants (one of whom may have been Ennis's father): "this thing grabs on to us again in the wrong place, we'll be dead" (87). That likelihood seems to be what Ennis means by the laconic line, "If you can't fix it . . . you gotta stand it," for that violence, along with Ennis's surety of its being inevitable if not also warranted, is what stands between them (54).[4]

Few scenes in recent literature or cinema have as potently shown the function of fag-bashing. Like lynching, fag-bashing is terrorist violence (Gorton, "The Hate Crime" 14), visited at random on one individual less to justify than to naturalize the inferior social or political status of all members of the victim's sexual (or, in the case of lynching or other hate crimes, ethnic or religious) cohort. But the leverage wielded by fag-bashing is importantly, structurally dissimilar to the impact of hate crimes against other groups, specifically in the effect on spectators not belonging to the victim's group, in this case, on nonhomosexuals. While non–African Americans may have been repulsed by lynchings, it's doubtful that any feared for their own safety (on the contrary, quite the opposite). And, instances of passing aside, whites never fear that their blackness may be discovered; they certainly are not culturally coached to live in fear that they might be black. Yet this is precisely the wide net cast here, since homophobia implants in every Western male the fear, lived with for shorter or longer, or recurrent, periods depending on the individual, that he might be gay. As defined so acutely by Eve Sedgwick, that fear is "homosexual panic," the "structural residue of terrorist potential . . . of Western maleness," the "most private, psychologized form in which many western men experience their vulnerability to the social pressure of homophobic blackmail" (*Between Men* 89). Just as gay-bashing works, ostensibly, to legitimate a panicked aggressor's straightness, Ennis suffers the intended sequela. He lives in quiet panic, fearing that at any moment his homosexuality will be detected, if for no other reason than it is something that must be detected, a state of being so antithetical to collective society that it can only exist in hiding.

Equally striking, though, is Jack's lack of fear. One might say that, by comparison, Jack Twist represents a "pure" (unrealistic or advanced?) gay consciousness inasmuch as he seems not to have internalized any of the guilt heterosexual discourse teaches us all, if somewhat more quietly than in the past, to associate with homosexuality. Ennis speaks as the inscribed subject, unquestioningly mouthing the dogma with which he has been inculcated, the law of the father. Gay happiness cannot exist because men like Ennis's father will kill it. Ennis's fear of meeting a fate like Earl's is palpable and realistic. At the same time, Ennis's vision typifies the violence with which the dominant discourse refuses to afford homosexuals any unsubjugated place. What Ennis presents as the pragmatic implausibility of gay love is also a fair reflection of its cognitive impossibility—at least on its own terms, terms that are not dictated by a phobic, pathologizing regime. The question is whether, Jack's bravado and self-acceptance aside, Ennis speaks to the power of a discourse largely beyond either man's control.

When Coming Out Is Hard to Do

As queer theorist David Halperin suggests, and as day-to-day queer experience corroborates, coming out is not only an always unfinished, differential experience but also one that can fail to live up to its pop-psychological reputation as an act of self-empowerment:

> if there is something self-affirming or *liberating* about coming *out* of the closet, that is not because coming out enables one to emerge from a state of servitude into a state of untrammeled liberty. On the contrary: to come out is precisely to expose oneself to a different set of dangers and constraints, to make oneself a convenient screen onto which straight people can project all the fantasies they routinely entertain about gay people, and to suffer one's every gesture, statement, expression, and opinion to be totally and irrevocably marked by the overwhelmingly social significance of one's openly acknowledged homosexual identity. If to come out is to release oneself from a state of unfreedom, that is not because coming out constitutes an escape from the reach of power to a place outside of power: rather, coming out puts into play a different set of power relations and alters the dynamic of personal and political struggle. (*Saint Foucault* 30)[5]

Being out or being visible (arguably quite different) does not obviate the fact that many queers cannot see a place in the culture, in the republic, where they're unequivocally brooked. Media visibility can be a valuable public relations tool for education, but inclusion of fictional characters is not tangible, is neither political voice nor economic equity. From Ennis's point of view, he and Jack face the immediate possibility of being harassed or killed for, as one critic puts it, "liv[ing] life on their own terms" (Ansen par. 3). And even though queers' lives are still devalued, threatened, and taken, queer viewers of *Brokeback* can't help but wonder: in 2005, after decades of incremental but demonstrable progress in representations of homosexuality, are these the characters we get? In their mournful, tight-lipped, doe-eyed (and admittedly affecting) pain, Ennis and Jack feel reminiscent of pre-Stonewall characters, loving conflictedly (like Beth in Ann Bannon's *Odd Girl Out* or Charlie in Gordon Merrick's *The Lord Won't Mind*) or flatly refusing to acknowledge their love (like Marcher in James's "The Beast in the Jungle"). Halperin's Foucauldian perspective might explain the backward-looking affect of the film's protagonists more reassuringly—as a mark of the "different set of dangers and constraints" queers face now. But this chapter reads Ennis and Jack as a reactionary response to lesbians and gays' increasing visibility and our continued, sometimes heeded demands for rights and dignity—an atavistic "project[ion]," to borrow from Halperin, of "straight . . . fantasies about gay people" onto a queer public body that has become increasingly salient and human, both defying and galvanizing the dissemination of phobic images (by antigay marriage and adoption organizations, for example).

Like fellow queer theorists Lee Edelman and Michael Warner, Halperin counters that being "release[d] . . . from a state of unfreedom" yet not beyond "the reach of power" is hardly a hopeless situation.[6] It can actually be a productive one, provided we adopt an honest, efficacious stance:

> The most radical reversal of homophobic discourses consists not in asserting, with the Gay Liberation Front of 1968, that "gay is good" . . . but in assuming and empowering a marginal positionality—not in rehabilitating an already demarcated, if devalued, identity but in taking advantage of the purely oppositional location homosexuality has been made to occupy by the logic and the supplement and by the fantasmatic character of homophobic discourse. (Halperin 61)

It is this latter oppositional stance that the film and most critics fail to adopt, instead taking as given, or at least not questioning, the tragic, marginal vein in which *Brokeback* depicts gay desire. Eliciting pity and regret, far from "empower[ing]" gay marginality, simply enervates it. The tonal grandeur and cathartic timbre that Lee's film lends to Ennis's tragic journey may solidify that marginality, but Ennis's failure to challenge the homophobic pressures inculcated in him generate it. To that extent, he is responsible for his own misery. This last point may seem belligerent without good cause, since reviewers including Daniel Mendelsohn, Roy Grundmann, Andrew Holleran, and Anthony Lane have acknowledged Ennis's impossible fight against a barrage of negative cultural messages. Yet because most critics accept the inexorability of Ennis's losing that struggle, their responses translate too easily into an affirmation of the normative, phobic idea that there's something tragic, if noble, at the core of gay identity. What is the value of—and worse, what is the damage inflicted by—portraying queer liminality and oppression as a predicament one "can't fix," as Ennis declares, and therefore has "gotta stand"?

An Unnecessary Death

Positioning tragedy in *Brokeback* within a classical context seems inappropriate if for no other reason than its singular focus (Ennis as tragic hero). What gets lost in such a reading is the more mundane tragedy of Jack's death. Lureen, Jack's wife, relays the details of his death to Ennis over the phone: Jack was inflating a flat tire when it blew, knocking the tire rim into his face, breaking his nose, and leaving him on his back, unconscious, to choke on his own blood. Proulx and Lee both juxtapose this story with the image of Jack being beaten to death by tire iron-wielding homophobes, an attack Mendelsohn refers to as "clearly represented, in a flashback" (par. 7).[7] Yet, in handling Jack's death, McMurtry and Ossana's script, as well as Lee's realization of it, is faithful to Proulx's story: this image is marked as Ennis's imagination of what really happened. After Lureen's lines describing Jack's death, Ennis "wonders . . . if it was the tire iron":

> SHARP CUT TO
>
> ENNIS'S POV . . .
>
> A FLASH . . . ENNIS and WE SEE, in the evening shadows, a MAN being beaten unmercifully by THREE ASSAILANTS, one of whom uses a tire iron.
>
> SHARP CUT BACK TO
>
> . . . ENNIS [who] doesn't know which way it was, the tire iron—or a real accident, blood choking down JACK'S throat and nobody to turn him over. (McMurtry and Ossana 87–88)

On film, Lee clarifies that the beating image originates from Ennis by cutting to it and back to Lureen during her lines. Although the circumstances of Jack's death may seem unusual, neither Proulx, the screenwriters, nor Lee give us any reason to believe Lureen is lying.[8] To be fair, it's true that Lureen's version of events is a reconstruction after the fact, and thus open to doubt (we're told that Jack's body was found after he'd died). In Proulx's original story, hearing Lureen's description of Jack's death, Ennis is even more emphatic about the veracity of his own interpretation of events than he is in the screenplay: Proulx writes, in a one-sentence paragraph, "No, he thought, they got him with the tire iron." The later statement that Ennis, hearing about Jack's new lover, "now . . . knew it had been the tire iron" is not any more conclusive (Proulx, "Brokeback Mountain" 23, 25). Ennis's certainty is no more factually based than Lureen's. One might even argue that it is less so: whatever scenario Ennis was confronted with, he could not interpret it as anything other than a fag-bashing. He must square it with the way he has been taught the world treats queers, a way he must confirm at every turn if he's to make his denial of Jack and himself palatable. Aside from the fact that the death-by-beating seems to emanate from Ennis's fear-driven mind (Proulx's story is written in limited third person, focused mostly on Ennis), this scene serves as an obvious bookend to the film's first flashback of homophobic violence (the mutilated gay rancher), one of only three flashbacks in the entire movie, two of which belong to Ennis.[9]

Regardless of the plausibility of Jack's death as Ennis imagines it, how Jack dies is not only unknowable or speculative but, finally, immaterial. That he dies at all is the point. To call the circumstances of Jack's death "immaterial" might seem insensitive or at least inappropriate; there's certainly a material difference between being killed in a freak accident, or being killed for any reason besides one's sexuality, and being killed because one is queer. But "immaterial" is the appropriate word inasmuch as Ennis can read Jack's death, however it occurs, only as the result of homophobia. The bashing scene is most instructive for what it reveals about Ennis: in a sense, he needs to have Jack die that way for verification of his own father's warning. In death Jack serves as a substitute for Ennis, who, never having shed the power of the father, believes he deserves to die.

The discussion thus far raises the matter of whether *Brokeback* is not so much a gay polemic as it is a cautionary tale—not necessarily a conscious warning but, equally culpable, one passed on by writers and filmmakers unconsciously transmitting ubiquitous homophobic cultural energies. Deliberately or not, Jack's death (much more so than Ennis's self-imposed exile) exposes a belief that undergirds *Brokeback*, a notion that, despite the honest, vehement demur of many an individual, seems nearly everywhere woven into heteronormative culture: gay happiness is unimaginable. As Christian Draz writes, "It's as if, for all their good will, [the filmmakers] were unable to understand these two gay characters as anything *other* than tragic" (13; emphasis added). Peter Swaab's enlightening reference to Willa Cather disputes the inevitability of Proulx's ending:

> Proulx's mountain reminds me of the New Mexican mesa where Tom Outland and Roddy Blake live amorously in Willa Cather's novel *The Professor's House* (1925). Cather's fictions imagine a real if compromised place for all sorts of outsiders, racial and sexual, in pioneering America; but in *Brokeback Mountain* there is simply no place for Jack and Ennis to continue their love, in the Wyoming of their time. (42)

Swaab, like others, seems too prompt to add the "simply" to "there is no place for . . . their love," too ready to accept that that is "simply" the way things are. This is not to petulantly insist that stories must end happily just because they can. But, given the definitional "double bind" that imbricates heterosexuality and homosexuality, queer love is rarely, if ever, "simply" impossible, at least not inherently, on its own. All manner of dicta, traditions, and circumstances—warnings and threats both adventitious and witting, transmitted and perceived by the lovers and by the larger culture—impact its expression and survival. Further, as pointed out by Matt Foreman, a "native Westerner whose parents have ranched in Wyoming" and executive director of the National Gay and Lesbian Task Force from 2003 to 2008, Jack's proposal is not beyond the realm of possibilities, even in 1967 Wyoming (qtd. in Vary par. 22).[10] More lamentable is our willingness to cheer a depiction of queer life as backward as Cather imagined eighty-some years ago. Since when is "no place" better than a "real if compromised place" where one can "live amorously"?

While a number of happy queer films have emerged fairly recently (such as *The Broken Hearts Club*, *The Ski Trip*, *Connie & Carla*, and *Another Gay Movie*), one should note that these are all comedies or at least seriocomic works. It's an old saw that serious art rarely features happy endings because happiness lacks conflict and without conflict narrative is banal. And part of my argument, admittedly, is that unhappy endings for queer characters may more accurately reflect literally and/or symbolically the continued legal and cultural marginalization of American queers. Yet none of these qualifications can dissipate the lingering feeling that, after a handful of mainstream gay films in the past two decades (*Philadelphia* being the most prominent of these), happy endings for queers lie beyond the compass of the American mind. Roy Grundmann, writing for *Cineaste*, finds it "petty to fault [the film] for its reticence on the availability of alternative sexual venues for its lovers," and one must concede that the paucity of queer stories puts an undue amount of pressure on each new work of art to be representative and/or satisfying (par. 15). But that's not what galls here. The 1980s saw a number of queer films hailed rightly or wrongly as "groundbreaking," including *Personal Best*, *My Beautiful Laundrette*, *Desert Hearts*, *Parting Glances*, and *Prick Up Your Ears*.[11] Even a movie such as *Making Love*—not without its flaws but starring established straight actors Harry Hamlin, Michael Ontkean, and Kate Jackson—is worthier of the "groundbreaking" label than *Brokeback*. The gay characters played by Ontkean and Hamlin don't end up together, but neither one dies: one "play[s] the field" while the other "finds himself a rich architect and marries the guy" (Russo 272). What's galling about *Brokeback* is that Proulx first—and then McMurtry and Ossana, who chose to remain faithful to Proulx's original vision in this detail—envisioned an ending for Jack but chose to extinguish it. Regardless of the realities of rural life in 1960s Wyoming, or the continuing menace of homophobia and violence, choosing to tell this story at this moment feels oddly incognizant of the past twenty years in gay art and history. David Ansen's *Newsweek* review exemplifies this disquieting equation of loss and progress: "the reason [*Brokeback*] feels like a breakthrough is that Lee has made it for the right reasons: he recognizes a heartbreaking love story when he sees one" (par. 2). By this dubious logic, queer tragedy is a narrative "breakthrough." "[H]eartbreaking" gay stories are the "right" ones to film, while, implicitly, heartwarming ones are the wrong ones. While Grundmann is right that the "paradox of all great romances" is "the promise of a happily-ever-after and the mandate that this must never come to pass," a doomed gay romance, especially one recounted by straight storytellers, risks carrying a valuative, if not also proscriptive, charge absent from heterosexual romance (par. 10). The latter, though subject to individual instances of failure, never faces the charge that it categorically cannot or ought not to be.

What makes calling *Brokeback* the "right" gay story more perturbing is that Jack has a happy ending—or almost does. After Jack's death, Ennis learns from Jack's father, John, that Jack had recently found "another fella" willing to move to Lightning Flat with him, to begin the life together Ennis had rejected as incapable of realization without fatal consequences (McMurtry and Ossana 90). Although the idea may run counter to a slavish habituation to generic convention (doomed romance) and to enduring (gay and straight) acculturation to queer inferiority, Jack's death is not necessary. Jack's finding someone else to live with, even if only as a substitute for Ennis, is sufficient to produce the unhappy ending that Ennis's claustrophobically constricted mentality demands. Jack's sullen father snips that, "like most a Jack's ideas," leaving his wife and working the family ranch with another man "never come to pass" (McMurtry and Ossana 90). But this is fallacious reasoning on John Twist's part. Neither his pessimism nor Jack's own admission of his historic bad luck expunges the fact that this plan, as far as we can tell, was about to "come to pass." This reading might seem baselessly optimistic, but it's worth noting that we're given no reason, other than John's cynicism, to think that Jack's notion of setting up house with another man was not going to be realized. McMurtry and Ossana lend substance to the possibility of this plan's actualization by inserting a scene in which Randall Malone—presumably the "ranch neighbor . . . from down in Texas" Jack had asked to live with him—makes a pass at Jack (McMurtry and Ossana 76, 90). If Jack were to live, much less live happily, such an ending (Jack finds love; Ennis knows only paralysis) would punish Ennis sufficiently to convey the oppressiveness and the personal cost of homophobia. At minimum, happiness is possible for Jack in a way it cannot be for Ennis. That Jack would find someone other than Ennis to love is a reasonable assumption, if only because he seeks it, because he, unlike Ennis, can envision it.

That Proulx could envision a happy ending for Jack Twist but could not envision him realizing that ending is perhaps the most saddening dimension of the narrative—because it renders Jack's death entirely gratuitous. In regard to the ending, Proulx writes, "While I was working on this story, I was occasionally close to tears. I felt guilty that their lives were so difficult, yet *there was nothing I could do about it. It couldn't end any other way*" (qtd. in Sean Smith par. 3). Proulx's reflection is patently a statement of bad faith, however heartfelt. Brushing aside the facile suggestion that stories write themselves, we're faced with the bald admission that Proulx cannot visualize, let alone, write another ending—just as Ennis cannot visualize it. In effect, we're being told that Ennis functions as Proulx's mouthpiece in the text, that Proulx is incapable of inhabiting Jack Twist, seeing the world from his point of view. The narrative circumstances of Jack's death, in which a future is imagined and then cancelled out (apparently by irrevocable Fate, not authorial volition), undermine Proulx's otherwise apparently antihomophobic motives. Cultural antipathy to homosexuals is so deeply and sometimes covertly ingrained that the numbing fatalism of "it couldn't end any other way" passes for an inexorable aesthetic law rather than the inflection of the old phobic aphorism that it is: gay life is solitary and sad—and there's nothing anyone can do about it.[12] Rather than merely a tale, as Proulx puts it, of "destructive rural homophobia," her story and Lee's film both embody, if unwittingly, the appalling extent to which homophobia imbues even the willfully most antihomophobic context (Proulx, "Getting Movied" 130). Although many of them have joined the rush to lionize Annie Proulx for her courage, sympathy, or insight, queers should intuit more easily than anyone how unenterprising, formulaic, and orthodox her conception of gay life is. It is deracinated, joyless, fugitive, trite; without hope of outlet, fulfillment, articulation, or sanctuary.

Always the Bridesmaid

One of the film's most significant additions to the original story—the final scene between Ennis and his daughter, Alma Jr.—likewise comes off as less heartwarming than intended. Alma Jr. visits her hermitlike father in his solitary trailer home to invite him to her upcoming wedding. After gruffly claiming he can't get time off work, Ennis thaws toward his daughter and agrees to attend. Once she drives off, Jack notices she's forgotten her sweater. Opening his locker to store it, he sees the hanger with his old flannel shirt (which Jack had secretly stolen after their first summer on the mountain) and a shirt of Jack's layered beneath it. To signal both Ennis's closeted sexuality and his deeply internalized love for Jack, Ennis has reversed the layering of the shirts as he initially found them in Jack's closet at the Twist home (Ennis's shirt inside Jack's). Looking at the shirts, along with the postcard of Brokeback Mountain pinned on the locker door, Ennis starts to tear up and delivers the film's truncated last line, "Jack, I swear. . . ." (McMurtry and Ossana 97). Grundmann shrewdly diagnoses this scene's "political instrumentality" (par. 16). Ennis's "I swear," juxtaposed with talk of his daughter's impending wedding, evokes marital vows ("And do you take this man . . . ?" "I do.")—a token, for Grundmann, of the screenwriters' "liberal-minded nod to gay mainstream politics" in "legitimiz[ing] the gay marriage that would have been by linking it to the straight wedding that will be" (pars. 16, 17). No other critic seems to have made the connection between Alma Jr.'s marriage and the partnership Ennis will never have, or to have remarked in this context on gay marriage's less desirable implications: inducting gays and lesbians into the institution of marriage grants equality only to those who choose to marry; the married are still rewarded and valued in ways that the unmarried are not.[13] Grundmann also correctly (if a bit testily) attributes any political freight in the scene to the screenwriters. While Proulx ends the source story with the image of the two shirts, the scene between Ennis and his daughter is the invention of McMurtry and Ossana. But it's possible to read this added scene even more cynically—and truthfully. Proulx allows the two lovers (Ennis remembering Jack) to close the story. In the screenplay, by contrast, heterosexuality and the society Ennis has avoided so long intrude into his last private space (the closet within which his locker doubly closets his love for Jack), coaxing him back into the straight fold with the proverbial ties that bind (parent–child affection and duty), requiring his presence at heterosexuality's central sacralizing, promulgating event (marriage).

At the same time, a happy ending for Ennis and Jack might seem inappropriate at present. Queers are outsiders in America. (Michael Warner would suggest that oppositionality, or "thorough resistance to regimes of the normal," is the proper and perhaps only authentic way for queer culture to survive—which makes *Brokeback* a wrongly mournful account of exclusion, as if there can be no newly made culture, no contentment outside heteronormativity [Introduction xxvi].) Obviously much has changed over the past forty-odd years. Yet whatever the material circumstances or political gains of the past decade (most prominently, the Supreme Court decision in *Lawrence et al. v. Texas*), queers remain the symbolic and—to judge from the number of state-level laws and amendments against gay marriage, civil unions, and domestic partner benefits—also the material pariahs of heteronormativity. It's in this vein, in the historically familiar stereotype of scary (or toxic) gay, that *Brokeback* presents gay men: as a corrosive agent undermining the family, eroding it from within and without. Finally confronting Ennis with her knowledge of his affair with Jack, Alma hisses, "Jack Twist? . . . Jack Nasty," identifying Jack as the "nast[iness]" that wormed its way into the Del Mar domestic sanctum, destroying their marriage. Ennis, having become nasty himself, is enraged with Alma for discovering his secret, wrenches her arm, and must be expelled: "Get out of my house, Ennis Del Mar!" (McMurtry and Ossana 68–69). The fact that Alma is pregnant with a third child, her first with second husband Monroe, renders the expulsion of Ennis, of "nast[iness]," doubly vital, not merely to domestic tranquility but to fetal life, to the future of (straight) hearth and civilization. Like Ennis in Alma's view, in rhetoric and in images that not everyone promotes and many find offensive but that continue to resonate, queers still stand poised to destroy civilization.[14]

That Old, Familiar (Tragic) Feeling

The Era of Good Feelings inaugurated by *Brokeback*'s success is unwise for queers and unfortunate for straights. In neither group does the film incite anger at current discrimination, violence, or exclusion. The film's somber affect and painterly eye, along with its status as a genre and period piece, encourages—or at the very least permits—distance. We're invited to regret that it didn't work out for Ennis and Jack and how sad it was back then. If a common first reaction is "how sad," this is uncomfortably close to that common phobic refrain that being gay is a hard life (as if it were a choice; no one says such things about being a person of color or female precisely because that would nonsensically imply one has a choice in such matters). Richard Schneider, editor of *Gay and Lesbian Worldview*, falls victim to a tantalizing yet falsely content sense of progress by virtue of cultural distance from "back then" when he writes, "Proulx . . . create[s] the worst possible environment to be gay, reducing that struggle to a stark choice between living a lie and risking one's life. There but for the grace of God, one can't help thinking, but for the fact that times have changed. *Brokeback Mountain* reminds us of the progress we've made, and the film's very existence is a case in point" (10). Faced with the excluded middle Proulx constructs, either alternative ("risking one's life" by living openly like Jack or "living a lie" like Ennis) is a strong contestant for a pis aller. Schneider may have hit on *Brokeback*'s catch-22: Jack's death at once upbraids and vindicates Ennis for staying in the closet. Queers understandably welcome the advent of the gay blockbuster, but might we wonder whether it has to be tragic gay? For all its beauty, or partly because of it, *Brokeback* is fundamentally reactionary, both on paper and film, reinscribing homosexuality within conventional, all too familiar parameters. More damning still is what one might call the film's ethical irresponsibility. Despite the fact that filmmakers were roundly lionized for delivering a gay love story capable of changing minds, reaching those phobic or indifferent to homosexuality, no one seemed prepared to entertain a less pleasant truth: namely, that a homophobic viewer could watch *Brokeback* and leave the theater with his homophobia utterly intact. Whether or not the gay-bashing was Ennis's interpretation of Jack's death, Jack still dies. Jack's death can be read, by such viewers, as not just a gay-bashing but a justified one. Ennis ends up isolated from homosexuality yet, in the film version, reconnected with his daughter. Thus, not only is the film unlikely to appeal to viewers who are not already sympathetic, it makes no attempt to disable homophobic readings. There is at least one hopeful note to be found in *Brokeback*, however—surprisingly, in Ennis's enigmatic, final words, "Jack, I swear. . . ." If one interprets Ennis here to be swearing regret at not having acted more courageously, at denying himself and Jack both what the latter was so ready to grasp, then screenwriters and directors might learn from Ennis's and *Brokeback*'s shortcomings and dare, next time, to conceive of and dramatize gay happiness, to redeem it from its historically and continued chimeric status in the national imaginary.

Even though gay happiness may be difficult to imagine for straight mainstream filmmakers and fiction writers (and gay unhappiness, dismayingly plausible for American audiences, both gay and straight), national politics is another case entirely. As chapter 5 illustrates, in public political discourse queers are all too credible—and not just as, in chapter 2, limp-wristed, emasculated nellies unfit to be the chief executive. When sex potentially enters the picture—sex with teenagers, no less—the American imagination is instantly kindled with vivid phantoms: pedophile, pervert, sex predator. That the factual basis of these unfounded phobic specters has been repeatedly debunked seems to make little difference.

5

The IMs Are Coming from Inside the House

Recruitment, the Closet, and the Right

If the specter of homosexual recruitment has long haunted heteronormative American culture, Anita Bryant's 1977 Save Our Children campaign against a gay and lesbian antidiscrimination law was a watershed moment. This campaign, launched in response to a Miami-Dade County, Florida, ordinance and moving quickly to other counties and states, helped galvanize the burgeoning conservative Christian political movement and its monomaniacal fixation on homosexuality as the paramount social evil. Bryant's battle cry heralded the imminent risk that gays and lesbians posed to children, particularly by becoming adoptive parents: "Since homosexuals cannot reproduce, they must recruit and freshen their ranks. The recruitment of our children is absolutely necessary for the survival and growth of homosexuality" (qtd. in Highleyman par. 5). Following an uncommonly counterintuitive line of homophobic reasoning, Bryant hypothesized that if gays and lesbians never adopted children—which facilitated molesting, brainwashing, and thereby converting them to homosexuality—then no children would ever be gay (because, of course, all children are heterosexual to begin with).

The 2006 sex scandal involving U.S. Representative Mark Foley (R-FL) provides a compelling parallel and bookend to the banner raised by Bryant thirty years ago and kept aloft since then by the Republican Party and conservative lobbying organizations such as the Family Research Council. (For more in-depth discussion of "fissures and rifts" over issues of gender and sexuality in the American conservative movement from Barry Goldwater to Ralph Reed, see Angela

Dillard's *Guess Who's Coming to Dinner* Now?, particularly 137–70.) Personal scandal did not undermine Bryant's cause: voters overturned Miami-Dade County's antidiscrimination ordinance; in return, gay activists led a boycott that cost Bryant her career as a celebrity spokesperson for the Florida Citrus Commission, Coca-Cola, Kraft, and Tupperware. Yet the continuity could not be more striking between her bid to "save our children" and the efforts of the House Caucus on Missing and Exploited Children, headed by Foley, to criminalize suggestive Internet images of minors. The scandalous pith of Foleygate is not, as right-wing goons such as James Dobson and Matt Drudge have suggested, that Foley is gay (fulfilling the homophobic myth that homosexuals are child molesters) or that Foley is the victim of a prank by gay Republican staffers (Drudge's record of gay-baiting after his own outing in 2000 requires a descriptor other than "projection"). Rather, the potential catastrophe for the GOP—and the relevance of this episode for a theorization of recruitment—is the cover-up. Preliminary evidence suggests that Republican House leaders and colleagues, including Speaker Dennis Hastert (R-IL), had known about Foley's prurient Internet correspondence with congressional pages for perhaps possibly up to six years—which means that a long-known ephebophile was tasked with cracking down on the cyberpredation of minors. More significant than the fact that Foley's actions were covered up is that they were condoned. Foley is one of the latest in a succession of outed Republican officials, including Spokane Mayor Jim West and Virginia Representative Ed Schrock, only to be followed by Reverend Ted Haggard and Senator Larry Craig (R-ID), who have been spouting party-line homophobia and working to restrict queer citizens' rights while violating, in private, the very "family values" platform they publicly valorize, in this instance by being gay.

My point here is emphatically not to equate homosexuality with ephebophilia or pedophilia, as heteronormative culture and the Right routinely do, but simply to note that a party obsessed with codifying a severely restricted model of human sexuality as the basis for political and economic franchise seems to be disproportionately populated with adulterers and homosexuals. While hard evidence might be lacking for an empirical claim such as this, experience seems to bear it out. Perhaps Republican adulterers and homosexuals are exposed or arrested more often than Democratic ones. The GOP's vilification of gays as corrosively antithetical to family and nation might well lend greater schadenfreude (or newsworthiness, if there's a difference) to their exposure. As conservative pundits have been quick to point out, Democrats have had their share of sex scandals (e.g., Representatives Jerry Studds and Barney Frank and President Bill Clinton). But Democrats, unlike Republicans, have not claimed unique moral immaculacy, so while Studds, Frank, and Clinton can be shamed, they cannot be accused of hypocrisy.

The most salient point would be, following the theoretical work of Michael Warner, Eve Sedgwick, and Lee Edelman, that heterosexuals denouncing queers for recruiting is textbook projective behavior. The energy expended in almost every instance of daily discourse, from national political rhetoric to water cooler small talk, reinscribes the naturalness of heterosexuality (a naturalness, following Judith Butler's discussions of gender, rhetorically undermined by its compulsive repetition). Though perhaps karmically gratifying, the Foley incident is symptomatic of a party and a larger sexual culture that seem unwilling, if not constitutionally unable, to see their own umbilical dependence on recruitment. By considering the competing narratives of homosexual corruption, the cult of the child, and "traditional values" against the backdrop of the Foley scandal as well as the outings of Reverend Ted Haggard, Matt Sanchez, and Senator Larry Craig, this chapter seeks to develop a theoretical model to explain a set of pressing questions: Why do Republicans keep recruiting homosexuals? Is there something self-recruiting about gay conservatives that draws them to groups that openly despise them? What if a party in whose platform homophobia is a load-bearing plank must recruit gays to survive (much less be able to recognize the "threat" it wishes to target)? The familiar psychoanalytic mechanism of projection seems finally insufficient to describe the way in which not just hypocrisy but recruitment subtends contemporary right-wing ideology.[1]

Bracketing the unproductive debate about the age of Foley's Internet correspondents (defenders are claiming that the pages Foley IM'd and had sex with were eighteen or older at the time) as well as the question of whether Foley is a pedophile or an ephebophile, the moral hypocrisy of the Republican House leadership's shielding of Foley, if not their giving him power in the first place, shows a constitutional lack of commitment to the fundamentalist and "traditional" values argument upon which Republicans have built their party for the past quarter of a century. One wonders why Republicans didn't simply replace Foley—or, better yet, expose him, make an example out of him, and thereby solidify their evangelical and conservative base. Why turn a blind eye, if for no other reason than that such a move would be congruent with Capitol Hill corruption on both sides of the aisle (lobbying, infidelities, gay and straight prostitution)? By targeting Internet predators through congressional legislation, Foley was acting not merely out of self-hatred or Roy Cohn–like diversionary persecution. It's my suggestion that he and those complicit in the cover-up—like Ted Haggard and Matt Sanchez—have been playing the ultimate closet game. They have co-opted the closet for the pleasure of transgressing with impunity, of "doing it and getting away with it" (which other closeted gay men may also do, but many of whose double lives are more often enforced by concrete or general threats). This chapter will, then, build on Slavoj Žižek's theory of political misidentification and the work of Eve Sedgwick to theorize a model for conservative colonization of the queer closet from within, a new wrinkle in the homophobic project for which, with new energy and more pointedly eugenic politics, the closet has come to stand.

Tastes Like Teen Spirit

The bare facts of the Foley scandal are prurience, denial, and recrimination. For an initially unclear period of time, Mark Foley was e-mailing and instant messaging several young pages, during and after their tenure in the congressional page program. He doesn't seem to have had sex with any of them, at least when they were still minors. Speaker of the House Dennis Hastert was warned more than once by aides and other congressmen about Foley's activities and urged to intervene. Once ABC News aired IMs between Foley and one of the pages,[2] leading Foley to resign posthaste, Hastert fumblingly disputed the timeline of his involvement and the severity of the events themselves. In general, the efforts of Hastert[3] and other congressmen and aides to conceal, obfuscate, or simply plead ignorance of Foley's actions are equally, embarrassingly indicative, as Eugene Robinson writes in the *Washington Post*, of "stunning cynicism" and "woeful incompetence" (par. 5). But it seems that as early as 2000, Foley's actions were noted and fretted over behind the scenes: former Hastert clerk Jeff Trandhal "periodically called [Kirk] Fordham"—former chief of staff to Mark Foley and then Representative Tom Reynolds (R-NY), who headed the National Republican Congressional Committee—"to say Foley was spending too much time with pages . . . and Fordham would have to 'pull him back a little'" (Weisman par. 9). Fordham supposedly urged Foley to be "'conscious of appearances. Everyone knows you're gay'" (Weisman par. 9). In 2000 or 2001, Congressman Jim Kolbe (R-AZ), who is openly gay, or "someone in his office" approached Foley about "what were described as 'creepy' e-mails to a page," according to Kolbe's press secretary (Margasak par. 12). Members of Hastert's staff reportedly "warned the page class of 2001–2002 to stay away from Foley" (Aravosis par. 4). In 2003 Foley was "seen drunk outside the pages' dormitory after their 10 p.m. curfew, trying to get in" (par. 10). Fordham met with Hastert's chief of staff, Scott Palmer, "in 2003 or earlier to intervene, after Fordham's own efforts to stop Foley's behavior had failed" (Palmer denies the meeting occurred) (Weisman par. 3). In November 2005, Representative John Shimkus (R-IL), head of the House Page Board, and Trandhal, who along with Shimkus ran the page program, confronted Foley in response to complaints by a former page from Louisiana. Representative Tom Reynolds and House Majority Leader John Boehner (R-OH) went to Hastert directly in the spring of 2006 to inform him, if not to urge action.[4]

Rushing to Foley's defense, party zealots offered a host of red herrings. Newt Gingrich suggested the e-mails and instant messages were leaked as a Democratic ploy timed to hurt Republicans in the upcoming midterm elections. Ann Coulter, in addition to pointing the finger at wealthy Democratic donor George Soros, accused Foley's critics of gay-bashing. Falling back on the expected conspiracy theories, most of those who rushed to defend Foley also decried the leak as an invasion of his privacy. Whether knowingly disingenuous or the effect of selective amnesia, homilies on the sacredness of individual privacy are rich coming from Republican loyalists of the kind who, in 1986, rejoiced over the Supreme Court's ruling (*Bowers v. Hardwick*) that gays and lesbians lack the right to sexual privacy enjoyed by heterosexuals, and who, more recently, have defended President Bush's illegal wiretapping program. To further demonize these lavender assassins (the supposed leakers), extremists on the Right claimed that Republican leaders had not intervened against Foley earlier because they feared being called homophobic—a cover-up due, then, not to Republican apathy or moral bankruptcy but to an oppressive culture of liberal political correctness.[5] Yet more colorful than either allegations of partisan intrigue or claims of thwarted virtue was the theory—circulated by such luminaries as "Internet gossip" Matt Drudge, radio host Mike Savage, James Dobson, Representative Patrick McHenry (R-NC), and *Wall Street Journal* deputy editor Daniel Henninger—that Foley had simply been pranked by gay Republican staffers—whacked by gay Sopranos, if you will ("Echoing Drudge" par. 1).[6] Henninger called the mere "rumor" that Foley had been "pranked by the House pages"—"goaded unwitting[ly]" into "typ[ing] embarrassing comments" as "sort of a joke," as Drudge put it—"the first plausible thing I've heard in seven days" (qtd. in "Echoing Drudge" par. 2; Drudge par. 2). As Jon Stewart insightfully joked on *The Daily Show*, the obvious absurdity of the gay mafia rumor evoked a sobering, contrary truth: surely a "velvet mafia" powerful enough to shield Foley for the past several years would also have sought to block, if not reverse, homophobic federal and state policies and initiatives (qtd. in Edwards par. 1; see also "Right Wing Blames Gays for Foley Scandal").

Despite the speciousness of a "velvet mafia" hit on Foley, a plausible argument might be made for gay complicity in the cover-up before the leak. Kirk Fordham and Jeff Trandhal, the two congressional aides central to the cover-up and chief witnesses in the postleak investigation, are themselves gay. Yet rather than engineering a gay conspiracy of the kind painted by right-wing figures, Trandhal and Fordham tried not to shield or condone Foley's actions but put a stop to them. A more cynical reading would be that they simply wished Foley to keep a lower predatory profile. More moderately, one might contend that their admirable unease about what Foley was doing (moral discomfort with sexual harassment or advances toward minors) was matched by anxiety over the damage public knowledge of Foley's behavior and its breach of Republicans' superior moral stance might wreak on the political futures of their party, their bosses, and themselves. For Fordham, certainly, party loyalty comes first: after leaving Foley's office, he served as finance director for Senator Mel Martinez (R-FL) in a 2004 campaign that accused Martinez's rival of favoring the "radical homosexual lobby" (qtd. in Leibovich par. 14). More abstract forms of harassment, such as defamation and hate-mongering via campaign rhetoric, are apparently easier to stomach. Before evaluating the complex position(ing) of gay Republican "insiders" such as Trandhal, Fordham, and Foley himself, it is worthwhile, first, to consider the phobic totems of pedophilia and recruitment.

Worshipped not just by those on the Right, these fetishes are relied on by commentators from across the spectrum—deeply embedded cultural fetishes that surface, sooner or later, in even the most civilized and ostensibly liberal discussions of homosexuality.

The most common feature of commentary on Foleygate is the slippage—in the popular imagination as well as in much conservative rhetoric—between Foley's predatory behavior (whether it involved intercourse or not), homosexuality, and pedophilia. Publicity about Foley's sexuality (though he had been outed once before, in 2003; see Naff and Sain; Ryan-Vollmar; Skoloff) no doubt caused discomfort for Republicans,[7] who have expanded their base in recent decades among hard-Right political and religious conservatives with gay-baiting initiatives such as the Federal Marriage Amendment, state constitutional bans on same-sex marriage and civil unions, and prohibitions on domestic partner benefits. What made Foley's 2006 outing more embarrassing, and potentially damaging, was the revelation of his online pursuit of congressional pages. The party of "family values" was harboring not simply a homosexual but a man actively pursuing sex with minors—and not just any man, but the congressman tasked with cracking down on Internet predation of minors. Symbolically as well as literally, that illicit call was coming from inside the House, inside the sacralized domestic realm.

The text of the IM sessions, first aired on ABC, was undeniably prurient, and Foley's online interlocutor was still under eighteen.[8] In a series of chats with a former page, whose identity ABC concealed with the anonymous screen name "Xxxxxxxxx," Mark Foley, as "Maf54," asked for details of the teen's sexual life:

Maf54: did any girl give you a hand job this weekend

Xxxxxxxxx: lol no

Xxxxxxxxx: im single right now

Xxxxxxxxx: my last gf [girlfriend] and i broke up a few weeks ag[o]

* * *

Maf54: good so you're getting horny

Xxxxxxxxx: lol a bit

Maf54: did you spank it yourself this weekend

Xxxxxxxxx: no

Xxxxxxxxx: been too tired and too busy

Maf54: wow . . .

Maf54: i am never to busy haha

Xxxxxxxxx: haha

Maf54: or tired . . . helps me sleep

* * *

Xxxxxxxxx: i dont do it very often normally though

Maf54: why not

Maf54: at your age it seems like it would be daily

In a prolonged exchange, Foley then asks the teen for details about his masturbation habits. As an extended sample makes clear, the IM sessions were sexually explicit enough that the White House's initial stance—when White House press secretary Tony Snow characterized the e-mails that were leaked in advance of the IM sessions as "simply naughty"—was no longer tenable:

Maf54: do you really do it face down [on the bed]

* * *

Xxxxxxxxx: well i dont use my hand . . . i use the bed itself

Maf54: where do you unload it

Xxxxxxxxx: towel

Maf54: really

Maf54: completely naked?

Xxxxxxxxx: well ya

Maf54: very nice

Xxxxxxxxx: lol

Maf54: cute butt bouncing in the air

* * *

Maf54: well I have a . . . totally stiff wood now

* * *

Maf54: is your little guy limp . . . or growing

Xxxxxxxxx: eh growing

Maf54: hmm

Mafv54: so you got a stiff one now

* * *

Maf54: i am hard as a rock . . . so tell me when your[s] reaches rock

* * *

Maf54: what are you wearing

Xxxxxxxxx: normal clothes

Xxxxxxxxx: tshirt and shorts

Maf54: um so a big buldge

Xxxxxxxxx: ya

Maf54: um

Maf54: love to slip them off of you

Xxxxxxxxx: haha

Maf54: and gra[b] the one eyed snake

Xxxxxxxxx: not tonight . . . don't get to excited

Maf54: well your hard

Xxxxxxxxx: that is true

Maf54: and a little horny

Xxxxxxxxx: and also tru

Maf54: get a ruler and measure it for me

Xxxxxxxxx: ive already told you that

Maf54: tell me again

Xxxxxxxxx: 7 and ½ [inches]

Maf54: ummmmmmmmmmmmmm

Maf54: beautiful

Xxxxxxxxx: lol

Maf54: thats a great size

Xxxxxxxxx: thank you

Maf54: still stiff

Xxxxxxxxx: ya

Maf54: take it out

Xxxxxxxxx: brb [be right back] . . . my mom is yelling

Regardless of the teen's willingness to engage in sexual banter with Foley (the anonymity of the Internet makes palatable much that one might be unwilling to say in person), Foley clearly initiates the discussion's more unsavory turns, and at least one of the teens pursued by Foley complained to those in charge of the page program. Setting aside what for most Americans is the contentious, if not unthinkable, question of the sexual subjectivity of teenagers, Foley's conversations with the former page are disturbing, but not for the reason most coverage seems to insinuate. The word "predatory," so commonly used to describe Foley's behavior, has implications both gay and straight commentators might want to avoid—or perhaps not, if their animus is, respectively, to distance themselves or their gay associates from the twin taboos of pedophilia and preadult sexuality. Certainly, given Foley's political status as a congressman and (in a sense) the page's former supervisor, Foley's advances also constitute a form of sexual harassment.[9] To be clear: Foley's advances could fairly be characterized as inappropriate, creepy, and possibly actionable. But to label Foley a pedophile is inaccurate (and homophobic, as I discuss below): a seventeen-year-old, though legally a minor, is not a child, certainly not in the way a five-year-old or an eight-year-old is. Foley qualifies as an ephebophile, someone attracted to young men in their late teens. Of greater concern is that when commentators refer to Foley as a pedophile, a man with a taste for young boys, the error may be due not merely to a historic American panic over preadult sexuality but rather to a studied imprecision, an equally historic phobic conflation of two very distinct nonnormative sexualities (pedophilia and homosexuality).

The homosexual-as-pedophile image has long been a favorite truncheon of less subtle homophobes, from Anita Bryant to fundamentalist and "family values" lobbying entities such as the Family Research Council, the Traditional Values Coalition, and Concerned Women for America. These heavily funded organizations continue to preach the cliché that most child molesters are homosexual—86 percent, according to James Dobson. But Dobson lumps gay men together with bisexuals, a cheat that only draws attention to the difficulty of positioning men who are socially straight-identified (i.e., married to or dating a woman) but have an active sexual life with men. Are these men bisexual or "actually" gay? (As always with sexuality surveys, respondents' reluctance to openly identify as gay or bisexual skews data in a way that may fail to reflect their full sexual lives.) Echoing Dobson, Peter LaBarbera, president of Americans For Truth, pronounces Foley's behavior "'typical of homosexuals'" (qtd. in "Congressional Page Scandal" par. 13). Tony Perkins, who heads the Family Research Council, puzzlingly pins the blame on liberal-enforced "tolerance and diversity"—even though Foley was a Republican in a GOP-controlled Congress. The culture of liberality that, according to Perkins, not only allowed Foley to acquire political power but encouraged his online activities ensures that neither Republicans nor Democrats are "likely to address the real issue, which is the link between homosexuality and child abuse" ("Congressional Page Scandal" par. 12). It's stunning that anyone is still able to make this kind of claim, or is willing to listen to such drivel, unless they're also able or willing to discount a series of studies, from the late 1970s to one by the American Medical Association in 1998, finding that between 90 percent and 99 percent of child molesters are heterosexual. (Again, classification as "heterosexual" here, one supposes, is aligned with a subject's self-identification, public life, and sexual history with spouses or opposite-sex partners. One might be safe in assuming that Dobson, LaBarbera, and Perkins would classify as "homosexual" only someone living an avowedly gay life—not the man with a wife and children who attends church but secretly cruises rest stops for sex with men.)

The more malevolent edge of the gay pedophile cliché is not so much predation as it is recruitment. In the heteronormative imaginary, recruitment—a menace conjured by Anita Bryant in 1977 and kept alive by social conservatives—refers to the notion that homosexuals make other homosexuals, that we reproduce by battening on and stealing the fruits of others' "natural" (re)production, that is, their children. Being gay or lesbian, in the recruitment narrative, means also being a child molester, for it's by brainwashing and/or having sex with children that one makes them gay.[10] To most rational adults, the recruitment myth is likely to seem, as Eugene Robinson writes in the *Washington Post*, "far beyond ridiculous" (par. 8). And yet for the past two decades at least, religious and social conservatives have grown more vocal and indignant, embattled by, among other things, what they feel to be the demotion of the nuclear family from its Copernican centrality by the cultural, if not always institutional, recognition of difference (race, ethnicity, gender, sexuality). As the concept of "America" becomes more complex (and resembles less the blanched, homogeneous nation these besieged souls wish it to be), the fiction of recruitment feels as comforting and credible as when it fell from the lips of a beauty queen thirty years ago. But it's part of this chapter's argument that this facile rhetoric remains credible and compelling, or at least palatable, to a wider audience than groups such as the Traditional Values Coalition (TVC). The filtering of recruitment ideology into mainstream forums of discussion—and the failure, with some exceptions, to denounce it for the repulsive, insulting nonsense it is—suggests a dismaying trend.

In the past few years, while continuing to oppose gay parenting and marriage, social and religious conservatives have shifted their tack to the educational arena, implementing the recruitment myth in response to the efforts of GLSEN (the Gay, Lesbian, and Straight Educational Network) and other organizations to enlighten teens and children about homophobia, tolerance, and diversity. The TVC calls GLSEN's workshops "pro-homosexual sensitivity training" ("Parents: Get the Truth" par. 3). Clearly, the TVC would prefer children to receive homosexual *in*sensitivity training—for which its Web site suggests it boasts ample expertise. Writing online in 2000 for *Accuracy in Media*, a right-wing media watchdog, Reed Irvine and Cliff Kincaid lambaste "Teach Out," a

GLSEN-sponsored "workshop held at Tufts University [in] March [2000] for high school students where," so Irvine and Kincaid claim, "state employees [HIV educators from the Departments of Public Health and Education] taught them the techniques of homosexual sex" (par. 1).[11] True to form, Irvine and Kincaid claim that visibility itself constitutes proselytizing: "[H]omosexuals are recruiting children in the public schools of Massachusetts. . . . [T]his is being promoted with public funds in the guise of a program to make school safe for gay students" (par. 1). Irvine and Kincaid are frank about the more indisputable details: GLSEN annually receives "$1.5 million . . . from the Governor's Commission for Gay and Lesbian Youth" (par. 2), so in that sense the conference was state-funded (whereas the state employees leading workshops had volunteered their services). But about the precise content of the workshop (which is "too shocking for us to discuss on the air" or in print), Irvine and Kincaid are oddly prudish, relying fallaciously on absent evidence. Frank York, writing for *World Net Daily*, is not so squeamish, reporting the experience of Scott Whiteman, who attended the conference as a member of the Massachusetts-based Parents Rights Coalition and secretly taped several workshops. In one workshop, "What They Didn't Tell You About Queer Sex & Sexuality in Health Class: A Workshop for Youth Only, Ages 14–21," facilitators discussed practices including fisting and the "pros and cons of ingesting male body fluid during oral sex" (par. 11).[12] According to Whiteman, facilitators forced this information on the teens; the facilitators claim "these kids were just asking questions and being told honest answers" (qtd. in York par. 17). That question may never be settled, since a judge, upholding the confidentiality policy agreed to by Teach Out participants, "issued a preliminary injunction barring dissemination of the tape" (Irvine and Kincaid par. 6).[13] Regardless of the content of this or other workshops (most workshops were actually nonsexual in nature[14]), the mere discussion of gay sex (even safe sex), the admission that nonprocreative sex exists (much less that it can be pleasurable), becomes, for these hysterics, a "recruitment tactic" to swell homosexual ranks (TVC, "Let's End" par. 6). The characteristic, inane assumption that knowledge of gay sex will make one want to have it go unexamined: if this logic were true, seeing a gay pride parade would turn any spectator gay. The mainstream success of *Will & Grace* and *Queer Eye for the Straight Guy*, should, then, have "turned" straight Americans gay by the millions.[15]

But groups such as the Traditional Values Coalition, Concerned Women for America, and the American Family Association oppose even discussions of homosexuality where the focus is not on sex. For the TVC, simply encouraging tolerance or discussing gender identity is a recruitment tool:

> establishing homosexual clubs with adult advisors and mentors [helps] initiate children into the strange world of homosexual sex. These children are to be lured into the movement and indoctrinated until they view their own parents as a "constant source of exasperation and amusement."

> According to [Gerald] Hannon [author of an essay in *Lavender Culture*[16]], one of the main goals of proselytizing is to separate children from their parents and the values they have been taught at home.
>
> Homosexual zealots are operating an amazingly efficient brainwashing and recruitment machine—and parents are getting to foot the bill. ("Let's End" pars. 10–12)

In the same vein, *Whistleblower*, a magazine produced by *World Net Daily*, devoted an entire issue to the dire threat of recruitment. Stephen Baldwin, executive director of the Council for National Policy, laments that

> it is difficult to convey the dark side of the homosexual culture without appearing harsh. However, it is time to acknowledge that homosexual behavior threatens the foundation of Western civilization—the nuclear family. An unmistakable manifestation of the attack on the family unit is the homosexual community's efforts to target children both for their own pleasure and to enlarge the homosexual movement. (qtd. in Dougherty par. 4)

As usual, the recruitment myth ignores—as, one supposes, it must in order to function—the obvious fact that gays and lesbians are born and bred by straights. We may not be made gay or lesbian in the sense of being "turned" by some error in parenting or child rearing, but we are certainly biologically made and raised (most of us) by straights. As for Baldwin and the TVC, perhaps the greatest damage feared from antihomophobic health and diversity education is the contradiction of the official heteronormative narrative under which students have been socialized and often raised.

Conservative blogger Daniel Levesque is likewise incensed that his accepted definition of what is natural or normal might be questioned:

> if you are a homosexual, I don't care what you do behind closed doors even though I find it morally repugnant and think it violates basic laws of nature. However, DO NOT FORCE YOUR WAY INTO MY KID'S SCHOOL (K–12) AND TRY TO RECRUIT HIM! My kids, my beliefs. If any of them make different choices despite my best efforts they can live with the consequences, but the last thing my child needs is someone trying to convince him to adopt an unhealthy, immoral lifestyle that cuts years or decades off people's life expectancies.
>
> . . . In prohomosexual schools there is a video called "My Family," a video that promotes alternative families.[17] Books like "Gloria Goes to Gay Pride" are on the district approved lists for material for teachers to read to first graders. Entire primary schools are forced to participate in and promote gay pride parades. Children are given

questionnaires about their sexuality that challenge their notion of being a heterosexual. (par. 4)

Besides the habitually shrill, fallacious equation between visibility (or even iteration) and proselytizing,[18] and between homosexuality and AIDS, Levesque is blithe about holding the menacingly nonspecific threat of "consequences"—AIDS? abandonment? fag-bashing?—over the heads of his (and implicitly, all) children. The final sentence quoted above exposes the fear that most vigorously animates the recruitment myth: not that activist groups such as GLSEN challenge children's "*notion* of being a heterosexual," but rather the notion that heterosexuality is all there is. But as Anna Marie Smith explains, that presumption depends on its own impossibility—not just on normalcy's susceptibility to subversion but its constitutive dependency on subversion:

> obsessive surveillance of young people's sexuality is a logical corollary to the assumption that homosexuality is essentially predatory and that virtually every young person is open to corruption. Homosexuality must be displaced from the childhood space in which the "true" sexuality is carefully nurtured; if homosexuality is to emerge, it must do so later. . . . The paradoxes are obvious: homosexuality is represented as potentially present in the originary moment of childhood, and yet must be made to come later; heterosexuality, the "natural" sexuality, does not "naturally" develop but must be produced through intervention; if every "normal" child can be seduced by the "not-normal," then there is something in the essence of normalcy that turns the "normal" against itself; the "normal" would not be "normal" without its relation to the "not-normal"; thus the very idea of normalcy depends on an ever-present threat from the "not-normal"; with the play of contamination and dependency between the two terms, the distinction between the "normal" and the "not-normal" ultimately fails and so on. This self-contradictory thinking does not collapse into incoherence, however, but fuels an obsessive concern for the production of normalcy in a world in which nothing can be taken for granted, especially in the sexual development of the apparently most "normal" child. "Natural" sexual development, then, cannot be left to "nature" but must be actively created through an intensively interventionist project of social transformation. (*New Right Discourse* 202)

What better name for an "interventionist project of social transformation" than recruitment? Levesque's fear that children might be talked into becoming gay masks a deeper terror that they might learn, despite what their families and churches may have told them, that not everyone is straight, that children might begin to question the ways culture daily propagandizes, in ways writ large and small, both the value of being straight and—its indispensable corollary—the despicable worthlessness of being queer. There is some comfort, perhaps, in the fact that the battle fought by Levesque and company can never be won. As long as queerness remains, evangelists of the normal will be ill at ease. For that reason if no other, homosexuality should be kept in view and kept queer. The visibility of queers in inoffensive, assimilable forms is as much an index of normalcy's (apparent) triumph as their unmitigated erasure.

The notion of homosexual recruitment thus ignores the ways heteronormative culture interpellates subjects as inherently heterosexual. Heterosexuality is an identity gays and lesbians must negotiate their way out of; coming out or even realizing they are queer requires defining themselves against that which they have been assumed to be from birth: straight. The apparition of gay recruitment is, on the simplest level, a projection of heteronormative (here, American) culture's incessant recruiting behavior. Etymologically, *recruit* comes from the French *recrute* and, before that, from the Latin *rescrescere*, meaning "to grow again." In addition to its familiar literal and figurative connotation (drafting, with always an edge of coercion), other meanings are equally apt in this context: to increase population by reproduction or immigration; to incorporate cells into a tissue or a body from elsewhere in the body.

Efforts by Republicans to minimize damage from Foleygate make strategic sense. Labeling Foley a "predator" (which, in the popular imagination, is nearly synonymous with "pedophile") is an attempt to distance him from the party, but Foley is still a gay man, belonging to a class of person regularly reviled and disenfranchised by Republicans since at least the 1970s. The hope may be that the pall of pedophilia will overshadow the fact that, once again, another homosexual has been found "on the inside." As the *Washington Post*'s Eugene Robinson noted, "the recruitment myth helps explain why social conservatives, who make up the most loyal and energetic segment of the Republican Party base, are so up in arms" (par. 11). The other kinds of recruitment at work among Republicans and conservatives that Foleygate made manifest will be discussed in the following section. Before moving on, however, it seems only responsible to think through the wider currency, in venues beyond the Far and New Right, of the conjoined myths of homosexual recruitment and homosexual-as-pedophile.

More than simply a redoubtable heavy of the Right, recruitment surfaces in mainstream political discussions and journalism of Foley's misconduct, albeit in subdued, comparatively benevolent forms. The bogeyman of recruitment—the repressive and imprecise slippage it permits between pedophile, predator, and homosexual—exercises considerable power, too, over journalists and activists, gay and straight. Gay activist John Aravosis, founder of Americablog, has been relentless in outing or focusing media attention on closeted gay Republicans such as Jeff Gannon and Mary Cheney. Yet when covering Foley, Aravosis perfunctorily refers to him as a "child sex predator" (par. 6). By the laws Foley himself shepherded through committee, Foley qualifies as a predator, but not of children. This inexactness risks the collapse of the very categories (pedophile, sexual predator, and homosexual) that gay activists have struggled for decades to convey the true differences between. Denis Dison, vice president of the Gay and Lesbian Victory Fund and Leadership Institute, reacting to the claim that Republicans failed to reprimand Foley earlier out of political correctness, commits a similar slip: "It's an absurd notion to say that the leadership is so afraid of offending gay people that they'd let a child predator stay in office, while they aren't afraid of trying to amend the Constitution" (qtd. in Epstein par. 18). With similar imprecision, Craig Bowman, executive director of the National Youth Advocacy Coalition (for GLBT youth), categorizes Foley's behavior as being "like that of a predator, who should be arrested and prosecuted for his criminal behavior. . . . Some may believe this is a gay issue. It is not. This is an issue about protecting children from those who seek to do them harm. It should be a priority for our country. Somehow it seems to have gotten lost" ("Congressional Page Scandal" pars. 22–23). In light of the historic—and for, those such as James Dobson and Tony Perkins, the continued—homophobic characterizations of gays as predatory pedophiles, it makes sense that gays would want to distance themselves from these associations and, by doing so, refute the idea of recruitment. To borrow Bowman's language, however, "what's getting lost" is not merely the crisis of online sexual predation of children (this was, after all, a legislatively targeted issue). Rather, when one relies on the word *predator*, even for antihomophobic purposes, one risks the historic, lingering slippage between homosexuality and pedophilia—a slippage one has no sure way of averting or, despite decades of activism, definitively uncoupling.

When a social conservative such as Peter LaBarbera, speaking to the Christian Newswire, carps that "'gay activists' ridicule anyone [such as Dobson, Perkins, or himself] who suggests that there is a predatory component to male homosexuality," obviously LaBarbera's intent in using *predator* differs from that of Aravosis, Dison, or Bowman (qtd. in "Congressional Page Scandal" par. 15). My point is that, given the recalcitrance of homophobic rhetoric, our best efforts to combat, resist, and transform it are only made more difficult by promulgating the predatory—and, on some level, fundamentally homophobic—image evoked by pedophilia and recruitment. E. J. Dionne, similarly well intentioned, argues for antihomophobic liberals to embrace and recuperate "family values" rhetoric. Dionne would rehabilitate the notion of "saving the children" from its current right-wing inflection: namely, defending children from the swarm of predatory forces (perverts, pornographers, pro-choice advocates, homosexuals) whose chief priority is the destruction of innocence. By contrast, Dionne intones, "I am a married father of three, and that's more important to me than the fact that I am a liberal. Our kids matter infinitely more to my wife and me than the results of an election, even an election we both care a lot about" (par. 6). What Dionne seems to undervalue is the intimate connection between recent Republican-dominated presidential and congressional elections and the political culture that installed and shielded Foley. The election Dionne finds less important than "our kids" is, in part, what condoned and constituted a threat to them. Attempting to reappropriate "family values" language, to drain from it the homophobic ichor with which the Right has filled it, is an admirable endeavor. But simply adopting that language, aping its very terms and totems (safeguarding children, the domestic), does little to defuse or transform it. Dionne is right to note that "[m]isbehavior and irresponsibility by married heterosexuals"—even though Foley is unmarried and gay—"do far more damage to families and children" than same-sex marriage (par. 12). Still, the enmity "family values" rhetoric carries, at its core, toward gays and lesbians—a cultural animosity not diluted simply by permitting same-sex couples inside the picket fence—indicates the care to be taken, even when discussing "obvious" perversion, particularly when the same cognitive structures have been (and still are) wielded against other nonnormative or socially abject populations.[19]

Another nonnormative population whose sexuality the Foleygate coverage effectively silences is that of adolescents. Part of the trouble is that, for LaBarbera and company, teen sexuality itself is problematic. Even though it makes little sense to declare that something as arbitrary as a birthday categorically enables one, suddenly, to understand or "process" sex in a way one had been unable to do before (all the more arbitrary since the age of majority varies cross-culturally), that is precisely LaBarbera's argument. And I suspect that even those who dismiss his homophobia would be unwilling to question his account of preadult sexuality. For it is a culturally pervasive one, almost universally so. For gays, the discomfort occasioned by Foley is that of being associated not just with an old gay stereotype (the pedophile) but with the forces of darkness an embattled heteronormativity can blame for deflowering its children. As Donald Hall observes, although feminists and queer theorists have done much to problematize distinctions between "the natural" and "the unnatural" as socially constructed rather than essential, few activists and writers (other than Guy Hocquenghem, Gayle Rubin, and Pat Califa) have dared tackle the topic of "sex with and among minors" (106). Hall continues,

> the field of queer theorization has generally avoided issues of age-of-consent laws and intergenerational desire, and perhaps for understandable reasons. Even with the protection of "tenure" and the shield of "academic freedom," queer theorists are usually employed by institutions—often publicly funded universities—that put many forms of overt and covert pressure on them to avoid discussing topics that might engender hysterical (often media-driven) public reactions. And even if that pressure is not palpable, certain silences exist that simply derive from the internalization among even self-styled "queer" academics of broader social designations of the acceptable and the unacceptable. (106)

Implicit in Hall's gesture toward "broader social designations" is the heterosexual authorship of those designations. Part of the added shock factor in this case is the age of Foley's inamorati—shocking because their proximity to the age of consent troubles a rather prelapsarian narrative that not only equates sex with corruption and knowledge with the death of innocence but that locates heterosexuality as the *fons et origo* of human civilization. The readiness with which even gay-sympathetic straights, in discussing Foley, fell back on the pedophile narrative marks how viscerally heterosexuals, regardless of their feelings about homosexuality, cringe before the bogeymen of intergenerational sex and teen eroticism. Perhaps because these kinds of sex hit too close to home by threatening to eroticize members of the nuclear family other than the parents, to wrest control over erotic knowledge from parental authority, sexual ideation or activity among minors can be perceived only as precocity and therefore as violative, a sign of corruption that has to come, predator-like, from without. We might well apply Richard Mohr's conclusions in "The Pedophilia of Everyday Life" to not just children but to teens, to any preadult individual:

> In light of the current cultural view that sexual interest in children flows only from, is contingent solely on, the mind of the pedophile, for anyone to admit that he or she has any frisson at all from looking at children is necessarily to be branded as deviant. Were society to allow itself to articulate that it does have sexual interests in children—little adults are not sexy, but innocence and purity are—society would have met the enemy and seen that he is us.
>
> ... America's hysteria over kiddie porn [or pedophilia] ... is not simply the result of the country's epicyclical prudishness about matters sexual. Rather, it is the result of our general worries about purity, innocence, and identity—who we are. Childhood—the social concept—cannot do the moral work society created it to do.... [T]o serve as an ethical prop and security blanket, we have created a moral museum of innocence and purity—our Eden—and we have labeled it *childhood.* (29)

Preadult sexuality qualifies as yet another "queer" (as in not yet normalized) kind of sexuality screened off, along with homosexuality, in discussions of Foleygate.

Thus, it is not simply the Grand Guignol fantasies of Dobson and his kind we should be worried about. The outwardly sympathetic exertions can tug, intentionally or in panicked reflex, on more brutal filaments, loosening the tether in one place only to cinch it tighter at unanticipated junctures. More concretely, inasmuch as the Right, along with a cooperative, corporatized media, has normalized homophobia in public discourse by voicing it as a defense of liberal individualism, "[h]omophobic forces now tend to avoid blatant genocidal language in favor of pseudodemocratic denunciations of 'special rights' of lesbians and gay men" (Anna Marie Smith, "Why Did Armey Apologize?" 152). One potential danger, then, of outwardly compassionate exertions, even by nonhomophobes, is their proximity to, and potential for subsiding into, the New-Right form of tolerance, that is, homophobia in tolerant clothing. Smith emphasizes that the Right's "pseudotolerant gestures" don't just speak "recod[ed]" "intolerant discourse" to their base; such gestures "transfor[m] the entire political terrain . . . threatening to obliterate the few remaining progressive moments of the liberal democratic tradition" (168–69). Without overstating the case (as ideological determinism), it's safe to say that tolerance by individuals does not negate the ambient cultural hatred fed by the Right's homophobic efforts, efforts that also encourage the disassociation of individuals from their intolerance by seeing it as free-floating or as justified by liberal democratic principles. This is not to say that tolerance is not discursively or materially possible, for individuals or even institutions. But the odds are not in its favor.

It's hardly my intent to suggest sympathy for Foley, but rather to recommend considering the resemblance between the panoply of cultural and rhetorical energies leveraged against Foley and those so often brought to bear against queers—in this case, gays as well as teenagers. Ostracizing an ephebophile in order to keep the name of the gay community unsullied should not be done in terms still pullulating with homophobia. Otherwise, one is engaging in another negative externality, ignoring the boundaries that, although one might imagine having passed or transcended them, still exist—boundaries that marginalize in ways often as impoverishing as they are generative.

Pulpits, Porn, and the Colonized Closet

If the specter of gay recruitment helps shore up heterosexuals' sense of their own naturalness and centrality, it also distracts one from the recruitment practiced by Republicans and social conservatives themselves. What Foleygate exposes, potentially more detrimental to the moral credibility of the GOP, is its own penchant for—one might even say, dependence on—recruitment. If heterosexuality incessantly recruits, hawks its ideology, its benefits (material, symbolic, and imagined), it's to be expected that other ambitious entities such as the conservative/Republican movement would follow suit. Recent outings suggest that the Right is recruiting gays—or if they are not actively recruiting them, they might as well be. If Foley seems, on one level, just another gay Republican who got caught, when coupled with the outings of Jeff Gannon, Ted Haggard, Matt Sanchez, and Larry Craig, Foleygate raises the question of what draws queers to the Republican Party, or, rather, how conservative ideology itself recruits queers.[20]

After the spate of outings, just in the past five years, of closeted gay Republicans (see page 99 for a partial list), one might well wonder how many more "pink elephants" or "homocons"[21] (that is, homosexual conservatives) are hiding in the darker corners of the big tent or, on the contrary, standing front and center as the party's antigay ringmasters. Foleygate, rather coincidentally, brought attention to other gay "insiders," such as congressional aides Jeff Trandhal and Kirk Fordham, high up in the power structure, poised (if they wished) to influence opinion (as the gay Mormon clerk to Supreme Court justice Byron White did in 1986, canvassing other justices to ensure an antigay verdict in *Bowers v. Hardwick*). Among the outings from 2004–2005, the most salacious has to be that of Jeff Gannon/Jeff Guckert, the gay escort and Republican shill who, although he ran a partisan mouthpiece Web site (Talon News), was given weekly passes to attend White House press conferences in order to lob soft, often anti-Democratic questions at White House press secretary Scott McClellan. But the outings weren't over. The midterm elections of 2006 were immediately preceded and soon followed by scandals surrounding two more homocons—one influential, though unknown to many Americans; the other hardly a key player, but intimately familiar to consumers of gay pornography.

Less than a week before the midterm election, gay escort Michael Jones alleged that Pastor Ted Haggard, leader of the fourteen-thousand-member New Life Church in Colorado Springs, Colorado, had been paying him for sex on a monthly basis for the past three years. Jones also said Haggard had given him money to buy crystal meth, which Haggard then used. Though he publicly denied all charges at first, Haggard resigned his post after a private meeting with church overseers where he confessed to "sexually immoral conduct" with Jones (Plunkett and Gorski par. 6). Haggard was not just any minister, however, nor just another peccant evangelical on the pattern of Jimmy Swaggart or Jim Bakker. As president of the National Association of Evangelicals, "a 30-million member 'para-church' organization,'" Haggard participated in regular White House conference calls in which Bush conferred with evangelical leaders on matters of policy, and, in 2005, *Time* included Haggard in its list of the twenty-five most influential evangelicals ("Evangelical Leader Admits" par. 1). Jones, the escort, said he came forward after seeing Haggard (who had used the alias "Art") on television and learning of his real identity. A factor in Jones's decision to go public, he said, was Haggard's vocal support for proposed Colorado Amendment 43, which would define marriage as heterosexual.[22] Despite his regular sexual encounters with Jones, Haggard stayed true to a certain stereotype of evangelicals, regularly denouncing homosexuality in his sermons.

A comparably minor player next to Haggard, Matt Sanchez experienced a much more accelerated rise in, and fall from, the right-wing firmament. On December 4, 2006, the *New York Post* printed an op-ed piece in which, Sanchez, a thirty-six-year-old Columbia University student and U.S. Marine reservist, claimed that in fall 2005 a member of the International Socialist Organization, an antiwar student group, had ridiculed his military service and called him a "baby killer."[23] In January 2007, Sanchez was booked on conservative talk shows including *Hannity & Colmes* and *The O'Reilly Factor* (Rupert Murdoch owns both FOX and the *New York Post*), "where he received praise for coming forward and complaining about his treatment at the hands of Columbia's 'radical anti-military students'" (Joe par. 1). Sanchez was further lionized at the March 2007 Conservative Political Action Committee (CPAC) conference, where he received the first Jeanne Kirkpatrick Academic Freedom Award for his bravery in standing up to what, according to conservatives such as David Horowitz, is the oppressive liberal bias of American higher education. This was the same CPAC conference where Ann Coulter infamously referred to presidential hopeful John Edwards as a "faggot"[24]; Coulter also gleefully posed for a photo-op with the hunky Sanchez. Yet Sanchez's right-wing accolades were soon tarnished by revelations about his "lengthy career in gay porn, working under the names Rod Majors and Pierre LaBranche, starring in such art films as *Jawbreaker*, *Donkey Dick*, and *Glory Holes of Fame 3*, where his '11-inch uncut monster cock'"—that's porn inches, of course—"earned him a devoted following" (Joe par. 2). Apparently, Sanchez's television appearances triggered his outing: bloggers Joe (of *Joe My God*) and Tom Bacchus began to receive e-mail from gay men who found something oddly familiar about Corporal Matt Sanchez, even though in his previous on-camera appearances he routinely wore less clothing and rarely discussed politics. Conservatives largely defended the outed Sanchez, crying invasion of privacy—a laughable claim on behalf of an advertising gay escort and a performer in over thirty porn movies for most of the major gay studios, including Titan, Falcon, Catalina, and Kristen Bjorn.[25]

Unlike Haggard or Foley, the former star of *Tijuana Toilet Tramps* took to the Internet—the tool that made his exposure so easy—to answer his critics. Claiming that "any putative gayness" was in his past, Sanchez sophistically offered a summary of long-term relationships—"Boyfriends: 0; fiancées: 2; wife: 1"—as evidence of his long-term heterosexuality (Wilcox par. 6). The ci-devant porn star spoke out on his own blog and on *Salon.com*, denouncing his adult film career as both spiritually bankrupt and completely irrelevant to his current politics:

> I don't like porn, it reduces the mind, flattens the soul. That's not hypocrisy talking, that's experience. If I started off with liberal leanings, being on a gay porn set should have been heaven. In porn, everything is trivialized and everything trivial is projected. How does a conservative trace his roots to such distasteful beginnings? Like all followers of a cult, it's tough to figure out when you stopped believing in the party-line, but I can tell you by the time I finished my summer tour of the major studios, I was pretty disgusted with myself. It was an emotional low. . . . Why did I become a conservative? Just look at what I left, and look at who is attacking me today? [*sic*] Let's face it people, you're all cynical enough to know that if I had espoused liberal causes, spoken out against the military, got a liberal award for courage and then outed with a porn-past, you'd be clamoring for my memoir, and nominating me for a diversity ticket with Barack Obama. Instead those who complain about wire-tapping reserve the right to eavesdrop on my private life for political brownie points. Sure, I took a picture with Ann Coulter, I don't endorse what she said, but anyone in the military

> would defend her right to say it. I realize that sounds prohibitively phony, but gee it's really true! (par. 6)

Aside from Sanchez foreshortening his porn career to the span of a single, misguided summer (his films appeared throughout the 1990s), his claiming invasion of privacy is insultingly disingenuous. Sanchez had sex on camera for film companies with international distribution. He posted his escort ads, complete with nude pictures, prices, and contact information, on the Internet. It was hardly necessary to resort to "eavesdrop[ping]," as Sanchez hyperbolizes, to discover what he omitted from his political curriculum vitae. In both cases, Sanchez willingly forfeited his right to privacy by stepping into the marketplace. Furthermore, for Sanchez to support Coulter's right to use homophobic slurs is not "phony," as he puts it, but rather a hollow gesture. In the military culture of "Don't Ask, Don't Tell," under which discharges for homosexuality have actually increased, Sanchez could hardly object.[26]

As enjoyably ribald as all this may be, it's only fair to point out that Sanchez's past in and of itself is not the issue. Anyone has the right to change his career or his beliefs. Making porn is a legal endeavor (prostitution is not, but, illegality aside, can be a consensual act). What's most shocking about this episode is not what Sanchez did for a living (although the still photos gay blogger Tom Bacchus posted from Sanchez's films and escort ads are not for the erotically sheltered) but instead that, as with Jeff Gannon and Mark Foley, the GOP has found itself in bed with someone whose behavior or identity it habitually crusades against. Journalist Max Blumenthal no doubt speaks for many sensible Americans when, writing for the *Huffington Post*, he puzzles over the involvement of Sanchez with a vocally antigay party:

> There is of course nothing wrong with Sanchez being a gay porn star or a male escort. His past is only notable because he chose to join a movement that exploits anti-gay sentiment for political gain. Coulter's now-famous "faggot" remark was not an aberration, but rather a symbol of the politics of resentment that propels the conservative movement and its elected Republican surrogates; a reflection of the bigotry conservatives have sought to write into the Constitution through the so-called Federal Marriage Amendment. (par. 7)

The counterfactual Sanchez proposes (that a liberal peacenik with a porn star past would be feted by liberals as he himself was by CPAC) is an unconvincing polemic feint. Many liberals might well shy away from making a porn star their political poster child, even if he was antiwar. But an adult film actor being drawn to liberal causes would not be as puzzling as the current turn of events. It's not that a porn star can't be conservative. Sexuality need have no deliberate connection to other facets of one's being. But even if Sanchez is not gay (many gay porn stars claim to be straight, though fewer make this claim now than in decades past), he is at least bisexual—whether by the Kinsey scale or by virtue of his intimate, albeit commercialized, connection to men. What Blumenthal, myself, and others find objectionable and perplexing is not Sanchez's past. It's that a man who has been erotically intimate with men (even if, some of the time, for money), who has socialized with gay men as escorts and strippers do, could sign on, without a qualm, to a vociferously homophobic organization. Not only has the GOP's moral centerpiece for the past decade been a crusade to save civilization from the clutches of pedophilic, sexually predatory homosexuals, Sanchez was embraced by those who, were he not saying what they wanted to hear, would have called him a "faggot," too. Likewise, whom Ted Haggard chooses to have sex with is, finally, his own business. What's perplexing is that, while regularly having gay sex, he not only denounced homosexuality from the pulpit but used his position of influence to campaign for antigay state legislation. In the passage from Sanchez's blog quoted above, the former Rod Majors opines that porn "reduces the mind [and] flattens the soul." One might say the same for any party line—especially one that, like party lines espoused by many social conservatives, evangelicals, and Republicans, flattens human nature by ruling certain kinds of intimacy as being out of bounds, that reduces any who diverge from certain norms to monstrous stereotypes, unworthy of basic dignities and rights.

Why, then, does the Republican Party appear to be full of homosexuals? What is it about the Republican Party or about conservatism, as opposed to more liberal groups and philosophies, that attracts men like Foley, Sanchez, Haggard, and Gannon? Are they drawn by a sheer sense of ideological as well as material power? Or does a party that wears its disdain for gays and lesbians on its collective sleeve seem like the perfect hiding place, the last place one would expect to find queers? One is tempted to speculate that gays and lesbians drawn to a group that openly denigrates them must be self-loathing on some level, or, to be less pejorative, deeply conflicted. How else is one to explain the number of gay Republicans and conservatives who foment hatred by advocating or implementing queer disenfranchisement and discrimination, or who, in silent or vocal complicity, work for the judges and politicians who do so?

In *Gay Conservatives: Group Consciousness and Assimilation* (2007), sociologist Kenneth Cimino tries to answer some of these questions. In order to discover why "conservative LGBTs might join political groups that not only do not support [pro-LGBT] policies . . . but also . . . advocate prejudicial policies and make statements that are actively detrimental to the LGBT community," Cimino looks at attitudes toward GLBT issues, activism, and discrimination among gays and lesbians of varied educational background and economic and relationship status (1). Although it appears from Cimino's data that conservative GLBTs are among the minority (in a 2002 Kaiser Foundation survey, 7 percent identified as conservative compared to 66 percent identifying as liberal), two conclusions Cimino draws about the group consciousness of gay conservatives are of interest here. Gay conservatives tend, for various reasons, not to see themselves as part of the gay and lesbian community or movement, inasmuch as the latter is perceived (rightly or wrongly) to comprise predominantly liberal activists committed to a marginal perspective and agitation for greater government protection. Though gay conservatism in America has roots going back at least to the Mattachine Society in the 1950s, a swell of gay conservatism occurred "in the early 1990s [when] a small group of LGBT conservatives and libertarians," including Andrew Sullivan and Bruce Bawer, "rebel[led] against 'queer theory'" and the confrontational activism of groups such as Queer Nation.[27] Those such as Bawer and Sullivan argued

> that LGBTs must begin to live in the "real world" and accept the dominant culture of heterosexuals. Hence, the "assimilationists" started a campaign to normalize homosexual behavior and present a better image to heterosexual society. The LGBT needed to get out of the "Disneyland" of the urban ghetto and try to assimilate. Thus, in their view, it was LGBT similarities, not differences, with heterosexuals that are important. (Cimino 45)

Gay conservatives are likely to be sympathetic to complaints such as Bawer's (that some gay men's promiscuity and flamboyance are responsible for perpetuating negative stereotypes) and advice such as Sullivan's (that if queers assimilate to heterosexual norms of dress and behavior, straights will be less offended and more tolerant). Demographically, Cimino concludes that, despite a diversity of opinion among conservative gays regarding their political beliefs, core issues, and relationship to the gay community, most "conservative LGBTs do not see a need to group identify with their sexual identity and identify [instead] with some other variable . . . such as class and social and/or economic status" (Cimino 85). Loyalties to group identities other than a homosexual one are coupled, generally, with a failure to see one's primary identity as gay, a failure to consider oneself—or gays and lesbians—as significantly marginalized, oppressed, or discriminated against. Far from advocating that one has to be "into the gay scene" (to borrow the phrase used mainly by those gays who aren't), it's my position that it is only ethical for a member of a marginalized minority such as queers—even if unaffiliated, alienated, and/or repulsed by the gay community or some aspect(s) of gay subculture—to identify, at least politically, with a larger queer community, even if that community is a patchwork, a unity reified for strategic purposes. Michael Warner, in *The Trouble with Normal*, has argued—even more strongly—that it is unethical and hazardous not to identify in such a way, to refuse identification in an attempt to barter for social respectability and political clout.

In seeking to better comprehend the processes of gay conservative identity formation, we might turn to Angela Dillard's *Guess Who's Coming to Dinner* Now?: *Multicultural Conservatism in America* (2001). For delineating the motivations of gay (in addition to a variety of other kinds of unexpected) conservatives, Dillard points us to Hannah Arendt's "perspective on the efficacy of group consciousness," in particular, Arendt's distinction between the parvenu and the pariah. "Parvenu" is Arendt's term for minority individuals who "ape the mannerisms of the majority culture in order to be accepted" (Dillard 124). Black, Latino, or gay conservatives, for example, often defend assimilation based on the claim that identifying primarily as American allows them to connect to the myth of American prosperity and liberal individualism in a way that—according to the "conservative critique of group consciousness"—identifying as black, Latino, or gay supposedly does not. Identifying on bases other than nationality (race, ethnicity, sexuality) is seen by the parvenu as selfish loyalty to a special interest, a fragmentary identity that both disconnects one from other Americans and undermines national unity. For Arendt, however, this "form of assimilation" "entail[s] distance from one's origins" and "inevitably obscures political realities" (Dillard 124). Arendt is writing about Jews and anti-Semitism, but her explication of the "'politically naive'" nature of such assimilation seems more than apt in describing the consequences of assimilation for any stigmatized minority:

> No assimilation could be achieved merely by surrendering one's past but ignoring the alien past. In a society on the whole hostile to Jews . . . it is possible to assimilate *only by assimilating to anti-Semitism also.* If one wishes to be a normal person precisely like everybody else, there is scarcely any alternative to exchanging old prejudices for new ones. If that is not done, one involuntarily becomes a rebel . . . and remains a Jew. And if one really assimilates, taking all the consequences of denial of one's own origin and cutting oneself off from those who have not or have not yet done it, one becomes a scoundrel. (qtd. in Dillard 125)

In Dillard's gloss on Arendt, assimilation—valuing the "'senseless freedom of the individual' at the expense of the group"—"damag[es] not only . . . the individual but also the group or culture the individual seeks to escape. . . . If assimilation means identification with a culture which is not just American but also racist and homophobic, the *pariah*, by contrast, embraces his identity as 'the outsider, the outcast, the marginal'" (125, 124). Viewing gay conservatives, then, as parvenus avoids the insulting imputation of "false consciousness": far from being tricked into acting against what seem, to others, his best interests, the queer parvenu appears to sincerely believe that majority (that is, heterosexual) interests are his best interests. As Arendt bluntly insists, though, the parvenu has chosen to adopt "an alien past" as his own: the past of a culture that is alien to the parvenu precisely because it views him as the alien, because it has a long history of antipathy toward his kind, no matter how congenial he may think or wish that history to be. By this logic, for gays to assimilate is by definition to become, at least in some measure, conservative, closeted, homophobic.

In another attempt to fathom the proliferation of gay conservatives, Max Blumenthal, in his coverage of the CPAC conference featuring Sanchez and Coulter, proposes a personality type—"CCC," or "Conflicted Conservative in Crisis"—to describe conservatives such as Ann Coulter and Matt Sanchez who often act against their ostensible self-interest as women, people of color, or homosexuals (par. 12). CCC's "act aggressively toward groups they privately identify with, such as sexual minorities or independent women," but are "simultaneously submissive to those who might otherwise persecute them" (par. 13). Coulter, who trumpets the sanctity of marriage but "has had three broken engagements [and] has never been married,"

> assiduously cultivated the approval of James Dobson, an anti-feminist demagogue who advocates "women's submission"; Sanchez enlisted in the Marines, then joined the right's campus culture war; and Haggard inveighed against homosexuality from the pulpit. These CCC's scurried away from freedom for the tight confines of an authoritarian movement. For CCC's, backlash politics is a crude form of therapy. (par. 13)

Yet what looks, from a liberal or moderate angle, like a glaring conflict of interest does not bother many gay Republicans: "'You learn to compartmentalize really well,' said one Republican strategist who, like most gay Republicans interviewed [for a story in the *New York Times*], would speak only anonymously for fear of adversely affecting his career" (Leibovich par. 13). This sentiment, though perhaps not representative of all gay conservatives, would seem to call for a model beyond simply identification with "class and social or economic status" to the exclusion of sexuality (as Cimino suggests), a model, rather, that encompasses nested levels of incongruous or antagonistic affiliations, between which conflict is acknowledged (and perhaps grieved) but actively ignored.

An alternative explanation is that the gay Republican isn't ignoring conflict. What if he feels unconflicted not because he fails to acknowledge the contradiction of loyalty to a group that villainizes him but, rather, because he doesn't care? What if he's aware of the conflict, yet his conservative beliefs hold fast despite the homophobia enunciated by many conservatives? A model that goes some way toward explaining this state of mind comes from Slavoj Žižek's *The Object of Ideology*, which Anna Marie Smith draws on in *New Right Discourse* to account for the ability of any political subject to maintain beliefs that are demonstrably irrational or contradictory. Smith's interpretation of Žižek elucidates the important difference between "false consciousness" (for Žižek, an improper and insulting diagnosis) and misidentification:

> Contradictory identifications with political discourses are not incoherent performances by inadequately rational individuals who require the intervention of a privileged knower—the intellectual, the party,

> and so on—to straighten out their allegiance. . . . With Žižek . . . all political identifications are structured in terms of a fundamental cynicism: "the cynical subject is quite aware of the distance between the ideological mask and the social reality, but [she] none the less still insists upon the mask." . . . The cynical subject already knows the falsehood behind the truth claims and is already well aware that particular interests are being represented as universal interests, but she still refuses to renounce the claims.
>
> . . . Instead of proposing an elitist schema in which the privileged knower detects the contradictions within the masses' discourse, Žižek insists that we pay attention to the unconscious dimension of political discourse. The subject's deep investment in hegemonic discourse cannot be weakened by a straightforward appeal to her conscious rationality. We might show her that certain racist and homophobic claims are utterly untrue; she might still respond, "well, even so, I still think that affirmative action for blacks has gone too far, lesbians should not be allowed to be parents, gay men with AIDS ought to be quarantined" and so on. . . . The force of a hegemonic discourse lies not in its actual content, but in its form. . . . Political subjects become cynical supporters, because, at an unconscious level, they crave the order, or at least the "minimum of consistency," which the hegemonic project introduces into an otherwise chaotic political terrain. As long as alternative political projects remain stigmatized as incoherent and illegitimate, the subject's investment in the hegemonic project's order will stand firm regardless of her contradictory policy preferences. (*New Right Discourse* 37–38)

Žižek's innovation in this instance is to read the Lacanian "mirror stage" politically:

> The Lacanian conception of (mis-)identification should not be read as yet another type of false consciousness theory. The Lacanian point is that *all* identifications with political discourses are mis-identifications. Every political discourse holds out a false promise of resolving dislocation in favor of total coherence; in Lacanian terms, they catch social fragments up in the "lure" of an orderly society when of course their perfect fantasies and totalistic imaginaries can never be fully realized. (Smith, *New Right Discourse* 39)

Žižek's model allows us to make sense of how the gay Republican makes sense of his own position. Through misidentification, the hegemonic discourse (in this case, Republican ideology) promises the gay conservative subject an orderliness to his world that cannot be undermined by that ideology's homophobic elements and incarnations. One might say, then, that gay Republicans are not so much compartmentalizing as prioritizing. According to Žižek, however, that's par for being a political subject, regardless of one's sexuality.

That being said, Žižek's theory of political misidentification fails to take into account the particular circumstances of the closeted political subject. A Republican may remain faithful to the GOP despite specific inconsistencies or scandals, but the conflict lies in most such cases outside the subject: this politician or that policy, and not the subject himself, straying from the overarching ideology. In the gay Republican's case, by contrast, there's an added internal conflict, for he himself contravenes the party line—in his sexual desires and acts, in his very sensibility. And he does so secretly. He actively harbors that which, ideologically, he abhors. Perhaps that secret is what drives the gay Republican. After all, who could execrate the enemies of the Right more genuinely than one of its enemies? Who could hate more authentically than one who knows more intimately than his fellows what it is he avows hatred for, because he is what they hate? If a gay conservative makes, oddly, for a more dedicated conservative, Žižek also clarifies the centrality of the homocon to conservative political ideology. If all political discourses require some scapegoat to "stitch up the inconsistency of [their] own ideological system[s]" (Žižek 48), it's not simply the case that Republicans espouse gay marginality and erasure. They don't just want gays and lesbians out of sight, hidden. They need them hidden—internally, within the party. Closeted queer Republicans are in a sense necessary to the GOP because they show the work yet to be done, not just out there in the polity but in its most sacred, faithful inner sanctum. If the party itself is contaminated, the expunging of homosexuality takes on an even more violent urgency. By the same token, that work can never be fully accomplished. The Right might soften the edges of its homophobia, but the end of homosexual demonization would deprive the Right of one its most energizing nuclei. Debunking this or that homophobic myth has no effect on a right-wing subject's conviction that homosexuality threatens society in some more general (often unenunciated) way. The Right's internalization of homosexuality, in the form of the homocon, only strengthens that conviction by rendering concrete the right-wing subject's worst fear: the fear of contamination, the fear of homosexual penetration.

A model that goes still further in elucidating the nuanced terrain of gay conservative identity is afforded by the closet. Eve Sedgwick's cogent theorization of the closet as a contested, culturally endemic representational space may need to be augmented in light of Foleygate and similar scandals. Amid the media punditry surrounding Foley, outrage focused on the Republican leadership's foreknowledge, through complaints and attempts at intervention, of Foley's proclivities. But the explanation lies not solely in partisan incompetence, corruption, or inertia, as journalists and commentators commonly proposed. Not ousting Foley, or not simply removing him from the House Caucus for Missing and Exploited Children, may have merely been a matter of expedience on the Republicans' part. Exposing or censuring Foley might have risked showing up neocons' commitment to the "family values" agenda (and its war on porn, abortion, gay rights, and so on) as little more than lip service required to court wedge-issue voters. It may seem flip to suggest that, in concealing Foley's indiscretions, Republican leaders were also preserving a sort of gay pipeline. Yet my contention is precisely that what the exposure of Foley, like that of Haggard and Sanchez, reveals is the Right's colonization of the closet. In this line of thinking, one might posit Foley's official, "family values" side, his respectable public face, as a sort of Dr. Jekyll figure, and the gay, IMing Foley as Mr. Hyde, the mastermind cloaking his secret vices behind a predator-hunting persona. And yet such an analogy, though colorful, begs the question of agency—a question, problematized by Foleygate, to which we do some disservice if we refer it immediately back to a bifurcated homo/hetero template. What's required is some further articulation of the spaces that are the closet—as well as the spaces that exist within, adjacent to, or askew the closet, that surround or otherwise intersect with it, that obscure, disempower, and/or empower its former or present inhabitants.

Discussions of the closet, both theoretical and pragmatic (if one insists on some difference between these), do well to return to Sedgwick's *The Epistemology of the Closet*, which positions itself explicitly as a prolegomenon to other endeavors in queer studies.[28] Of particular saliency is the idea that the closet is constituted and superintended from without as much as from within, serving as indispensable a diapason of functions for heterosexuals as it does for homosexuality. Queer inquiries, Sedgwick enjoins, should resist "focusing scrutiny on those who inhabit the closet (however equivocally) to the exclusion of those in the ambient heterosexist culture who enjoin it and whose intimate representational needs it serves in a way less extortinate to themselves" (68–69). Foley's peripatetic turns both inside and outside, into and out of, closets of differing transparency illustrate a certain privileged relation to the closet beyond that available to most gays and lesbians. In terms of the closet as a rich site for both punitive and enriching cultural identifications, Sedgwick notes that

> a lot of the energy of attention and demarcation that has swirled around issues of homosexuality since the end of the nineteenth century, in Europe and the United States, has been impelled by the distinctively indicative relation of homosexuality to wider mappings of secrecy and disclosure, and of the private and the public, that were and critically are problematic for the gender, sexual, and economic structures of the heterosexist culture at large, mappings whose enabling but dangerous incoherence has become oppressively, durably condensed in certain figures of homosexuality. The "closet" and "coming out," now verging on all-purpose phrases for the potent crossing and recrossing of almost any politically charged lines of representation, have been the gravest and most magnetic of those features. (*The Epistemology of the Closet* 71)

To apply this to the case at hand, one can say that the differential powers wielded by Foley (as a congressman, the head of a House caucus, and an affluent white man of middle age) allowed him, until ABC released the text of the infamous IMs, to manage a series of identities and milieux—and to do so at his own benefit, without cost to himself, and at varying costs to others. Foley's homosexuality and ephebophilia were fully known to several congressional pages, open secrets to many others in Congress, and closed secrets to his constituents and the general public. But more than political corruption or partisan cynicism, what Foley's unmasking truly reveals is the co-optation of the closet by the forces outside it—here, specifically, by Republican and conservative agencies and their attendant moral impulsions.

The sheer number of gay Republicans discloses the closet's unique dimensional complexity, especially as refracted through the medium of the Internet. Many, if not most, of these homocons are known to be gay by the party higher-ups. No one involved in the story or its media coverage expressed shock over the fact that Trandhal and Fordham, the two staffers involved in covering up Foley's antics, were gay. That wasn't the unwelcome surprise. Within the beltway and other corridors of power, everyone knows who the homosexuals are; the closet is projected outward to the unknowing masses. Thus, the closet from and in which all these Pink Elephants operate really functions more like the "open secret" discussed by Sedgwick: a set of spaces at once transparent and opaque. The gayness of gay Republicans is utterly pellucid to those in the know but indiscernible to the poor suckers out there in the Republic who think the GOP is genuinely dedicated to stopping those slavering, degenerate fags from single-handedly destroying marriage and enlightening kindergartners on the ins and outs of anal sex.

A still more trenchant question might be why Republicans would want to colonize the closet, inasmuch as colonization implies ownership and usurpation. What practical purpose does its annexation serve? If the GOP's operative strategy is the bait and switch—presenting a particular kind of political/cultural face to the world while, in fact, acting in complete contradiction to that persona—then its motivating principle is deception. And doubleness is something a closeted queer knows all about. So if the Republican Party wants at its operational core people who understand all too well the efficacy of deception on a daily (if not hourly) basis, not to mention the prowess to pull off said deception, then it makes absolute sense that it would recruit so many gay men into its ranks. Because (following Cimino) these closet cases primarily identify with groups that are not linked by sexual identity but, instead, by economic status or political affiliation, their loyalty to the party will always trump any loyalty to a "brotherhood" of queens. On some level, the GOP needs closeted queers stage-managing the show because these are the people who know best how to keep the scam running, people whose disdain for all things gay-political ensures that their actions will be directed toward Republican political goals and no others. The cultural ideology of the GOP helps create the closet, but then the party colonizes it, expands it, makes it more luxurious (via the rewards of party loyalty), and turns it into an arm of the political machine. A Republican-colonized closet helps the larger party stay in perpetual motion.

One might go so far as to regard Foley himself as a double bind, an embodiment of the "mechanisms of self-contradictory definition" afforded by the binarisms (homo/hetero, secret/open, private/public, monitor/transgressor) that "provide lasting potentials for powerful manipulation" (Sedgwick, *The Epistemology of the Closet* 10).[29] Viewing the IM session as a closet depends on more than a coincidence of terminology. IMing is also known as "privating," and, in the Internet's early days, online conversations took place in chat rooms. The IM session's equivocal properties resemble those of the closet: differently closed and open, private and public. IM sessions, as Foley discovered, are erratically not within one's control in consequential ways: by virtue of the IMer's consent to the terms and conditions stipulated by America Online, Yahoo!, or Microsoft, one's "private" conversations and personas are, from the start, corporate property, subject to subpoena and disclosure. Likewise, what happens inside the closet is steadily subject to exposure, the closet subject to control by what lies outside it. Questions requiring further analysis remain—questions with implications beyond Foleygate (and, within other contexts, necessarily different answers)—such as the nature of online fantasy and its relation to one's "being" or identity. Is chatting a form of play that impinges on, or expresses part of, the self, or not? Without proposing that Foley was playing the *role* of a middle-aged man lusting after young men on the cusp of majority (an argument Foley's defenders surprisingly didn't make), I'm suggesting that the vectored relation of online personalities to one's (admittedly equally malleable) "actual" self acquires a heightened state of interest and political consequence in regard to the closet.[30]

It is in the context of theorizing the closet that Sanchez's and Foley's claims on behalf of privacy become both flawed and informatively complex. The careers of these two men imply the array of possible functionalities and relationships between the closet and the Internet—a technology that provides multiform ways of rendering, particularizing, and (perhaps most importantly for closeted conservatives) compartmentalizing the self far beyond those previously available in conventional social settings. Sedgwick's evocation of the "the imponderable and convulsive" "geographies" of the "glass closet" are apropos not simply to "open secret[s]" such as Foley's but to the as yet incompletely articulated links and quantum leaps that prevail, with Heisenbergian uncertainty, between the closet, chat/IMing, and social, sexual, and online identities (80).[31] Both in terms of Foley's having already been outed in 2003 and in terms of the putative privacy of an IM session, the glass closet might be said to consist of at least two closets, one within and transverse to the other. Similarly, for Sanchez, one might look productively at the assumed and actual optics of the glass porn set; for Haggard, the glass pulpit. For it's not just that claims by these men of privacy invasion are ludicrous; it's that these ludicrous claims are empowered by a conservative ideology that makes starkly inequitable claims about sexual privacy based on one's relationship to the closet. What other state of affairs than the Republican colonization of the closet could account for the ability of the right-wing, on the one hand, to regard having gay sex on film intended for commercial distribution as private and, on the other hand (in *Bowers v. Hardwick*), to deem the unfilmed, private sexual behavior of other gay men as failing to qualify for the same protection as gay Republicans or heterosexuals—deserving, instead, vilification, disenfranchisement, and even extermination. As much as IM chat personas offer a degree of anonymity and free play especially genial to queer theory's dedication to the abrasion of norms, the Internet provides a closet in its creative as well as pernicious capabilities: a defensive, even nurturing, shelter from deleterious cultural forces, but also an imperfectly negotiable space that can, like the closet, shield the originators and conduits of those very potencies. The "power of our enemies over us" that, according to Sedgwick, the closet enables—the leverage of "ignorances" and opacities that, far from true ignorance, are "produced by and correspond to particular knowledges" (*The Epistemology of the Closet* 7–8)—is not quite fully sufficient as an explanation in theorizing the closet's right-wing colonization. Here opacities and ignorances are not just being trained on or pointed into the closet from the outside but, in addition, are issuing out of it—wielded at those not in it by those (in greater or smaller measure) still hiding inside.

It would seem that Republicans have not, then, so much colonized the closet as they've erected and owned it from the start. The string of outings of multiple Republican and conservative figures—which one would expect to produce moments of irrecoverable chagrin—seems to have made little more than a dent in the Right's ability to woo constituents. Foley and Haggard are exposed as precisely the type of scabrous debauchee they and their morality-hawking colleagues have made careers, followings, and sometimes fortunes execrating, yet the ideological edifice whose cornerstone is the evil of homosexuality stands unshaken, solidly square on its righteous plinth. More often than not, response from conservatives is not disgust or outrage that the unclean has infiltrated the temple, but pity for a tortured soul or sorrow over violated privacy. An occupation such as porn star, which would be denigrated or titillating in other contexts, is defended—as long as the porn star has hitched his wagon to the elephantine star. Belief in the tenets of homophobia and the spotless moral justification of conservatism never seems to falter. Of course, this is how ideologies survive, by being more durable than their embodiments, instruments, and emanations. Also, embarrassed parties reflexively close ranks, repudiating the scandalized or their attackers but never their principles. While it might be consoling to think this exoneration is knowingly hypocritical on the part of party leaders, pundits, or everyday citizens, the opposite may, dispiritingly, be nearer to the truth.

Senator Larry Craig's arrest in June 2007 for soliciting sex from a male undercover policeman in a public restroom in the Minneapolis airport launched a spate of jokes when the story was made public in August, yet the incident failed to spawn the same moral posturing as Foleygate—despite Craig's antigay congressional voting record. After an initial bluster of outrage by politicians and reporters, and after Craig's promise to resign from office, Republicans were surprisingly quiet when in October Craig changed his mind and announced he would not step down. Maybe Republicans sensed that further discussion would only draw attention to the kind of story for which the party had received too much attention already. Perhaps Craig's arrest failed to generate prolonged media attention because, unlike Foley, his homosexuality could not be linked to pedophilia—a sad reflection on media homophobia, unconscious or not. But Craig fundamentally is no different than Foley or Haggard: a gay Republican denying his homosexuality ("I'm not gay. I don't do those kind of things") in the face of a history of having sex with men (qtd. in Daly par. 3). Six months after his arrest, when the scandal seemed to have faded, the Idaho *Statesman* reported on eight men who claimed they "had sex with . . . Craig or were targets of sexual advances by [him] at various times during his political career" ("Paper: 8 Men Claim Encounters with Craig" par. 1). As in Foley's case, Craig is a career Republican and a career closet case. That one of the men quoted in the *Statesman* was Mike Jones, the male escort who exposed Ted Haggard, had little impact in this case. Craig plans to stay in office at least until the end of his current term.

Judging by the resilience of Republican homophobia in the face of repeated, seismic embarrassments, as queerly satisfying as their embarrassments may be, the dark likelihood exists that they may not be undone by them, now or ever. For one thing, it's fair to say that, as much as conservatives need the closet, they also need homosexuality. In "Tremble, Hetero Swine!" Cindy Patton proposes that, perhaps to a surprising extent, the relationship between gays and the Right is just as symbiotic as it is antagonistic:

> Both gay and new-right identity operate by invoking parodies of the other; but gay identity frequently also uses the narrative device of "coming out" stories as instructive parables. The new right must cope with these claims to empirical self-understanding; homosexual self-knowledge is reconstructed as a kind of delusion that, in "coming out" and committing itself to the public state, forms positive evidence of perversion for the nonhomosexual, who, as part of his/her reciprocal identity, is capable of "seeing through" the cultural denial of the danger of always present but unacknowledged homosexuality. This maneuver is epistemologically central to the new right's identity claim and situates the new right as able and required to reinstruct a morally lobotomized society that has forgotten the danger of the homosexual.
>
> It is ironic that the new right have seems to have gained power in part in response to the moderate gains of the gay civil rights movement and the increased visibility it has afforded many lesbians and gay

> men. But similarly, the gay movement capitalized on the bold and vicious opposition to it that was generated by a general societal homophobia, even if this strategy and the movement's rhetoric could not erase the reality that violence was exacted on gay people by homophobes, but not the reverse. (144–45)

In the end, this mutual dependency comes down to a sort of reverse recruitment:

> [T]he mutual focus on the new-right/gay-movement oppositional dyad not only helped consolidate the internal identities of each group, but was also used by each to promote general societal *dis*identification with the other: if neither group could reasonably hope to recruit many outsiders to its identity, promoting disidentification produced at least temporary allies. (145)

The closet, then, will continue to exist for numerous reasons, some positive, some damaging, but it seems that its power to shelter those who would injure its current, former, and future residents cannot be uncoupled from its curative, even curatorial, functions. The closet—like homophobia—encloses and protects, even (if not especially) in the name of what seems most antithetical to it. Relying solely on outing, visibility—the hope that if enough queers come out, or if enough "pink elephants" are outed, homophobic discrimination and violence will cease, as if by the breaking of a maleficent spell—amounts to another queer negative externality. Such a scenario also relies on a patently fallacious equation between invisibility and victimization, as if one can hate, intimidate, or abuse only those one can't see. Bracketing the terroristic intent of homophobic acts (the dire fate of a visible queer might intimidate less visible ones into staying, even temporarily, hidden), both logic and the history of the American gay and lesbian political movement (or, more specifically, the spectral visibility of the homosexual in the AIDS-panicked 1980s) corroborate how much easier it is to declare open season on targets one can see to aim at than on those cloaked in caliginous silences and omissions.

Like the teens in the utopian novels of David Levithan and Alex Sanchez, queers who rely on this hope risk forgetting that what separates can also protect, and what protects can also separate. If the closet and the gay ghetto, like sexual identities themselves, cannot be definitively dissolved, then they might be worth embracing—materially, symbolically, strategically. For as much as queers and sympathetic others might wish to see the cynical hypocrisy, sham moralizing, and gay-baiting of the Right crumble, such an eventuality would also be irreplaceably impoverishing. Without the risk of disenfranchisement, we might forfeit the entangled promise for critique and transformation. The most profound though perhaps initially unwelcome insight afforded by Foleygate may be a greater clarity into the closet's true, ambivalent character: semipermeable but ineradicable; fortifying yet opportunistically, sometimes disadvantageously, opaque.

Conclusion

Like a Faggot from the Ashes

IF THE ARGUMENT of *Queer Externalities* is somewhat unexpected—less for its novelty than its incongruity with recent trends in gay and lesbian politics and theory—that's very much to the point. Many of the cultural artifacts that, amid continuing battles over same-sex marriage and domestic partner benefits, appear to constitute progress, also signify something quite the opposite. The heady haze of acceptance betokened by certain films, television shows, and young adult novels clouds our vision, disguising the extent to which tolerance functions (as Wendy Brown asserts) as a social control mechanism, impeding our ability to parse out the punitive implications of cultural encounters from their favorable ones, to distinguish long-term, subtler side effects from the immediate, often fraudulent rush. Likewise, the sight of gay conservatives caught with their homophobic pants down provides an undeniable thrill, but such outings have done little not only to hobble the Right's homophobic crusade but also to dull the animus vectored at queers in both acrid and more muted forms from across the cultural and political spectrum. Exhorting caution in the face of American culture's apparent tolerance for queerness will no doubt strike some as cynical; the threat, overstated. It would be disingenuous to deny local decreases in homophobia, or the polls and anecdotes adduced to establish a generational shift toward acceptance. Yet a contrarian stance is not necessarily a cynical one. *Queer Externalities* exhorts holding onto difference, but not willfully or irascibly, and certainly not unconditionally. The recommendation is for a productive, opportunistic separatism, a tactical—that is, selective and strategic—deployment of essentialism in its practical, nonidealist capacities. Keeping attuned to the menacing undertow of cultural encounters doesn't involve just assessing the status of historically disenfranchised populations such as gays and lesbians, although that's hardly unimportant work. The goal, at least here, has been to heighten awareness of the tension between homophobic cultural tonalities and more well-meaning ones, to spotlight the antinomy between the invidious and the compassionate within the same encounter. It's my feeling that the promise both for motivating queers and for actuating change lies within these contradictions—within the aporia of America's relation to gay and lesbian citizens, within the tension, for queers and homophobes alike, between fantasies of well-being and a sense of collective hazard. In closing, then, it seems incumbent to consider the implications of my argument for queer theory and queer politics: What disjunctures and affinities are generated by thinking of queer in this particular way (as opposed to postmodern and constructionist readings more common to queer theory)? And, given that distinction, what might constitute queer action, queer citizenship?

It bears reiterating that, whereas my use of the term "queer" is mostly (but not exclusively) gay and lesbian specific, for some the term bears a broader meaning, encompassing not only gays and lesbians but individuals and groups whose desires, bodies, and/or erotic practices the larger culture has deemed nonnormative. I've made clear in the introductory chapter my reservations about too expansive an application of the term, although I sympathize with the intent of such an interpretation: not simply to curry allies outside the gay community but to widen the premise on which political and ideological resistance to norms qua norms might be mounted. I'm not saying that "queer" can't include or mean any person or group that troubles heteronormativity and its sense of what's normal, that reveals the laboriously, continually constructed character of ostensibly natural sexual desires and gender identities. I think there's room for both uses of the term. And yet, despite my difference on this matter with those such as Donald Hall, Judith Halberstam, and (to a lesser degree) Michael Warner, I feel there's an overlap between these two uses—evidenced, partly, by the fact that not all gays and lesbians, at least not all the time, see themselves as "queer" in the sense of existentially or willfully thwarting norms. Moreover, regardless of what additional nonnormative individuals or groups find shelter under the umbrella of queer, the queerest sexuality, in American culture at least, remains homosexuality.

As a point of information, it's noteworthy that this mixture of the discrete and the heterogeneous—what Sedgwick dubs the tension between "minoritizing" and "universalizing" views of homosexuality—has been present in queer theory from the start (*The Epistemology of the Closet* 1, 82–86). Teresa de Lauretis, who first coined the phrase "queer theory" in a 1991 issue of *differences* to suggest something less categorical and essentializing than "gay and lesbian studies," nonetheless also describes "gay sexuality in its specific female and male cultural (or subcultural) forms" as an "agency of social process whose mode of functioning is both interactive and yet resistant, both participatory and yet distinct, claiming at once equality and difference, demanding political representation while insisting on its material and historical specificity" (iii). "Both interactive and yet resistant, both participatory and yet distinct"—this is precisely the way in which I'm suggesting "queer" works, in which, despite the critical fretting, queer theory, politics, and activism can and do work.

If recommending, as I've done, a reevaluation of the possibilities afforded by identity, community, and visibility seems problematic, the intention has been to be productively so. This is not to suggest that "queer" is monolithic or static, obdurate or universal, fully knowable or all-encompassing. Speaking of "the queer community" and "queers" is to some degree a necessary argumentative move, an intervention not presumed to be permanent. Even (or maybe especially) in the historical sense, "queer," depending on a host of other identitarian, social, and epistemological factors, does not always permit the same modality of affiliation, does not always furnish a single or uniform, much less compulsory, way of connecting with the larger culture, individuals, or other subcultures. Indeed, it may conflict or at least fail to comport equally, symmetrically, or consistently with one or more other axes of identification (see Halberstam, "Shame and White Gay Masculinity"; Perez). It should be unsurprising then if, in the process of contesting and abrading norms, queerness is itself queered. Furthermore, those who negotiate queerness do so at varied angles and in tandem or in sequence with a range of other axes of affiliation (such as class, age, race, nation, kink, sexual position, mannerism). The extent to which these other identificatory planes and subcultures are more or less labile and capable of resistance to reification—as well as how they cut across, disallow, or parallel "queer"—are matters to be pursued elsewhere. *Queer Externalities* hardly disallows these or other modes and temporalities of alliance (or dis-alliance) that may interrupt or further denature the shape of queerness. Invoking apparently fixed entities such as "queer" and "community" is not to foreclose the possibility of nonalgorithmic interventions in addition to those that are telic or merely routine.

There's room for both the queering of roles and identities and the perpetuation of such identities. We shouldn't stop trying to queer or question norms, by any means. Yet the ultimate recalcitrance of the homo/hetero binary may lie, most tellingly, in our inability to think of terms outside that paradigm to violate. Our position is, on some level, necessarily myopic, as interpellated subjects of the very sexual ideology we seek to trouble. As Sedgwick argues in *The Epistemology of the Closet*, the revision of gay and lesbian identity constructs finds greatest resistance from those to whom it may be the most invaluable: heterosexuals. It's "the paranoid insistence," Sedgwick writes, "with which the definitional barriers between 'the homosexual' (minority) and 'the heterosexual' (majority) are fortified . . . by nonhomosexuals, and especially by men against men that most saps one's ability to believe in 'the homosexual' as an unproblematically discrete category of person" (83–84). Essential categories of sexual definition may do homophobic service for heterosexuals, but, as Sedgwick admits, such categories also serve antihomophobic purposes as well. *Queer Externalities* suggests that it is politically and culturally as well as psychologically productive to hold to gay and lesbian identities as realized both abstractly and concretely, both theoretically and practically, while also remaining aware of the "faultlines" (to borrow from Alan Sinfield). "Faultlines" refers to those contingencies for resistance if not escape, those opportunities for local transformation or deformation, that are possible—whether they're random or programmatic, ad hoc or premeditated, frivolous or pragmatic, ephemeral or more durable. Part of the possibility of such opportunities for queering the paradigm, or for queer iterations of the paradigm, owes to the fact that a paradigm exists in the first place. (That system, as historians of sexuality demonstrate, has changed in the past and so is likely to change again. As the work of David Halperin and Judith Butler suggests, such change has, previously at least, occurred not by voluntaristic fiat and not by single iterations that problematize the "normal" categories in which human gender and sexuality get codified, but through a process of accretion.)

This is not to say that the postmodern reading of identity common to queer theory lacks a sympathetic, even persuasive, argument. Take, for instance, Donald Hall's urge to "imagine queer theories proliferating and to see that proliferation as itself valuable," "to hold as our highest priority a respect for and understanding of multiplicity—of identities among and identities within" (108). Here we see queer theory's struggle to unravel categorical constraints while still valuing the animating, transformative differences capable of enunciation through those very categories. Even transgender theorist Susan Stryker, who praises the invigorating "rhetoric of queer inclusivity and gender diversity," voices concern over the lack or "erasure of specificity" that might result from "queer inclusivity," from stretching "queer" too far (153). The model I've suggested of preserved yet opportunistically permeable boundaries permits "active intellectual and political exchange," an exchange that Hall insists may "alter" "unspoken norms and lingering prejudices" (108). Furthermore, the model outlined here does not forbid the addition or redrawing of other boundaries or affiliations, either within, outside, or athwart existing boundaries. Holding onto difference with one hand, so to speak, seems crucial because of the reductive, exclusive torsion by which reactionary as well as some progressive ideologies manage the nonnormative or divergent. Maybe I'm less optimistic than Hall that "complexity wins out over time, that mounting evidence of variability and different *value*-ability slowly erodes simplistic, tendentious categories, and the institutions that enforce and reinforce them" (132). I viscerally appreciate the impulsion toward a less regimented, less exclusively dichotomized comprehension of sexuality, but one irksome fact remains: that is the model by which gay and lesbian Americans are popularly known, by which our lives, bodies, and rights are proscribed and regimented, and, for the present at least, by which we find sex partners, friends, lovers, communities, histories, and politics.

Queer theory has long acknowledged the tension between its own postmodern, constructionist claims—which are quite valid in their own right—and essentialist identity claims that not only make propriodescriptive sense to many queers but are the linchpin of the modern gay and lesbian movement's human rights claims. The tension between essentialism and constructionism has carried a particular onus for gays and lesbians, often in terms of a schism between praxis and theory (see Hall 45–46; Sedgwick *The Epistemology of the Closet* 86). Historically, there has been a perception that queer theory and GLBT politics are antithetical, especially among activists concerned that queer theory undermines one of the more solid foundations for advocating the rights of GLBT citizens. On a practical level, queer theorists such as Eve Sedgwick and Janet E. Halley (*The Epistemology of the Closet* and "The Construction of Heterosexuality," respectively) acknowledge that essentialist and postidentity approaches are each, in differing contexts, serviceable to widely divergent ends—homophobic as well as gay-positive. The fact that this definitional incoherence serves homophobic ends as well as antihomophobic ones cannot be helped. That there is a contest is what's important.

If the best conclusion we can reach is that identity has both constructed and essential content, is both a fiction and a lived reality, is that a conclusion we can live with? That is, can we become citizens, running on a split ticket? Must one voice be silenced, as it has been by queer or feminist activists who scoff at theory as apolitical, nonproductive, even counterproductive? Or, paradoxically, might we not uproot identity (or at least, certain programmatic, routinizing concepts of it) by clinging to it? Need the lived concreteness of being gay in America in the early twenty-first century—the boundedness of the gayborhood, for example—be antithetical to understanding the polymorphousness of human experience? Perhaps my feelings come to rest, finally, at the hard fact that multiplicity, unboundedness—queerness—cannot be legally described or protected. And whatever the flaws of a positivist model of additive democratic inclusion, suturing this group, then that one, into laws that apply to "citizens" is the model we must work with (see Turner 54). The gap between self-understanding and praxis may seem incommensurable, but it's not necessarily overwhelming. For it's by using theory practically—inflicting it on the resilient medium of the shifting text of law, ideology, and culture that we might denaturalize (or "deterritorialize," to use a term from Gilles Deleuze and Félix Guattari) the fiction of identity while remaining pragmatic about its political reality, its cultural consequences.

The next theoretically distinctive feature of *Queer Externalities* also impinges on the political. As my examples should make clear, the argument I've advanced is trained on the present. One should be careful about extrapolating terms such as "queer" and "community" onto earlier periods in American gay sexual and social life—as Scott Herring reminds us in *Queering the Underworld: Slumming, Literature, and the Undoing of Lesbian and Gay History* (2007). Herring argues that early twentieth-century texts such as Djuna Barnes's *Nightwood* and Willa Cather's "Paul's Case," while commonly read as "bohemian slumming narrative[s]" (the slumming genre promising ostensibly normative readers privileged access to a decadent demimonde), actually frustrate visibility and defy knowability—the panopticon-like objectives of the genre (102). Privileging invisibility and the "anticommunal" in order to combat the claustral force of (bourgeois, heteronormative) technologies of epistemology, consumption, and affiliation (82), the texts Herring investigates seek to baffle not just the prying, juridical gaze of a moral majority but communal, subcultural models of gay and lesbian identity that, though promising freedom, nonetheless abide under that gaze. Historically framed, Herring's project seems properly circumspect. Wary of transhistorical false equivalencies of the kind David Halperin and George Chauncey caution against, Herring seeks to "unhing[e] the word [*queer*] from its nominal role in the sexual 'identity formation' of any queer 'group subject' across race, nation-state, region, class, or historical time" (22). Yet Herring stakes out an even stronger objective: "to rui[n] the business of communal visibility" (210).

Emphasis on unknowing and on evasion of the gaze and its legal-moral force is understandable in an early-twentieth-century setting (although Chauncey's *Gay New York* suggests otherwise; for some male urban homosexuals at least, visibility did not always foreclose autonomy). However, given the comparatively privileged (or at least unprosecuted) present status of some American queers (white, affluent gays and lesbians) and the socioeconomic marginalization of others (queer minorities and transgenders), and the ideological erasure/demonization of all queers, valorizing invisibility and nonidentity this blithely seems derelict. To eschew visibility makes sense as an escape route from late modern epistemological regimes, but in thus escaping (presuming such escape is finally possible, or possible by fiat) one credits too far the continuity and stability of those regimes, whose aims to "know" the homosexual can be intermittently unraveled, either by counterproductive excess of their own efforts or by the kind of queer reading—reading against the grain—promoted in *Queer Externalities.* Opting for "suspicion of sexual hermeneutics" (Herring 14), one underestimates the fragmentation to which dominant structures of knowing and being are liable, the frustration and play available to alterity even as that alterity is supposedly "known" and "fixed" by the dominant discourse. One abandons both the pragmatic ends queers (or other abject populations) might accomplish to their own political or social benefit within identitarian epistemological frameworks, such as securing domestic partner benefits, as well as the deferrals to be wrested, at times, from discursive limits through critical resistance, through refusing to play what Anne Marie Smith describes as homophobic rhetoric's "self-reinforcing" (that is, fixed) "game" of "truths and counter-truths" (*New Right Discourse* 192). An approach that credits identity, whether closeted, pronounced, or some admixture thereof, attempts to retain more possibilities than a model that valorizes invisibility and elusiveness only.

Against the background of present-day American sexual-social politics and culture, the latter model seems weaker. Take, for instance, Herring's analysis of a discussion of the DL, or "down-low," phenomenon that occurred on *Oprah* ("down-low" being African American slang for straight-identified men who secretly have sex with men):

> *Oprah* tires to solicit true confessions from [J. L.] King [author of *Secrets* and *Coming Up from the Down Low*] that will "blow the lid off" the down low, but King refuses to say anything about his sexual self or his affiliations with any sexual group identity. . . . As Winfrey tries to excavate King's personal sexual history, King becomes more and more undetectable. When asked to "tell," he interrupts Winfrey with a repeated series of "buts." He undoes the set parameters of the talk show Q&A by interviewing Winfrey ("Why do I—and so why do I have to label myself?"). He refuses to elaborate on Winfrey's questions by answering in repetitive monosyllables. He feigns ignorance about the proper definitions of activities such as "date." He forces Winfrey to clarify herself to the point of absurdity ("Am I intimately involved with men and women?" "Ok. Yeah."). He answers inquires with non sequiturs ("What do you call it?" "Yes." "Yes." "Yeah." "Ok"). And he ends [the] interview on the same note of irresolution with which he began. The exchange goes nowhere. It's an articulation that functions as sexual disarticulation, a "never apologize, never explain" stance that refuses *Oprah*'s slumming desire for sexual comprehension. And in so doing, King "emerges" at what Judith Butler elsewhere called "the limits of intelligibility." (204–05)

To chastise Oprah for slumming is not a wholly unfair charge—but then one has to pause and consider whether the legitimate target is a particular talk show or the talk-show format itself, the exposé (slumming) style by which J. L. King promotes himself and his books. And yes, Oprah is slumming on behalf of an unmarked (white, straight) audience. Both genres—not just Oprah's—are freighted with slumming's promise of epistemological security. But it would seem that Herring is making a somewhat ahistorical comparison between modernist-era literary culture and an early twenty-first century middle-class (sub)urban sexual landscape. It's King who qualifies for more legitimate criticism, it seems. Herring reads Oprah as cornering King even as the latter dodges her proprietary grasp. Yet, especially given King's own complicity in exposé and his appearance on the show in order to promote his book and presumably explain what life on the "down-low" is like, one might regard Oprah in a different light: as simply trying to get a straight, or rather, a gay answer from an uncooperative interlocutor. Herring writes that he has "little desire to valorize King," only "to highlight his calculated refusals to narrate what, exactly, black male sexuality is," to "situate himself outside mass-mediated surveillance[]" of the "'shocking' . . . underworld" to which Oprah promises her audience access (206, 204). But there's a difference between intentionally queering or attempting to impede a prescriptive identitarian police action and not answering a question. King appears to be doing the latter.

My intent is not to diminish a long tradition of critiquing rigidity in systems of sexual identification. From Carl Wittman's liberationist "Refugees from Amerika: A Gay Manifesto" (1970) to more recent academic discussions, such as Beth Firestein's *Bisexuality: The Psychology and Politics of an Invisible Minority* (1996), Brett Beemyn and Mickey Eliason's *Queer Studies: A Lesbian, Gay, Bisexual, and Transgender Anthology* (1996), and Marjorie Garber's *Vice Versa: Bisexuality and the Eroticism of Everyday Life* (1995), contemporary gay, queer, and gender theorists and activists have legimitately troubled the dichotomy corseting Western thought about sexuality for over a century. Particularly noteworthy is Maria Pramaggiore and Donald E. Hall's collection *RePresenting Bisexualities: Subjects and Cultures of Fluid Desire* (1996), which delivers a series of provocative readings "from the fence," attempting to theorize bisexuality on its own merits, without heterosexuality or homosexuality as a default position. In *Queer Theories* Hall himself criticizes a tendency, particularly among gay men, to label straight-identified MSMs (men who have sex with men) as self-deluding, as "really" gay:

> [T]he implications of [Alfred] Kinsey's research—that sexuality can change dramatically over time and in respect to context, and that sexual activity does not necessarily have to lead to self-identification—have yet to be fully acknowledged and grappled with by most sexual rights movements even today. . . . It is easy but finally reductive to read onto complex human behavior and emotions the artificial binary "heterosexual/homosexual" and categorize diverse activities and multi-faceted identities as belonging to one "side" alone. Indeed, self-validation along those lines by lesbians and gay men has often led to a facile diagnosis of "not accepting" one's "true" homosexual self if one has occasional or passing erotic contact with members of both sexes. Even one homosexual encounter can be taken by some as proof of "really" being lesbian or gay, and of living in an unhealthy state of denial if one fails to self-identify as such. (40)

Hall justifiably balks at the rigidly dichotomizing impulses of our late Western approach to sexuality, especially the habit—in queer theory as well as in the gay bar—to read sexual acts as determinants of sexual identity. Any lesbian or gay man who, at some point, has had heterosexual encounters should know better than to make such facile or absolute equations. Hall writes: "'Repressed' hardly captures the complexity" of the "identity positions" of MSMs who "never identify as 'homosexual' or 'bisexual. In fact,"

> there is no evidence that a "heterosexual" man receiving oral sex from another man is "repressing" anything; he could just as easily be considered less "repressed" than others since he is allowing a rather wide

> field for possible sexual gratification. Indeed, we have no "queer theory" to date that would even account for the unremarkable experience of "situational" or "circumstantial" homosexuality, such as that which occurs in prison and other single-sex environments. Certainly, if we limit our discussion of sexual "identity" to the standard definition encouraged by identity politics—that of self-identification—the point is moot. . . .
>
> But my point here is that self-identification, explicit or potential, should *not* limit us in the ways we theorize about desire, that self-identification is a potentially powerful political position, but that it is also an intellectual problem. . . . [Q]ueer coalition building can be furthered by expressing and exploring more vigorously the many ways that "heterosexual" and "homosexual" are terms that do not capture the complexity of most human lives when viewed diachronically for past behaviors and always inherent future potential. (100–01)[1]

During Alfred Kinsey's time, for a straight, married man to receive oral sex from a gay man may have less clearly been a conflict or inconsistency—or at least, understandable following the 1930s legal crackdown on gay visibility in American public life (see Chauncey 331–54). Other factors should be taken into account as well, such as the role of shifting cultural understandings of gender behavior (versus object choice) in determining one's "choices" of identification—that is, both the sexual positionalities open within a culture and what individual subjects see as choices open to themselves personally. Without invalidating the cogent work of these bisexual theorists, *Queer Externalities* is less concerned with sexual subjectivity per se than with sexual subjects' political and cultural alliances, with the pragmatic, sometimes involuntary workings of social coalition. How straight-identified men feel when being blown by other men is of less concern for my purposes than how they might compartmentalize their erotic investments in ways that deny the present-day cultural and political costs of gay sex. Such a dissociative move not only ignores the extent to which gay sex is as politicized as the rights denied to gay citizens, but, regardless of individual intent, it perpetuates the stigmatization of gay sex. If only gay men will openly admit to having gay sex, then they alone bear the brunt of cultural homophobia—as well as the responsibility for advocacy and activism. Rather than undermining the homo/hetero binary and facilitating affiliation beyond the gay community, one might argue that refusals to identify further ossify the straight/queer dichotomy and, in fact, occlude opportunities for intercommunal rapport and affiliation. Not worrying somewhat about the repercussions of engaging in gay sex—or being apathetic, silent, or even hostile to gay political and cultural interests—is to ignore a negative queer externality.

To return to Herring's discussion of J. L. King, one can dress up such evasiveness if one wants to, but let's be candid. From a certain—not unsympathetic, if politically incorrect—viewpoint, isn't the down-low or a concept like pansexuality just the closet? Or, to put it less severely, isn't either position, though capable of being sincerely inhabited as an affective/sexual category, equally capable of being hijacked to serve as a closet, to shield oneself from the taint of abjection? Shirking the fabled prescriptive force of labels is a noble stand, but one's motive in doing so seems very much to the point. There's a significant difference between not wanting to be labeled and not wanting to be labeled as gay. As with *Rubyfruit Jungle*'s Molly Bolt or the teens Savin-Williams writes about, it may be hard to discern one impulsion from the other. Then again, maybe there isn't much of a difference, in which case evading categorization is a move toward the closet, however framed. Just as whiteness is the racially unmarked signifier, to be labeled in terms of sexuality is to be labeled as queer, as gay or lesbian, as nonnormative.

My concern is more specific and targeted, however, than all MSMs. Anecdotally at least, many (though hardly all) of the men who identify as bisexual do so anonymously or, during casual sexual encounters, emphasize their need to be "discreet." In such cases, "discreet" means "closeted." What it also too often means is "I'm married" to or "in a relationship" with a woman who doesn't know that her husband or boyfriend is bisexual, or just doesn't know that he's nonmonogamous. Let me be explicit: in no way am I questioning the legitimacy of bisexuality as an experiential or identitarian category. (The question of whether bisexuality, despite its perhaps wrongly spurned status among much of the gay and lesbian community, ends up reaffirming the very dichotomy it would problematize is one to debate elsewhere.) If a man is bisexual, however, but his wife and his close friends don't know—if no one knows except his male sexual partners—then it seems spurious to refer to the man in question as bisexual. He's not socially identified as such. He's a straight man secretly having gay sex. And while that's not the same as being gay, it's certainly gay-adjacent. While it might seem invidious to equate the average man on the down-low or the college frat boy who "messes around with his buddy" now and then to closet colonizers such as Mark Foley, Ted Haggard, or Larry Craig, the comparison bears consideration. All these men, to varying degrees, are cashing in without conscience on the privileges of heterosexuality, indifferent to those who forfeit those privileges by their manifest queerness.

To worry the question of historical periodization a bit further still, there is something to be said for George Chauncey's observation in *Gay New York* (12–15) that the homo/hetero binary crystallized, at least for working-class men, even later than Foucault or Halperin have dated it: as recently as the 1940s. Does this mean that homosexuality as invoked by gays and lesbians since Stonewall, if not earlier, requires a closet? And if so, does coming out somehow become an insincere or at least ineffective act? Can there be no out-and-proud lesbian Latinas or Folsom Street daddies without men such as King on the DL, without teen wrestlers such as the one in *Rainbow Road* hiding deep within the closet, or without political leaders such as Mark Foley and Larry Craig powerful enough (at least for a time) to kick over the traces of their perambulations in and out of the closet? Though Chauncey seems right about the uneven historical development of sexual roles and subcultures, it would strain credulity to claim (and Chauncey adamantly does not) that gays and lesbians' cultural visibility, legal equality, and social legitimacy depend on the secrecy or invisibility of those who have not come out or do not wish to declare their affiliation. (Chauncey is setting out, after all, to revise the truism that being gay before Stonewall was only to be closeted, self-loathing, secretive.) For it's arguable that many closeted homosexuals, by virtue of being closeted, enjoy as known heterosexuals the visibility, equality, and legitimacy their out queer counterparts lack.

This is not, then, to mandate knowability of the sort Herring and the writers he examines resist. As I hope to have made clear in the previous chapters, in both substance and ethos, my argument willfully departs from the prevailing gay and lesbian take on present-day queer life as a Golconda of commercial clout and social acceptance. Media visibility at once promises both recognition and erasure by the dominant heteronormative discourse. Whether we can escape or transform that double bind is a matter of debate, or simply time, but I think the models of community and identity that many queers appear eager to shed are not so paralyzing as they make them out to be. Nor are they innately, effortlessly liberatory. The reinventability of queerness—its capacity to rise from the representational ashes to which the culture (or to which queers themselves) may periodically consign it—lies in its ability to be as useful or useless, as obtrusive or slippery, as one desires. I'm recommending informed skepticism over brute pessimism. What's finally more hazardous for queers than the negative externalities examined here is their own lack of insight into the threats posed by queers' cultural abjection. It's not as surprising that heteronormativity would blind those who most (unconsciously) enjoy its imprimatur, but when gays, lesbians, open bisexuals, and others versed in the blighting powers of norms lapse into false complacency over their cultural status, there is ample cause to worry.

My intent is hardly to make a call for outing, voluntary or forced. Many still live and work where they cannot be openly queer without hazard to their physical safety or financial stability. Factors such as these may well render coming out a gestural luxury for some, though it remains a legitimating constative and political move. My aim is hardly to pin all the woes of gay Americans on closeted bisexual men. There are pressures for such men to keep the gay part of their erotic life secret from their partners and associates. Often focused through the normalizing force of children and the call to protect the heterosexual family's untroubled innocence, these forces take more concrete forms as well (job loss, gay-bashing). However, without invalidating closeted lives or lives that traverse the closet (as many of ours, in successive contexts, do), it's possible to uphold a distinction between using the closet to hide from real personal threats and manipulating its screening capacity in order to evade the stigma of actual or perceived association with an open gay community. For those men who are socially identified as straight, who can afford visibility and activism, to be open about the gay element of their erotic lives would demand a reconstruction of sexuality, of tolerance—even of citizenship—in welcome and unpredictable ways.

Further, as I hope the preceding chapters have made clear, the discussion of closeted male bisexuality is only one of the alluring yet hazardous positions I discuss (along with the postgay mentality and gay comfort with mainstream commercial visibility). Though soothing, these positions not only ignore significant corporeal and emblematic threats to queer Americans, they also solidify assimilationist, appeasement-driven queer politics as the only game in town. By further isolating self-identified gays and lesbians as those solely responsible for activism and political representation of difference in regard to sexuality, these false positions undermine the possibility of alliances in terms beyond the narrow dichotomy of gay/straight. This is a call, rather, to soberly evaluate, more than has been our habit, the route gays and lesbians face to not only tolerance and acceptance, but also to citizenship, a route that is both frustratingly and redemptively anfractuous. An indirect, considered approach permits us to ask at what price social and political "arrival" come, formulated on whose terms, and to whose detriment? What will it mean for queers finally to "join the nation"? Would queer citizenship mean being civilized in the passive sense, being interpellated as good gays within a dichotomy whose stark alternative is the subversive faggot? Or might we in some way queer the nation, affect not just the idea of nation or community but the very composition of that entity, the "citizen"? Perhaps we should seek ways of joining nation and community queerly (even on the local and subcultural levels), our critical perspective and accumulated collective knowledge intact. We might look, then, to "join queerly" in multiple, disputational senses: to join or bring to visibility our queer communities, whether literally or gesturally; to become part of the nation in a way that productively troubles ideological and organizational narratives. Moving beyond the historically pernicious phantasmatic of "the nation," we might at least point toward the pulling together of other kinds of communities in queerly unanticipated and heteroclite arrangements, as capable of pleasure and disruption as of praxis.

What might this line of thinking mean for queer politics in more concrete terms? Rather than programmatically set out particular solutions, however—and thereby continue the single-issue, mainstream model whose usefulness, if unmodified, has proven to have clear limits—my final move is less concrete but, I hope, nonetheless generative. The following section sketches the two poles between which queer action must stage itself (whether political, cultural, or otherwise) in order to be productive, protective, and self-sustaining. While these poles—coalition and withdrawal—have historically been the antithetical forces pulling on any minority group seeking recognition or redress from hegemonic American culture, or seeking to trouble the hegemonic exempla of that culture, recent political theory provides two models of nation, democracy, and citizenship that dramatically revise traditional notions of coalition and separatism, thereby licensing, instead, new, invigorating conceptions of queer political action.

One concept that requires a rethinking of coalition is radical democratic theory. Developed largely by Ernesto Laclau and Chantal Mouffe and astutely explicated by Anna Marie Smith in *Laclau and Mouffe: The Radical Democratic Imaginary* (1998), radical democratic theory attempts to "bring the most democratic moments" of socialism and democracy "to the fore" (Smith 15). This "retrieval project" would essentially infuse democracy with the best insights of socialism, so as to sidestep the limitations of each tradition (respectively, allowing the continuance of inequality via capitalism and liberal subjectivity, and failing to address conflict or inequality along axes other than class). One of the obstacles to significant progressive change, as Laclau and Mouffe note, is the friction inherent in liberal democracy's commitment to both equality (which requires difference and autonomy) and unity (which demands, on some scale, the elision of the very same). Given the theoretical and practical value of both commitments, their incongruous stipulations

> call for the kind of political strategy that can achieve unity and preserve autonomy at the same time—that is, a radical democratic pluralist hegemonic strategy. . . . [I]t is only by conceptualizing unity in terms of hegemonic articulation that the goal of unifying different movements becomes compatible with the goal of preserving their autonomy.
>
> . . . [This model] would allow for effective solidarity without asking any individual movement to pay the price of tokenism, co-optation and assimilation. No single struggle should be allowed to impose its agenda over all of the others. While each struggle should learn from the others—it should share political values and tools, engage in collaborative strategies, and reform its identity as it takes on board the democratic demands of other struggles—it should also continue to develop its own distinctive worldview and pursue its own projects. A leading struggle may emerge . . . but will be so deeply affected by its negotiations with other progressive struggles that its philosophy, program and tactics—its very identity—would be reshaped in the process.
>
> In this sense, each of the democratic struggles would constantly reconstruct their identities through a democratic process of mutual education with the others. This process could not, however, be characterized as the formation of a coalition between pre-constituted interest groups. It would take the form instead of continuous negotiations that give rise to new hybrid identities and temporary blocs. (Smith, *Laclau and Mouffe* 32)

Despite the postmodern drift of "new hybrid identities"—a phrase that feels very much in line with queer theory's historical assault on identity categories—Laclau and Mouffe also seem to run counter to that line by insisting on the preservation of distinct group "worldviews." The unspoken hybrid here is actually that between queer theory and more pragmatic notions of identity: the retention of particularity amid the process of negotiation with other groups; the articulation of resemblance across margins of difference, of common cause voiced athwart disagreement, even rancor. Within a radicalized democracy, "[f]ar from isolating themselves from the dominant community," the struggles of minority groups such as gays and lesbians

> often attempt to subject dominant groups and hegemonic authoritarian values to the democratic critique that can be found in the discourses of the disempowered. Minority rights claims sometimes take the form of a demand for separation, but they can also be phrased as radical communitarian demands for the authorization of an anti-racist, anti-sexist, anti-homophobic and anti-capitalist definition of "our common tradition" or "our shared values." . . . [T]he aim is to value difference so that the operation of power—discrimination, exploitation and erasure—can be brought to light. (Smith, *Laclau and Mouffe* 192)

My primary emphasis has been on the "demand for separation." If this comes across as an overemphasis, that's quite to the point. The effort has been to counterbalance the dominant tone in contemporary gay and lesbian politics ("communitarian demands"—though not always "radical"—"for the authorization of an . . . anti-homophobic definition" of American polity) in order to accentuate currently less popular priorities (valuing difference, retaining goals specific to individual minority groups). While *Queer Externalities* is not centrally a socialist enterprise, its version of queer community and identity is hospitable to radical democracy's wider political agenda. Certainly, my objective analytically and politically has been "to value difference" in order to expose, as Smith puts it, the "operation of power." In this case, that power is heteronormativity, as propagated by gays as well as by straights, in antihomophobic as well as overtly homophobic contexts. The innovation of Laclau and Mouffe's model of coalition is that it infuses the project of inclusion with the soundest insights and attestable benefits of separatism, thereby avoiding the enervating effect assimilation can have (and has had) on gay and lesbian politics.

If coalition is a concept that can stand to be modified, and thus rendered a greater implement for change, separatism is another. In its most commonly conceived form, separatism implies isolation, alienation—a hostile minority drawn in on itself, immured politically and often socially. But, as Michael Warner evidences in *The Trouble with Normal*, the separatist impulse is valuable if, instead of isolated, it vectors its energy—and the insights allowed by critical distance—toward social and political norms. In terms of gay sex, for example, Warner's politics—

> a frank embrace of queer sex in all its apparent indignity, together with a frank challenge to the damaging hierarchies of respectability—can result in neither assimilation nor separatism if carried through consistently. . . . Straight culture . . . needs to learn a new standard of dignity, and it won't do this as long as gay people think that their "acceptance" needs to be won on the terms of straight culture's politics of shame. (74)

A "frank challenge" to norms, whether of sexuality, gender, or personhood, serves to connect queer politics to the object of its critique. Separatism is worth cultivating inasmuch as it incites the drive for progress without narrowing too sharply the possibilities of what progress might look like.

Amy Brandzel likewise asks us to conceive of separatism as something both more valuable and more productively radical than we may be accustomed to doing. In "Queering Citizenship?: Same-Sex Marriage and the State" (2005), Brandzel caps off her critique of same-sex marriage (along the lines of Warner) with the following cautionary note: "advocacy for same-sex marriage rights has not critiqued citizenship and its tendency to exclude or differentiate, but it has reproduced the myth of universal citizenship as a great equalizer" (par. 60). Since "citizenship itself is necessarily exclusive, privileged, and normative" (par. 3), Brandzel regards "'queer' and 'citizen' [as] antithetical concepts" (par. 62). She asks

> queers, especially those who are privileged and well off enough to do so, [to] refuse citizenship and actively subvert the normalization, legitimization, and regulation that it requires. In claiming that queer is anticitizen, I am referencing a more nuanced understanding of what it means to be a citizen. To be a citizen is not simply a matter of enjoying a specific legal status; it includes the wide variety of practices and imaginings required by citizenship. That is, one must imagine oneself as a citizen as well as be imagined by the American citizenry as a member of it. . . . While an intersectional queer critique aims to make connections among practices, experiences, and identifications, it must not equalize these experiences or treat them as if they were the same. In fact . . . citizenship displaces nonwhite, nonheterosexual, nonmale peoples via intersections of normativities, but it does so in very different and meaningful ways.
>
> A radical queer critique of citizenship has a stake not in saving it or in redefining it, but in undermining its production and promotion of normativity. Queers are seen as oppositional and/or antagonistic to U.S. community-building practices and institutions. In the American imaginary, they often epitomize indulgence and selfishness, traits seen

> as extensions of their excessive sexual identifications. While queers do not choose to be positioned outside or in opposition to U.S. citizenship, their positioning can and should be used to critique normative citizenship practices and institutions. Queerness as an identification and a politics allows for a reflective stance that can represent the paradox of citizenship: that the great umbrella of American ideals does not shelter everyone. It allows for a position from which we, as deviants, can work to undermine and expose—that is, queer—the normativities of citizenship.
>
> Queer citizenship requires a critique of citizenship, of the nation-state, of normalization and heteronormativity. To queer citizenship, then, we need to work to conceive of a citizenship that does not require universalization, false imaginaries, or immersion in and acceptance of the progress narratives of U.S. citizenship. . . . Queer citizenship requires a constant critique not only of the break between queer and normative citizens but of the boundary maintenance inherent in citizenship. If the history of citizenship is in fact the history of normalization, of legitimization, of differentiation, then to queer citizenship would transform these practices radically. A queer citizenry would refuse to participate in the prioritizing of one group or form of intimacy over another; it would refuse to participate in the differentiation of peoples, groups, or individuals; it would refuse citizenship altogether. (pars. 62–64)

Brandzel makes several important points that resonate with *Queer Externalities*: the failure of American culture to imagine gay citizenship; the distinctiveness of particular minority claims and experiences from one another; and, most importantly, the centrality of maintaining a stake in difference to an animating progressive political vision. Not treating race as if it were the same as queerness is important, but so is not treating queer the same as if it were straight (as much of an ideal as that seems). Otherwise, how profoundly can one "undermin[e]" the "production and promotion of normativity" without the preservation of boundaries such as the gayborhood and gay and lesbian identitarian positions? All the same, Brandzel recommends withdrawal not from the political process per se but from that process, and from the nation, as imaginatively constituted. Instead of inducing the nation to imagine queer citizens (an imagining likely to draw on heteronormative terms), queers should seek, instead, to "undermine" the concept of citizen as the normative, exclusive unit of the nation. "Citizen" is a concept, as both Brandzel and Lee Edelman point out, structurally antithetical to and defined against queers. Neither the marketing of queer in the entertainment industry nor perhaps even the institution of same-sex marriage can truly normalize queer. There will be gays and lesbians who don't wish to get married; the United States will still be constituted against a number of excluded inhabitants, unimaginable citizens. "Conceiv[ing] of a citizenship that does not require universalization, false imaginaries, or . . . acceptance of the progress narratives of U.S. citizenship" is precisely what the opportunistic deployment of essentialism can procure, when paired with a healthy cognizance of categories' fabricated status and exclusionary character (Brandzel par. 64). To "refuse citizenship altogether" is not to opt out of the nation, but to ask what other ways of imagining collectivities are available to us. And gay and lesbian identity—homosexuality broadly and communally conceived—is one source of collectivity that has sustained life and mobilized action in ways and through channels alien to the larger culture. At the same time, the confines of gay and lesbian identity should not fully dictate imaginative limits for queer politics or organization, but rather serve as a home base—at once starting point, refuge, and bellwether. Critical reading of cultural artifacts from a full, even conflicting, set of perspectives is indispensable to tracing normativity's pervasive yet irregular rhetorical effects and, correspondingly, the efficacy of various strategies and allies, both old and new, both local and wide-ranging.

Without proposing too neat a symmetry, one might trace a useful parallel, on the one hand, between the ad hoc essentialism I'm advocating and the postmodern, constructionist insights regarding identity (which are also of strategic value) and, on the other hand, the two primary avenues of resistance outlined by Foucault in *The History of Sexuality, Volume 1:* reverse discourse and counterdiscourse. Reverse discourse entails taking advantage of discourse's "tactical polyvalence," or instability, by using hegemonic rhetoric for purposes of resistance (such as the adoption by gays and lesbians of nineteenth-century psychiatric descriptions of "the homosexual" not only to defy such categorization but for their own positive affiliative and subcultural purposes). Counterdiscourse, by contrast, assaults the foundation of a dominant discourse, refuting its legitimacy by proposing an alternative authorizing narrative (such as Brandzel's call for a less exclusionary principle of social organization or Hall and Pramaggiore's pursuit of a less dichotomized understanding of sexuality). It should be clear by now that neither an essentialist nor a constructionist approach to queer politics and identity, neither reverse discourse nor counterdiscourse, is by itself sufficient. Each not only honors different aspects of our experience and possesses distinct political effects, but also works to counterbalance repressive, hegemonic uses of identity as either essential or constructed. Thus, the reformulations of coalition and withdrawal allowed by Laclau, Mouffe, and Brandzel move from traditional senses of those terms (articulating differences either to a common greater good or to the priorities of a smaller group) toward a more transformative sense (the potential to alter one's own and others' particularized identities even while negotiating public discourse through the dominant identitarian paradigm). While not as satisfactory to readers seeking a practicum in waging political battle against concrete queer issues such as job discrimination, domestic partner benefits, or access to HIV medication, that has not been this book's aim. Thinking theoretically about the political, however—about how we approach communal as well as national discourse—can invigorate not just the political process but what one conceives of as being political, what subjects, persons, and structures we consider open (or, possibly, closed) to address and debate. We might, while retaining an essentialist, serviceable base of identity, seek ways of allocating agency (or agencies) differently, which might well include abrogating agency, even cultivating counteragencies (see Janet Jakobsen's "Sex + Freedom = Regulation: Why?" for one example of this line of thinking).

Debate is pivotal to queer politics and queer theory, and my intent has been to provoke such rethinking (not exclusive of my own argument). Moving discussion beyond rigid and/or unexamined commitments to assimilation and heteronormativity often requires an obstreperousness that, I hope, will not be mistaken for sheer stridency. Take, for instance, Didier Eribon's pronouncement on assimilation: "assimilation is an impossible project, a trap gay people set for themselves . . . and one's time is better spent turning one's back on the kinds of claims whose aim would be to integrate gay people to the social order and, instead, learning to enjoy the benefits of marginality" (120). This sort of prodding is easily dismissed as truculent, isolationist, unproductive. But Eribon is making a more subtle point. If assimilation is a "trap," it's not so much that gay people who fall for its charms are stupid, for its charms are hailed throughout the culture as unequaled and, more deceptively, as the coin of the realm in political and psychological welfare. Nor is it the case that those who don't succumb to such charms are superior. Assimilation's most impoverishing aspect is its selfishness, the demand—or at least the likelihood—that petitioners relinquish other, empowering possibilities: an internally defined dignity, a less crippling standard of personhood than that which is everywhere embedded in the culture, even in ourselves. We find a gentler version of Eribon's statement in *Everybody Loves You*, the third volume in Ethan Mordden's *Buddies* short story cycle. Concerning a group of friends traveling abroad, Mordden observes how gay men become

> tourists, disintegrated from the place we were in and thus made to become complete unto ourselves.
>
> It was easy to do it. Gay men do it, in fact, every day of their lives. No gay can ever be a part of his nation unless he gives away something of himself, his self-esteem, perhaps. We are always disintegrated from the status quo, always complete to ourselves. In the straight world—in the world—we are tourists till we close Them off behind our doors. (289)

Tourists travel yet always, periodically at least, return home. Honoring queer theory's commitment to open-endedness doesn't have to also mean forswearing incumbent or quondam strategies. Two of the "we" referred to above are Little Kiwi and Cosgrove, the "live-ins" of Mordden's narrator—a fictional version of Mordden himself—and his best friend Dennis Savage (*live-in* is Mordden's word for part houseboy, part lover). What seems valuable here for *Queer Externalities* is that part of being a tourist is learning one's way around, and part of doing so is finding guides: mentors, friends, fuck buddies, lovers. In addition to gossip, allegiance, sex, and camaraderie, guides educate us in bridging the gap between new and old worlds, shifting between strange and familiar registers. They alert us to zones of safety and to remaining pockets of danger.

It's apt, therefore, that *Queer Externalities* begins and ends by looking at instances involving young adults: in chapter 1, the fictional teens from gay YA literature, and in chapter 5, the real-life male teens approached online by former Representative Mark Foley. Interesting that demographic—real teens and twentysomethings, that is—is a pressing task for queer activists who are interested in more than mere assimilation. These young queers, raised on *Will & Grace* and *Queer as Folk*, are, anecdotally at least, unmotivated by the gay political agenda set by national groups such as the HRC. Even though, from their personal lives, some teens may know that harassment, violence, and discrimination have hardly been eradicated by media visibility and economic interpellation, perhaps they're cynical about the ability of politics to address their concerns. If young queers are casting their lots in other battles (against the Iraq War, on behalf of the medically uninsured), it's not necessarily the case that they've left their queerness behind, forsaken queer interests and investments. What's required, possibly, is that this generation must find something of interest in being queer. Regardless of their own political (dis)interest, they must not lose sight of the fact that the culture at large as well as certain specific entities (from the GOP to the TVC) regard them—their sexuality, their person—as political, as fodder for palpable discrimination and invidious, socially poisonous rhetorical attacks. As Eve Sedgwick reminds us in "How to Bring Your Kids Up Gay," despite certain undeniable signs of gay acceptance, there is little institutionalized "resistance to the wish endemic in the culture," "the wish that gay people not exist":

> the number of persons or institutions by whom the existence of gay people is treated as a precious desideratum, a needed condition of life is small. The presiding asymmetry of value assignment between hetero and homo goes unchallenged everywhere: advice on how to help your kids turn out gay, not to mention your students, your parishioners, your therapy clients, or your military subordinates is less ubiquitous than one might think. On the other hand, the scope of institutions whose programmatic undertaking is to prevent the development of gay people is unimaginably large. (75–76)

Young queers need to excavate a history already sinking beneath the horizon—the gay and lesbian movement's past alliances and commitments, triumphs and frailties—and to avoid the numbing lure of uncritical, assimilationist consumer and political engagement. They need to resist the apoliticizing of queer, if not all, Americans. Resisting is not easy: media punditry and government policy seem distant from everyday life. Politicians may seem, at best, jokes; at worst, corrupt hypocrites with little obligation to or interest in "the people." Retaining a sense of what it means to be queer needn't interfere with competing or kindred attachments, with establishing amalgams or partitions. Still, young queers ought not lose sight of their queerness, both as that which potentially maps onto other progressively minded struggles (via race, class, age, gender, or disability) yet whose elemental remainder is homosexuality: gay and lesbian sex and speech, queer culture and politics. They might find—and teachers and activists might help them discover—the energizing irateness, the appetite for neutrality and justice, and the regard for the merits of partiality that queer embraces. As Sedgwick notes above, however, reaching young queers is difficult (at least until they leave high school), given the barriers in public and private education to substantive discussions of homosexuality in the classroom—or, for that matter, in entertainment media aimed at teens—barriers erected and maintained out of supposedly antiquated fears of contamination, promotion, and recruitment.

Have no fear: that maudlin, heteronormative, and (as Lee Edelman observes) ultimately toxic bromide "the children are our future" does not underwrite the current project. It simply cannot. For the children in that cliché are implicitly heterosexual; that is, they will go on to have children themselves. It goes without saying, the cliché insinuates, that they've been produced by heterosexual intercourse. But queer children cannot be reached in the same way as the nonqueer. They cannot be addressed so abstractly. Inasmuch as queer children have, heteronormatively speaking, no future, they are not the children of the platitude. Queer youth, in many places in America, have more resources than they might have had twenty or more years ago, but the culture at large still does not address queerness in ways other than the superficial or cosmetic. Queer youth might turn up anywhere. They might, even now, be beaten, intimidated, convinced that silence or pretense is their safest or easiest option. Less ominous, but equally damaging, is the possibility they might be convinced that being queer isn't the most (or even *an*) important fact about themselves. But why shouldn't it be? Because it sets straights on edge, because it makes queer youth stand too much apart from their peers, their surroundings? I would ask them to consider the inimical consequences of willingly making oneself less unsettling, or at least minimizing one's nonnormativity. But even if comfortably queer, they might find their initial political or identitarian awakening along some other axis. We must keep looking. We must also give them something to look for, should they—when they—glance our way.

Notes

Introduction

1. Other major corporations that provide domestic partnership benefits include 3M, Boeing, Cisco Systems, Coca-Cola, Dow, Dupont, Ford, General Motors, Goldman Sachs, Hewlett-Packard, Johnson & Johnson, McDonald's, Merck, Target, and Verizon. The Human Rights Campaign Web site provides a comprehensive listing of private and public employers that have policies covering the same-sex domestic partners of employees (<http://www.hrc.org/Template.cfm?Section=Work_Life>).

2. Strides made toward domestic partner benefits might, of course, just as easily be seen as far from the spoils of victory. While an ethical step toward economic parity with heterosexuals, such benefits are only a stopgap measure necessitated by the legal nonrecognition of gay and lesbian partnerships as marriage. In chapter 3 of *The Trouble with Normal*, Michael Warner delivers a lucid polemic against the mad dash toward the altar in which most of the gay community seemed headily engaged during the 1990s—ignoring both the gay and lesbian movement's historic critique of normativity and state-regulated sexuality and the fact that securing marriage rights for gays and lesbians does nothing to rectify the inequity with which the bundling of a whole host of legal and economic rights and privileges with marriage still discriminates against the unmarried, whether queer or straight.

3. Cogent analyses of the gay conservative movement have been made by Lisa Duggan, Richard Goldstein, and Paul Robinson. Jack Malebranche, writing ostensibly as neither a conservative nor a liberal but, he says, on behalf of "androphiles" (non–gay-identified men who have sex with men), might well agree with gay conservatives critical of gay activism. For Malebranche, unlike some gay conservatives, it's not that gay activism exacerbates or creates homophobia; rather, it's that gay activism is no longer necessary. There's no oppression to fight:

> The Gay Advocacy Industry must maintain the illusion of oppression and victimization so that hundreds of thousands of checkbook revolutionaries can believe they are fighting for their own freedom. But the truth is that they're already free to do just about anything. So, like any movement that has achieved its goals but can't just close up shop,

> the Gay Advocacy Industry looks for new problems, and creates them (or exaggerates their importance) if necessary. The Gay Advocacy Industry's biggest problem is not the Religious Right, it is the possibility that same-sex-oriented people don't need them for much of anything. If homos don't feel victimized or oppressed, they'll stop writing all those checks. (33–34)

4. For a more detailed explanation of externality in its economic sense, see Richard Cornes and Todd Sandler's *The Theory of Externalities, Public Goods, and Club Goods* (1996).

5. The focus of *Queer Externalities*—reaching back temporally and conceptually only as far as the 1970s—suggests in no way a prescriptive limit, either for studies of the cultural forces examined here or for the lexicon through which cultural studies and queer studies appraise their subject matter. Histories of sexuality such as George Chauncey's landmark study *Gay New York* suggest that our understanding of gay sex as integral to homosexuality—in effect, as defining its participants as gay—is a fairly recent development. Chauncey documents that, in early-twentieth-century New York City for example, gender roles rather than sexual acts tended to determine sexual identification. Thus, although for middle-class American gay men the shift toward sex-based identification came earlier than it did among working-class males in this period, "the gay world was only one of the worlds in which most gay men moved, a richly supportive and engaging world for many, but not their only source of identity" (274). Chauncey argues that we should be wary of measuring gay American men in the early 1900s (or, implicitly, in any period or context outside our own) against present-day standards of identification:

> Many in a later generation of gay men considered it a betrayal of their identities not to be "out" to their straight associates at work and in other social settings, but the salient division between gay men in the prewar years [WWII] tended to be between men who covertly acknowledged their homosexuality to other gay men and those who refused to do even that. Most middle-class men believe for good reason that their survival depended on hiding their homosexuality from hostile straight outsiders, and they respected the decision of other men to do so as well. Indeed, a central requirement of the moral code that governed gay life and bound gay men to one another was that they honor other men's decisions to keep their homosexuality a secret and do all they could to help protect that secret from outsiders. (276)

To clarify the boundaries of my own project, my statements about coming out (a concept whose shifting meaning Chauncey also traces) are not intended as universalizing claims about homosexuality: the closet and "coming out" are post-Stonewall concepts whose specificity qualifies their applicability to earlier generations of gay men and men-who-have-sex-with-men (MSMs) (see

Chauncey 5-8). (MSMs includes not just straight-identified men on the "down low" but gay and bisexual men who, for a variety of reasons, either are out to no or relatively few people or who disidentify with the "gay scene," the gay community, or with so-called typical queers.) Chauncey notes, however, that, despite the periodization of such concepts, gay men in the prewar era already

> disagreed about whether a man was morally obliged to reveal his homosexuality to other gay men. Some men felt no such obligation, but they were bitterly resented by others who considered them hypocrites and cowards for not acknowledging their membership in "the club" to other members. "What was criminal was denying it to your sisters," one man in the latter camp declared. "Nobody cared about coming out to straights."
>
> Such debates hinged on men's different perceptions of the boundaries of the gay world and the requirements of "membership" in it. (276)

Still today, many MSMs might well face very real impediments to coming out as gay or simply as MSMs (fear of violence, job loss, being disowned by family or community of origin). For these men, a "double life" remains a valid "tactical response to the dangers posed by the revelation of their homosexuality to straight people" (273). Chauncey's portrait of a vibrant gay urban world in early-twentieth-century Manhattan is a welcome caution against "misinterpret[ing] silence as acquiescence" by "constru[ing] resistance in the narrowest of terms—as the organization of formal political groups and petitions" (5). But it's difficult to say the same for all present-day MSMs. Naturally, there are other ways to resist than by political action or by nelling out in public; thus it's partly because gay political organization and public presence are now thinkable—and partly because they are still unthinkable and fiercely resisted by many Americans—that MSMs' identification with gay men, at least politically if not communally, is of graver importance than ever. The lack, if not inconceivability, of a gay rights movement during the period Chauncey writes about, did not preclude a gay public presence or the gay world's transversal of straight public life. As I discuss further in the concluding chapter, my aim is not to legislate behavior or merely to resuscitate the post-Stonewall war cry of activism through outing (or by voluntarily coming out)—although the latter is arguably a viable tool in a wider set of strategic moves. One way of getting at my point is to think of the closet in a broader sense: MSMs such as Mark Foley and Matt Sanchez (see chapter 5) are quite different from Chauncey's prewar subjects; perhaps that goes without saying. Though known to be gay by political insiders or paying tricks, Foley and Sanchez are closeted in the sense of not being connected to a gay world. That connection—and the willingness to enunciate it (for those who are safely able to do so)—is the ethical aspiration of *Queer Externalities*: to own the stigma that gay sex still bears, to make common cause with the value of there being something outside and distinct from the norm.

6. Matthew Breen discusses several other British bands and individual musicians who have come out with no impact on sales or popularity.

7. Malebranche's paean to "real" masculinity—the kind gays need, he says, to reclaim as their so-called organic right—seems proud of its deadening essentialism:

> Homosexual males are males who have been robbed of a masculine ideal. Most are lost boys without a sense of what it means to be men—Peter Pans who never become men and leave the never-neverland of the Gay Party Life.
>
> Homosexual males don't become men because they're never expected to, because they don't recognize themselves as "real" men; they regard straight men as MEN and regard themselves as *something else.* Because they've been stigmatized as being effeminate, they play at being womanlike. . . . But all of [their] innate maleness—that aggressive, restless energy—finds an outlet in promiscuous sex, drug use, alcohol abuse, and generally adolescent behavior.
>
> . . . Because homosexual men have traditionally been beyond the pale of conventional morality, there are no codes of morality that govern them as a group. There's no ideal or model to guide their behavior. Productive male role models are virtually nonexistent. Gay icons are virtually all tortured, self-destructive artists, and most are female.
>
> . . . The purpose here is to reclaim masculinity for *androphiles*, to reclaim manhood—this religion of man—and adapt it to their condition. Prohibition against homosexuality . . . [is] breaking down. . . . Only the divisive gay identity stands in the way of homosexual males taking their rightful place beside men and truly becoming men in their own right. By perceiving themselves as men . . . and dropping all of the baggage that comes with gayness, they can look to all men, straight men and homos alike, for productive models of masculinity that are compatible with their own *essential masculinity.* They can look to great men, manly men, for guidance. They can build their own personal pantheon of male gods and mold their own sense of what it means to be a man in the image of those gods, as other men do. (78–80)

Overestimating the progress of tolerance, Malebranche is as much a gay assimilationist as Andrew Sullivan, Bruce Bawer, or James Collard. Itching to be allowed access to the macho inner circle, Malebranche seems willfully unaware of the ways in which so many "real" men are still homophobic (whether violently or not) and the degree to which heteronormative masculinity itself still rests squarely on a disavowal of homosexuality. Malebranche wants to belong to a club that wouldn't have someone like him as a member.

8. As David Halperin puts it, "If contemporary gay and lesbian identity seems to hover in suspense between these different and discontinuous discourses

of sodomy, gender inversion, and same-sex love, the same can be said even more emphatically about homosexual identity as we attempt to trace it back in time. The essence of the constructionist approach to the history of homosexuality, after all, was to argue that homosexuality is a modern construction, not because no same-sex sexual acts or erotic labels existed before 1869, when the term 'homosexuality' first appeared in print but because no single category of discourse or experience existed in the pre-modern and non-Western worlds that comprehended exactly the same range of same-sex sexual behaviors, desires, psychologies, and socialities, as well as the various forms of gender deviance, that now fall within the capacious definitional boundaries of homosexuality" (*How to Do* 106).

9. The core of Halperin's advance in (homo)sexuality studies can be found in the fourth chapter of *How to Do the History of Homosexuality* entitled "How to Do the History of Male Homosexuality" (104–37).

10. In theoretical terms, this disagreement—over how subversively interpellated subjects can use the terms of the ideological structures they inhabit and are, in some views, constituted by—is one between New Historicism and cultural materialism. Cultural materialism views the possibilities for slippage, contestation, and resistance more optimistically than New Historicism. Similarly, in an essay on Freud, Michael Warner draws attention to the problem of analyzing sexuality from within its discursive bounds: "how difficult it is to analyze a discourse of sexuality, when our own tools of analysis *are* that discourse" ("Homo-Narcissism" 191).

11. See Thomas C. Greene's "Mass Murder in the Skies: Was the Plot Feasible?"

12. The zombie film *28 Weeks Later* (2007; dir. Juan Carlos Fresnadillo), a sequel to Roddy Doyle's *28 Days Later* (2002), draws a similar connection, this time between the War on Terror and a virus that turns humans into flesh-eating monsters. Plot points revolve around the threat of carriers (of the virus) and the imperfection of barriers designed to keep toxicity at bay. Interestingly, it's the nuclear family—more, specifically, the children—that defies an imposed quarantine, breaks the barrier, and brings about (re)infection.

1. At the End of the Rainbow

1. Other contemporary gay YA titles, though not examined here, include Joe Babcock's *The Boys and the Bees* (2005), James Howe's *Totally Joe* (2005), Lisa Papademetriou and Chris Tebbetts's *M or F?* (2005), and Brian Sloan's *Tale of Two Summers* (2006). As I discussed in the introduction, with the exception of *Rubyfruit Jungle*, the texts and events to which *Queer Externalities* responds—though read for their implications for queers in general—are gay-themed. A worthwhile subject for future scholarship is the lesbian-themed YA novels published over the past decade, including Bett Williams's *Girl Walking Backwards*

(1998), Julia Watts's *Finding H.F.* (2001), Bonnie Shimko's *Letters in the Attic* (2002), Lauren Myracle's *Kissing Kate* (2003), two titles by Julie Anne Peters—*Keeping You a Secret* (2003) and *Far from Xanadu* (2005)—and a twenty-fifth anniversary reissue, in 2007, of Nancy Garden's once censored 1982 novel, *Annie on My Mind.* Work remains to be done in mapping out how these texts connect to, reconfigure, or refuse notions of utopianism, identitarianism, and normative heterosexuality—and whether they do so in ways that parallel or diverge from the gay YA works examined here. (Though perhaps misrepresentative, a cursory review of lesbian YA titles suggests a more realistic, less utopian ethos.) It should also be noted that my focus is on specific gay YA titles—*Geography Club*, *Boy Meets Boy*, and the *Rainbow* series—which were not just displayed at major retailers such as Barnes & Noble but also cross-marketed in gay and lesbian bookstores (where they're placed side by side with adult titles).

2. In her argument for moving beyond the constructionist-essentialist debate regarding homosexuality, Eve Sedgwick cites the "unimaginably large" "scope of institutions whose programmatic undertaking is to prevent the development of gay people." One could argue that gay utopian novels such as those of Sanchez and Levithan (and to a lesser extreme, Hartinger) rely on the idea of "cultural malleability"—which, for Sedgwick, when regarded as "the only conceivable theatre for effective politics" (even "gay-loving" politics), risks "end[ing] in the overarching, hygienic Western fantasy of a world without any more homosexuals in it" (*The Epistemology of the Closet* 42). *Queer Externalities* generally recommends not losing sight, amid the euphoria of media visibility and incremental legal advances, of what Sedgwick calls the "relatively unchallenged aegis of a culture's desire that gay people *not be*, [the fact that] there is no unthreatened, unthreatening conceptual home for a concept of gay origins" (43).

3. It's true that utopian events are, by definition, unlikely to come to pass. An additional, more practical stumbling block is the umbilical dependence (noted by Derrida, Sedgwick, and others) of oppressive—in this case, conservative social or religious—ideology on an abject(ed) "other."

4. As Didier Eribon observes in *Insult and the Making of the Gay Self*, the conservative objection to "the 'ghettoization' of gays and lesbians in big cities" is "often nothing more than a disguised insult produced by a phobic reaction to the collective visibility of gays and lesbians," a visibility that calls into question notions about gay shame, self-hatred, and abnormality that underpin a good deal of conventional religious and political ideology. Yet Eribon shrewdly points out that liberal objections to gay and lesbian urban ghettoization, at base, stem from the same discomfort (if less hatefully justified). The tolerant, pitying stance of not wanting to see gays and lesbians ostensibly confined by the limits of the ghetto plays, even if unconsciously, on the desire not to see gays and lesbians:

> Visibility is an escape path from the terrible interior ghetto that is experienced by a soul that has been subjected by shame. What the

> discourse of liberal tolerance would recommend is nothing other than the perpetuation of precisely that interior ghetto: its recommendations amount to a suggestion that this inferiorized identity be maintained within the "invisible" space of private life, the space accorded to gay people by heterosexuals, to the minority by the majority. This call for discretion would annihilate the historical victories that today allow one to leave behind the psychological ghetto. (101)

Likewise, well-meaning liberals who cringe at flamboyant—or even measured but still public—displays of homosexuality are motivated by the same cultural impulse toward gay erasure: "When gays and lesbians are reproached for displaying their private lives in public, for crossing the line between public and private, we are again dealing with the protection of privilege—of heterosexual privilege" (102).

5. The only substantive critical readings I have been able to discover are those by Louise Kawada, Judith Roof, and Leslie Fishbein. Among these, Fishbein alone takes issue with the novel's reputation as one of the greatest contributions to lesbian writing.

6. Although calling a woman Molly suspects of being a lesbian a "'closet fairy'" may be the most egregious example, the following quotes also show Brown's appropriation of gay (male) argot and camp humor (128): "'She's been down with everything but the Titanic'" (80); "'Honey, I didn't know whether to go blind, shit, or run for my life'" (119); "'Better wear your chastity belt.'/'Haven't got one. Do you think B.O. will do the trick?'" (166).

7. Brown's vision is more exacting even than other "radical utopias" discussed by Diane Crowder—both those from the early 1970s, which "envision a world where gender does not exist," and those from the mid- to late 1970s, where "we find a proliferation of lesbian and feminist utopias depicting attractive worlds, but which are often based upon a philosophy—essentialism—that deprives readers of any realistic means of attaining the better world" (240, 244).

8. Credos similar to Wittman's can be found in a number of other liberation-era writings: "We want to reach the homosexual entombed in you [heterosexuals], to liberate our brothers and sisters, locked in the prisons of your skulls. We want you to understand what it is to be our kind of outcast—but also to understand our kind of love, to hunger for your own sex. Because unless you understand this, you will continue to look at us with uncomprehending eyes, fake liberal smiles; you will be incapable of loving us. *We will never go straight until you go gay*" (Shelley 34; emphasis added).

9. In his analysis of *Rubyfruit Jungle* and other gay and lesbian novels, Jonathan Dollimore concludes that

> binary oppositions are a "violent hierarchy" [Derrida] where one of the two terms forcefully governs the other. A crucial stage in their deconstruction involves an overturning, an inversion which "brings low what

> was high." The political effect of ignoring this stage, of trying to jump beyond the hierarchy into a world quite free of it, is simply to leave it intact in the only world we have. . . . [T]he reversal of the authentic/inauthentic opposition in *Rubyfruit Jungle* . . . [is an example of] . . . overturning in [this] sense. [It is one of several] stages in a *process* of resistance, one whose effects can never be guaranteed. . . . (98)

I agree with Dollimore's critique of "trying to jump beyond . . . hierarchy into a world quite free of it," but I think he has misapplied that critique in the case of *Rubyfruit.* A more sophisticated response—not jumping beyond but working within—motivates Caryl Churchill's play *Cloud Nine* (1981).

10. This deconstructive reading of identity is typical of many queer theorists, including Donald Hall, Judith Butler (*Bodies That Matter* and *Gender Trouble*), and Michael Warner.

11. Karl Woelz's afterword to *M2M: New Literary Fiction* intervenes in this long-standing debate. Woelz notes that after nearly two decades (the 1980s and 1990s) of mainstream publishing support for gay and lesbian authors, most houses have "deemed [gay and lesbian readers] an unprofitable market segment": "All three critically acclaimed gay short fiction anthologies of the 1980s and 1990s no longer exist, almost all periodical venues for gay short fiction have dried up, and many (if not all) of the mainstream publishing houses have either abandoned gay-themed titles altogether or so drastically reduced support for them that it amounts to the same thing" (322).

12. Woelz has commented astutely on the current situation of gay and lesbian publishing, whereby the gay and lesbian market is deluged almost entirely with genre fiction (particularly erotica, romance, and self-help) while queer literary fiction (which publishers have deemed unprofitable) becomes increasingly more scarce.

13. In *The Feel-Good Curriculum*, Maureen Stout analyzes pernicious trends in American educational methods over the last decade or two, including the cult of self-esteem, the devaluation of knowledge, and the fetishizing of individualism at the cost of any notion of community. Of particular interest here are chapter 1 ("What Is School for Anyway?") and chapter 7 ("Too Many Degrees of Separation").

14. Levithan's *Wide Awake* (2006), also set in the future, offers a similarly mixed state of affairs. For instance, there's worldwide health care, and a Jewish gay man has been elected president—suggesting a burgeoning of political liberalism, religious tolerance, and gay positivity. At the same time, formidable conservative resistance and prejudice continue: the President-Elect's conservative opponent calls for a recount of contested votes in Kansas, and the opponent's supporters (known as "Decents") pepper their rhetoric with anti-Semitism and homophobia. The Decents are defeated and the President-Elect confirmed, but only because his opponent is seen on camera admitting his scheme to steal the election.

15. For parenthetical references to Sanchez's trilogy, I have used the following abbreviations: RB for *Rainbow Boys*, RH for *Rainbow High*, and RR for *Rainbow Road.*

16. A study by C. J. Pascoe reveals the extent to which homophobia in high school still takes "the form of blatant antigay practices and, more commonly the staging of taken-for-granted heteronormative school ceremonies and traditions. . . . In this ferociously heteronormative context GSA [Gay-Straight Alliance] members had to struggle to get their club approved and have it recognized in school announcements" (161). As Pascoe notes elsewhere (30–31), administrators at the school where she conducted her research approved the GSA *only* when threatened with a lawsuit. In another sobering contrast to Sanchez's *Rainbow* world, "[s]everal gay pride events" at the school Pascoe writes about, "such as the Day of Silence and the celebration of National Coming Out Day, were barred from campus" (161).

17. See Butler, *Bodies That Matter*, 118.

18. Nelson may be functionally pushed aside by the Jason-Kyle romance and symbolically demoted as a nonjock; nevertheless, he functions as a character in his own right. Openly gay before the series begins, he has mentored Kyle, listened to him pine over Jason, and introduced him to elements of gay history and culture. After having unsafe casual sex with a man he meets online (an episode meant to rehearse the pop psychology cliché about the dangers of low self-esteem), Nelson enjoys a romantic arc that spans the first two novels. But in terms of the three protagonists, and despite the fact that he narrates one-third of each novel, he is inevitably the third wheel—harboring romantic feelings for Kyle, his best friend, and, later, more fleeting desires for Jason. Conveniently, Nelson survives both infatuations and, by the end of the final novel, finds a boyfriend in California and ends up staying there, putting a continent between the gay jocks and the femme. Similarly, while Jason's coming out may atone for distancing himself from "Nelly," it's only in the third novel that Jason learns to tolerate Nelson "'bobbing his head and snapping his fingers'" (RR 13). Once the butch can stomach the queen and his "24/7 gayness" (RR 86), the two can bond—through a basketball lesson, no less. Still, until Nelson finds a boyfriend, at the end of the third novel, he can only fantasize about acceptance. When the three friends stumble onto a Radical Faerie sanctuary in rural Tennessee, Nelson "imagin[es] a place where no one hassled you for being crazily queer, a place where you could be totally yourself" (RR 70). Though it sounds very much like what Molly Bolt is searching for, the Radical Faerie sanctuary is merely a way station for Nelson. Meeting the faeries helps Jason become more accepting of Nelson's flamboyance, seeing him in the context not of heterosexuals and straight-acting jocks like himself and Kyle but surrounded by other eccentric gay men. Perhaps without meaning to, however, the episode also marks the dearth of middle ground between jocks and the "'anti-mainstream radical fringe of free-spirited queers'" (RR 68).

19. See Halperin, *Saint Foucault*, 29–38; and Eve Sedgwick, *The Epistemology of the Closet*, 79, 83–84.

20. Eribon contextualizes these comments in terms of the historic tension within the gay and lesbian movement between "integration and subversion, assimilation and separatism" (118).

> Gay people . . . must set themselves up as a specific group in order to ask that they be seen and treated as no different from anyone else. Such demands will unleash reactions that both insist that they are different and insist that they not ask to be treated as different. That is to say, they are inevitably forced back to their point of departure: the perpetual choice between silence and "rebellion," between returning to the closet and affirming who they are. That is how gay people remain torn between two different levels of what is commonly referred to as "assimilation." There is assimilation by way of invisibility—to be silent, not to exist as gay. And there is the assimilation a certain number aspire to, the assimilation that would come with achieving equal legal rights. Some no longer care for the first form and find the second violently refused to them by the homophobic majority. This is an insurmountable paradox. Yet it is in this paradox that one finds all the political and cultural stakes of gay 'resubjectification' today, whether it be individual or collective. (118)

In *What Do Gay Men Want?* David Halperin suggests some ways around this impasse to gay subjectivity.

21. Although Kenneth Cimino (*Gay Conservatives: Group Consciousness and Assimilation* [2007]) regards the postgay movement as "short-lived" (i.e., defunct), recent works such as Bert Archer's *The End of Gay* (2003) suggest that the cause has not been abandoned entirely and may still be attractive to some (Cimino 124). Ritch Savin-Williams (*The New Gay Teenager* [2005]) believes that many gay, lesbian, bisexual, and questioning teens, although unlikely to couch their ideas in the long historical context Archer does, adhere to something like a postgay consciousness. As a matter of accuracy, while James Collard did not coin the term *postgay*, as one of the postgay movement's most vocal proponents, he did much to popularize it. For a detailed lineage of the term's provenance and early use, see Gary Drum, "He's In. He's Out. He's Post-Gay: The Misadventures of James Collard's Post-Gay Journey to America." Michael Warner (*The Trouble with Normal* 61–71) delivers a fairly caustic analysis of postgay rhetoric: it "appeals to those gay men and lesbians who were least happy to be political in the first place, who have enough of a safe place in the world—thanks in part to past struggle—to think of their own lives no longer in terms of struggle" (62).

22. See, for instance, Hall's *Queer Theories*.

23. An uncritical, if unconscious, cathexis to norms founders on another obstacle: there is something endemic to homosexuality about insult. It's not that

the closet is a wholly salubrious, or wholly deforming, space; either assessment oversimplifies the matter. As Didier Eribon argues, visibility—"insofar as it is a manner of assuming and laying claim to an identity that has been stigmatized by insult"—may "partially defuse . . . the charge of social violence that insult carries" (66). Nonetheless, "'Visibility' does not, of course, disable oppression, and it is not capable of thwarting the subjugating processes of surveillance, of policing, of the norm, for it cannot in and of itself cause insult or the social dissymmetry of which it is a symptom to disappear" (66).

24. Eribon states that "heterosexuality is one of the major, foundational characteristics of what is referred to as public space. In that space, heterosexuality is displayed, recalled, manifested, at every moment, in every gesture, in every conversation—as any trip to the cinema, to a café, to a restaurant, any bus ride, any conversation at work can attest" (104). On the functional centrality of insult to public (heterosexual) discourse, see Eribon 61–69.

25. On the betrayal of the gay and lesbian movement's past insights on the value of resistance to the norm (which does not necessarily mean escape), see Warner, *The Trouble with Normal*, 59–60, 66–71, 87–91.

26. For material from Savin-Williams most relevant to the current discussion, see 70–92, 156–77, and 194–223. My interpretive and philosophical disagreement with Savin-Williams on certain points does not apply to his work as a whole. *The New Gay Teenager* insightfully amends flaws in previous models of assessing teen sexuality—for instance, reconsidering the misleading but influential "suicidal gay teen" profile, revising Vivienne Cass's now-standard six-stage development model, and considering the impact of race and ethnicity on conventional thinking about teen sexuality.

27. For Warner, "to have a politics of" identity without "a politics of shame" is "to doom oneself to incoherence and weakness. It is to challenge the stigma on identity, but only by reinforcing the shame of sex"—and, one might add, the shame of difference, of being nonnormative (31). Warner's criticism of the assimilationist wish that homosexuality could be defined by more than sex and sexuality is equally applicable to the postgay movement and to the q-topian boy-novels: in both cases, a vision beyond labels such as *gay* and *lesbian* relies on "the utopian notion that somewhere, one might not be defined by one's sexuality, that stigma might simply vanish from among the living. But since that utopia exists nowhere in *this* culture's near future, the idea reads as wishfulness, or even as self-contradiction. It is hard to claim that homosexuality is irrelevant as long you feel the need to make the claim. If sexuality were 'irrelevant . . .' we wouldn't have much to say to one another" (46).

28. Concurring voices include those of Andrew Sullivan (*Same-Sex Marriage: Pro and Con*, xxi–xxx), Jonathan Rauch, and Evan Wolfson. Of the three, Wolfson makes a rights-based argument as well as an emotional/normative one. The argument for gay marriage least enthralled to heteronormativity is that by Evan Gerstmann.

29. Halperin outlines the historicity of homosexuality—a contested concept, admittedly—in *How to Do the History of Homosexuality*, 10–12, 105–10, 130–34.

30. For an insightful reading of the gay sidekick trend and the subordination of gay desire (on television, in this case), see Ron Becker 190–94.

31. In regard to the complex and not always liberating ramifications of coming out, Sedgwick reminds us of the

> radical uncertainty closeted gay people are likely to feel about who is in control of information about their sexuality identity. This has something to do with a realism about secrets . . . but it has much more to do with the complications in the notion of gay identity, so that no one person can take control over all the multiple, often contradictory codes by which information about sexuality identity and activity can seem to be conveyed. In many, if not most, relationships, coming out is a matter of crystallizing intuitions or convictions that had been in the air for a while already and had already established their own power-circuits of silent contempt, silent blackmail, silent glamorization, silent complicity. After all, the position of those who think they *know something about one that one may not know oneself* is an excited and empowered one—whether what they think one doesn't know is that one somehow *is* homosexual, or merely that one's supposed secret is known to them. The glass closet can license insult ("I'd never have said those things if I'd *known* you were gay!"—yeah, sure!); it can also license far warmer relations, but relations whose potential for exploitiveness is built into the optics of the asymmetrical, the specularized, and the inexplicit. (79–80)

32. Though presumed gay by fellow students once the GSA goes public at the end of *Geography Club*, Russel is not fully out in the second novel (*The Order of the Poison Oak*); for instance, at his summer job as a camp counselor, only his friends from the GSA, Min and Gunnar, know he's gay. Russel comes out to his parents during the third novel in the Russel Middlebrook series, *Split Screen* (2007).

2. "In my day it used to be called a limp wrist"

1. Gay voters, among others, may have found Kerry's apparent equivocations on this issue worrisome, and, materially, Kerry was divided on the issue: on the one hand, he supported state constitutional amendments banning gay marriage (because, he argued, "historically . . . the application of marriage laws has always been state defined"); on the other hand, he voted against the Defense of Marriage Act, criticized the proposed Federal Marriage Amendment, and promised to "provid[e] federal benefits" to same-sex couples by "fight[ing] for" federal civil-union legislation (Keen pars. 15, 23). (For analyses of Kerry on the marriage question, consult Patrick Healy and Frank Phillips; Lisa Keen; "Kerry

Signed Letter Backing Gay Marriage"; Rick Klein; and Carla Marinucci.) Kerry's position seems less a flip-flop than the nuanced stance typical of any politician trying to reach voters who are divided, as even Democrats are on this question. Also divided was the Bush/Cheney ticket. During the 2000 campaign Cheney said the issue should be left up to the states. When in early 2004 Bush violated party ethos by endorsing the Federal Marriage Amendment and thus federal encroachment on state prerogative, Cheney held firm to his state-centered position (see Kaufman and Allen). Neither Bush's flip-flop, Cheney's variance from the new party line, nor even the fact that Cheney had an out gay daughter gave much pause to those making hay of, and sometimes just making up, Kerry's about-faces.

2. Duggan provides an overview of the roots and advent of neoliberalism in the introduction and chapter 1 ("Downsizing Democracy"). She also contends that internal divisions on the progressive Left—"unproductive battles over economic versus cultural politics, identity-based vs. Left universalist rhetoric, theoretical critiques vs. practical organizing campaigns"—have ill-equipped progressives to counter the success of neoliberal policies (xix). Facing little substantive opposition, neoliberals have managed to "shrink the spaces for public life, democratic debate, and cultural expression . . . *through* their own versions of identity politics and cultural policies, inextricably connected to economic goals for upward redistribution of resources" (xx). That is, neoliberalism's "overt rhetoric of separation between economic policy on the one hand, and political and cultural life on the other" has been, in practice, simply untrue (xiv). By comparison, the Left has largely been unable to connect its own commitment to identity politics to its progressive economic goals—the sort of transformative synthesis that Laclau and Mouffe's radical democratic theory seeks to accomplish (see my conclusion).

3. As Eve Sedgwick among others notes (*The Epistemology of the Closet* 31, 34), we must be careful to distinguish gender from sexuality, articulate when and where they differ and overlap. Bush campaign rhetoric in 2004 targeted Kerry's sexuality primarily, or (in a foreseeably reductive, knowingly potent slip) gender tied to or construed as sexuality.

4. All of these shows are now off the air. Having been spoiled by an embarrassment of gay riches on network and cable television over the past decade, one wonders what effect this sudden and at least momentary decrease in queer visibility will have, if any, on the continuing battle for GLBT rights and public discourse regarding homosexuality from both the Right and the Left.

5. It should be noted that I am not basing the "queering" of Kerry on the much discussed article by Jeff Gannon/James Guckert suggesting that Kerry would be "the first gay president" (qtd. in Corn, "Gannon-Guckert-Gate" par. 12). David Corn, typically unwavering in his animadversions of the Bush administration (see Corn's *The Lies of George W. Bush*), finds nothing inappropriate about a working male escort, unaccredited reporter, and partisan operative being

given months' worth of day passes to attend White House press conferences and lob soft, flattering questions when Bush or McClellan gets boxed in. Nonetheless, Corn is right on the subtext of the "first gay president" quote. Gannon/Guckert coined the phrase to shorthand Kerry's public image as a supporter of gay rights (in the same way that "'Bill [Clinton] is considered by some members of the African-American community to be "the first black president" because of their perceptions of his positions with regard to minority issues'" [qtd. in Corn, "Gannon-Guckert-Gate" par. 13]).

6. In *The Trouble with Normal*, Michael Warner expounds on the enormous cultural energy spent on "selling" heterosexuality—in short, the cardinal social humor of heteronormativity: "People are constantly encouraged to believe that heterosexual desire, dating, marriage, reproduction, childrearing, and home life are not only valuable to themselves, but the bedrock on which every other value in the world rests. Heterosexual desire and romance are thought to be the very core of humanity. . . . It is the one thing celebrated in every film plot, every sitcom, every advertisement. It is the one thing to which every politician pays obeisance, couching every dispute over guns and butter as an effort to protect family, home, and children" (47). The excess of positive messages about straight desire risks gilding the lily of the latter's status as biological imperative.

7. Fritz and Nyhan track the Kerry-as-French story as it wended its way through both conservative and mainstream media outlets. Robert Greenwald's 2004 documentary *Outfoxed: Rupert Murdoch's War on Journalism* provides an accessible, condensed example of FOX News' Francophobic coverage of Kerry. (See also Melanie; Judy; and Robert Furs.) Unsurprisingly, this sort of pabulum played best with FOX News and other conservative and religious broadcasters and news sources (for example, Dale Hurd on CBN, the Christian Broadcasting Network; Diana West, for *Townhall.com*; Elizabeth Bryant at the *Washington Times*; and, of course, Brit Hume on *FOX News Sunday*). While noninflammatory coverage of the so-called story was reassuringly spotty and short-lived, media outlets such as ABC, *CNSNews.com* (Cybercast News Service), and the Raleigh, North Carolina, *News & Observer* were eager to carry water for the RNC and their operatives (for stories from these outlets, see Fritz and Nyhan, Eva Cahen, and Rob Christensen, respectively). Robert Furs points out that this smear, as with the attack on Kerry's military service, could be seen as a case of projection: Kerry, appearing on MSNBC's *Hardball*, pointed out that Bush aide and hagiographer Karen Hughes "'was born in Paris'" (par. 3). While American Francophobia might seem so prevalent as to be taken for granted, Richard Z. Chesnoff's *The Arrogance of the French: Why They Can't Stand Us—And Why the Feeling Is Mutual* (2005) stands as a recent example.

8. Paul Robinson's sound observations about the emergence of a vocal gay conservative movement provide an instructive corollary: "gay conservatives seek to rescue homosexuality from its association with gender deviance—with effeminate men and mannish women" (2). Given that gays themselves "have often

been divided in their feelings about effeminacy" (25), stridently heterosexual Manion is predictably phobic in railing against all things feminine or effeminate. In chapter 1 of *The Wimp Factor*, Stephen Ducat traces the ubiquity and interrelation of femiphobia and homophobia in twentieth-century American culture and politics; chapter 6 analyzes the striking correlation between homophobia, femiphobia, and increased political conservatism among American males over the past decade.

9. Bernard Chapin's characterization of feminism is similarly overblown, though infinitely more tasteless and clinically paranoid: "Once again we see that radical feminism is little different from Nazism in that you substitute 'Jew' for 'white male' and get the same evil product" (par. 1). Rarely has the odious subtext of the "Feminazi" slur been so vividly realized.

10. Depending on the listener, what Stacy Lorenz describes as Bush's "cowboy masculinity" can demonstrate either tenacity or simplemindedness (par. 14).

11. The bare mention of "gay romance" by Maureen Dowd (in reference to reputed liberal support for same-sex marriage) sends Chapin into a classic tailspin: "No conservative gives a gosh darn what kind of romance occurs with gay members of the population. Our only request is that we shouldn't be forced to watch, participate or give legal sanction to it" (par. 6). The old saw of homophobia ("be silent and invisible, and we'll suffer your deviance") is given a new though unintentionally counterintuitive twist: "stay invisible, and don't ask for any rights that, since you're invisible, would impact my life in no tangible way."

12. As *Newsweek*'s cover story for November 15, 2004, put it—with a lingering reluctance to make distinctions between lies and truth—"the Swift Boat ads . . . were misleading, but they were very effective. The Kerry high command failed to see the potential damage until it was too late" (Thomas par. 3).

13. Sedgwick also comments on the nature of the double bind in *The Epistemology of the Closet* (9–10).

14. More shocking than any single smear for which Drudge is responsible is the fact that time and again his unsupported claims have found their way, due to laziness, bias, or some combination thereof, into the columns of credentialed mainstream journalists.

15. The pervasiveness, though not the spirit, of homophobic anti-Kerry political rhetoric is partly due to the multiple platforms of media delivery to which the Bush administration and the RNC have access: FOX News, the *Washington Times*, and other de facto organs of the Bush administration, including the recently discredited Talon News, the news service which was not a news service but a mouthpiece for GOPUSA, a Texas-based Republican organization. Nonpartisan causes, especially for the promulgation of baseless rumor and partisan talking points on formerly respectable networks such as CNN, include the echo chamber of the twenty-four-hour cable news cycle and, perhaps, a simple lack of integrity.

16. Edelman is quoting from Lacan's *Seminar, Book XX*, 120.

17. As the documentary *Outfoxed* (2004) pointed out with preinterview footage between Cameron and Bush, whom Cameron covered for FOX during the 2000 campaign while his wife was working in Bush's reelection campaign, Cameron's lack of objectivity is habitual. In an attempt to avoid a conflict of interest the next go round, FOX assigned Cameron to the Kerry trail in 2004. The ersatz quotes about Kerry make it clear that no one in Cameron's family was working for the Democrats at the time.

18. For dismissals of Rove's canard (in addition to his own denial, that is), see Mark Mellman and James Q. Wilson; for an early warning about precisely such a backlash, see Stanley Kurtz.

19. Discrete events may indeed foster surges of cultural homophobia. The U.S. Supreme Court's ruling on *Bowers v. Hardwick* (1986), which upheld the discriminatory criminalization of gay sex in spite of Georgia's gender-neutral definition of sodomy, constituted an "ostentatious declaration, for the private sector, of an organized open season on gay men" (Sedgwick, *Epistemology* 5). Despite (or perhaps because of) *Bowers*'s emergence at a time of alternating silence and hysteria about AIDS, the nation held its breath waiting to see if it had finally "caught it" (homosexuality, the "gay plague," if they were not already equated in the cultural imaginary). Yet the bated-breath anxiety of the mid-1980s seemed mild compared to the much more vocal, self-righteous wave of hatred and moral demagoguery unleashed by the Massachusetts Supreme Court's mandate to allow same-sex marriage on equal protection grounds and by *Lawrence et al. v. Texas* (2003), the ruling that reversed *Bowers* in striking down as unconstitutional any sodomy law (defined exclusively as same-sex or not). Although homophobia, like other prejudices, may be clearly punctuated by single historical acts, I would suggest that in America, at least since Stonewall if not well before, it is always open season (whether enunciated or basal) on queers.

20. For articles and postings about some but not all of these outings, see Adrian Brune, John Byrne, Rebecca Dana and Jose Antonio Vargas, John Hansen, John in D.C., Scheer, and the BuzzFlash editorials "Matt Drudge, A Gay Who Backs the Gay Bashers" and "Matt Drudge, Are You Gay?" A related, equally intriguing club is that constituted by antigay activist Phyllis Schlafly and antiabortion crusader Randall Terry, both of whom have gay sons. Terry, though most well-known for his work with Operation Rescue, raised eyebrows when he commented to Alan Colmes on the latter's radio show that "it's time that you and I admit to the whole world that's listening that we used to be homosexual lovers" (qtd. in Ellen).

In yet a further wrinkle, Kerry was accused of doing a little gay-baiting of his own when, in the third presidential debate, he mentioned Mary Cheney in his response to the question of whether he believed that homosexuality "is a choice": "We're all God's children," Kerry responded. "And I think that if you were to talk to Dick Cheney's daughter [Mary], who is a lesbian, she would tell you that she's being who she was, she's being who she was born as. I think if you talk to anybody, it's not a choice" (qtd. in Hollar par. 3). The very next morning Dick Cheney claimed to be a "'pretty angry father'" and his wife, Lynne (who herself once penned a lesbian romance novel), dubbed Kerry "'not a good man'" and his answer, a "'cheap political trick'" (Goodman par. 3; Laris par. 3; see also "Having It Both Ways"). First launched on CNN, Cheney's talking point—that Kerry is "'a man who will do anything to get elected'" (Hollar par. 5)—was soon wending its slimy way through the conservative media (see N.C.'s posting on *Media Matters for America*). Some of the press corps' more thoughtful members laid bare the inanity and outright falsehood of charges that Kerry violated Mary Cheney's privacy by outing her. As Julie Hollar, among others, points out, Mary Cheney has been out for years, serving as "liaison to the gay community for Coors Beer" and, in 2002 and 2003, "on the board of the Republican Unity Coalition . . . a gay organization founded to support George W. Bush. . . . Dick Cheney himself had spoken openly about Mary's sexuality, most recently at a campaign stop in Iowa (AP, Oct. 15, 2004)" (par. 16).

21. This bill apparently did not pass the Senate in 2005, given that in May 2007 the House passed a similar bill. Although the Senate was expected to approve the bill, President Bush threatened to veto it.

3. Queer Eye on the Prize

1. Not all response has been negative, obviously. The show's pilot episode garnered Bravo its second highest ratings ever, and NBC, which had recently acquired Bravo, was quickly running thirty-minute–formatted episodes after summer repeats of its own highly rated show *Will & Grace*, creating the first network gay programming block. In December 2003 the American Film Institute supplemented its annual 10-best lists in TV and film with a list of nine "moments of significance": *Queer Eye* was number two.

2. While some of the *Queer Eye* commentary dealt with comes from the academy or from industrial media organs such as the *Advocate*, a number of responses come from Internet-based publications such as *popMatters* or *PopPolitics.com* or discussion threads on sites such as *Snarkfest*—from what I would argue are, comparatively, "everyday" viewers. That is, the latter voices, borne on the medium of the Internet, are more democratic, whether they are freelance professionals or amateurs.

3. One notable exception is Christopher Kelly, writing in August 2003: "In the summer when a conservative Supreme Court has struck down Texas' anti-sodomy laws—surely the most momentous step forward for gay civil rights in this country—here is a show that portrays straight people and gay people as one happy community, bonding over foie gras, Lucky Brands Jeans and the virtues of eyebrow waxing" (par. 5).

4. Warner prefers the term "normalizing" to "assimilationist" (*The Trouble with Normal* 52). Semantics aside, the same "hierarchy of respectability" that

Warner delineates in the history of American gay and lesbian politics can be seen at work in discussions of *Queer Eye*, both in gay and mixed forums—discussions that, as this chapter shows, are "built on embarrassment" (49). As Warner observes, negotiations of the past twenty years for gay rights have, on the national level certainly, involved a quest for "respectability," "bargain[ing] for a debased psuedo-dignity, the kind that is awarded as a bribe for disavowing the indignity of sex and the double indignity of a politics built around sex"—and by extension, of a politics built around queers as sexualized beings (78, 66). I would connect much of the negative response to *Queer Eye* to the impulse, felt and acted on by the most well-meaning politically aware queers and straights alike, to hold at arm's length those more embarrassing members of queer culture, individuals whom it is too easy—and yet incorrect, inauthentic, and impoverishing—to dismiss as stereotypes. "The others, the queers who have sex in public toilets" (or at least joke about it as Carson does), "the boys who flaunt it as pansies or as leathermen," those "whose gender deviance makes them unassimilable to the menu of sexual orientations, the clones in the so-called gay ghetto . . .—all these flaming creatures are told that their great moment of liberation will come later . . . when we get to be about 'more than sexuality'" (Warner, *The Trouble with Normal* 66).

5. See Chasin 33–40. The studies to which Chasin refers, as well as other relevant analyses of gay marketing trends, are discussed in more detail by Dan Baker, "A History in Ads: The Growth of the Gay and Lesbian Market" and M.V. Lee Badgett, "Beyond Biased Samples." See also Badgett's "Income Inflation," "The Myth of Gay and Lesbian Affluence," and *Money, Myths, and Change*. Katherine Sender's *Business, Not Politics* provides a comprehensive history of gay niche marketing and analyzes its political and economic implications.

6. The negative reactions to the 1960s television show *Julia* illustrate the way in which even apparently progressive images are doomed to be labeled as damaging stereotypes. Yet as Ben Patrick Johnson, writing online for *Kiosque*, observes, using either Diahann Carroll or the Fab Five as benchmarks of inauthenticity is unfair and illogical: "Collectively, [the Fab Five] don't represent gay men as a whole, any more than Diahann Carroll represented black women when her fictional character Julia appeared . . . in 1968. No one TV program can demonstrate the breadth of a culture [or subculture]. . . . Thankfully, *Queer Eye* knows better than to pretend to such importance—to do so would be absurd" (par. 12).

7. Among the gripes about representation, the most valid come from Hemal Jhaveri and José Estaban Muñoz. According to Jhaveri, *Queer Eye* observes what seems to be "the rule for gay men on TV: cute, white, charming, and totally asexual" (par. 9). Aside from failing to explain how Jai Rodriguez qualifies as "white," Jhaveri is correct about the generally overbearing whiteness of (gay) pop culture representation. And yet the same charge can be levied at straight shows (*Friends*) as well as gay ones (*Will & Grace*). For another invocation of minstrelsy, see Sawyer pars. 1 and 12.

8. Andrew Sullivan is quite right to point out that the airing of *Queer Eye* hardly equals the legalization of marriage. On the other hand, Sullivan's advocacy of gay marriage (see *Same-Sex Marriage*) is driven—in a way that perceptive analysts such as Michael Warner find particularly troubling—by a quest more to be seen as normal than to secure equity under the law. In this context, Sullivan's reading of the show's invidious dynamic is simply another (albeit, more Foucauldian) version of Kelly's minstrelsy analogy or Sawyer's and Kanner's "body servant" trope: "It seems as if heterosexuals are willing to tolerate homosexuals, but only from a position of power. . . . [A]rguing that [a] lesbian couple is morally indistinguishable from a straight couple is where many draw the line" (35). Sullivan could not be more on target in unmasking the unspoken homophobia and entitlement that make even the most tolerant citizens, or those who admit the rational basis of queer claims to legal parity, balk at the line in the sand that is gay marriage. Yet as an analyst of *Queer Eye*, Sullivan conflates its appropriation of the heterosexual narrative (get the girl) with an endorsement of heteronormativity as the natural order from which the Fab Five accept their exclusion. My discussion of the realities of stereotyping and camp humor in *Queer Eye* demonstrates, I hope, that the latter is not the case.

9. While it's worthwhile being cautious about the risk of co-optation, in my reading, *Queer Eye*'s self-consciousness about its commercial context allows its play with and interrogation of sexual and gender stereotypes to avoid being compromised. Contrary readings, such as that by Robert Bateman, take a more cynical view:

> At the end of each episode, the Fab Five retire to a comfortable living room where, by television, they watch as their aesethetically reconstituted straight man reunites happily, though at times ambivalently, with his spouse or girlfriend. The viewers witness not only this reunion but also the Fab Five witnessing this reunion. Thus, *QE* serves up the image of gay men looking longingly at the spectacle of heterosexual romance. Queer men are positioned comfortably outside this spectacle; they are onlookers, accomplices, facilitators, but alas, not participants. The Fab Five are ultimately portrayed as desiring beings, but their desire, it appears, is to be straight or to have the type of relationships straight people have, or maybe, to have no relationships at all. Or perhaps their desire is for the straight man whom they must regretfully relinquish to his female paramour. On the other hand, with the depiction of gay men staring longingly at heterosexual romance, perhaps *QE* is urging a social recognition of the need for cultural institutions that would enable gay men to have the same type of intimate relationships. Maybe, just maybe, *QE* betrays sympathy for something like gay marriage. However, I am more inclined to argue that *QE* views gay men as radically exterior to and incapable of such relationships. (17)

Healthy suspicion of normative energies in even apparently antihomophobic situations is admirable—and, as my other chapters illustrate, an attitude I more than sympathize with. Bateman's reading, however, seems to interpret *Queer Eye* according to a well-worn cultural script rather than on its own particular merits. Heteronormativity may posit gay men as existing outside a romantic scenario in which they themselves can never act, but this doesn't mean that spatial separation in itself entails actual disenfranchisement or social marginalizaton. The Fab Five, it's true, observe the final segment of the show (the "reveal," in makeover lingo) by remote feed, but this seems to be an aesthetic decision without ideological motive or consequence. After all, the Fab Five are observers only for the final minutes of each episode; the rest of the time, they are fully present "in" the social space that Bateman reads them as being exiled from.

Ron Becker's reading of *Queer Eye*, by contrast, balances wariness about marginalization with a more objective assessment of what the show is able to accomplish. While Becker, like Bateman, notes that "the last segment of each episode segregate[s] the Fab Five in their well-appointed urban loft watching via video while their now-metrosexual charge return[s] to his nearly always all-straight world," Becker also admits that the show "provides a guide for escaping male homosexual panic and a solution for those straight panic anxieties about what it means to be straight in a culture where being gay was no longer unequivocally stigmatized" (221). Similarly, Becker chafes at the show's positioning of gay men as "midwives to . . . heterosexual marriage" yet argues, all the same, that *Queer Eye* "offers an interesting reversal of the trope of the helpful heterosexual, but whereas such narratives had [previously] offered straight characters agency and narrative centrality, the helpful homosexuals on *Queer Eye* become narratively central but (as far as marriage was concerned) remain socially marginal" (221–23). Becker's description of the setting of each episode's final segment (a "well-appointed urban loft") is a useful reminder that separation is not inherently *un*equal. Rather than being banished to a dank, featureless cell, might we not view the Fab Five as returning, at the end of each show, to a sort of gay Bat Cave?—an image that would seem more empowering than Kanner allows (see my page 112).

10. The Fab Five's "stereotypical" occupations, along with their camping and frank sexual humor, render them threatening—and, to borrow Christopher Kelly's word, "execrable"—enough to a gay movement that has spent the last decade courting the mainstream in media and politics to justify the sort of attacks we see here. Michael Warner locates this sort of "identity ambivalence" at the heart of the contemporary national gay and lesbian movement (43). Garnering political representation and mainstream cultural presence for gays and lesbians in the 1990s was accompanied by (and Warner argues, dependent on) a shift toward "stigmaphobia," a quest for queer dignity apart from sex that is both grounded in and generative of shame about the "apparent indignity" of queer sex (74). (The term "stigmaphobia," along with the corollary "stigmaphilia," derives from Erving Goffman's *Stigma: Notes on the Management of a Spoiled Identity* [1963; New York: Touchstone, 1986].)

11. In a workshop I conducted in April 2004 for undergraduates involved in college and university GLBT activism and education, a number of participants (student and adult) voiced their discomfort with Carson's physical contact with the straight men, stating that Carson was "going too far" or that they, as viewers, "could tell [the man] was uncomfortable."

12. I would further question such a portrayal of consumer culture's absolute deadening power. If those who criticize *Queer Eye* are not turned into mindless shopping drones, why should it follow that viewers who enjoy the show are?

13. Gay men flirting with straight men is radical and subversive when some see this as reason enough to kill: on trial for the 1999 murder of Matthew Shepard, Aaron McKinney and Russell Henderson claimed "homosexual panic" as their defense. The legal failure of this tactic does not diminish the fact that it was, even to the perpetrators, a credible and intuitive defense.

14. To Kanner, "Carson Kressley's wit is sharp and quick . . . delivered in a style that's undoubtedly too flamboyant for many straight viewers and too stereotypical for many gay ones" (35). And to judge from a series of postings on *Snarkfest.com*, she may be right. Jason, who initiates the discussion thread after reading the Terry Sawyer piece cited earlier, complains that "the presumption of the Fab Five and the largely female audience watching is that there is something majorly wrong with straight men . . . based completely on the way that they dress up and accessorize their lives" ("Few Straight Guys Watching Queer Eye" par. 4). Isn't what's really threatening not a makeover per se (after all, the ultracasual, just-rolled-out-of-bed look now in vogue was itself tweaked if not created by the industry) but a makeover explicitly at the hands of gay men? If what lurks unverbalized in the comments on *Snarkfest* is not the clichéd fear of "catching it" then it is a deeply ingrained, if unconscious, distaste for the company of openly gay men—which amounts to the same thing: according to Erin, the Fab Five "are a bunch of wannabe women, judging straight guys on their appreance [*sic*]. . . . [H]ere we have 5 gay guys walking into a male hetero-sexual's [*sic*] life, verbally bashing it, and taking away any last bit of manhood he had left. . . . What kind of hetero-sexual [*sic*] man, in his right mind, would allow another gay man to judge him . . . ?" (par. 25). Queer sexuality has made the gay man eligible for membership in that most repulsive of categories: the castrating bitch.

At the same time that these comments reemphasize how much work there is still to do in terms of overcoming homophobia and opening channels of communication, the vehemence of the comments attests to *Queer Eye*'s popularity with straight women, whose whetted desire for a well-groomed boyfriend is manifest: "A friend said to me that when she watches the show she is in total agreeance [*sic*] with everything the fab five says. She can see everything that's wrong about the guy and that they are all things that women complain about all the time. They are the things that every woman wants to change about her man" (par. 9). The greatest threat may not be a haircut or a coffee table; it may be conciliation, change, or even the contemplation of changing anything within the male perimeter. What emerges from the postings most clearly—and is perhaps most disheartening in terms of overcoming rigid conceptions of gender and sexuality—is an almost divine feeling of being (or wanting to feel) impervious to change: "if [one] checked on these guys 6 months later she would find them in their overalls and jeans, probably with bushy eyebrows and unkempt facial hair. They may still have the clothes and the shoes . . . but they probably haven't done any more. . . . [I]f it wasn't already part of their general routine, they would not be adding trips to the upscale shop to buy new shirts. . . . They are making these changes to make someone else happy and not themselves" (pars. 12–13).

15. *Queer Eye* is not ashamed to ally itself with what Warner describes as the "stigmaphile space . . . where we find a commonality with those who suffer from stigma, and in this alternative realm learn to value the very things the rest of the world despises—not just because the world despises them, but because the world's pseudo-morality is a phobic and inauthentic way of life" (*The Trouble with Normal* 43).

4. *Broke*(n)*Back* Faggots

1. Nathan Lee remarks on this ambivalence: "On the one hand [the film] isn't very queer. . . . On the other hand, the one that's lubed up with saliva, could *Brokeback Mountain* be any queerer? . . . [W]e don't actually see Ennis . . . bareback Jack . . . [but] *the many millions of 'mos on the planet* [have] *just been given* . . . the epic romantic tragedy straight people have taken for granted all their lives." Lee's admirably queer take is compromised by the price he seems willing to pay (not expecting "pedigree[d]" heterosexuals to play graphic sexuality) for getting to play tragic just like straights (42).

2. See Eve Sedgwick on the "void[ing]" effect of "universalizing" readings (*The Epistemology of the Closet* 165).

3. *Brokeback* "universalists"—including Anthony Lane, Richard Alleva, Roger Ebert, and Lee Harris—typically argue that Jack and Ennis are not "'really' gay" (Mendelsohn par. 13). The thinnest version of this argument turns on the pair's scarcely credulous "morning after" dialogue ("I ain't queer," "Me neither") (McMurtry and Ossana 20). Not wanting Jack and Ennis to be gay and wanting them to be seen as more than just gay both amount to wanting gayness out of the picture. While some might object that reading Ennis and Jack as gay collapses alternative alignments of identity, sexuality, and gender among rural Americans into a more familiar urban-centric model, it seems possible both to discuss what *Brokeback* offers or is read as offering to all queer Americans about their cultural liminality (in a discourse that seldom differentiates between those who identify as queer and those perceived as such) without ignoring Judith Halberstam's insight into the urbanist prejudice of models of gay identity (*In a Queer Time and Place* 22–46).

4. Ennis's identificatory crisis begs the question of amending Sedgwick's assertion that gay men are the only men "exempt" from the "wasting rigors" of homosexual panic (Sedgwick, *The Epistemology of the Closet*, 188).

5. See also Sedgwick, *The Epistemology of the Closet* 67–70, 78–86.

6. See Michael Warner, *The Trouble with Normal* 33–40, 61–80 and *Publics and Counterpublics* 7–63, 187–223; and Edelman 1–31.

7. Although "[e]asily misinterpreted as omniscient narration, these fleeting pictures" of Jack's death by gay-bashing are, "in fact, Ennis's imagination" (Grundmann par. 17).

8. Distrusting Lureen's version of Jack's death as a cover story requires reading the fag-bashing images as emanating from her consciousness—which would make little sense since the film grants her no other flashbacks.

9. The exception is Jack's memory of his and Ennis's "dozy embrace" by the campfire their first summer on the mountain (Proulx, "Brokeback Mountain" 22). This is Jack's only moment of interiority or flashback in Proulx's story—an odd exception to the text's overall structure, which is framed as one extended flashback by Ennis. Lee retains this quiet moment as Jack's: the embrace by the campfire in 1963 cuts directly back to Jack's face as he watches Ennis drive away in 1981.

10. See also Grundmann par. 20.

11. See Vary pars. 19, 12; and Russo 248–323.

12. Following Sedgwick, one might go further and read in Jack's death a "fantasy trajectory toward a life *after the homosexual*," "a culture's desire that gay people *not be*" (*The Epistemology of the Closet* 127, 43).

13. Although he does not cite Warner, Grundmann's discussion of gay marriage seems indebted to Warner's in *The Trouble with Normal* (81–147); see also Butler, *Undoing Gender* 105–112.

14. See Edelman 2–7, 13–17.

5. The IMs Are Coming from Inside the House

1. Characteristic rightist rants include FRC head James Dobson's e-mail employing the spurious "link between child sexual abuse and homosexuality" to deflect blame from Republican leadership (qtd. in Will Bunch); pieces by Reed Irvine and Cliff Kincaid (for *Accuracy in Media*) and Daniel Levesque; as well as "'Gay' Rights' [*sic*] Secret Agenda" (*World Net Daily*) and several items from the Traditional Values Coalition Web site (including "Homosexual Urban Legends: 'Born Gay,'" "Parents: Get the Truth about the Gay, Lesbian, and Straight Education Network [GLSEN]!" and "Let's End Taxpayer Supported Homosexual Recruitment in Public Schools"). For sample gay press coverage of various stages of Foleygate, see Cain; Chibbaro, "Gay Blogger Sought to Protect Privacy"; Chibbaro, "Gay Staffers to Help in Foley Inquiries"; LaPadula and Chibbaro; and Perry.

2. For transcripts of the IM sessions aired by ABC News, see John in D.C. ("House GOP Leadership Knew about Foley"); and "Foley's Exchange with Underage Page."

3. Frank James analyzes Speaker Hastert's prevarications during his press conference (for which James provides a full transcript) following Foley's resignation.

4. Aside from Weisman ("Hastert Aides Interest Ethics Panel" and "Staffer Cites Earlier Role by Hastert's Office"), details about the (contested) timeline by which Foleygate unfolded and about the cover-up are available in Aravosis; Hunter; Margasak; Yang and Ross; and "DNC: Where's the Outrage?"

5. Tony Perkins of the Family Research Council was one proponent of the "tolerant cover up" theory (see Epstein par. 5). As pointed out by Denis Dison, vice president of the Gay and Lesbian Victory Fund and Leadership Institute, the "charge . . . makes no sense" given the Republican party's position on same-sex marriage and its push for a Federal Marriage Amendment (qtd. in Epstein par. 17).

6. See Will Bunch; Matt Drudge, "Claim: Filthy Foley Online Chats Were Page 'Prank Gone Awry'"; "Echoing Drudge and Savage, Dobson and Henninger Claimed Foley Scandal is 'Sort of a Joke' and a 'Prank[]' by Pages"; Mark Leibovich (par. 5); and Patrick McHenry.

7. San Francisco supervisor Bevan Dufty suggests that Republican leaders "use[d] Foley's then-hidden sexuality against him in 2003" when he campaigned for Bob Graham's Florida Senate seat: "They bashed him [behind the scenes]," Dufty says. "They made it clear it would be ugly for him if he ran" (qtd. in Epstein pars. 19, 20). That Mel Martinez was the White House favorite for Graham's seat and a Cuban American in a state where Republicans needed to court minority voters lends credibility to Dufty's claim. But corroborating evidence is lacking. Foley was outed first in the gay alternative press.

8. Given the nonstandard English spelling and punctuation endemic to instant messaging, and in order to avoid the excessive use of "[*sic*]," I have made only occasional annotations. Quotes are taken from "Foley's Exchange with Underage Page."

9. In 2008 Florida authorities concluded there was "'insufficiant evidence' to charge [Foley] with breaking [state] laws"; the Justice Department also "confirmed that [he] would not face any federal charges" (Sexton pars. 1, 5). Both Foley and Congress stonewalled requests for access to electronic records, and pages from Florida interviewed by state authorities failed to report "inappropriate activity or conversations" with Foley (par. 10). Nonetheless, in at least one of the IM sessions made public, he solicited sex from a former page. ("E-mails Show Foley Sought to Rendezvous with Page").

10. For an example of typical recruitment-by-molestation propaganda, see Traditional Values Coalition ("Homosexual Urban Legends: 'Born Gay'").

11. Additional (hysterical) coverage of the Teach Out workshop is available from Frank York as well as the Traditional Values Coalition ("Let's End

Taxpayer Supported Homosexual Recruitment in Public Schools"). For other conservative diatribes against GLSEN, see Stephen Bennett, Rod Dreher, Julie Foster, Warren Throckmorton, and Kimberly S. Wygert.

12. While HIV educators and physicians generally agree the virus is much more difficult to catch or transmit during oral sex compared to anal sex (due to the lower vulnerability of tissues in the oral cavity and to HIV's weakness outside the bloodstream), they strongly discourage allowing partners to ejaculate in one's mouth and/or ingesting their semen. HIV has been isolated in precum as well as semen, although precum is usually produced in much smaller amounts. But even though, as Michael Shernoff notes, "the debate over what is and is not 'high-risk' sex continues, notably around fellatio," "only a handful of [HIV] transmissions [via fellatio] have been documented," and those few are agreed to be controversial (11; see also 44–45). Fellatio that involves withdrawal before ejaculation is thus considered fairly low-risk. Given deeply ingrained American prejudices against honestly discussing sexuality (and even more so, homosexuality) with teens and children, at least in educational settings, it's unsurprising that American youth are asking questions about the risks of various behaviors vis-à-vis AIDS. It is furthermore commendable that teens are asking questions about the relative risks and that educators are answering those questions.

13. Whiteman, along with Brian Camenker (president of the Parents Rights Coalition), defied the gag order, and both were threatened with criminal charges for violating state wiretap laws and invading the teen participants' privacy. Official reaction was mixed, though less hysterical. The Massachusetts State Board of Education was uninterested in Whiteman and Camenker's complaint. Massachusetts commissioner of Education David Driscoll pronounced the workshop in question "prurient . . . and not educational," according to Irvine and Kincaid (par. 4). Irvine and Kincaid attribute the quote to Driscoll, but fail to make clear where the quote originated (in an interview or public statement). Whatever his initial reaction may have been, Driscoll's actions spoke clearly. He dismissed two of the state employees who led workshops (the third resigned) and directed his staff to refocus their educational efforts on those adults who have the most daily contact with students (such as parents, teachers, health educators, guidance counselors, and coaches) (Irvine and Kincaid par. 4). "Our role," Driscoll stated, "will *not* be to interact directly with students on issues related to sexuality" (Driscoll par. 6). While the commissioner reaffirmed his support of "age-appropriate, school-based AIDS/HIV education," and while other authorities (such as the district attorney) failed to take Whiteman and Camenker seriously, Driscoll's response suggests at least a partial retreat when confronted with the specter of recruitment (Driscoll par. 7). Education by proxy is hardly the same as direct education: what if the informed adults choose not to pass on the information they've been given, or feel it shouldn't be passed on? Isn't that the same as not disseminating the information at all?

14. Other workshops included "Ask the Transssexuals," "Early Childhood Educators: How to Decide Whether to Come Out or Not," "Lesbian Avengers:

How to Promote Queer-Friendly Activism in Your Schools and in Your Lives," "Diesel Dykes and Lipstick Lesbians: Defining and Exploring Butch/Femme Identity," "Starting a Gay/Straight Alliance in Your School," and—no doubt, the favorite of GLSEN's conservative critics—"The Religious Wrong: Dealing Effectively with Opposition in Your Community" (York par. 16).

15. As Michael Warner notes, the mere existence or visibility of alternatives threatens heteronormativity:

> The received wisdom in straight culture, is that all of its different norms line up, that one is synonymous with the others. If you are born with male genitalia, the logic goes, you will behave in masculine ways, desire women, desire feminine women, desire them exclusively, have sex in what are thought to be normally active and insertive ways and within officially sanctioned contexts, think of yourself as heterosexual, identify with other heterosexuals no matter how tolerant you might wish to be, and never change any part of this package from childhood to senescence. Heterosexuality is often a name for this entire package, even though attachment to the other sex is only one element. If you deviate at any point from this program, you do so at your own cost. And one of the things straight culture hates most is any sign that the different parts of the package might be recombined in an infinite number of ways. But experience shows that this is just what tends to happen. If heterosexuality requires the entire sequence, then it is very fragile. No wonder it needs so much terror to induce compliance (37–38)

16. The so-called evidence used by the Traditional Values Coalition dates from the late 1970s and, in fact, is antihomophobic. In this case, they're referring to the New York University Press 1994 reissue of Karla Jay and Allen Young's 1978 gay-liberation anthology *Lavender Culture*—and in particular, an essay by gay activist Gerald Hannon on the importance of education and support for gay youth.

17. This video, which included Spongebob Squarepants, is discussed in chapter 2.

18. See Eribon 101–06.

19. As Lee Edelman has suggested in *No Future*, the "cult of the Child" that so extensively underwrites the entire project of Western culture, both materially and in the realm of the Symbolic, seems fundamentally inimical to queers. Edelman puts this argument in its strongest form—one from which my activist sensibility demurs (if sometimes only slightly)—but his point is well taken given the current cultural and rhetorical landscape for American queers.

20. For coverage of the Haggard scandal, consult "Evangelical Leader Admits to Some 'Indiscretion' in Gay Sex Scandal"; Gorski, Cardona, and Gonzales; Holusha and Banerjee; Plunkett and Gorski; and "Second New Life Pastor Resigns over 'Sexual Misconduct.'" Gay bloggers Joe (of *Joe.My.God*) and Tom Bacchus

broke the story of Matt Sanchez's (not so) secret past as a gay porn star and escort. Joe also interviewed Sanchez for *Joe.My.God.* See also Barbara Wilcox, Max Blumenthal (who covered the Conservative Political Action Committee conference at which Sanchez was honored), and Big Dog's attack on Blumenthal and defense of Sanchez. Sanchez's response was available on his own blog and at *Salon.com.*

21. The term "homocon" originates from Richard Goldstein's *The Attack Queers* (30).

22. Two days after Haggard's confession, Colorado's Amendment 43 passed with 56 percent of the vote. It's only fair to note that Haggard, unlike other supporters of the marriage ban, did not support a ban on domestic partnership rights for gay and lesbian couples.

23. As an antimilitary epithet, "baby killer" smacks more of Vietnam-era antimilitary sentiment than it does of antiwar activism surrounding America's invasion and occupation of Iraq. Given the Bush administration's penchant for fabricating heroes (Jessica Lynch, Pat Tillman), this anachronistic detail casts some doubt on the factuality of Sanchez's story.

24. Coulter's exact words were "I was going to have a few comments on the other Democratic presidential candidate John Edwards, but it turns out you have to go into rehab if you use the word 'faggot,' so I—so kind of an impasse, can't really talk about Edwards." The video of Coulter's comments at CPAC was available on numerous Web sites; I accessed it through *ThinkProgress.org*, where blogger Nico also reprinted the comment in question. In a move indicative of Coulter's continued success as a media pundit (despite her regularly advocating the murder of Arabs and liberals), Coulter showed that spewing hate doesn't keep her from staying current with primetime network TV. Her slur against Edwards was a tasteless riff on an incident on the set of ABC's *Grey's Anatomy*, where, in October 2006, actor Isaiah Washington referred to costar T. R. Knight as a "faggot" (Tabloid Baby).

25. Some films are compilations, but, even setting these aside, Sanchez appeared in at least a dozen original films.

26. As a case in point of the extreme and irrational dedication of Republicans and other conservatives to homophobia—at a time when the government was aggressively recruiting Arab-language specialists as part of the War on Terror—the military, since 2002, has discharged a total of fifty-eight gay linguists specializing in Arabic. Given that the "Don't Ask, Don't Tell" policy fails to distinguish (as Sanchez does) between gay sex and gay identity, Sanchez's outing as Rod Majors/Pierre LaBranche generated speculation that he, too, might be discharged.

27. See Paul Robinson's *Queer Wars*, Richard Goldstein's *The Attack Queers*, and Michael Warner's *The Trouble with Normal* (chap. 2) for further discussion of the gay conservative movement—of which Andrew Sullivan's *Virtually Normal* and Bruce Bawer's *A Place at the Table* are central texts.

28. Sedgwick presents *The Epistemology of the Closet* as (and it was taken as) an entrée to the then-infant field of queer studies:

> A real measure of the success of such an analysis would lie in its ability, in the hands of an inquirer with different needs, talents, or positionings, to clarify the distinctive kinds of resistance offered to it from different spaces on the social map, even though such a project might require revisions or rupturings of the analysis first proffered. . . . If the book were able to fulfill its most expansive ambitions, it would make certain specific kinds of readings and interrogations, perhaps new, available in a heuristically powerful, productive, and significant form for other readers to perform on literary and social texts with, ideally, other results. The meaning, the legitimacy, and in many ways the possibility for good faith of the positionings this book makes depend radically on the production, by other antihomophobic readers who may be very differently situated, of the widest possible range of other and even contradictory availabilities. (14)

29. Double binds, Sedgwick notes elsewhere in *The Epistemology of the Closet*, "systematically oppress . . . gay people, identities, and acts" not just by defining homo- and heterosexuality in terms of one another but "by undermining through contradictory restraints on discourse their very being" (70).

30. Related questions would be: What parts of our selves are not currently technologically mediated? How does this mediation affect even our response to this question, or determine what responses we will discover now and at later instances?

31. See Julie Rak's rather essentialist argument about blogs and (queer) identity. J. D. Applen, Danah Boyd, Toby Huff, and Burt Kimmelman have begun to flesh out, in different directions, the evolutionary impact of online discourse such as instant messaging, blogs, and Web sites like MySpace and Facebook on social interaction, political activism, and theories and practices of group, cohort, and individual identity.

Conclusion

1. Similarly, David Halperin pinpoints the difficulty, when considering pre-nineteenth-century relationships, in seeing beyond the purview of our modern homo/hetero paradigm:

> It is difficult for us moderns—with our heavily psychologistic model of the human personality, our notion of unconscious drives, our tendency to associate desire with sexuality, and our heightened sensitivity to anything that might seem to contravene the strict protocols of heterosexual masculinity—it is difficult for us to avoid reading into . . . passionate expressions of male love [before the mid-nineteenth century] a suggestion of "homoeroticism" at the very least, if not of "latent homosexuality," those being the formulations that often act as a cover for our own perplexity about how to interpret same-sex emotions that do not quite square with canonical conceptions of sexual subjectivity. (*How to Do* 120)

Works Cited

"AFI's Top Film, TV, Moments of 2003." *HollywoodReporter.com.* 16 Dec. 2003. 16 Dec. 2003 <http://www.hollywoodreporter.com/thr/film/article_display.jsp?vnu_content_id=2-52526>.

Alleva, Richard. "Emotional Apartheid." Rev. of *Brokeback Mountain*, dir. Ang Lee. *Commonweal* 10 Feb. 2006. *Academic Search Premier*. EBSCOhost. Lehman Library, Shippensburg University. 6 Apr. 2006 <http://www.epnet.com>.

The Angry Liberal. "Congressman Foley Overreacts to Media Smear!" *Buzzflash.com.* 2 Oct. 2006. 1 Jan. 2007 <http://www.buzzflash.com/articles/theangryliberal/001>.

Ansen, David. "The Heart Is a Lonely Hunter." Rev. of *Brokeback Mountain*, dir. Ang Lee. *Newsweek* 19 Dec. 2005. *Academic Search Premier*. EBSCOhost. Lehman Library, Shippensburg University. 6 Apr. 2006 <http://www.epnet.com>.

Anziulewicz, Chuck. "A Love Story." Letter. *Commonweal* 10 Mar. 2006. *Academic Search Premier*. EBSCOhost. Lehman Library, Shippensburg University. 6 Apr. 2006 <http://www.epnet.com>.

Applen, J. D. "The Effects and Dynamics of Networks, Texting, and Power Relationships on the Construction of Identity." *Post Identity* 4.1 (Spring 2004).

Aravosis, John. "Hastert: The Buck Stops with My Staff." *Americablog.* 5 Oct. 2006. 8 Oct. 2006 <http://www.americablog.com/2006/10/hastert-buck-stops-with-my-staff.html>.

Archer, Bert. *The End of Gay (and the Death of Heterosexuality).* New York: Avalon, 2003.

"Are John Kerry and John Edwards Gay?" 2004. 9 Feb. 2005 <http://www.fun.lol.com/funpages/john-kerry-and-john-edwards-are-gay.html>.

Babcock, Joe. *The Boys and the Bees.* New York: Carroll and Graf, 2005.

Bacchus, Tom. "Dirty Sanchez." *Tom Bacchus on the Vine.* 5 Mar. 2007. 21 Mar. 2007 <http://tombacchus.blogspot.com/2007/03/dirty-sanchez.hml>.

Badgett, M. V. Lee. "Beyond Biased Samples: Challenging the Myths on the Economic Status of Lesbians and Gay Men." *Homo Economics: Capitalism, Community, and Lesbian and Gay Life.* Ed. Amy Gluckman and Betsy Reed. New York: Routledge, 1997. 65–71.

———. "Income Inflation: The Myth of Affluence Among Gay, Lesbian, and Bisexual Americans." New York: Policy Institute of the National Gay and Lesbian Task Force and the Institute for Gay and Lesbian Strategic Studies, 1998.

———. *Money, Myths, and Change: The Economic Lives of Lesbians and Gay Men.* Chicago: University of Chicago Press, 2001.

———. "The Myth of Gay and Lesbian Affluence." *Gay and Lesbian Review* (Spring 2000): 22–25.

———. "The Wage Effects of Sexual Orientation Discrimination." *Industrial and Labor Relations Review* 48.4 (July 1995): 726–39.

Baker, Dan. "A History in Ads: The Growth of the Gay and Lesbian Market." *Homo Economics: Capitalism, Community, and Lesbian and Gay Life.* Ed. Amy Gluckman and Betsy Reed. New York: Routledge, 1997. 11–20.

Bateman, Robert Benjamin. "What Do Gay Men Desire?: Peering Behind the Queer Eye." *The New Queer Aesthetic in Television: Essays on Recent Programming*. Ed. James R. Keller and Leslie Stratyner. Jefferson, NC: McFarland, 2006. 9–19.

Bauer, Gary. "Family Research Council Fundraising Appeal Letter from Gary Bauer." 2 June 1997. 16 Sept. 2005 <http://www.bridges-across.org/ba/frc970602.htm>.

Bawer, Bruce. *A Place at the Table: The Gay Individual in American Society.* New York: Simon and Schuster, 1993.

Beck, Timothy James. *It Had to Be You.* New York: Kensington, 2001.

Becker, Ron. *Gay TV and Straight America.* New Brunswick: Rutgers University Press, 2006.

Beemyn, Brett, and Mickey Eliason. *Queer Studies: A Lesbian, Gay, Bisexual, and Transgender Anthology.* New York: New York University Press, 1996.

Bennett, Stephen. "Homosexual Agenda: Bill O'Reilly: He Still Doesn't Get It." *AFA* [American Family Association] *Online.* 13 Feb. 2004. 6 June 2007 <htttp://www.afa.net/homosexual_agenda/GetArticle.asp?id=115>.

Big Dog. "Hitman Max Blumenthal and the Party of Tolerance." Online posting. 9 Mar. 2007. 21 Mar. 2007 <http://www.onebigdog.net/2007/03/09/hitman-max-blumenthal-and-the-party-of-tolerance/.>

Blumenthal, Max. "CPAC's Gay Porn Star Honoree, Ann Coulter, and the Politics of Personal Crisis." *Huffington Post.* 7 Mar. 2007. 21 Mar. 2007 <http://www.huffingtonpost.com/max-blumenthal/cpacs-gay-porn-star-hono_b_42842.html.>

Boswell, John. *Christianity, Social Tolerance, and Homosexuality: Gay People in Western Europe from the Beginning of the Christian Era to 14th Century.* Chicago: University of Chicago Press, 1981.

Boyd, Danah. "Sexing the Internet: Reflections on the Role of Identification in Online Communities." Presentation. Sexualities, Medias and

Technologies: Theorizing Old and New Practices. University of Surrey. 21–22 June 2001. <www.danah.org/papers>.

Brandt, Doreen. "Administration Balks at 'Gay' in Gay Suicide Conference." *365gay.com*. 16 Feb. 2005. 18 Mar. 2005 <http://www.365gay.com/newscon05/02/021605suicide.htm>.

Brandzel, Amy L. "Queering Citizenship?: Same-Sex Marriage and the State." *GLQ: A Journal of Gay and Lesbian Studies* 11.2 (2005): 171–204.

Breen, Matthew. "Pop's New Queen." *Out* July 2007. *Out.com*. 19 June 2007 <http://www.out.com/detail.asp?id=22629>.

Brock, David. *The Republican Noise Machine: Right-Wing Media and How It Corrupts Democracy*. New York: Crown, 2004.

Brokeback Mountain. Dir. Ang Lee. Perf. Heath Ledger and Jake Gyllenhaal. Focus Features, 2005.

Brown, Rita Mae. *Rubyfruit Jungle*. 1973. New York: Bantam, 1977.

Brown, Wendy. *Regulating Aversion: Tolerance in the Age of Identity and Empire*. Princeton: Princeton University Press, 2006.

Brune, Adrian. "Outed Hill Staffer Condemns Campaign." *Washington Blade* 9 July 2004. *Washington Blade Online*. 15 Feb. 2005 <http://www.washingtonblade.com/2004/7-9/news/localnews/outed.cfm>.

———. "Two Members of Congress Outed." *New York Blade* 9 July 2004: 11. *GLBT Life with Full Text*. Lehman Library, Shippensburg University. 19 Dec. 2006 <http://www.epnet.com>.

Bryant, Elizabeth. "Kerry Boasts French Support." *Washington Times* 24 Feb. 2004. 27 Feb. 2005 <http://www.washtimes.com/world/20040224-113724-8812r.htm>.

Bunch, Will. "Family Research Council: Blame 'the Gay' for Foleygate." *Attytood.com*. October 2006. 1 Jan. 2007 <http:www.attytood.com/2006/10/family_research_council_blame.html>.

Burack, Cynthia. *Sin, Sex, and Democracy: Antigay Rhetoric and the Christian Right*. Albany: State University of New York Press, 2008.

Butler, Judith. *Bodies That Matter: On the Discursive Limits of "Sex."* London: Routledge, 1993.

———. *Gender Trouble: Feminism and the Subversion of Identity*. New York: Routledge, 1990.

———. *Undoing Gender*. New York: Routledge, 2004.

Butler, Judith, Ernesto Laclau, and Slavoj Žižek. *Contingency, Hegemony, Universality: Contemporary Dialogues on the Left*. London; New York: Verso, 2000.

Byrne, John. "Chief Financial Officer of Republican National Committee Admits He's Gay, Stays Quiet." *The Blue Lemur: Progressive Politics and Media News*. 24 Sept. 2004. 15 Feb. 2005 <http://www.bluelemur.com/index.php?p=305>.

Cahen, Eva. "French Back Kerry by Large Margin." *CNSNews.com*. 19 Oct. 2004. 27 Feb. 2005 <http://www.cnsnews.com/ViewPrint.asp?Page=

%5CForeignBureaus%5Carchive%5C200410%5CFOR20041019c.html>.

Cain, Chris. "Mark Foley's Crazy Closet." *Washington Blade* 30 May 2003: 42. *GLBT Life with Full Text.* Lehman Library, Shippensburg University. 19 Dec. 2006 <http://www.epnet.com>.

Chapin, Bernard. "Maureen Himmler." *Men's News Daily.* 28 Aug. 2003. 12 Feb. 2005. <http://www.mensnewsdaily.com/archive/c-e/chapin/03/chapin082803.htm>.

Chasin, Alexandra. *Selling Out: The Gay and Lesbian Movement Goes to Market.* New York: Palgrave, 2000.

Chaudry, Lakshmi. "What John Kerry Needs: The Estrogen Factor." *AlterNet.* 11 May 2004. 11 Feb. 2005 <http://www.alternet.org/story/18666>.

Chauncey, George. *Gay New York: Gender, Urban Culture, and the Making of the Gay Male World, 1890–1940.* New York: Basic Books, 1994.

Chesnoff, Richard Z. *The Arrogance of the French: Why They Can't Stand Us—And Why the Feeling Is Mutual.* New York: Sentinel-Penguin, 2005.

Chibbaro, Lou, Jr. "Gay Blogger Sought to Protect Pages." *Washington Blade* 10 Nov. 2006: 1+. *GLBT Life with Full Text.* Lehman Library, Shippensburg University. 19 Dec. 2006 <http://www.epnet.com>.

———. "Gay Staffers to Help in Foley Inquiries." *New York Blade* 16 Nov. 2006: 11. *GLBT Life with Full Text.* Lehman Library, Shippensburg University. 19 Dec. 2006 <http://www.epnet.com>.

Christensen, Rob. "Macho's Role in Politics." *News & Observer* [Raleigh, NC] 3 Oct. 2004. *LexisNexis.* Lehman Library, Shippensburg University. 15 Aug. 2005 <http://web.lexisnexis.com/universe/document?_m=34474561033968b2ae9f30f08d44bd9e&_docnum=20&wchp=dGLbVlz-zSkVb&_md5=d881606d701b3755a57c0cab9c1da338>.

Churchill, Caryl. *Cloud 9.* 1981. New York: Theatre Communications Group, 1995.

Cimino, Kenneth W. *Gay Conservatives: Group Consciousness and Assimilation.* New York: Harrington Park Press, 2007.

Collingsworth, Stephen. Letter. *Boston Globe* 6 Nov. 2004, 3rd ed., A14. *LexisNexis.* Lehman Library, Shippensburg University. 15 Aug. 2005 <http://www.lexis-nexis.com/universe/document?_m=b497edf7d4ccf72444a11d488c28c40a&_docnum=109&wchp=dGLbVlz-zSkVb&_m5=76496a43dfb55d9baa4601dfb9146d68>.

"Congressional Page Scandal Takes on Anti-Gay Bent as Details Emerge." *Dallas Voice.* 6 Oct. 2006. 8 Oct. 2006 <http://www.dallasvoice.com/artman/publish/article_3555.php>.

Corn, David. "Gannon-Guckert-Gate." *The Nation. CBSNews.com.* 25 Feb. 2005. April 16 2005 <http://www.cbsnews.com/stories/2005/02/25/opinion/main676554.shtml>.

———. *The Lies of George W. Bush: Mastering the Politics of Deception.* New York: Three Rivers, 2003.

Cornes, David, and Todd Sandler. *The Theory of Externalities, Public Goods, and Club Goods.* 2nd ed. Cambridge: Cambridge University Press, 1996.

Coulter, Ann. "One Last Flip-Flop." *World Net Daily.* 3 Nov. 2004. 15 Aug. 2005 <http://www.worldnetdaily.com/news/article.asp?ARTICLE_ID=41281>.

Crowder, Diane Griffin. "Separatism and Feminist Utopian Fiction." *Sexual Practice/Textual Theory: Lesbian Cultural Criticism.* Ed. Susan J. Wolfe and Julia Penelope. Cambridge, MA: Blackwell, 1993.

Crowley, Mart. *The Boys in the Band.* 1968. New York: Samuel French, 1996.

Cuseo, Allan A. *Homosexual Characters in YA Novels: A Literary Analysis, 1969–1982.* Lanham, MD: Rowman and Littlefield, 1992.

Dadich, Scott. "What You See Is What You Get." *New York Times* 9 Oct. 2004. *LexisNexis.* Lehman Library, Shippensburg University. 15 Aug. 2005 <http://web.lexis-nexis.com/universe/document?_m=344745610e3968b2ae9f30f08d44bd9e&_docnum=11&wchp=dGLbVlz-zSkVb&_md5=b8d4c90c569c4d244fdcaeb7e8ce5fe>.

Daly, Matthew. "Officer Accused Craig of Lying." Associated Press. *Yahoo! News.* 30 Aug. 2007. 30 Aug. 2007. <http://news.yahoo.com/s/ap/20070830/ap_on_the_go/craig_arrest>.

Dana, Rebecca, and Jose Antonio Vargas. "Capitol Hill Insiders Irked by Campaign To 'Out' Them." *Washington Post* 15 July 2004: C1. 15 Feb. 2005 <http://www.washingtonpost.com/wp-dyn/articles/A50299-2004Jul14.html>.

Deleuze, Gilles, and Felix Guattari. *A Thousand Plateaus: Capitalism and Schizophrenia.* 1980. Trans. Brian Massumi. Minneapolis: University of Minnesota Press, 1987.

Dillard, Angela. *Guess Who's Coming to Dinner Now?: Multicultural Conservatism in America.* New York: New York University Press, 2001.

Dionne, E. J. "'Family Values' for All of Us." *Washington Post* 7 Oct. 2006: A23. 8 Oct. 2006. <http://www.washingtonpost.com/wp-dyn/content/article/2006/10/06/AR2006100601371.html>.

Dixon, Wheeler Winston. "Hyperconsumption in Reality Television: The Tranformation of the Self through Televisual Consumerism." *Quarterly Review of Film and Television* 25.1 (Jan. 2008): 52–63.

"DNC: Where's the Outrage? Why is the White House Protecting Republicans Instead of Children." *Buzzflash.com.* 2 Oct. 2006. 1 Jan. 2007 <http://www.buzzflash.com/Articles/releases/026>.

Dollimore, Jonathan. "The Dominant and the Deviant: A Violent Dialectic." *Critical Quarterly* 28.1–2: 179–92. Rpt. in *Homosexual Themes in Literary Studies.* Ed. Wayne R. Dynes and Stephen Donaldson. New York: Garland, 1992. 87–100.

Dougherty, Jon. "Report: Pedophilia More Common Among 'Gays.'" *World Net Daily*. 29 Apr. 2002. 15 Aug. 2005. <http://www.worldnetdaily.com/news/article.asp?ARTICLE_ID=27431>.

Dowd, Maureen. "Gotta Lotta Stigmata." *New York Times* 24 Aug. 2003. *NYTimes.com*. 11 Feb. 2005 <http://www.nytimes.com/2003/08/24/opinion/24DOWD.html?ex=1108443600&en=9df6c67ef9ede05c&ei=5070>.

Draz, Christian. "Lost in Adaptation." Rev. of *Brokeback Mountain*, dir. Ang Lee. *Gay and Lesbian Review Worldwide* 13.2 (Mar. 2006): 12–13.

Dreher, Rod. "Banned in Boston: Better Not Complain about the Gay Agenda for Massachsetts Schools." *Weekly Standard* 3 July 2000. 7 June 2007. <http://www.weeklystandard.com/Utilities/printer_preview.asp?idArticle=11094&R=1137C60A9>.

Driscoll, David P. "A Statement on the March 25 GLSEN Conference." *Massachusetts Department of Education*. 19 May 2000. 7 June 2007. <http://www.doe.mass.edu/news/news.asp?id=545>.

Drudge, Matt. "Can't Keep Hands Off Each Other." *Drudge Report*. 8 July 2004. 11 Feb. 2005 <http://www.drudgereportarchives.com/data/2004/07/09/20040709_011402_kerry.htm>.

———. "Claim: Filthy Foley Online Chats Were Page 'Prank Gone Awry.'" *Drudge Report*. 5 Oct. 2006. 8 June 2007 <http://www.drudgereportarchives.com/data/2006/10/06/20061006_211622_page.htm>.

Drum, Gary. "He's In. He's Out. He's Post-Gay: The Misadventures of James Collard's Post-Gay Journey to America." 1 June 2007. <http://www.hardyboy.com/postgay.html.>

Ducat, Stephen J. *The Wimp Factor: Gender Gaps, Holy Wars, and the Politics of Anxious Masculinity*. Boston: Beacon, 2004.

Duggan, Lisa. *The Twilight of Equality?: Neoliberalism, Cultural Politics, and the Attack on Democracy*. Boston: Beacon, 2003.

Duralde, Alonso. "Queer Tunes for the Straight Ear." *Advocate* 30 March 2003: 61.

Ebert, Roger. Rev. of *Brokeback Mountain*, dir. Ang Lee. *Chicago Sun-Times* 16 Dec. 2005. 30 July 2006 <http://rogerebert.suntimes.com/apps/pbcs.dll/article?AID=/20051215/REVIEWS/510190/06/1023>.

"Echoing Drudge and Savage, Dobson and Henninger Claimed Foley Scandal is 'Sort of a Joke' and a 'Prank[]' by Pages." *Media Matters for America*. 6 Oct. 2006. 8 Oct. 2006 <http://mediamatters.org/items/200610060004>.

Edelman, Lee. *No Future: Queer Theory and the Death Drive*. Durham: Duke University Press, 2004.

Edwards, David. "Video: Daily Show Reveals 'Opus Gay' Network Shielded Foley." *TVNewsLies.org*. 11 Oct. 2006. 1 Nov. 2006. <http://tvnewslies.com/forum/viewtopic.php?f=18&t=5231>.

Ellen. "Radical Christian, Anti-Gay Activist and Schiavo Spokesperson Randall Terry Jokes About Being Homosexual." *News Hounds*. 25 Mar.

2005. 20 Apr. 2005 <http:/www.newshounds.us/2005/03/25/radical_christian_right_antigay_activist_and_schiavo_spokesperson_randall_terryjokes_about_being_homosexual.php>.

"E-mails Show Foley Sought to Rendezvous with Page." *Blotter*. 2 Oct. 2006. 1 Jan. 2007 <http://www.abcnews.com/theblotter/2006/10/emails_show_fol.html>.

Epstein, Edward. "Ex-Foley Aide Says He Told on his Boss before 2004." *San Francisco Chronicle*. 5 Oct. 2006. 8 Oct. 2006 <http://www.sfgate.com/cg-bin/article.cgi?file=/c/a/2006/10/05/ <NGBOLINSN1.DTL>.

Eribon, Didier. *Insult and the Making of the Gay Self.* Trans. Michael Lucey. Durham: Duke University Press, 2004.

"Evangelical Leader Admits to Some 'Indiscretion' in Gay Sex Scandal." 4–6 Nov. 2006. *Advocate.com*. 1 Jan. 2007 <http://www.advocate.com/news_detail_ektid38645.asp>.

"Few Straight Guys Watching Queer Eye." Online posting. 30 July–30 Nov. 2003. 3 Dec. 2003 <http://www.snarkfest.com/reruns/000337.php>.

Firestein, Beth A. *Bisexuality: The Psychology and Politics of an Invisible Minority*. Thousand Oaks, CA: SAGE, 1996.

Fishbein, Leslie. "*Rubyfruit Jungle*: Lesbianism, Feminism, and Narcissism." *International Journal of Women's Studies* 7.2 (March/April 1984): 155–59.

"Foley's Exchange with Underage Page." ABC News <http://www.abcnews.go.com/WNT/BrianRoss/story?id=2509586&page=1> or <http://www.pnetz.org/media/_blogs/Sicht_Weise/FoleyIMsWithPate.doc>.

Forrest, Susan. "SAMHSA: No Gay/Transgender Suicide Prevention." *Sandiego.indymedia.org*. 16 Feb. 2005. 18 Mar. 2005 <http://www.sandiego.indymedia.org/en/2005/02/107664.shtml>.

Foster, Julie. "California Schools' New Homosexual Curriculum: 2 Bills Take 'Diversity' Training to Classroom Effective Jan. 1." *World Net Daily*. 26 Dec. 2000. 6 June 2007 <http://www.worldnetdaily.com/news/article.asp?ARTICLE_ID=21132>.

"FOX Chief Political Correspondent Who Interviewed Bush in 2000 and Bragged that His Wife Was Volunteering for George, Now—in 2004—Made Up RNC Message Point Quotes That John Kerry Never Said." A BuzzFlash News Analysis. *BuzzFlash.com*. 2 Oct. 2004. 13 Feb. 2005 <http://www.buzzflash.com/analysis/04/10/ana04019.html>.

Freccero, Carla. *Queer/Early/Modern.* Durham, NC: Duke University Press, 2006.

Fritz, Ben, and Brendan Nyhan. "John Kerry's French Connection." *Spinsanity*. 24 Mar. 2004. 27 Feb. 2005. <http://www.spinsanity.org/columns/20040325.html>.

Furs, Robert. "Who's French Now, Karen?" *Counterbias.com*. 28 Apr. 2004. 15 Feb 2005 <http://www.counterbias.com/019.html.>

Fuss, Diana. *Essentially Speaking: Feminism, Nature, and Difference*. New York: Routledge, 1989.

———. "Inside/Out." *Inside/Out: Lesbian Theories, Gay Theories*. Ed. Diana Fuss. New York: Routledge, 1991. 1–10.

Garber, Marjorie. *Vice Versa: Bisexuality and the Eroticism of Everyday Life*. New York: Simon & Schuster, 1995.

Garden, Nancy. *Annie on My Mind*. 1982. New York: Farrar, Straus, and Giroux, 2007.

"'Gay' Rights' [sic] Secret Agenda: How the Homosexual Activist Movement Has Targeted America's Children." *World Net Daily*. 28 July 2002. 01 Jan. 2007 <http://www.worldnetdaily.com/news/article.asp?ARTICLE_ID=28069.>

Gerstmann, Evan. *Same-Sex Marriage and the Constitution*. Cambridge: Cambridge University Press, 2004.

Giltz, Michael. "Queer Eye Confidential." *Advocate* 2 Sept. 2003: 40–44.

GLAAD (Gay and Lesbian Alliance Against Defamation). "Network Responsibility Index: Primetime Programming, 2006-2007." *GLAAD.org*. 6 Aug. 2007. 20 Dec. 2007 <http://www.glaad.org/2007/2007PDFS/GLAAD_NRI2007.pdf>.

———. "Where We Are on TV: GLAAD's Annual Study Examines Diversity of the 2006-2007 Primetime Television Season." *GLAAD.org*. 6 Aug. 2007. 20 Dec. 2007 <http://www.glaad.org/documents/media/DiversityStudy_06-07.pdf>.

Goldstein, Richard. *The Attack Queers: Liberal Society and the Gay Right*. London: Verso, 2002.

———. "What Queer Eye?: Are the Fab Five a Breakthrough or a Stereotype?" *Village Voice*. 23–29 July 2003. 3 Dec. 2003. <http://www.villagevoice.com/issues/0330/goldstein.php>.

Goldstein, Steve. "Gay-Rights Opponent Santorum Stands by Outed Aide." *Tribune* [San Luis Obispo]. *SanLuisObispo.com*. 15 July 2005. 16 Sept. 2005 <http://www.sanluuisobispo/mid/sanluisobispo/news/politics/12144709.htm>.

Goodman, Ellen. "Who's Insensitive to Gays?" *Boston Globe* 21 Oct. 2004. *LexisNexis*.Lehman Library, Shippensburg University. 15 Aug. 2005 <http://web.lexis-nexis.com/universe/document?_m=99661e58e34664cfcc964e3dca5508df&_docnum=75&wchp=dGLbVlz-zSkVb&_md5=73d5f53fc4e4da2f8df8d752ce6d7812>.

Gorski, Eric, Felisa Cardona, and Manny Gonzales. "Pastor Takes Leave Amid Allegations of Gay Sex." *Denver Post*. 3 Nov. 2006. 1 Jan. 2007 <http://www.denverpost.com/ci_4588998>.

Gorton, Dan. "The Gay Republican Conundrum." *Gay and Lesbian Review Worldwide* 14.1 (Jan./Feb. 2007). 03 April 2007 <http://www.glreview.com/issues/14.1/14.1-gorton.php>.

———. "The Hate Crime." Rev. of *Brokeback Mountain*, dir. Ang Lee. *Gay and Lesbian Review Worldwide* 13.2 (Mar. 2006): 13–14.

"A Great Mess in Great Neck." *Queer Eye for the Straight Guy*. Bravo-TV. Episode 102. 15 July 2003.

Greene, Thomas C. "Mass Murder in the Skies: Was the Plot Feasible?" *The Register*. 17 Aug. 2006. 20 Aug. 2006 <http://www.register.com/2006/08/17/flying_toilet_terror_labs/>.

Griggers, Cathy. "Lesbian Bodies in the Age of (Post)mechanical Reproduction." *Fear of a Queer Planet: Queer Polities and Social Theory*. Ed. Michael Warner. Minneapolis: University of Minnesota Press, 1993. 178–92.

Grundmann, Roy. Rev. of *Brokeback Mountain*, dir. Ang Lee. *Cineaste* 31.2 (Spring 2006). *Academic Search Premier*. EBSCOhost. Lehman Library, Shippensburg University. 11 May 2006 <http://www.epnet.com>.

Gutter Dyke Collective. "This Is the Year to Stamp Out the 'Y' Chromosome." 1973. Rpt. in *For Lesbians Only: A Separatist Anthology*. London: Everywoman Press, 1988.

"Hair Today, Art Tomorrow." *Queer Eye for the Straight Guy*. Bravo-TV. Episode 101. 15 July 2003.

Halberstam, Judith. *In a Queer Time and Place: Transgender Bodies, Subcultural Lives*. New York: New York University Press, 2005.

———. "Shame and White Gay Masculinity." *Social Text* 84–85 23.3–4 (Fall/Winter 2005): 219–33.

Hall, Donald E. *Queer Theories*. London: Palgrave Macmillan, 2003.

Hall, Radclyffe. *The Well of Loneliness*. 1928. New York: Knopf, 1990.

Halley, Janet E. "The Construction of Heterosexuality." *Fear of a Queer Planet: Queer Politics and Social Theory*. Ed. Michael Warner. Minneapolis: University of Minnesota Press, 1993. 82–102.

Halperin, David M. *How to Do the History of Homosexuality*. Chicago: University of Chicago Press, 2002.

———. *Saint Foucault: Toward a Gay Hagiography*. New York: Oxford University Press, 1995.

———. *What Do Gay Men Want?: An Essay on Sex, Risk, and Subjectivity*. Madison: University of Wisconsin Press, 2007.

Hansen, John. "U.S. Rep. Schrock Drops Re-election Bid over Allegations." *Virginian-Pilot* 31 Aug. 2004. *HamptonRoads.com*. 17 Feb. 2005 <http://home.hamptonroads.com/stories/story.cfm?story=74982&ran=126361>.

Harris, Lee. "Misunderstanding *Brokeback Mountain*." Rev. of *Brokeback Mountain*, dir. Ang Lee. *TCS Daily* 17 Jan. 2006. 11 May 2006 <http://www.tcsdaily.com/article.aspx?id=011606D>.

Hartinger, Brent. *Geography Club*. New York: HarperTempest-HarperCollins, 2003.

———. *The Order of the Poison Oak*. New York: HarperTempest-HarperCollins, 2005.

———. *Split Screen: Attack of the Soul-Sucking Brain Zombies/Bride of the Soul-Sucking Brain Zombies*. New York: HarperTempest-HarperCollins, 2007.

"Having It Both Ways: The GOP Hypocrisy over Kerry's Talk of Cheney's Daughter." Editorial. *Pittsburgh Post-Gazette* 20 Oct. 2004. *LexisNexis*. Lehman Library, Shippensburg University. 15 Aug. 2005 <http://web.lexisnexis.com/universe/document?_m=99661e58e34664cfcc964e3dca5508df&_docnum=73&wchp=dGLbVlz-zSkVb&_md5=312e4b3ec586e550219c0144d7b66066.>

Healy, Patrick, and Frank Phillips. "Kerry Backs State Ban on Gay Marriage." *Boston.com*. 26 Feb. 2004. 23 Sept. 2005 <http://www.boston.com/news/politics/president/articles/2004/02/26/kerry_backs_state_ban_on_gay_marriage.>

Herring, Scott. *Queering the Underworld: Slumming, Literature, and the Undoing of Lesbian and Gay History*. Chicago: University of Chicago Press, 2007.

"HHS Backs Down on Gay Funding Threats." *365gay.com*. 18 Feb. 2005. 18 Mar. 2005 <http://www.365gay.com/newscon05/02/021805frankHHS.htm.>

Highleyman, Liz. "What Was the 'Save Our Children' Campaign?" *Seattle Gay News* 18 Mar. 2005. 16 May 2007 <http://www.sgn.org/sgnnews11/page18.cfm>.

Hilton, Perez. "Mika Comes Out." *PerezHilton.com*. 6 June 2007. 19 June 2007 <http://perezhilton.com/topics/mika/mika_comes_out_20070606.php>.

Hollar, Julie. "With Respect to Mary Cheney: Pundits Use Kerry's Lesbian 'Gaffe' to Rewrite Debate." *Extra!* Jan./Feb. 2005. *FAIR: Fairness & Accuracy In Reporting*. 20 Aug. 2005 <http://www.fair.org/index.phppage=2483.>

Holleran, Andrew. "The Magic Mountain." Rev. of *Brokeback Mountain*, dir. Ang Lee. *Gay and Lesbian Review Worldwide* 13.2 (Mar. 2006): 12–15.

Holusha, John, and Neela Banerjee. "Evangelical Leader Says He Bought Drugs." *New York Times*. 3 Nov. 2006. 1 Jan. 2007 <http://www.nytimes.com/2006/11/03/us/04pastorcnd.html?ex=1167800400&en=ad9b3cc97cd37e5f&ei=5070.>

Hooper, Charlotte. *Manly States: Masculinities, International Relations, and Gender Politics*. New York: Columbia University Press, 2001.

Howe, James. *Totally Joe*. 2005. New York: Aladdin Mix-Simon and Schuster, 2007.

"How Gay Republicans Saved America." *The Guide* 26.12 (Dec. 2006): 8–9. *GLBT Life with Full Text*. Lehman Library, Shippensburg University. 19 Dec. 2006 <http://www.epnet.com>.

Huff, Toby E. "The Internet and the Public Sphere: Technologies of Control or Liberation and Development." *Hybridity* 1.1 (2000): 2–16.

Hunter. "Hastert Unhinged." *Daily Kos.* 6 Oct. 2006. 8 Oct. 2006 <http://www.dailykos.com/Storyonly/2006/10/6/4515/67734>.

Hurd, Dale. "John Kerry's French Connection." *CBN.com.* 27 Feb. 2004 <http://www.cbn.com/CBNNews/News/040601a.asp.>

Irvine, Reed, and Cliff Kincaid. "Homosexual Recruitment in Schools." *Accuracy in Media.* 20 June 2000. 01 Jan. 2007 <http://www.aim.org/media_monitor/A3030_0_2_0_C>.

Jakobsen, Janet R. "Sex + Freedom = Regulation: Why?" *Social Text* 84–85 23.3–4 (Fall/Winter 2005): 285–308.

James, Frank. "Hastert Briefing Raises More Questions." *Chicagotribune.com.* 5 Oct. 2006. 8 Oct. 2006 <http://newsblogs.chicagotribune.com/news_theswamp/2006/10/hastert_briefin.html>.

J. C. "Hume on Kerry: 'He'd Have to Clear Everything' with Jacques Chirac." *Media Matters for America.* 16 Aug. 2004. 27 Feb. 2005 <http://www.mediamatters.org/items/200408160002>.

Jhaveri, Hemal. "Searching for a Gay Man." *PopPolitics.com.* 16 Nov. 2003. 3 Dec. 2003 <http://www.poppolitics.com/articles/2003-10-22-gaytv.shtmhl>.

Joe. "Jeff Gannon Redux." *JoeMyGod.* 6 Mar. 2007. 21 Mar. 2007 <http//joemygod.blogspot.com/search/label/11%22%20uncut%20monster%20cock>.

John in D.C. "House GOP Leadership Knew about Foley Almost a Year Ago, Let Foley Remain in House Leadership, Let Him Remain as Chair of House Sex Offender Caucus." 29 Sept. 2006. 1 Jan. 2007 <http://americablog.blogspot.com/2006/09/house-gop-leadership-knew-about-foley.html>.

Johnson, Ben Patrick. "A Queer Eye on Stereotypes and Ad Revenue: How Gay TV Breaks Ground on Main Street and Madison Avenue." *Kiosque.* 3 Dec. 2003. 4 Dec. 2003 <http://www.culturekiosque.com/nouvelle/tele/queereye.html>.

Judy. "Kerry's French Connection." *News Hounds.* 4 Oct. 2004. 15 Aug. 2005 <http://www.newshounds.us/2004/10/04/kerrys_french_connection.php>.

Juergens, Brian. "Mika: In Which We Decline to Play Mika-boo Any Further." *AfterElton.com.* 12 June 2007. 21 June 2007 <http://www.afterelton.com/taxonomy/term/325>.

———. "Mika: 'Post-Gay' or Just 'Post-Interesting'?" *AfterElton.com.* 7 June 2007. 21 June 2007 <http://www.afterelton.com/taxonomy/term/325>.

———. "Mika: Why Don't the Gays Love Him?" *AfterElton.com.* 29 May 2007. 21 June 2007 <http://www.afterelton.com/taxonomy/term/325>.

Kanner, Melinda. "Questions for Queer Eye." *Gay and Lesbian Review Worldwide* 9.2 (Mar.–Apr. 2004): 35–37.

Kattelman, Beth A. "Rita Mae Brown." *The Gay and Lesbian Literary Heritage.* Ed. Charles J. Summer. London: Bloomsbury, 1997. 118–19.

Katz, Phyllis. "Smash Phallic Imperialism." Rpt. in *Out of the Closets: Voices of Gay Liberation*. Ed. Jay Karla and Allen Young. New York: New York University Press, 1992. 259–62.

Kaufman, Marc, and Mike Allen. "Cheney Sees Gay Marriage as State Issue." *Washington Post* 25 Aug. 2004: A1. 23 Sept. 2005 <http://www.washingtonpost.com/wp-dyn/articles/A29862-2004Aug24.html>.

Kawada, Louise. "Liberating Laughter: Comedic Form in Some Lesbian Novels." *Sexual Practice/Textual Theory: Lesbian Cultural Criticism*. Ed. Susan J. Wolfe and Julia Penelope. Cambridge, MA: Blackwell, 1993. 251–62.

Keen, Lisa. "Kerry Explains Support for Mass., Mo. Marriage Bans." Interview with John Kerry. *WashingtonBlade.com*. 24 Sept. 2004. 23 Sept. 2005 <http://www.washblade.com/2004/9-24/news/national/kerry.cfm>.

Kelly, Christopher. "Gay TV Making Great Strides in Exactly the Wrong Direction." *Miami Herald.com*. 26 Aug. 2003. 15 March 2004 <http://www.miami.com/mld/miamiherald/entertainment/6618804.htm>.

"Kerry & Edwards in Love." 2004. 9 Feb. 2005 <http://www.goyk.com/flash.asp?path=862>.

"The Kerry Gay Conspiracy Revealed." 8 Sept. 2004. 9 Feb. 2005. <http://www.kerrysucks.com/modules.php?name=News&file=print&sid=11>.

"Kerry Signed Letter Backing Gay Marriage." *USA Today* 11 Feb. 2004. 23 Sept. 2005 <http://www.usatoday.com/news/politicselections/nation/president/2004-02-11-kerry-gay-marriage_x.htm>.

Kimmelman, Burt. "The Internet, Selfhood, and the (Re)Textualizing of Experience." *College English Notes* 27.2 (Oct. 2000): 6–9 <http://web.njit.edu/%7Ekimmelma/literacyessay.html>.

Klein, Rick. "Democrats' Platform Shouldn't Back Gay Marriage, Kerry Says." *Boston Globe* 6 May 2005. Common Dreams News Center. 23 Sept. 2005 <http://www.commondreams.org/headlines05/0506-05.htm>.

Kooijman, Jaap. "They're Here, They're Queer, and Straight America Loves It." *GLQ: A Journal of Gay and Lesbian Studies* 11.1 (2005): 106–09.

Krawczeniuk, Borys. "Santorum Calls Gay Staffer a 'Trusted Employee.'" *Citizens' Voice*. 19 July 2005. 16 Sept. 2005 <http://www.citizensvoice.com/site/news.cfm?newsid=14880487&BRD=2259&PAG=461&dept_id=455154&rfi=6>.

Kurtz, Stanley. "The 'Gay' Election: Bad Timing for the Democrats." *National Review Online*. 10 Feb. 20004. 15 Aug. 2005 <http://www.nationalreview.com/kurtz/kurtz200402100850.asp>.

Lacan, Jacques. *The Seminar of Jacques Lacan. Book XX: On Feminine Sexuality, the Limits of Love and Knowledge, 1972–73, Encore*. Ed. Jacques-Allain Miller. Trans. Bruce Fink. New York: Norton, 1998.

Laclau, Ernesto, and Chantal Mouffe. *Hegemony and Socialist Strategy: Toward a Radical Democratic Politics*. 1985. London: Verso, 2001.

Lane, Anthony. "New Frontiers." *New Yorker*. 12 Dec. 2005. *Academic Search Premier*, EBSCOhost. Lehman Library, Shippensburg University. 6 Apr. 2006 <http://www.epnet.com>.

LaPadula, Phil, and Lou Chibbaro Jr. "Foley Comes Out Against Federal Marriage Amendment." *Houston Voice* 2 Apr. 2004: 6. *GLBT Life with Full Text*. Lehman Library, Shippensburg University. 19 Dec. 2006 <http://www.epnet.com>.

Laris, Michael. "Mention of Gay Daughter a Cheap Trick, Lynne Cheney Says." *Washington Post* 14 Oct. 2004: A6. 15 Aug. 2005 <http://www.washingtonpost.com/wp-dyn/articles/A31310-2004Oct13.html>.

Lauretis, Teresa de. "Queer Theory, Lesbian and Gay Studies: An Introduction." *differences: A Journal of Feminist Cultural Studies* 3.2 (Summer 1991): iii–xviii.

Leavitt, David. "The Marble Quilt." *The Marble Quilt*. New York: Houghton Mifflin, 2001. Rpt. in *Collected Stories*. New York: Bloomsbury, 2003. 489–525.

Lee, Nathan. Untitled rev. of *Brokeback Mountain*, dir. Ang Lee. *Film Comment* 42.1 (Jan./Feb. 2006): 42.

Leibovich, Mark. "Foley Case Upsets Balance of Gay Republicans." *New York Times* 8 Oct. 2006. 8 Oct. 2006 <http://www.nytimes.com/2006/10/08/washington/08culture.html?hp&ex=1160366400&en=04a2c0bca257d759&ei=5094&partner=homepage>.

LeVay, Simon. "A Difference in Hypothalamic Structure Between Heterosexual and Homosexual Men." *Science* 30 Aug. 1991: 1034+.

Levesque, Daniel. "Homosexual Recruiting at Public Schools." 2 Oct. 2005. 01 Jan. 2007 <http://www.ravingconservative.blogspot.com/2005/10/homosexual-recruiting-at-public.html>.

Levithan, David. *Boy Meets Boy*. London: HarperCollins, 2003.

———. *Wide Awake*. New York: Knopf, 2006.

Liddy, G. Gordon. Interview with Chris Matthews. *Hardball*. MSNBC. 8 May 2003.

Lochhead, Carolyn. "Did Gay Marriage Issue Help Re-elect Bush?" *San Francisco Chronicle* 4 Nov. 2004. *LexisNexis*. Lehman Library, Shippensburg University. 15 Aug. 2005<http://web.lexis-nexis.com/universe/document?_m=B497edf7d4ccf72444a11d488c28c40a&_docnum=116&wchp=dGLbVlz-zSkVb&_md5=A3a49788035329f12f65662df965a3>.

Lorenz, Stacy. "Obsession with 'Manliness' Follows Old Pattern in U. S. Politics: Presidential Rivals Have Long Branded Each Other as Feeble, Feminine." *Edmonton Journal* 2 Nov. 2004. *LexisNexis*. Lehman Library, Shippensburg University. 11 Feb. 2005 <http://web.lexis-nexis.com/universe/document?_m=344745610e3968b2ae9f30f08d44bd9e&_docnum=8&wchp=dGLbVlz-zSkVb&_md5=2202c3f3a4c4583871ee2fc8277d32c>.

"Make Room for Lisa." *Queer Eye for the Straight Guy*. Bravo-TV. Episode 103. 22 July 2003.

Malebranche, Jack. *Androphilia: A Manifesto: Rejecting the Gay Identity, Reclaiming Masculinity*. Baltimore: Scapegoat, 2006.

Manion, Jim. "Men Are from Mars, John Kerry Is from Paris." *Men's News Daily*. 13 Oct. 2004. 11 Feb. 2005 <http://www.mensnewsdaily.com/archive/m-n/manion/2004/manion1010404.htm>.

Margasak, Larry. "Former Pages Surveyed in Foley Probe." 10 Oct. 2006. *Advocate.com*. 10 Oct. 2006 <http://www.advocate.com/news_detail_ektid37356.asp>.

Marinucci, Carla. "Kerry Backs Full Rights for Same-Sex Couples; Candidate's Stance Against Gay Marriage No Worry, Leno Says." *San Francisco Chronicle* 4 Mar. 2004. *SFGate.com*. 23 Sept. 2005 <http://www.sfgate.com/cgi-bin/article.cgi?file=/chronicle/archive/2004/03/04/MNG8H5E0RC1.DTL>.

"Matt Drudge, a Gay Who Backs the Gay Bashers." Editorial. *BuzzFlash.com*. 13 July 2004. 15 Feb. 2005 <http://www.buzzflash.com/editorial/04/07/edi04050.html>.

"Matt Drudge, Are You Gay?" Editorial. *BuzzFlash.com*. 10 June 2000. 15 Feb. 2005 <http://www.buzzflash.com/editorial/04/07/edi04050.html>.

McCarthy, Anna. "Crab People from the Center of the Earth." *GLQ: A Journal of Gay and Lesbian Studies* 11.1 (2005): 97–101.

McHenry, Patrick. Interview with Wolf Blitzer. *Late Edition*. CNN. 8 Oct. 2006. Rpt. in "McHenry Speechless When Asked to Provide Evidence That Foley Scandal Was Election Ploy." *Think Progress*. 8 Oct. 2006. 8 June 2007 <http://thinkprogress.org/2006/10/08/mchenry-pelosi>.

McMurtry, Larry, and Diana Ossana. *Brokeback Mountain*. Screenplay. Rpt. in *Brokeback Mountain: Story to Screenplay*, by Annie Proulx, Larry McMurtry, and Diana Ossana. New York: Scribner, 2005.

McNally, Terrence. *Love! Valour! Compassion!* and *A Perfect Ganesh*. New York: Plume, 1995.

Melanie. "Don't Forget—Kerry's Still a French Flip-Flopper." *News Hounds*. 27 Oct. 2005. 15 Aug. 2005 <http://www.newshounds.us/2004/10/27/don't_forget_kerrys_still_a_french_flip_flopper.php>.

Mellman, Mark. "Gay Marriage Isn't What Beat Kerry." *The Hill*. 3 Aug. 2005. 15 Aug. 2005 <http://www.hillnews.com/thehill/export/TheHill/Comment/Pollsters/MarkMellman/080305.html>.

Mendelsohn, Daniel. "An Affair to Remember." Rev. of *Brokeback Mountain*, dir. Ang Lee. *New York Review of Books*. 23 Feb. 2006. 6 Apr. 2006 <http://www.nybooks.com/articles/18712>.

Millbank. Dana. "GOP Expose: Kerry, Closet Frenchman." *Washington Post* 23 Mar. 2004: A17. 15 Feb. 2005 <http://www.washingtonpost.com/ac2/

wp-dyn?pagename=article&contented=A16135-2004Mar22&notFound=true>.

Miller, Mark Crispin. *Cruel and Unusual: Bush/Cheney's New World Order*. New York: Norton, 2004.

Mohr, Richard D. *The Long Arc of Justice: Lesbian and Gay Marriage, Equality, and Rights*. New York: Columbia University Press, 2005.

———. "The Pedophilia of Everyday Life." *Curiouser: On the Queerness of Children*. Ed. Steven Bruhm and Natasha Hurley. Minneapolis: University of Minnesota Press, 2004.

Mordden, Ethan. *Buddies*. New York: St. Martin's, 1987.

———. *Everybody Loves You*. New York: St. Martin's, 1988.

Muñoz, José Estaban. "Queer Minstrels for the Straight Eye: Race as Surplus in Gay TV." *GLQ: A Journal of Gay and Lesbian Studies* 11.1 (2005): 101–02.

Myracle, Lauren. *Kissing Kate*. New York: Dutton, 2003.

N. C. "Despite Conservative Accusations, Kerry Didn't 'Out' Mary Cheney." *Media Matters for America*. 15 Oct. 2005. 20 Aug. 2005 <http://mediamatters.org/items/200410150004>.

Naff, Kevin, and Ken Sain. "Newspaper Outs Foley." *New York Blade* 2 Jan. 2004: 7. *GLBT Life with Full Text*. Lehman Library, Shippensburg University. 19 Dec. 2006 <http://www.epnet.com>.

Nico. "Coulter: I Would Talk about Edwards but 'You Have to Go into Rehab if You Use the Word 'Faggot.'" *Think Progress*. 2 March 2007. 12 June 2007 <http://thinkprogress.org/2007/03/02/coulter-edwards/>.

Nussbaum, Martha C. *Hiding from Humanity: Disgust, Shame, and the Law*. Princeton: Princeton University Press, 2004.

Outfoxed: Rupert Murdoch's War on Journalism. Dir. Robert Greenwald. The Disinformation Company, 2004.

Packer, Vin. *Spring Fire*. 1952. San Francisco: Cleis Press, 2004.

Papademetriou, Lisa, and Chris Tebbetts. *M or F?* New York: Razorbill-Penguin, 2005.

"Paper: 8 Men Claim Encounters with Craig." Associated Press. 20 Dec. 2007. <http://ap.google.com/article/ALeqM5hnzMHYGd-aXQbgughBA40pWNvlxQD8T9UU200>.

Pascoe, C. J. *Dude, You're a Fag: Masculinity and Sexuality in High School*. Berkeley and Los Angeles: University of California Press, 2007.

Patton, Cindy. "Tremble, Hetero Swine!" *Fear of a Queer Planet: Queer Politics and Social Theory*. Ed. Michael Warner. Minneapolis: University of Minnesota Press, 1993. 143–77.

Perez, Hiram. "You Can Have My Brown Body and Eat It, Too!" *Social Text* 84–85 23.3–4 (Fall/Winter 2005): 171–91.

Perry, Elizabeth. "HRC Staffer Fired for Posting Foley E-mails." *New York Blade* 6 Nov. 2006: 12. *GLBT Life with Full Text*. Lehman Library, Shippensburg University. 19 Dec. 2006 <http://www.epnet.com>.

Peters, Julie Anne. *Far from Xanadu*. New York: Little, Brown, 2005.

———. *Keeping You a Secret*. New York: Little, Brown, 2003.

Pharr, Suzanne. *Homophobia: A Weapon of Sexism*. 1988. Expanded ed. Little Rock: Chardon Press, 1997.

The Plaid Adder. "Zero Tolerance." *Democratic Underground*. 2 Feb. 2005. 4 Feb. 2005 <http://www.democraticunderground.com/plaidder/05/39.html>.

Plante, Hank. "Pentagon Confirms It Sought to Build a 'Gay Bomb.'" *CBS5.com*. 8 June 2007. 13 June 2007 <http://cbs5.com/topstories/local_story_159222541.html>.

Plunkett, Chuck, and Eric Gorski. "Pastor Confessed: Church Review Says Admission Came Thursday." *Denver Post*. 5 Nov. 2006. 1 Jan. 2007 <http://www.denverpost.com/news/ci_4604135>.

Potts, Leanne. "'Queer Eye' Makes Over View of Homosexuals." *ABQJournal*. 12 Aug. 3 Dec. 2003 <http://www.abqjournal.co/shock/72103personalities08-12-03.html>.

Pramaggiore, Maria, and Donald E. Hall, eds. *RePresenting Bisexualities: Subjects and Cultures of Fluid Desire*. New York: New York University Press, 1996.

Proulx, Annie. "Brokeback Mountain." *Close Range: Wyoming Stories*. 1997. Rpt. in *Brokeback Mountain: Story to Screenplay*, by Annie Proulx, Larry McMurtry, and Diana Ossana. New York: Scribner, 2005. 1–28.

———. "Getting Movied." *Brokeback Mountain: Story to Screenplay*, by Annie Proulx, Larry McMurtry, and Diana Ossana. New York: Scribner, 2005. 129–38.

"Queer Eye for the Skate Guy." *Queer Eye for the Straight Guy*. Episode 123. Bravo-TV. 9 Mar. 2004.

Radicalesbians (New York City). "Leaving the Gay Men Behind." *Rpt. in Out of the Closets: Voices of Gay Liberation*. Ed. Jay Karla and Allen Young. New York: New York University Press, 1992. 290–93.

Rak, Julie. "The Digital Queer: Weblogs and Internet Identity." *Biography* 28.1 (Winter 2005): 167–82.

Rauch, Jonathan. *Gay Marriage: Why It Is Good for Gays, Good for Straights, and Good for America*. New York: Henry Holt, 2004.

Rich, Adrienne. "Compulsory Heterosexuality and Lesbian Existence." 1980. *Blood, Bread, and Poetry: Selected Prose 1979–1985*. New York: Norton, 1994.

Rich, Frank. "How Kerry Became a Girlie-Man." *New York Times* 5 Sept. 2004. *LexisNexis*. Lehman Library, Shippensburg University. 11 Feb. 2005 <http://web.lexis-nexis.com/universe/document?_m=7f177fda6153092d44c736c4ec90842&_docnum=19&wchp=dGLbVzz-zSkVA&_md5=c5930e2f7cele6fa204ae25e4fac8151>.

"Right Wing Blames Gays for Foley Scandal; Gay Activists Respond." *Empty Closet* Nov. 2006: A4–A5. *GLBT Life with Full Text*. Lehman Library, Shippensburg University. 19 Dec. 2006 <http://www.epnet.com>.

Robinson, Eugene. "GOP Bigotry That Backfired." *Washington Post* 6 Oct. 2006: A23. 6 Oct. 2006 <http://www.washingtonpost.com/wp-dyn/content/article/2006/10/05/AR2006100501548.html>.

Robinson, Paul. *Queer Wars: The New Gay Right and Its Critics*. Chicago: University of Chicago Press, 2005.

Roof, Judith. "'This is Not for You': The Sexuality of Mothering." *Narrating Mothers: Theorizing Maternal Subjectivites*. Ed. Brenda O. Daly and Maureen T. Reddy. Knoxville: University of Tennessee Press, 1991. 157–73.

Ruskola, Teemu. "Gay Rights versus Queer Theory: What's Left of Sodomy after *Lawrence v. Texas*?" *Social Text* 23.3–4 (Fall/Winter 2005): 235–49.

Russo, Vito. *The Celluloid Closet*. 1981. Rev. ed. New York: Harper & Row, 1987.

Ryan-Vollmar, Susan. "Mark Foley Wasn't Closeted." *Bay Windows* 5 Oct. 2006: 6. *GLBT Life with Full Text*. Lehman Library, Shippensburg University. Dec. 19, 2006. <http://www.epnet.com>.

Sanchez, Alex. *Rainbow Boys*. New York: Simon and Schuster, 2001.

———. *Rainbow High*. New York: Simon and Schuster, 2003.

———. *Rainbow Road*. New York: Simon and Schuster, 2005.

Sanchez, Matt. Online posting. *Salon.com*. 8 Mar. 2007. 21 Mar. 2007 <http://mattsanchez.Blogspot.com/2007/03/saloncom.html>.

Santorum, Rick. Interview with the Associated Press [excerpt]. 7 Apr. 2004. *USA Today.com*. 23 Apr. 2004. 16 Sept. 2005 <http://www.usatoday.com/news/Washington/2003-04-23-santorum-excerpt_x.htm>.

Savin-Williams, Ritch C. *The New Gay Teenager*. Cambridge, MA: Harvard University Press, 2005.

Sawyer, Terry. "Blind Leading the Bland." *PopMatters*. 22 July 2003. 3 Dec. 2003 <http://www.popmatters.com/tv/reviews/q/queer-eye-for-the-straigt-guy.shtml>.

Scheer, Robert. "GOP Gays and the 'Finkelstein Phenomenon.'" *Los Angeles Times. Latimes.com*. 19 Apr. 2005. 20 Apr. 2005 <http://www.latimes.com/news/opinion/commentary/la-oe-scheer19apr19,0,2839125.column?coll=la-news-comment-opinions>.

Schell, Andy. *My Best Man*. New York: Kensington, 2000.

Schneider, Richard, Jr. "Not Quitting Brokeback." *Gay and Lesbian Review Worldwide* 13.2 (Mar. 2006): 10.

"Second New Life Pastor Resigns over 'Sexual Misconduct.'" *Chicago Sun-Times*. 20 Dec. 2006. 1 Jan. 2007 <http://www.suntimes.com/news/nation/179189,CST-NWS-pastor20.article>.

Sedgwick, Eve Kosofsky. *Between Men: English Literature and Male Homosocial Desire*. New York: Columbia University Press, 1985.

———. *The Epistemology of the Closet*. Berkeley and Los Angeles: University of California Press, 1990.

———. "How to Bring Your Kids Up Gay." *Fear of a Queer Planet: Queer Politics and Social Theory*. Ed. Michael Warner. Minneapolis: University of Minnesota Press, 1993. 69–81.

Seidman, Steven. "Identity and Politics in a 'Postmodern' Gay Culture: Some Historical and Conceptual Notes." *Fear of a Queer Planet: Queer Politics and Social Theory*. Ed. Michael Warner. Minneapolis: University of Minnesota Press, 1993. 105–42.

Sender, Katherine. *Business, Not Politics: The Making of the Gay Market*. New York: Columbia University Press, 2004.

Sexton, Catherine Jordan. "Ex-Lawmaker Won't Face Charges in Page Case." *New York Times* 19 Sept. 2008. 13 May 2009 <http://www.nytimes.com/2008/09/20/us/20foley.html?_r=l>.

Shelley, Martha. "Gay is Good." 1972. Rpt. in *Out of the Closets: Voices of Gay Liberation*. Ed. Jay Karla and Allen Young. New York: New York University Press, 1992. 31–34.

Shernoff, Michael. *Without Condoms: Unprotected Sex, Gay Men, and Barebacking*. New York: Routledge, 2005.

Shimko, Bonnie. *Letters in the Attic*. Chicago: Academy Chicago, 2002.

Shorto, Russell. "What's the Movement to Outlaw Gay Marriage Really About? (Big Hint: It's Not Just About Marriage)." *New York Times Magazine* 19 June 2005: 34+.

Sinfield, Alan. *Faultlines: Cultural Materialism and the Politics of Dissident Reading*. Berkeley and Los Angeles: University of California Press, 1992.

Skoloff, Brian. "Former Rep. Foley at Dad's Grave: 'I disappointed him so much.'" *Philadelphia Gay News* 24 Nov. 2006: 23–30. *GLBT Life with Full Text*. Lehman Library, Shippensburg University. 19 Dec. 2006 <http://www.epnet.com>.

Sloan, Brian. *Tale of Two Summers*. New York: Simon and Schuster, 2006.

Spivak, Gayatri, and Ellen Rooney. "In a Word." *Differences* 1.2 (1989): 124–56.

Smith, Anna Marie. *Laclau and Mouffe: The Radical Democratic Imaginary*. London: Routledge, 1998.

———. *New Right Discourse on Race and Sexuality: Britain, 1968–1990*. New York: Cambridge University Press, 1994.

———. "Why Did Armey Apologize?: Hegemony, Homophobia, and the Religious Right." *Unraveling the Right: The New Conservatism in American Thought and Politics*. Ed. Amy E. Ansell. 1998. Boulder: Westview, 2001.

Smith, Sean. "Forbidden Territory." Rev. of *Brokeback Mountain*, dir. Ang Lee. *Newsweek* 21 Nov. 2005. *Academic Search Premier*. EBSCOhost. Lehman Library, Shippensburg University. 11 May 2006 <http://www.epnet.com>.

Steele, Bruce C. "The Gay Rights Makeover." *Advocate* 2 Sept. 2003: 42–43.

Stout, Maureen. *The Feel-Good Curriculum: The Dumbing Down of America's Kids in the Name of Self-Esteem*. Cambridge, MA: Perseus, 2000.

Stryker, Susan. "The Transgender Issue: An Introduction." *GLQ: A Journal of Gay and Lesbian Studies* 4.2 (1998): 145–58.

Sullivan, Andrew. "Beware the Straight Backlash." *Time* 11 Aug. 2003: 35.

———, ed. *Same-Sex Marriage: Pro and Con: A Reader*. 1997. Rev. ed. New York: Vintage, 2004.

———. *Virtually Normal: An Argument about Homosexuality*. New York: Knopf, 1995.

Swaab, Peter. "Homo on the Range." Rev. of *Brokeback Mountain*, dir. Ang Lee. *New Statesman* 12 Dec. 2005: 40–42.

Tabloid Baby. "Newsgasm: Slur Could Cost Washington His Grey's Gig." *TVgasm*. 18 Oct. 2006. 12 June 2007 <http://www.tvgasm.com/archives/greys_anatomy/002956.php>.

Tanner, Steve. "John Kerry Has No Recollection of Throwing Medals Like a Girl." *Broken Newz*. 27 Apr. 2004. 15 Aug. 2005 <http://www.brokennewz.com/displaystory.asp_Q_storyid_E_926kerrygma>.

"They Aren't Gay—They're FABULOUS!" *BlameBush!* 12 July 2004. 11 Feb. 2005. <http://www.blamebush.typepad.com/blamebush/2004/07/they_arent_gay.html>.

Thomas, Evan. "The Vets Attack." *Newsweek* 15 Nov. 2004. *LexisNexis*. Lehman Library, Shippensburg University. 15 Aug. 2005 <http://web.lexis-nexis.com/universe/document?_m=e3471d083146a4eb46409cb04d653279&_docnum=56&wchp=dGLbVlz-zSkVb&_md5=9311c3a40a4e7a9b0d8bbbcc6d623270>.

Throckmorton, Warren. "Teach Respect?: Bullying Should Be Stopped. But That's Not the Real Agenda Behind the Day of Silence." *Concerned Women for America*. 12 Apr. 2005. 6 June 2007 <http://www.cwfa.org/articles/7882/CFI/family/index.htm>.

Tinkcom, Matthew. *Working Like a Homosexual: Camp, Capital, Cinema*. Durham: Duke University Press, 2002.

Torres, Sasha. "Why Can't Johnny Shave?" *GLQ: A Journal of Gay and Lesbian Studies* 11.1 (2005): 95–97.

Traditional Values Coalition. "Homosexual Urban Legends: 'Born Gay.'" 1 Jan. 2007 <http://www.traditionalvalues.org/urban/three.php>.

———. "Let's End Taxpayer Supported Homosexual Recruitment Programs in Public Schools." 1 Jan. 2007. <http://www.traditionalvalues.org/modules.php?sid=103>.

———. "Parents: Get the Truth about the Gay, Lesbian, and Straight Education Network (GLSEN)." 1 Jan. 2007 <http://www.traditionalvalues.org>.

"Training Day." *Queer Eye for the Straight Guy*. Episode 123. Bravo-TV. 23 Mar. 2004.

Turner, William B. *A Genealogy of Queer Theory*. Philadelphia: Temple University Press, 2000.

Van Leer, David. *The Queening of America: Gay Culture in Straight Society*. New York: Routledge, 1995.

Vary, Adam B. "The *Brokeback Mountain* Effect." *Advocate* 28 Feb. 2006. *Academic Search Premier*. EBSCOhost. Lehman Library, Shippensburg University. 11 May 2006 <http://www.epnet.com>.

Warner, Michael. "Homo-Narcissism; or, Heterosexuality." *Engendering Men: The Question of Male Feminist Criticism*. Ed. Joseph A. Boone and Michael Cadden. New York: Routledge, 1990. 190–206.

———. Introduction. *Fear of a Queer Planet: Queer Politics and Social Theory*. Minneapolis: University of Minnesota Press, 1993. vii–xxxi.

———. *Publics and Counterpublics*. New York: Zone Books, 2002.

———. *The Trouble with Normal: Sex, Politics, and the Ethics of Queer Life*. Cambridge, MA: Harvard University Press, 1999.

Waters, Sarah. *Affinity*. New York: Riverhead, 1999.

———. *Fingersmith*. New York: Riverhead, 2002.

———. *Tipping the Velvet*. New York: Riverhead, 1998.

Watts, Julia. *Finding H.F.* New York: Alyson, 2001.

Weisman, Jonathan. "Hastert Aides Interest Ethics Panel: Staff Members' Knowledge of Foley's Actions with Former Pages in Question." *Washington Post* 12 Oct. 2006: A06. 12 Oct. 2006. 1 Jan. 2007 <http://www.washingtonpost.com/wpdyn/content/article/2006/10/11/AR2006101101639.html>.

——. "Staffer Cites Earlier Role by Hastert's Office." *Washington Post* 7 Oct. 2006: A01. 8 Oct. 2006 < http://www.washingtonpost.com/wp-dyn/content/article/2006/10/06/AR2006100601888.html>.

West, Diana. "Monsieur John Kerry: French Fried." *Townhall.com*. 9 Aug. 2004. 27 Feb. 2005 <http://www.townhall.com/columnists/dianawest/dw20040809.shtml>.

Wilchins, Riki. "Gender is What Drives Conservatives Nuts." *Advocate* 7 Dec. 2004. *GLBT Life with Full Text*. Lehman Library, Shippensburg University. 20 Apr. 2005 <http://www.epnet.com>.

Wilcox, Barbara. "Matt Sanchez: 'I'm Bad at Being Gay.'" *Advocate* 9 March 2007. *Advocate.com*. 21 Mar. 2007 <http://www.advocate.com/news_detail_ektid42752.asp>.

Wilgoren, Jodi. "Part Butler and Part Buddy, Aide Keeps Kerry Running." *New York Times* 28 Apr. 2004. 16 Aug. 2005 <http://www.nytimes.com/2004/04/28/politics/campaign/28CHIE.html?ex=1127966400&en=f43bac1f0ab7ef9&ei=5070>.

Williams, Bett. *Girl Walking Backwards*. New York: St. Martin's, 1998.

Wilson, James Q. "Why Did Kerry Lose? (Answer: It Wasn't 'Values')." *Wall Street Journal* 8 Nov. 2004. *American Enterprise Institute for Public Policy Research—Short Publications*. 15 Aug. 2005 <http://www.aei.org/publications/pubID.21512,filter.all/pub-detail.asp>.

Wittman, Carl. "Refugees from Amerika: A Gay Manifesto." *San Francisco Free Press* Dec. 22–Jan. 7, 1970. Rpt. in *The Homosexual Dialectic*. Ed. Joseph A. McCaffrey. Englewood Cliffs: Prentice Hall, 1972.

Woelz, Karl. Afterword. *M2M: New Literary Fiction*. Ed. Karl Woelz. San Francisco: AttaGirl, 2003. 321–32.

Wolfson, Evan. *Why Marriage Matters: America, Equality, and Gay People's Right to Marry*. New York: Simon and Schuster, 2004.

Wygert, Kimberly S. "Queering the Schools: The City Journal." *Number 2 Pencil*. 25 Apr. 2003. 6 June 2007 <http://www.kimberlyswygert.com/archives/000368.html>.

Yang, John, and Brian Ross. "Exclusive: Former House Clerk's Testimony." *Blotter*. 19 Oct. 2006. 1 Jan. 2007 <http://www.abcnews.com/theblotter/2006/10/house_clerks_te.html>.

York, Frank. "Public Employees Teach Kids 'Gay' Sex: Workshops Reportedly Instruct Youth in How to Perform Homosexual Acts." *World Net Daily*. 9 May 2000. 6 June 2007 <htttp://www.worldnetdaily.com/news/article.asp?ARTICLE_ID=17490>.

Index